RUSSIA

EXPERIMENT WITH A PEOPLE

Also by Robert Service

The Bolshevik Party in Revolution: A Study in Organisational Change

Lenin: A Political Life
Volume One: The Strengths of Contradiction
Volume Two: Worlds in Collision
Volume Three: The Iron Ring

The Russian Revolution, 1900–1927

A History of Twentieth-Century Russia

Lenin: A Biography

ROBERT SERVICE

RUSSIA

EXPERIMENT WITH A PEOPLE

FROM 1991 TO THE PRESENT

MACMILLAN

First published 2002 by Macmillan
an imprint of Pan Macmillan Ltd
Pan Macmillan, 20 New Wharf Road, London N1 9RR
Basingstoke and Oxford
Associated companies throughout the world
www.panmacmillan.com

ISBN 0 333 72626 X

1 3 5 7 9 8 6 4 2

A CIP catalogue record for this book is available from
the British Library.

Typeset by SetSystems Ltd, Saffron Walden, Essex
Printed and bound in Great Britain by
Mackays of Chatham plc, Chatham, Kent

CONTENTS

THREE: PERSUADING RUSSIA

FOUR: IN THE RUSSIAN DEPTHS

List of Illustrations

Section One

1. Boris Yeltsin, Russian President, 1991 to 1999.
2. Yeltsin, Lukashenka and Patriarch Alex II.
3. Vladimir Putin, Russian President from 2000.
4. Presidential Crest of the Russian Federation.
5. New Gate to Red Square.
6. Marshal Zhukov Statue.
7. Peter the Great Ensemble.
8. Underground supermarket complex on the Manège.
9. Advert for cigarettes named after Peter the Great.
10. Russian spoof version of James Bond (*Sem' dnei*, 6–12 May 2002).

Section Two

11. Upmarket women's magazine cover (*Limit*, November 2000).
12. Nationalist newspaper salutes Stalin (*Duel'*, December 1998).
13. Party leaders disguised as animals (*Literaturnaya gazeta*, 3–9 November 1999).
14. Nationalist newspaper denies that Russia will be dominated by the USA (*Sovetskaya Rossiya*, 7 February 2002).
15. Putin carries figure of Yeltsin over the cliff (*Sovetskaya Rossiya*, 21 March 2002).
16. Putin and Prime Minister Kasyanov attempt to speed up economic progress (*Argumenty i fakty*, April 2002).
17. Disagreement at chess game (*Taim-aut/Sportklub*, May 2001).
18. Bank robbery (*Literaturnaya gazeta*, 19 June 1996).
19. Financial transfers, Russian style (*Literaturnaya gazeta*, 22 May 1996).
20. Arrest of local politician (*Literaturnaya gazeta*, 15–21 December 1999).

Preface

This is a book I have long wanted to write. When reform came to the USSR in the mid-1980s, great undercurrents surfaced which have continued to clash and foam since the end of the Soviet order in 1991. They flooded across the entire life of the country that became known as the Russian Federation. Communism was overturned after seven decades of power, and new rulers came to govern a new state seeking to create a new way of existence for all its citizens.

There are already many accounts of high politics and macroeconomics (and these will also be topics in the following chapters). Yet the breadth and depth of Russia's transformation has failed to be registered. This has come about because insufficient attention has been given to the intimate linkage of politics, economics, culture, society and belief. Contemporary Russia is understood in several dimensions at once or it is not understood at all. Another problem has been the tendency to deal with the historical background as if it were a simple and self-evident matter. In fact the legacy of the past has many complexities important for current developments. Moreover, we read so much about the undeniable horrors of Russian society that the positive sides of recent experience have been largely overlooked – even by the Russians themselves. Russia is in a quite bad enough condition without its achievements needing to be belittled. My aim in this book is to make sense of the country as a whole, from the Kremlin down to provincial towns and villages and from the President's entourage down to ordinary Russians and the momentous changes in their circumstances since the USSR's abolition.

Diverse types of evidence will be examined. The primary sources from the press and other media are listed in the bibliography; they include not only conventional ones such as scholarly books and articles but also magazines, films, CDs and Web sites. I have also learnt from conversations with Russian friends and with strangers on the street, in shops, on the bus or in the metro. The process has been enlivened by the necessity to keep one's eye simultaneously on the pages of the draft and on the continuing changes in Russia itself.

This, though, is a moment to express thanks. Jonathan Aves, Archie Brown, Vladimir Buldakov, David Godwin, Heather Godwin, Marna Gowan, Geoffrey Hosking, Alex Pravda, Tanya Stobbs and Jeremy Trevathan improved the full draft. Above all, my wife Adele Biagi commented on several versions. Michael Bourdeaux, Philip Cavendish, Julian Graffy, Lindsey Hughes, Jeff Kahn, Catriona Kelly, Gerry Smith, Stephen Webber and Stephen Whitefield gave advice on specific matters. I am also indebted to staff in three British libraries. Jackie Willcox in the Russian and East European Centre Library at St Antony's College in Oxford suggested and obtained materials that would have escaped my notice. I had assistance, too, from Richard Ramage in the Slavonic Library and Angelina Gibson in the Bodleian Library. It would be unrealistic to expect every reader to agree with my conclusions, and in any case books on Russia which secure unanimity are probably not worth reading. My hope is that factual mistakes have been eliminated, but such of them as remain are my responsibility. End of Soviet-style self-criticism: on with the book.

Robert Service

1 October 2001

INTRODUCTION

There are no roads in Russia, only directions.

Russian proverb

On a trip to Moscow in the mid-1990s, I was strolling down the cobbled passage from Red Square towards the Manège. This is one of the districts in the capital I know best, and I was quite unprepared for the changes made since my visit the previous year. The passage was no longer clear. Where once the Soviet armed forces could parade their tanks and aeroplanes on May Day, now the sixteenth-century Resurrection Gate had been restored as it had been before Stalin demolished it.

Back on Red Square itself the Kazan Cathedral was being rebuilt brick by brick in its original form six decades after the communist regime had reduced it to rubble. Payment for materials and labour had not only come from the authorities and private businesses but also passers-by. The new premises would be used not as a museum – as had been the fate until recently of St Basil's Cathedral outside the Kremlin wall – but as a functioning place of Christian worship. Changes had also been made down in the Manège. It was there that a statue had been erected in honour of Marshal Georgi Zhukov, the Soviet commander who received the surrender of the German Wehrmacht in May 1945. Zhukov is one of those singular public figures of the Soviet period to have remained in official favour after communism's demise. More than that: Zhukov was the sole leading character in twentieth-century history still well regarded by nearly all sections of Russian public opinion. The defeat of Nazi Germany was almost the only one of the USSR's triumphs in receipt of popular approval, and his latter-day sculptor represented Marshal Zhukov on horseback.

Nearby a rumble of excavating machinery could be heard. Wooden barricades had been put up a hundred yards away in front of the Hotel

Moskva, and a crowd stood on a platform from which they could peek at what was going on. In the sunny morning light I joined dozens of inquisitive Russians. Below our gaze lay the foundations and scaffoldings of a vast underground 'commercial complex'.

This construction and reconstruction was a symbolic expression of the new official Russia. The restoration of the Resurrection Gate signalled the end of communism and the resumption of ties with the ancient order of the Romanov dynasty. Pre-communism and post-communism were combined. The Zhukov equestrian statue was a tribute to achievements in the intervening decades of communism. Although the communist period was not extolled, it was not systematically denounced. The statue was designed to suggest that much that happened had been to the benefit of Russia and the world. Then there was the subterranean complex of brash, expensive shops. It stood for contemporaneity, for Westernism and for capitalism; its subterranean location, which was reached by stairways festooned with advertisements, was the perfect symbol of a hidden, powerful force that would soon surface and spread across the country. But it would do so in a country that remained influenced by both its antique traditions and its twentieth-century history.

Such impressions were not accidental ones but the intended result of an attempt by the authorities to provide Russia's people with the ideal of a different way of life. Russians had to be convinced that the future would be radiant and that they remained a great nation with the highest potential in every area of human endeavour. Communism had to be buried. The people of Russia were being told they had a wonderful history, customs and attainments to their name, stretching back into the tsarist epoch and including feats of achievement even in the Soviet years.

This contrasted with Russia's conventional image at home and abroad as a land of exotic horror. State and society appeared irredeemably dysfunctional. Stories of official corruption, crude military violence and feckless 'masses' held attention in the media. These were not a new kind of narrative about Russia. The works of the classic nineteenth-century writers from Pushkin to Dostoevski abounded in grotesquerie, and foreign visitors filled their accounts with tales of unrelieved awfulness. Reportage on Russia continued in this vein in the revolutionary years from 1917. Commentators abroad, except for communist sympathisers, claimed that Leninist fanatics were reducing the country to an appalling condition. *Émigré* writers in particular reinforced the negative stereotype of Russia in international public opinion. Under Stalin in the

1930s, a measure of approval returned as Soviet attainments in industry and education were given recognition; and this trend grew stronger in the Second World War when the USSR formed the Grand Alliance with the United Kingdom and the USA against Germany and Japan. But the Cold War reversed all this from the late 1940s, when Russians were again depicted as either dangerous fanatics or indoctrinated zombies.[1]

Not until Gorbachëv's accession to power in 1985 was it again widely accepted that the Russian people were not an aggregate of freaks. Yet the changed treatment in the media did not last. With Gorbachëv's encouragement, the Soviet press itself searched out cases of repression and corruption since 1917 and exposed current abuses. The distasteful aspects of Russia's image were kept in focus after the abolition of the USSR at the end of 1991. There was Yeltsin the drunken, wild President. There were the military outrages in Chechen towns and cities. There were avoidable disasters such as the loss of the nuclear submarine *Kursk* and its crew. There were the abject beggars, hands held out for a few coins in the winter cold on city streets. Russia was reportrayed according to ancient stereotype.

These stories, while being individually true, made for a one-sided image. Russia as part of the USSR had been the backbone of a military superpower. It had had a massive industrial base and produced some of the finest science and literature of the twentieth century. Russians had been prominent among those peoples of the Soviet Union who took the brunt of the Nazi military rampages in the Second World War and made possible the victory of the Allies. Russia gave us Lenin and Stalin; but it also gave us Andrei Sakharov, Alexander Solzhenitsyn and countless fighters for the cause of human dignity. From Russia came the poet Anna Akhmatova, the aircraft designer Andrei Tupolev, the football goalkeeper Lev Yashin and the dancer Rudolf Nureyev. Then there were the millions of exceptional 'ordinary' Russians who managed to survive the horrors of the nation's history after 1900: the First World War, the Civil War, the famine of 1932–3, the Great Terror, the Second World War, the traumas of post-war repression and the economic collapse at the end of the 1980s. Russia is languishing. But no one ought to be surprised if and when, sometime in the future, it starts to fulfil its enormous potential.

So how is the conventional image to be redrawn? The essential thing is to question the assumptions that frame it. Most portraits began from the premise that Russia in 1992, after the end of the USSR, was simply re-emerging on to a path of natural development from which it had been dislodged by the October 1917 Revolution led by Lenin. The Soviet period was depicted as an artificial break. The idea that it would have been easy to establish a liberal democratic order and a thriving capitalism before the First World War gained much approval. The end of communism was also seen as an event that liberated Russia entirely from the entanglements of empire. Seemingly Russia was enabled to resume its old established boundaries and its people could smoothly revert to the positive sides of their character and traditions that had prevailed before 1917. The USSR's demise met with an unconditional welcome abroad, and it was supposed that almost all citizens of Russia shared this attitude at that time. The dominant assumption was that Russians had been given the opportunity to move towards the End of History: at last they could painlessly embrace democracy and the market.[2]

The brightest of these hopes were soon dashed. Russia acquired an economy run by robber capitalists who invested their gains in almost every country except Russia. Public life in Russia succumbed to degradation. Electoral fraud, bribery and assassinations became the norm and politicians were mired in scandal. Although Moscow flourished, whole regions and provinces languished and the countryside fell into neglect. The sense that no improvement was likely in the near future pervaded Russian society.

In 1991–2 practically every foreign analyst, unlike many Russian commentators, erred on the side of optimism. I should come clean at this point. When Gorbachëv fell from power in December 1991, it seemed to me something that was both inevitable and desirable. He had discharged a monumental task in democratising the USSR and become one of the great political figures of the twentieth century; but his steerage of the economy had been catastrophic and there was little prospect of his successfully altering course. He had ended in a political impasse.[3] The disintegration of the USSR and the taking of power in Russia by Yeltsin seemed preferable. Already it was obvious that Yeltsin would face difficulties. One problem was that 'Russia', even after the other Soviet Republics had broken away from Moscow, could not be an exclusively Russian nation state. Other peoples too lived there.[4] A further problem was that the functionaries of the USSR, being well organised, would not easily be dislodged from positions of influence. Already, too, it was clear that Yeltsin had his flaws and was less committed to democratic procedures than he professed.[5]

Yet I did not foresee the full scale of the ensuing disappointment, and from a very cautious optimism I moved to an equally cautious pessimism. This, though, was still pessimism tied to the feeling that things need not have turned out as badly as they had. Indeed, things can surely only get better. And so a cautious pessimism and a rejection of determinism lie at the heart of my book.

Commentators, as they recovered their breath, put forward various answers as to why Russia's encounter with reform has been so problematic. Both specialists on Russia and general analysts have written on this. One line of explanation emphasised the significance of the institutional arrangements made at the downfall of the Soviet regime. Thus it mattered, for instance, when and how Yeltsin offered himself and his supporters for re-election.[6] Another line stressed the political and economic policies put in place by the new rulers: failure to prioritise the access of ordinary people to the rewards of the new order was thought crucial.[7] Moreover, the character of the supreme leader, especially Yeltsin's self-indulgence, was picked out.[8] The focus was also widened to matters such as both the strength of civil society and relationships among the existing elites in Russia. The surviving importance of the old Soviet *nomenklatura* has been noted.[9] The presence of a common national purpose was added as a significant factor – and here, too, the Russians were found wanting.[10] In still wider terms it was contended that the deep history of any country is the single dominant factor explaining whether reform fails or succeeds.[11] Thus in the Russian case the grim path of political, economic and social development taken under Romanov tsars and Leninist commissars is seen as the greatest lasting obstacle to progress.[12]

It is usually assumed that Russia's internal affairs are the key to explaining the outcome.[13] But a further point has been made that the international environment of security, economics and diplomacy had a large impact – and the changes in Russia's relations after the September 2001 terrorist action in New York left the largest. For some, the West has been too accommodating to the Kremlin, whereas for others, Russia has been treated meanly; but they have agreed on the importance of external factors.[14] More generally it has been suggested that the establishment of a reasonably clean political and economic system is in any case the exception rather than the rule; it is not written into the natural order of things. Most people in the world live miserably.[15]

Dispute will go on about which factors were the most important; there will also be disagreement as to whether certain factors were of any importance whatever. In Russia's case, it seems to me, all the factors I have mentioned had an impact (and they are virtually impossible to disentangle from each other). Valuable specific works on Russia bear this out. Research is more abundant on politics and economics than on society, ideology and culture. Within the political field, the traditional concentration on personalities and events in the Kremlin has prevailed; and the central institutional nexus is beginning to be investigated in detail. The same is true for economics, where the decisions on central policy and the assessment of its results have dominated discussion. Local political and economic phenomena have not been overlooked, and works on society, ideology and culture are fortunately on the increase. Work is also being directed at 'the localities' as well as at Moscow. But much remains to be done. And although the significance of the historical context is recognised in principle, it has not yet attracted close scrutiny. The moment is right to take a look at Russia's general experience since the fall of communism.

The uncongenial historical background to the reform project is a good starting-point. It needs to be emphasised that 'Russia' is not a long-established entity in spatial terms. Russia changed its boundaries in every century, and in the twentieth century did this many times; it cannot be excluded that the frontier line will be altered again in the twenty-first. Nor should it be assumed that the 'Russian national character' is a fixed phenomenon definable without controversy. In 1900 most Russians were illiterate, church-going peasants who had never seen a city; a hundred years later an overwhelming proportion of them were urban, educated and religiously inactive. Habits and attitudes altered hugely in that lengthy period. This was as true among the political and intellectual elites as it was in the rest of society. Furthermore, most thinkers relegated matters of Russian nationhood to secondary import-ance; and those who wrote about 'the national question' usually advo-cated ideas hostile to conditions in the modern world. As if this was not enough, the general legacy of the USSR – in politics, economics and society – lay across the path of reform like a bulky roadblock. The Soviet way of life was never going to be very easily dislodged.

On to the problems of history were piled the problems of contem-porary public life. Political leadership degenerated fast under Yeltsin and his policies soon involved the abandonment of parts of the reform project. The Russian Federation was established in 1991–3 to the accompaniment of electoral fraud and political violence. Meanwhile the majority of Russians reacted unfavourably to the economic reforms of the 1990s and there was much hostility to the USSR's abolition. A plutocracy of ministers and financiers took power and the Russian people justifiably concluded that their rulers had cared more for themselves than for the common good. Russia was in confusion about its borders, national attitudes, institutional legitimacy and political purposes.

The country was already in disarray when it became independent and the odds were stacked against the reformers. They were aware of this, and knew they had to conduct a campaign of persuasion to convince Russians that a different form of state and society would benefit everybody. This aspect of the process is usually overlooked. In fact Yeltsin and his supporters in the media, schools and other institutions did much to remodel the official image of the country's past and its future; they also invented symbols for the new state in the form of flags, anthems and ceremonies. Unfortunately such activity took place with insufficient attention to popular sensibilities; and this gave a stick to opposition politicians, especially those on the extremes of the left and the right, to castigate what they alleged was a betrayal of the country's honour and traditions. Moreover, the younger generation of the artistic intelligentsia tended to lampoon the new Russia rather than to offer counsel about how to create a better society. Putin, after becoming President, restrained the iconoclasm of the Yeltsin era and proposed a more ambivalent vision of the Soviet past. But the damage had been done: most people had had enough of declarations by the political and intellectual elites.

Public institutions – the Orthodox Church, the armed forces, the Academy of Sciences, the press and the courts – proved too weak or reluctant to carry through the reform project in its entirety. The rulers were also hindered by the absence of a rudimentary consensus about the national purpose. There were as many interpretations of Russia's needs as there were political parties, and these parties too were divided. At the same time the government's reforms were balked in the regions. The bodies of local government went their own way; and criminal groups, arising from the underworld of the USSR, placed a stranglehold on the emergence of a free and legal order in Russia.

In such a situation it was no surprise that many traditions of the USSR, and indeed of the Russian Empire, were carried over into the new Russia. Faced with the unpleasantnesses of life after communism, Russians turned to their tested techniques of survival. They derided Yeltsin and although they welcomed Putin, their general scepticism about politics persisted. They decided that trust reposed in the authorities in Russia has usually been trust misplaced. Russians retreated into their families. They enthusiastically grasped the opportunities for personal privacy. Scornful of the state, they have stuck to their relatives and friends. The social groups based on patronage retained their functionality and survived the installation of the market economy. Workers in factories and on farms remained loyal to their bosses not out of affection but through fear that any alternative choice might bring worse results. The disrepute of Marxism-Leninism left a void which older Russian traditions, including ancient superstitions, filled. The rift between the politicians and their public grew wider, and the politicians, while aspiring to bring an end to ideology, put their cases for comprehensive political, economic, social and cultural change; and the result was that they produced ideological statements of their own.

Yet not everything was predetermined. The very chaos and uncertainty in the country in the early 1990s constituted an unrepeatable chance to realise reform, and Yeltsin, despite being late in developing his programme, seized that chance at least for a while. He was not a systematic thinker. In fact he was not a thinker at all. But although it is not fashionable to give him much credit,[16] this book will show how he and his advisers by and large succeeded in formulating a general reform project.

The project was broad and ambitious; it encompassed not only liberal democracy and the market economy but also ideological pluralism, local self-government, a legal order, ethnic tolerance, individual freedom and civic nationhood. The rulers in the Kremlin set up a new institutional framework. They sought out support in various organisations and social groups and organised propaganda for the project. They contrived a set of state symbols to break with the communist past. This substantial enterprise was tantamount to a project of nation-building even though the rulers did not refer to it as such. The project was not confined to politicians in power. Journalists, teachers and even some opposition politicians as individual activists assisted in its development. Among them, for a year or two, there existed a sense that they lived in a situation of realistic opportunity and that a wholly new way of life could be created.[17] This sense quickly faded, and not every advocate showed the necessary commitment even at the start of things. But for some time the excitement about the scope of possible change was communicated to the entire country. A new Russia was being fashioned, or so it seemed temporarily.

This means it is misleading to talk of Russia re-emerging or being reborn or remade. What should be accentuated is the sheer novelty of the general project. 'Russia' was being made as it emerged from the larger multinational state – originally the Russian Empire and then the USSR – in which it was encased. Russia's identity had previously been obfuscated by tsars and commissars who were afraid lest Russian nationalist impulses might destabilise the political order; and Russians had been deliberately inhibited from acquiring a sense of nationhood distinct from the interests of the Russian Empire or the USSR.[18] In 1992 this impediment was removed. Russia was finally allotted a territory, a state and an opportunity to create an independent future of its own.

Despite all the difficulties, some aspects of the Russian twentieth-century experience were helpful to the project. Russia embarked on reforms with several distinct assets. This was a country whose explorers and scientists had identified riches in natural resources. It had a solid administrative network. It had a workforce that was literate, numerate and co-operative. All Russians had some acquaintance with the nation's history and literary heritage and had been given at least a secondary education. They were also a fairly peaceful lot, at least until the troubles arose in Chechnya. They had barely noticed the loss of their 'outer' empire in Eastern Europe in 1989 and did not espouse the forcible reincorporation of Ukraine and other countries of the Soviet Union after 1991. They did not act as if they were a people hungry for an empire. They were not especially xenophobic. Most Russians wished for a harmonious relationship between Russia and the rest of the world. Extremists were distrusted unless they could pretend to be moderate. Violence met with deep disapproval.

Nor did everything change for the worse after 1991. It is one of my aims in this book to show that there were great successes as well as great failures. Building on the achievements of the Gorbachëv years, the Russian people gave priority to enjoying a private life and shutting the door on the state. For the first time since 1917 they could think and say what they liked. They could savour the cultural pluralism and enjoy the intellectual and religious freedom. They could engage in whatever recreations their income allowed. Gays and lesbians could 'come out' without fear of a prison sentence. Youth culture was finally loosed from its constraints. Foreign goods became available in shops and kiosks. Travel abroad was possible for everyone with sufficient money. Slowly but irreversibly the trend grew for enthusiasts to set up small, local organisations with their own cultural, environmental or social goals.

These were spring torrents of reform from below. They could have been turned into a flood if only the reformers in the Kremlin had so desired. Russia's people kept their vibrant ability to make the best of things. As they learned ever more about the rest of the world, they aspired to a lifestyle different from their experiences under communism. Russians, like every other people, are full of contradictions: they can also be fatalistic and passive, and these features have recently been in plentiful evidence. Yet the cardinal point of this book is that much optimism existed among the Russian people in the early 1990s. The ruling reformers spurned the opportunity to release and foster popular initiative for the country's transformation. Such an attempt would not have worked out perfectly. Difficulties would have been encountered as the political and economic elites pursued their interests at the expense of the public good. Yet it is regrettable that the attempt was not sustained. Fundamental improvement in Russia cannot come exclusively from on high. It must also proceed from the depths. Even now it is not too late for the attempt to be made.

PART ONE

THE PROJECT
OF REFORM

1. FOR A NEW RUSSIA

I am not presenting people with a global strategic goal. I am not setting my sights on some shining peak that must be scaled ... No. The chief goal of this restless president is Russia's tranquillity.

Boris Yeltsin, *The View From the Kremlin* (1995)

As the clock struck midnight in Moscow on 31 December 1991, a great state ceased to exist: the Soviet Union had suddenly vanished. This did not happen as a consequence of nuclear war with the USA. Nor did it result from revolutionary struggle in Russia. The whole scene was bizarrely uneventful. The red flag – with its hammer and sickle in the top right-hand corner – had already been lowered from its pole on the Kremlin ramparts and the tricolour of the Russian Federation – white, blue and red – had been hoisted in its place. Boris Yeltsin, Russian President, remained quietly at home outside the capital.

The man who had been ruling the USSR was Mikhail Gorbachëv. Appointed General Secretary of the Communist Party of the Soviet Union in 1985, he had never thought that the state under his leadership would disintegrate into separate countries. But in December 1991 he had to acknowledge defeat when the Presidents of Russia, Ukraine and Belarus decided to disband the USSR. This was an astonishing turnabout. The USSR had been a great military and economic power. Its Red Army had crushed Hitler's Wehrmacht. From 1945, only the USA had matched its weight in global affairs; the USSR had seemed a durable pillar of the world order. After leading the October 1917 Revolution, Vladimir Lenin had founded a new kind of state. His ultimate objective had been to do away with capitalism and to rid the globe of all oppression and exploitation. In subsequent years the Soviet state would repeat his party's claim to offer mankind the only sure way to bring about social and material contentment. The USSR stood as the model for communist

states established after the Second World War in Eastern Europe and
Asia. Although the number of its admirers in the West declined from
the late 1950s, it had continued to inspire respect and fear almost until
the last day of its existence.

But now the USSR had disappeared. Into the dustbin of history went
the October 1917 Revolution, Marxism-Leninism and the official cult of
Lenin. Seven extraordinary decades were dispatched to oblivion: the Civil
War, the Five-Year Plans and the Great Terror. Leaders of the Soviet
communist party – Lenin, Stalin, Khrushchëv and Gorbachëv – had once
evoked awe. But now the symbols of Soviet life had been tossed aside,
and the rest of the world began to forget the sputniks, the Olympic
gold medals, the achievements in physics and mathematics, the little
matrëshka dolls and the chess championships.

A proud state collapsed in tawdry confusion. This was exemplified
in the way Yeltsin rebuffed Gorbachëv, who stayed behind in the Kremlin
to offer to show him the arrangements for the 'black box' controlling
Soviet nuclear weaponry. Gorbachëv was not even given transport for
the removal of his personal belongings from the Presidential dacha.[1]
Gorbachëv had humiliated Yeltsin in autumn 1987 when they had both
belonged to the communist party leadership. He had also ordered Yeltsin
to be dragged from a hospital bed to face an inquisition by the Moscow
Party City Committee.[2] Their dispute continued after Yeltsin was
appointed, at Gorbachëv's behest, as First Deputy Chairman of the State
Construction Committee. Gorbachëv and Yeltsin were reconciled in
April 1991. Yet this rapprochement caused the most powerful of Gorbachëv's current ministers to dread that the result would be the disintegration of the USSR. In August they had organised a coup against him.
But the conspiracy failed. Although they successfully detained Gorbachëv
in his state dacha in Crimea, Yeltsin evaded arrest. Striding out from the
Russian White House, he clambered to the top of a tank and called upon
his fellow citizens to bring the plotters to justice. The coup petered out.
After Gorbachëv flew back from Crimea, Yeltsin derived visible pleasure
from giving him instructions before the lights of the world's television
cameras.

Gorbachëv and Yeltsin had previously agreed that the USSR should
be turned into a Union of Sovereign States. The proposed Union would,
in Gorbachëv's phrase, have 'a strong centre and strong republics'. A
treaty to this effect would have been signed on 20 August if the attempted
coup had not occurred. When Gorbachëv met Yeltsin again, they were
at loggerheads. Yeltsin wanted to weaken the powers of 'the centre'

still further. Grudgingly Gorbachëv made concessions but none proved sufficient for Yeltsin, who perpetually found motives to avoid finalising the text of any agreement. On 1 December, when 90 per cent of the electorate in Ukraine voted for secession from the USSR, Yeltsin decided to break up the entire Union. Meeting the Presidents of Ukraine and Belarus, he secured their consent,[3] and Gorbachëv had to accept their ultimatum. Yeltsin had won. Gorbachëv's final address to Soviet citizens was delivered on 25 December 1991.[4]

And so the New Year's celebrations in Russia were quite out of the ordinary. It had been traditional for the General Secretary of the Communist Party of the Soviet Union to broadcast a speech on the stroke of midnight. Under Leonid Brezhnev, Yuri Andropov and Konstantin Chernenko – the last General Secretaries before Gorbachëv – this custom had become an embarrassment. Brezhnev and Chernenko had geriatric conditions that made them slur their words at the best of times. It was only with Gorbachëv's advent that dignity was restored. Until 1990 he had remained the most popular politician in the USSR.[5] Gorbachëv was a masterful communicator in those earlier years when there appeared to be a prospect of a successful political and economic reform. But as things turned sour for him, he gained the reputation of a windbag, and if he had tried to talk to Soviet citizens on New Year's Eve 1991, he would have attracted still greater contempt than Brezhnev and Chernenko. For the first time in his career, the most charismatic leader in the country's history since Lenin and Trotski refrained from speaking in public.

The revellers in the rest of the country were in a divided mood. A large amount of vodka and brandy is consumed on such occasions in Russia. But most Russians were more worried than tipsy. An epoch was ending, and no one could predict what was going to happen next. Indeed people could not feel sure which country they would wake up in the following day. On 31 December 1991 they would carouse in the USSR. On 1 January 1992 they would arise from their beds in a different country. The Soviet Union would be no more.

It would be the task of Boris Yeltsin as President of Russia to allay popular concerns. These concerns were understandable. People urgently wanted to know what was going to be done with the economy. Since 1989 manufacturing output had gone into steep decline. Food supplies had shrunk. There had been much talk of 'the transition to the market' as being the sole route towards economic regeneration. But what, asked Russia's citizens, did this mean? What did it signify for wages, employment, food supplies, clothing, housing, transport and health-care? There had also been talk of the need for democracy. But what did this imply for the ability of people to control the way they were governed? There had been talk of law and order, of an end to corruption, of equal opportunities for all citizens regardless of their personal connections. Yet how this too was going to be achieved was undefined. Most citizens of Russia had little idea of what lay in store for them. The lack of clarity was a breeding ground for popular fear. Would 1992 be the year when catastrophe struck Russia?

Across the Russian Federation there was unhappiness about the disintegration of the USSR. Opinion polls were all pointing in the same direction. In October 1991 three-quarters of Russia's citizens favoured the retention of a Union of some kind or other.[6] In December, after the Ukrainian referendum, a swing away from this position occurred: nearly two-thirds of urban inhabitants in fourteen Russian cities pronounced themselves in favour of the creation of a Commonwealth of Independent States.[7] But this majority did not endure. Surveys conducted in Moscow from April 1992 through to the end of the year constantly indicated that between 60 and 70 per cent of people regretted the USSR's disintegration.[8] Yeltsin's personal popularity, while remaining higher than anybody else's, started to dip.[9] He could not permanently depend on the goodwill he had earned for his bravery during the crisis of August 1991; and he badly needed to carry out a campaign of public persuasion to convince Russian citizens that what was happening was in their interests. Yeltsin was the engineer of the Russian Federation's independence. But could he hold his electors with him on the course he was setting? Could he impress on them that their collective salvation would consist in the USSR's abolition?

Yeltsin was born in 1931 in the deep countryside fifty miles from Sverdlovsk in the Urals region. He came from a peasant family. The village priest was drunk at his christening and dropped him into the font; and but for the intervention of his grandmother, he would have drowned.[10] Boris grew up a mischievous boy, and one adventure nearly killed him. He and a couple of schoolfriends were wandering in the woods when they came across a hand-grenade. As the boys wanted to experiment with it, Boris pulled off the ring, setting off an explosion and losing two fingers.[11] He was not the only restless member of his family. His father Nikolai went to Nizhni Novgorod province, 400 miles away, to find work on building sites. The family hoped to escape the dreadful conditions that arose from the transformation of the USSR's agricultural land into collective farms. But Boris's father complained that the living conditions were nothing like what had been promised. They were dirty and ill equipped, and Nikolai said so. For this he was arrested and sent into a penal-labour settlement for three years in 1936.[12]

Boris, too, had a ready tongue. At school he was allotted the role of giving a speech of thanks to the teacher on behalf of his class at the end of the academic year. Typically he used the occasion to deliver a few choice words about the inconsistency of punishment.[13] He expected all authorities, including the teachers, to practise the high morality that they preached. He jibbed at any kind of restraint being applied to him. He was a zestful leader and a poor subordinate – and this was to prove the pattern in the rest of his eventful life.

Young Yeltsin was awarded a place at the Polytechnic Institute in Sverdlovsk. Coming from a poor family, he seemed a perfect recruit for the Stalinist order; for he managed to keep secret both his poor discipline at school and his father's conflict with the authorities. In fact he fitted uncomfortably into any mould. Having no money to take a summer holiday, he would creep along the platform at railway stations and clamber on to the nearest carriage top. It was illegal, but it was free and it was fun (apart from the need to avoid falling off in transit).[14] Each autumn he returned to his studies refreshed. He was fit and competitive, and having taken up volleyball, he joined one of the Sverdlovsk City teams. At the same time he studied to get the qualifications for work in the construction industry. Many young workers and peasants of his generation did the same. But when Yeltsin left the Institute for paid employment, he unusually declined the option of becoming a manager straight away. Instead he tried his hand at various labouring jobs. This stood him in good stead. When eventually he took up a managerial post, his workers found him hard to push around even if they threatened him for interfering with their various little scams.

Such a manager was bound to impress the authorities in Sverdlovsk. In 1961 Yeltsin joined the communist party. Just fifteen years later, in 1976, he became First Secretary of the Sverdlovsk Provincial Committee. Sverdlovsk was no mean city. It was the fifth largest in the USSR, and its political leader was among the most influential politicians outside Moscow. Immediately Yeltsin showed brilliance in extracting resources from the Kremlin. Having decided that Sverdlovsk needed a Metro system, he flew to Moscow to lobby Brezhnev himself. Brezhnev's health was already on the decline. Whispering his request in the old man's ear, Yeltsin secured a promise that the state planning bodies would release the necessary finance.[15] Towards his subordinates he was less diplomatic. He was exacting in his demands and could be extraordinarily bad-tempered when disobeyed or simply disappointed. He had a sharp eye for detail. His superiors were worn down by the profusion of his ideas for bettering productivity, and his willingness to contest any point of disagreement occasionally ended in a stand-up fight. There was a constant rage in him to get things done.

Yeltsin had never been abroad; he had not even travelled to Eastern Europe. All he knew was the USSR. The only ideology he knew was communism. For practical purposes he assumed, like other Soviet citizens, that whatever change for the better might occur in the USSR would come about within the framework of the existing political system.

But already he was a bit of an eccentric. On one occasion his car broke down forty miles from Sverdlovsk, after being driven into a ditch by his chauffeur on the eve of the celebration. It was the eve of the May Day holiday, when Yeltsin was scheduled to give the main speech. The nearest place of habitation was across several fields. At the dead of night Yeltsin and the chauffeur ran over and woke up the residents to get hold of an alternative vehicle. But no car was available. Yeltsin therefore sequestered a tractor. Unfortunately its vodka-loving driver had started to celebrate May Day a mite early. Yeltsin would not be put off, and commanded the farmer to transport him back to the city in time to change into a clean suit and make his traditional address.[16] The episode leaves open the possibility that the tractor-driver was not the only participant in the scene who was drunk. How did the chauffeur-driven car find its way into the ditch? Had Yeltsin and his chauffeur themselves been fully sober? Yeltsin's account leaves this unclear. What is clear, though, is that he already saw a close relationship with the general public as essential for a contemporary politician.

He appeared regularly on local television. He gave direct answers to questions put to him by the public, and allowed the agenda to be set by his audiences. His talent for improvisation was exceptional. He took notes of grievances. He had the common touch and listened intently. His aide Lev Sukhanov recounted that when he met people for the first time, he gave them his 'X-ray gaze'.[17] When he wanted to tell people something, he was equally effective. He used proverbs and anecdotes. His eyes twinkled and he was never too shy to embrace strangers. His style assured people that while he was one of them, he was also above them and could get things done for them. His physical presence was another asset: at a couple of inches above six feet he was considerably taller than the average Russian male of his generation, and he appealed strongly to women. His charm was famous in Sverdlovsk.

Such assets served him well when he moved to Moscow at Gorbachëv's request in 1985. He visited offices, industrial plants and supermarkets as the people's champion. He harangued managers who failed to meet targets in the provision of goods and services. He himself queued in shops. The word got around that he neither accepted bribes nor used the special medical facilities available in the Kremlin. Sometimes he took a bus into his party headquarters, clinging to the handrail among the ordinary passengers. He ensured all this was recorded by reporters. Cinemas, too, showed newsreels of him. I remember an evening in a Moscow cinema in October 1987 when *Repentance*, a feature film about the horrors of Stalinism by the Georgian director Tengiz Abuladze, was preceded by a news item about the failure of the city construction authorities to repair the roof of the great department store, GUM. The hero of the item was Yeltsin, who led the investigative team on to the store's premises and fired a barrage of questions at administrators. The audience applauded rapturously, thinking it worth the entrance fee for the newsreel alone.

Yeltsin had asked to be relieved of his candidate membership of the Party Politburo a month before that evening; he had fallen out with Gorbachëv, whom he had needled by attacking the privileges of the communist leaders and by criticising the influence of Gorbachëv's wife Raisa. Soon afterwards Yeltsin was hauled before the Moscow City Organisation and sacked from its leadership. But his appeal to the inhabitants of Moscow, far from declining, was increased by what was seen as his martyrdom. His autobiography became a best-seller.[18]

It was lucky for him that Gorbachëv proceeded to treat him gently. In 1989 Yeltsin was elected to the Congress of People's Deputies and joined the radical critics of Gorbachëv who called themselves the Inter-Regional Group. He shared the leadership with the prominent dissident Andrei Sakharov, who died in December and left Yeltsin without a serious rival. Yeltsin crossed another personal threshold in June 1990 by abandoning the communist party. His every step carried him nearer to the goal he wanted: the post of supreme state leader. But how was he to replace Gorbachëv? Although he had no fixed ideas about this, he could spot any gap when it presented itself. As Gorbachëv's difficulties with the non-Russian nations of the USSR mounted, so the politicians and intellectuals in the Russian Federation began to think that a specifically 'Russian' viewpoint on politics was required. Yeltsin became its principal exponent. In June 1991 he took this to its ultimate conclusion by standing in the elections for the Presidency of Russia within the still vaster Soviet Union. Six candidates put up against each other. Yeltsin was by far and away the most popular candidate, winning 55 per cent of the votes cast.

His prestige soared. His picture appeared on posters; poems were written about him, and a short verse became popular:

> People are fed up with fairy stories,
> It's time to stop living by higher command.
> Yeltsin knows what we need.
> So give a friendly vote for Boris![19]

Yeltsin, defying Gorbachëv's predictions, had risen from the political grave.

This was the man who had to argue the case for Russian independence to his electorate. His bravery in August 1991 had enhanced his popularity. The USSR was moving in the direction of disintegration, but Yeltsin's role had been decisive; and as he prepared to take power at New Year 1992, he faced problems of historic dimensions. Each of his ministers and advisers had impressive credentials of some sort. Yeltsin picked them up from the generation twenty years younger than himself. He had little choice about this: the former dissidents, brilliant though they had been in attacking the Soviet communist leadership, lacked practical administrative skills, and Yeltsin had to look elsewhere for his ministers. His appointees were young and energetic. They were committed reformers. They were not naïve: indeed they expected that their tenure of office would be short. They knew that the transformation of Russian society would involve painful adjustments that would not be universally welcomed. They did not expect the electorate to feel grateful to them. But although they were tough-minded, they had the great disadvantage of lacking the common touch: they could not communicate with people in simple, convincing language. Yeltsin alone had that ability.

He started with a handful of close supporters. Alexander Rutskoi was his Vice-President, Ruslan Khasbulatov the Speaker of the Russian Supreme Soviet; Yegor Gaidar was Acting Prime Minister and was charged with overseeing economic reform. Yeltsin's Deputy Prime Minister was Gennadi Burbulis. Anatoli Chubais headed the scheme for the privatisation of enterprises; Boris Fëdorov was Minister of Finance. Andrei Kozyrev was the new Minister of Foreign Affairs. All were convinced – or had temporarily persuaded themselves – that Russia's state independence was crucial to the attainment of a different social order.

But they were not only inexperienced: most of them were also bumptious. Gaidar, Yeltsin's favourite politician, was a case in point. His grandfather Arkadi had been a famous Bolshevik fighter in the Civil War and later a renowned children's writer. Gaidar himself had headed the editorial board of the communist party journal *Kommunist*. He was a child of the Soviet *nomenklatura* and never succeeded in commending himself to ordinary Russian citizens. While explaining to them that a basically new economic strategy was needed, Gaidar used the instructional style of a Soviet political propagandist. He had no natural feeling for words as spoken; the written newspaper article was his real *métier*, and few people read his works. He was obviously pleased with himself. He looked too smug. He made things even worse for his reputation through his obvious relish for wearing smart Western suits at a time when the general standard of living was falling. He was squat and pasty-faced – and most people felt that at the age of thirty-five he had not seen enough of life to have the wisdom needed for the governance of Russia.

The others in the team were scarcely more helpful. Vice-President Rutskoi had seen action as an airforce commander in Afghanistan and was bluff, moustachioed and plain-speaking. He was also developing doubts about the entire project of breaking up the USSR: already he was a divisive figure. Speaker Khasbulatov put himself out of favour by agreeing with Rutskoi. He had a grating voice and retained the style of the economics lecturer he had once been; he suffered from the additional political disadvantage of being a Chechen at a time when the Chechens were among the most reviled ethnic groups in the Russian Federation.

The rest of the team were closer to Yeltsin in policy but were of little use in convincing their fellow citizens of the correctness of their opinions. Burbulis was yet another former lecturer in Marxism-Leninism; his cantankerousness, in the fresh guise of a free marketeer, became notorious. Kozyrev had trained as a diplomat in the special school of the Ministry of Foreign Affairs. He was less belligerent than Gaidar and Burbulis, but his polished speeches and neat, well-groomed appearance strengthened his reputation as an untested youth. Fëdorov, who had worked mainly as an academic researcher, was too cerebral for most TV viewers. Even Chubais, who took trouble to explain the rationale of the government's scheme for the privatisation of the economy, was only a little more at ease with the general public. He, too, was a young lecturer. Gaidar, Burbulis, Kozyrev, Fëdorov and Chubais failed to reassure the public and their dress and demeanour irritated most citizens. Their youth was disconcerting. Vice-President Rutskoi referred to them as 'the little lads in pink shorts'.[20] These words were cruel, but they had a point.

Thus the principal burden of communicating with the citizens of the Russian Federation fell upon Yeltsin. Not one of his subordinates would have won an election. Each, while being more highly trained in academic terms, lacked the rudimentary capacity to put ideas across to people in a popular fashion. Without Yeltsin, the radical reformers in the government would have been lost before they had even begun.

The President was clever in the way he went about his task. Daily newspapers, including those beyond the control of the USSR authorities, had dropped the habit of carrying verbatim reports of speeches by leaders.[21] This did not bother Yeltsin. As President he had enough control over the Russian radio and TV stations to ensure live transmission of his perorations. And although he had a broad notion of his intended policies, he saw the need to use the literary skills of supporters.[22] His early career had been distinguished by a willingness to study the technical aspects of any task he had to discharge. As a construction engineer he mastered the small details of any building project before confronting his fellow managers. As a party boss in Sverdlovsk he looked into the minutiae of his subordinates' work. It is true that in Moscow in 1986–7 he had behaved like a bull in a china shop. But while bringing about the demise of the USSR in 1991, he reverted to a more cautious style because he understood the need to adopt an appealing tone and terminology in expressing ideas which many of the people who had elected him would find uncongenial. Careless phrases could cost him dear, and he knew it.

His first group of speech-writers included Alexander Ilin and Gennadi Kharin but the leading member was Lidia Pikhoya,[23] who came from Yeltsin's own Sverdlovsk Province and was married to the Russian Federation's minister for the state archives, Rudolf Pikhoya. She was a university teacher and, unlike Yeltsin, came from an academic background in the humanities and wrote fluently. They made a good pair: she could write while he had a feel for words and was a good editor of her scripts.[24] He was not entirely a politician in the Western style. He would not use an autocue. He refused to wear makeup on TV.[25] He disdained counsel to hire a professional image maker.[26] But he understood the vital need for getting the words right in his speeches, and Lidia Pikhoya had a remarkable empathy with him as he tried to give expression to his reform project; and the resultant speeches were the main medium whereby he influenced the attitudes of his fellow citizens in the half-year after the August 1991 coup attempt. In those crucial months he delivered twelve major speeches, starting with his oration at the funeral of three young men who had died under the wheels of tanks sent out to support the coup. There were also two short speeches and a lengthy television interview.[27]

Yeltsin surveyed the past, present and future of Russia. Unlike Soviet communist party General Secretaries, he avoided any laborious recapitulation of each and every stage in the country's twentieth-century history. He did things differently for two reasons. The first was his determination to demarcate himself from Gorbachëv. Yeltsin did not want to appear a know-all. The second reason was simply that he, the destroyer of the USSR, wished to interpret the Soviet years as a single period. From Lenin to Gorbachëv, according to Yeltsin, there had been a 'totalitarian regime'.[28] Thus the political turbulence of 1917 had been accompanied by nothing but 'tragedies', and the result was a regime of 'revolutionary obscurantism'. Soviet communism was 'a cruel experiment'.[29] An 'anti-human economy' had been established. The official state authorities had ignored all the sensible warnings that 'communism cannot be built'.[30] The communist era, declared Yeltsin, had to be relegated to oblivion. Under his Presidency a sharp and irreversible rupture was to be made with the past. The contrast with Gorbachëv was pronounced.

Yeltsin had the bit between his teeth. The USSR was to be replaced by fifteen independent states and chief among them would be Russia. Unless Russia went its own way, he asserted, reforms could not be fast or deep enough. On 28 October 1991, speaking to the Russian Congress of People's Deputies, he avowed that the other Soviet republics of the USSR were acting as a brake upon political and economic progress.[31] His concentration was given in subsequent months to convincing public opinion in Russia about this. In his Address to the People on 29 December 1991 he asserted: 'Russia is ill.'[32] Only state independence would provide the conditions for a successful cure. Faith in Russia was essential. So, too, were love and reverence for Russia. After the collapse of the August coup d'état Yeltsin announced emotionally: 'The word "Russia" is sacred.'[33] He dismissed any thought that Russia would be broken up; his slogan was 'Russia one and indivisible'.[34] From the first month of his Presidency Yeltsin encouraged the patriotism of Russia's citizens – and this patriotism was based upon Russia, not the USSR.

His argument, which he repeated frequently, was that Russians had been poorly treated in the Soviet period. The totalitarian nightmare had been comprehensive. The consequence, according to Yeltsin, was that there were 'no peoples, including the Russians, who could feel free'.[35] The disintegration of the USSR would enable the Russian nation to flourish at last.

Yet this patriotism was not to be confined to those citizens of Russia who were ethnic Russians. When he spoke on television, Yeltsin addressed his viewers not as *russkie* but as *rossiyane*. The linguistic distinction was deliberate. *Russkie* is the word for Russians implying ethnicity; it specifically excludes the other national and ethnic groups living in Russia. By contrast, *rossiyane* is an inclusive word and refers to all citizens of the Russian state. Yeltsin insisted that all citizens should enjoy equal 'rights in their entirety' and that a free Russia had to be 'a democracy, not an empire'.[36] It is true he mentioned the Russians more often than any other people. Indeed in that half-year after the August 1991 coup he avoided referring to specific major national groups inhabiting Russia such as the Tatars, the Jews and the Chechens. He recognised that his commitment to a multinational society should never leave the Russians without a sense that he would safeguard their interests. His main support came from Russians, and he was not going to forget the fact. Nevertheless he was aiming to create a new civic consciousness in Russia. He was no nationalistic demagogue. While indicating admiration for traditional Russian values, he did not wish to offend non-Russians in Russia.

His stated objective was the creation of a 'prosperous, law-governed, democratic and truly free state'.[37] There had to be 'decommunisation'.[38] He demanded 'a real democratisation of the entire society', and in September 1991 declared his government to be following 'the path of democracy, of the market economy, of the defence of human rights in accordance with international standards'.[39] Yeltsin preferred to stick to such generalisations and to avoid definitions and details. He said he simply wanted 'a normal life' for people in Russia.[40] Thus he argued that Russian society had the opportunity to rejoin the community of nations around the world. Russia could fulfil her potential as a 'civilised' country. He declared that this should be done with the minimum of fuss: he wanted 'social peace'.[41] This was to be a transformation without violence or polemics. He acknowledged that there existed 'groups and strata whose interests fail to coincide',[42] but he affirmed that differing interests could and should be accommodated. Tranquillity in public life was crucial. At the funeral for the victims of the August 1991 coup he solemnly asked: 'And forgive me, your President, that I could not defend, could not protect your sons.'[43]

Yeltsin did not pretend the economic reforms would be painless. He recognised that the movement from the economics of communism would require 'a harsh regime'. But generally he avoided unsettling language. He wanted to bind citizens together and to assure them that his reforms would eventually benefit everybody. None the less some social groups would benefit more than others; indeed the market economy would involve the promotion of groups which had been held in disgrace in the Soviet period. Agricultural regeneration, for example, would require the nurturing of a new class of 'farmers'.[44] Gorbachëv had called for 'peasants' to be allowed to take over the collective farms. This was audacious at the time since it implied that Stalin's elimination of the peasantry was reversible. But the word 'farmer' took things a stage further. Yeltsin was announcing a commitment to market economics (which were thought to bring harm even to the peasant economy). Entrepreneurship was brought back as a virtue. The market rather than the agencies of state was to be the motive force of the transformation. The government of newly independent Russia, Yeltsin insisted, would act quickly and decisively in pursuit of its aims in the domestic and foreign sectors of its policies. There was no time to be lost.

Knowing that worries existed about his project, Yeltsin employed the kind of language that would allay them. In the six months after the August 1991 coup Yeltsin talked a lot about the market economy. Not once did he call this economy by the name it had around the world: capitalism.[45] He knew that for seven decades the people of the Soviet Union had been instructed that there was no more evil thing in the world. Even in the tsarist period there had been official disquiet about the growth of capitalism in Russia. Capitalism had never had a decent ring to it in the Russian ear, and so Yeltsin recommended a capitalist economy without using the term. He also said nothing about inter-enterprise competition, about bankruptcies or about unemployment. He gave not the slightest hint that the economic policies in the short term might be accompanied by a reduction in the general standard of living. He did not mention the working class in industry and agriculture. Instead he talked somewhat opaquely about 'hired labour'. For that matter, he also drew no attention to the emerging social group of private bankers and private factory owners. Despite his rough-and-ready image, Yeltsin was displaying a subtlety which his ministers, surrounded by their Western advisers, lacked.

He could afford greater openness about his political aims. 'Democracy' was his watchword.[46] Like Gorbachëv, he stressed the need for the country to belong to a single global community of nations which respected each other and sought to realise their obligations in the field of 'human rights'. Russia, argued Yeltsin, had to learn from the 'experience of world civilisation'. Simultaneously he emphasised that Russia was in no way inferior to other countries, including the USA. Gorbachëv had done himself no favours with Russians in summer 1991 when he had gone to the G7 meeting of the world's largest financial powers with a request for a large loan. Thus he was thought to have made the country look like a beggar. The USSR had defeated Hitler and become an industrial giant and a military superpower; it had sent rockets into space. It was difficult for Russians to accept that the government could no longer manage the state budget without foreign assistance. Yeltsin did not want to repeat this mistake. Pride in Russia was all the more important to Yeltsin since he, more than anybody else, had been responsible for breaking up the USSR and declaring Russia's independence. A stirring vision of the future was crucial if he was to effect the changes that he wanted. His career would stand or fall by his success in the matter.

For this reason he held back from using the usual term for the advanced capitalist powers: the West.[47] His purpose was to present Russia as being already part of the global community of nations. The usual contrast between communism and capitalism or between the USSR and the Western countries was no longer appropriate. Russia was following the well-trodden path towards democracy.

The problem for Yeltsin was that while he could reasonably claim that Russia had gone some way towards adopting democratic forms of government, the market economy was in its rudimentary stage. He needed to say what kind of transition to the new forms of industry, agriculture and commerce he had in mind. It would have been foolish to have specified the USA or any other leading power as his proposed model. Instead he chose Mexico, South Korea, Poland, Czechoslovakia and East Germany.[48] The rationale of this choice was evident. The effectiveness of the Mexican and South Korean economic policies in the recent past was being widely praised in the Russian contemporary press – and there was even a Mexican soap opera on television. Yeltsin was suggesting that Russians could shortly have the same level of popular affluence. His reference to Poland, Czechoslovakia and East Germany was his way of confirming that it was by no means impossible for communist countries to undertake the passage from communism to the market economy. Russians had only to believe in this possibility and they would already be on the way towards achieving it – this was Yeltsin's message.

But they must, he urged, take their fate into their own hands. Yeltsin promised no help from abroad: citizens of Russian Federation alone would have to conduct Russia's regeneration. Although he did not forget that the USSR had been replaced by a Commonwealth of Independent States, in early 1992 he was keen to assert Russia's separation from her past. The Commonwealth of Independent States was not to become yet another entanglement which might delay political and economic reforms in Moscow. Consequently he showed no embarrassment at the fact that the headquarters of the Commonwealth was to be based in the Belarusian capital Minsk. Quite the contrary: nothing could symbolise better his determination that Russia was going to undertake her transformation entirely on her own terms. In his speeches in January and February 1992 Yeltsin scarcely mentioned Belarus or Ukraine. And he made no reference at all to Georgia, Azerbaijan and Armenia. Foreign countries, including those which had newly obtained independence from the USSR, were not going to be allowed to limit Russia's scope for untrammelled self-regeneration.[49]

This was the vision of the future presented to the Russian Federation by its President. He was not offering a party programme because he had not belonged to a party since walking out of the Communist Party of the Soviet Union in 1990. Repeatedly he stressed the wish to stand above the quotidian political struggle and to act as the embodiment of Russia in her process of self-regeneration.

Yeltsin understood that people were bored stiff by portentous declarations and that they wanted action from their government. He was trying to get through to them more impressionistically. He confessed to feeling his way towards a full set of fundamental policies. In November 1992 he disarmed an audience by admitting: 'We still have a rather poor understanding of the underlying philosophical meaning of what is happening to us and what is happening to Russia.'[50] The point was not to waste time elaborating an intellectual framework of reforms, but to get on with the business of carrying out the reforms. Yeltsin stressed that this had to be accomplished without confrontation. The violence of the October Revolution and the Civil War in the years after 1917 stood as a reminder of the potential dangers; and the Russian President often reminded citizens of the subsequent horrors of the Great Terror. In speech after speech, he called on them to join him in a great effort to pull Russia towards the ultimate objectives of a full-functioning democracy and a smoothly operating market economy.

Yeltsin was also offering himself as a nation-builder. Not as a nation-builder who gives privileges to one special national or ethnic group in the new state. Not as an imperialist, a demagogue, a xenophobe or a warmonger. Yeltsin was aiming at the construction of a new state based upon political democracy, social and inter-ethnic harmony, religious tolerance, freedom of ideas, a market economy and peace between Russia and her neighbours and the rest of the world. In the terminology of political science, Yeltsin's aim was to achieve a civic nationhood in the Russian Federation and to turn the Federation into a nation-state akin to democratic states elsewhere around the globe – and to achieve this within the space of a generation. His personal role would be paramount in the formative stage. He would not only be the ruler of the new state; he would be the prophet who interpreted the needs of citizens and expounded these needs to the citizens; and he would work to bring together all citizens of goodwill.

Comparable attempts have been made in other countries.[51] The most obvious resemblance is between Yeltsin and the other post-communist reformers. Poland's Lech Wałęsa and Czechoslovakia's Vaclav Havel come to mind. They, too, rose to prominence as advocates of a future for their countries without communism. But the popular constituency for such an agenda was much broader in Poland and Czechoslovakia for the simple reason that it had been the Red Army that had imported communism to them. The task was trickier in Russia, where communism as a state ideology had originated in 1917. Even so, it should be added that Havel's hope of keeping his country together was shattered on the rocks of antagonism between the politicians of the Czechs and the Slovaks. In 1993 the Czechoslovak federation broke up, and the Czech Republic and Slovakia went their separate ways. Havel had to content himself with the role of nation-builder for the Czechs alone. Perhaps a closer resemblance would be with the tasks facing Mustafa Kemal when he became President of Turkey after the collapse of the Ottoman Empire in 1919. Mustafa Kemal also ruled a country which had been the largest part of a collapsed empire; he too had to assign a fresh identity to his fellow citizens.

But there the resemblance ends. Unlike Yeltsin, Mustafa Kemal had not actively and prominently sought imperial disintegration. Unlike Russia in 1991, Turkey had sustained defeat in a world war. The Turks had little choice but to get on with making Turkey work. Russians had yet to feel comfortable with the very idea of an independent Russia. Yeltsin's chances of success were much less propitious than he or any contemporary commentators had imagined. It is to the nature of these difficulties that I now turn.

2. WHAT IS RUSSIA?

History doesn't give lessons,
But as the historian said – and there is
No reason not to believe him – our ignorance
Is punished by history.

Alexander Kushner[1]

The scale of Yeltsin's early problems becomes evident when the difficulty of answering a basic question is recognised: what is Russia? At
a superficial level this was a problem for decades before he became
President of the Russian Federation. The official maps of the USSR on
public sale were drawn with deliberate distortions. The same was true
of the city maps. As a postgraduate student in the mid-1970s I often
plodded through the snowy streets of midwinter Leningrad with a street
plan that showed my destination hundreds of metres nearer than it really
was; and several streets that were depicted as being straight turned out
to have bends. The centre of the city was represented in a particularly
unhelpful fashion: presumably the authorities worried that invaders
might follow Lenin's strategy in the October 1917 Revolution by seizing
the Winter Palace as the main priority. Thoughts of Alice in Wonderland
came to mind. If the authorities aimed to prevent foreign powers from
acquiring accurate maps, it was a futile endeavour in an era of U2 spy
planes and, later, orbital satellite reconnaissance. But the paranoia
continued through to the end of the USSR. Alone among the world's
great powers, the USSR regarded its geography as a state secret.

But there is also a deeper level to the difficulty. Quite apart from the
trickery in the Soviet decades, Russia had always been a hard place to
define spatially. The problems lie back in history. Russia emerged from
the unification of various princedoms of eastern Slavs who converted to
Christianity in the tenth century and eventually adopted Moscow as their
capital. Territory expanded and contracted, and foreign invasions were

frequent. In the thirteenth century the Mongols overran the Eurasian plain and conquered the Russians. From the fifteenth century the tsars of Russia successfully asserted themselves, threw off the Mongol yoke and steadily, despite many setbacks, pushed the boundaries outwards. Their rulers established an empire over many peoples. From then until the beginning of the twentieth century the Russian Empire annexed land after land by the Black Sea, by the Caspian Sea, throughout Siberia, Central Asia and the Caucasus, in Poland and across Finland. The Russian Empire came to cover a sixth of the world's land surface.

Yet Russian maps before the First World War gave no definitive shape to 'Russia' within the Russian Empire. Not until after the October 1917 Revolution did this start to happen properly. In the following year the communists set up the Russian Socialist Federative Soviet Republic (RSFSR),[2] and it was this entity which became the largest member of the Union of Soviet Socialist Republics (USSR) when it was brought into existence in 1924. The RSFSR was based in the area where Russians were the huge majority of the population. In practical terms this seemed tantamount to a decision on the boundaries of Russia within the USSR. Yet this decision was followed by several revisions so that Russia's boundaries were extraordinarily fluid through to the mid-1950s. The policy-makers in the Kremlin never consulted popular opinion or explained the rationale of their decisions. Indeed sometimes their decisions cut across national and ethnic contours; and the RSFSR was much smaller after the Second World War than it had been in the 1920s. When the RSFSR became an independent state under the name of the Russian Federation after the USSR's dissolution, there was reason for its citizens to feel confused and even resentful about their territorial boundaries.

Before 1917 the official maps disguised such complexity. Once conquered, countries were obliterated as individual entities. The Russian Empire was divided into provinces. Georgia did not appear as Georgia; instead there were the provinces of Tiflis, Kutais and Kars.[3] The result contrasted with the imperial experience elsewhere. The United Kingdom was proud to hold India in its grasp and India appeared thus on the maps. The French unashamedly kept Vietnam; the Dutch, the Dutch East Indies. But the tsars of Russia strove to avoid a distinction between a 'Russian' province and a 'Georgian' province. They wanted loyalty to themselves and their empire, not to a particular sense of nationhood. Perhaps they would have behaved differently if they had not ruled a landmass empire. Georgia and other subject areas were not overseas, like

British India, but contiguous with the rest of the Romanov lands. After 1853, when Nicholas I sold Alaska to the USA, no part of the Russian Empire was separated by sea from St Petersburg, and the tsars continued to obstruct the development of a separate identity in any region. The result was that no one could be sure where Russia ended and the other countries of the Russian Empire began. Often 'Russia' and 'the Russian Empire' were used interchangeably. It was all very confusing – and this was exactly as the Romanov tsars had intended.[4]

Still the Romanovs were wary of provoking rebellions by national or religious groups and recognised that several regions presented peculiar problems of administration. Just a few compromises were put in hand. In 1794 – when Poland was partitioned between Russia, Austria-Hungary and Prussia – the Polish provinces acquired by Emperor Paul of Russia were described in official statements as the Grand Duchy of Poland. Similarly Finland, which was annexed to the Russian Empire in 1804, was called the Grand Duchy of Finland. The Russian Empire's possessions across the Caucasus mountain range – the so-called Trans-caucasus – were not only divided into provinces but were also made subject to a Viceroy for the Transcaucasus. The areas occupied today by Tajikistan, Kyrgyzstan and Uzbekistan were called the Turkestani Region (*Krai*), a name which referred unmistakably to speakers of a language other than Russian. Terms such as 'duchy' and 'region' implied a deliberate downgrading in the status of such places; they also alluded to the fact that 'Russia' and the Russian Empire were not co-extensive. Not even the tsars felt able to claim that Poland, Finland and the Transcau-casus were Russian; and like emperors elsewhere at the time, they took pride in conquering countries and incorporating them into their empire.[5]

Even so, the largest parts of the Russian Empire remained undesig-nated by names other than as ordinary provinces. Ukraine did not appear as such; instead there was Little Russia for the region around Kiev and New Russia for the region around Odessa. Present-day Belarus was called White Russia.[6] The regions inhabited mostly by ethnic Rus-sians in the European segment of the empire were described as Great Russia. And so Russia under some appellation or other covered the regions inhabited principally by the Russians, Ukrainians and Belorus-sians; and the territory of today's Kazakhstan, which is the second largest successor state of the USSR, consisted of the huge provinces of Orenburg and Semipalatinsk. The Kazakhs – unlike the Russians, Ukrainians and Belorussians – were not Slavs and most of them were not Christian, but their lands were treated as provinces within Great Russia. Consequently what appeared to pass for 'Russia' in the Russian Empire included what we nowadays know as the Russian Federation, Ukraine, Belarus and Kazakhstan. Yet the tsars went only a certain way towards clarifying their empire's internal boundaries. In many of their statements and their maps 'Russia' was even larger than as I have described – and at times was equal to the full extent of the empire. This was reinforced by the way that foreigners referred to the Russian Empire: most of the time they used 'Russia' and 'the Russian Empire' interchangeably.

After the overthrow of the Romanov dynasty in the February 1917 Revolution, the Provisional Government of Prince Georgi Lvov and Alexander Kerenski lasted only eight months. It was left to Lenin and his communist party, after their October 1917 Revolution, to resolve what kind of administrative, territorial and national order should replace the Russian Empire. After setting up the Russian Socialist Federative Soviet Republic (RSFSR) in 1918, they successively established the Ukrainian, Estonian, Latvian, Lithuanian, Belorussian, Azerbaijani, Armenian and Georgian Soviet Republics. Successful anti-communist rebellions quickly occurred in Estonia, Latvia and Lithuania. The remainder of the Soviet Republics maintained bilateral treaties with the RSFSR; and it was the desire of Joseph Stalin – who served as People's Commissar of National-ity Affairs in the RSFSR – to restore a single unitary state administration by incorporating the independent Soviet Republics as internal autono-mous republics of the RSFSR. He regarded the existence of independent Soviet Republics as a tactical convenience until such time as the Reds might win the Civil War. With the end of the fighting, Stalin wanted the RSFSR to become the successor state to the Russian Empire.

Lenin, in his last political struggle before his death in 1924, opposed Stalin and successfully insisted that a different constitution should be adopted. The decision was taken at the end of 1922 to set up a Union of Soviet Socialist Republics (USSR) wherein the RSFSR was but one Soviet Republic among the rest. The USSR formally came into being on 1 January 1924.[7]

The significance of these measures after 1917 was that, for the first time for centuries, 'Russia' was clearly distinguished from the rest of the state territorially and administratively. The other Soviet Republics were explicitly based upon their being inhabited by a large titular nationality. Thus the Ukrainian Soviet Republic had been introduced in recognition of the region having a Ukrainian national majority. The same was true for the other Soviet Republics. The rationale was that the RSFSR was the Soviet Republic where ethnic Russians were the largest national group.

This republic covered a vast area from Vladivostok in the Far East to Smolensk, near to the Belorussian border; it stretched from Archangel in the north to the Crimea in the south. In truth it also spread across areas which were not populated principally by Russians. Large tracts of Siberia, for instance, were the ancestral abode of primitive peoples. Even Turkestani Region was retained as part of the RSFSR. The so-called 'national-territorial principle' of the administrative structure was not followed in every respect; but a rough-and-ready delineation of Russia was undoubtedly in the making in the 1920s.

There is a qualification to be made here. Russia was not called Russia. The RSFSR was Russia, but it was also not Russia – or else it would have been called that. The first word in the title was *Rossiiskaya* rather than *Russkaya*. The former referred to the state in which the Russians and other peoples lived; the second to Russian ethnicity. In the title, too, was the reference to federalism. This was yet another indication that the RSFSR was not meant to be a Russian national state but a state which embraced a multiplicity of nations.

But the territorial delineation had barely been made before it was altered. The RSFSR underwent a succession of boundary changes and these were not of a minor nature. The earliest loss to the RSFSR occurred in 1924–6. The discussions behind the scenes among communist politicians, demographers and geographers continued. Already in October 1924 it was decided by the Politburo in Moscow that something had to be done to reassure the Moslems of Central Asia that communism would not limit their autonomy; it may also be that the Politburo surmised that something had to be done to prevent these Moslems from forming a Pan-Turkic alliance against the Russians. Two new Soviet Republics were carved out of the body of the existing RSFSR: the Uzbek and Turkmen Soviet Republics. By 1929 it seemed to the Politburo that the Uzbek Soviet Republic itself was too unwieldy a national conglomeration, and the Tajik-inhabited region was cut off into a Tajik Soviet Republic. The RSFSR was also diminished by the transfer of Vitebsk, Gomel and Smolensk provinces to the Belorussian Soviet Republic. The internal boundaries of the USSR had scarcely been drawn up before they were redrawn – and in each case the RSFSR lost considerable portions of its newly assigned territory.

Boundaries went on being altered. The greatest spatial loss to the RSFSR occurred in 1936. It was then that a further apparent concession was made to the Moslem peoples of the USSR with the creation of the Kazakh Soviet Republic, which became the second-largest Soviet Republic and indeed bigger than the combined area of today's Germany, France, the United Kingdom and Spain. Stalin was not in fact yielding to irresistible pressure from the Kazakh nomads. Quite the opposite was true. The nomads had undergone oppression in the previous half a dozen years. Agricultural collectivisation had led to the death of nearly half the population in the region. It also resulted in the destruction of an entire way of life. Kazakhs were forcibly sedentarised; from horse-riding pastoralists they were turned into collective farmers who cultivated arable crops. But if Kazakhs had little reason to celebrate the creation of their Soviet Republic, the RSFSR had certainly lost a large area. And the sense of uncertainty as to the territorial definition of Russia persisted.

The process did not come to an end at that. Soviet foreign policy was turned upside-down with the signature of the Non-Aggression Treaty with Nazi Germany in August 1939. Stalin expanded the USSR's frontier into eastern Poland; he consolidated this by annexing Estonia, Latvia and Lithuania as new (or rather renewed) Soviet Republics. Thus they became the thirteenth, fourteenth and fifteenth constituent Republics of the USSR. The USSR also tried to annex Finland. A Soviet–Finnish war took place in the winter of 1939–40, and ended with hundreds of thousands of Red Army casualities. Unexpectedly the ill-equipped Finns repulsed the attack and a stalemate arose. Nevertheless the USSR negotiated a treaty with Finland which moved the frontier northwards so that Leningrad had a greater buffer-zone between itself and Finland. The RSFSR was thereby expanded for the first time since the end of the Russian Civil War. But there was also a diminution. In March 1940, while war with Finland was in progress, Stalin scooped a large region of the RSFSR – most of it uninhabited by ethnic Russians – into the new Karelo-Finnish Soviet Republic of the USSR. Altogether the RSFSR was spatially reduced as the result of the various changes.

Then in June 1941 Hitler invaded. The entire western area of the USSR was overrun and subjugated by the Third Reich. Russia in all its guises, past and potential, was on the point of disappearance. Especially in 1941–2, when the Germans occupied an area of the RSFSR where 30 per cent of its pre-war population had lived, Hitler's Ostministerium looked forward to further conquest and to the prospect of governing all the Russians.

But against the odds – at least as they appeared to most people at the time – the USSR broke the spine of the Wehrmacht. Nazi Germany was defeated. The USSR's frontiers were changed yet again and the RSFSR, too, underwent a territorial revision. In the first place the

RSFSR–Estonia frontier was stabilised in such a fashion as to give a little additional space to the RSFSR beyond the line of the RSFSR–Estonian Treaty of 1920. This was one of the areas left on the map for potential contention in the distant future. Estonia, Latvia and Lithuania had been re-annexed to the USSR in 1944, and the Western Allies had to accept this. It would have taken a full-scale war against the USSR to secure independence for these countries – something that was inconceivable at the time even though the Soviet Union did not yet have an active programme to produce a nuclear bomb. The most that the United Kingdom and the USA would contemplate was to refuse to give formal recognition to the annexation. This formal position never changed in subsequent years, and in 1945 Stalin knew he could proceed to dispose of Estonia, Latvia and Lithuania however he liked.

Substantial discussion, however, took place in the Grand Alliance about the region further to the west. As a result, the eastern border of Poland was shifted westwards. The main affected territories involved the Belorussian and Lithuanian Soviet Republics, which gained land from Poland. In compensation to Poland, which was being turned into a fraternal communist state, the eastern frontier of Germany, too, was pushed westward. It was as if Poland had been picked up and dropped 200 miles further west. But there was one part of pre-war Germany that Stalin decided to transfer to neither Poland nor Lithuania. This was Königsberg and the surrounding area. Stalin renamed it Kaliningrad, after the USSR head of state Mikhail Kalinin (who had not the slightest association with the city), and allocated it to the RSFSR. Geographically this was a strange idea. Kaliningrad province would become a 'Russian' enclave at the furthest western edge of the USSR, separated from the RSFSR by the Lithuanian Soviet Republic.

The boundary changes to the RSFSR in 1940 and 1944–5 were the only ones since the end of the Civil War which had resulted in the RSFSR's expansion; and even then the expansion was outbalanced by the creation of the Karelo-Finnish Republic from the body of the RSFSR in 1940. But the main point is that the RSFSR was having its frontiers changed yet again. There was no consultation of public opinion nor even any official explanation of the rationale for redrawing the map. The artificiality of those frontiers was highlighted by the accretion of distant Kaliningrad province, where until the end of the Second World War only Germans and Poles lived in any number. Kaliningrad province was more an assertion of the USSR's power than an ethnically reasonable decision. The city of the philosopher Immanuel Kant became the city of the USSR head of state Mikhail Kalinin, whose wife languished in a Gulag camp on Stalin's orders. It was the most bizarre redrawing of Europe's map of nation-states occurring after the Second World War.

There was just one other change of importance. At the time of the Yalta Conference in 1945, Churchill and Roosevelt assumed that, as German defeat became imminent, Soviet help would be necessary for Japan's final defeat. Stalin agreed, but exacted a price. The northern islands of Japan, he demanded, should be transferred to the USSR. These isles were within sight of Vladivostok, the RSFSR's great city on the Pacific Ocean; they were known to the Russians as the Kurile Islands – and to the Japanese as the Northern Territories.

The defeat of Japan proved easier than had been expected at Yalta. American scientists had worked intensively upon the production of an atomic bomb, and in August the USAAF dropped these horrific new devices on Hiroshima and Nagasaki. Emperor Hirohito offered his country's surrender and the USA's military occupation of Japan began. But Harry Truman, who succeeded to the US Presidency after Roosevelt's death in April 1945, abided by the Yalta Conference's commitment to the USSR. The Red Army had fought its way from Vladivostok on to the northern islands of Japan. Within weeks the Kurile Islands were in the hands of the USSR and were incorporated into the RSFSR's administrative boundaries. Before the Second World War Stalin had been confronted by a powerful, menacing Japan. He was determined to prevent such a threat being mounted ever again – and the RSFSR benefited territorially from his determination. Stalin relished the settlement he had achieved. He grabbed not only the Kurile Islands but also southern Sakhalin, which had been lost to Russia as the result of the Russo-Japanese war of 1904–5. The reconquest by the Red Army, Stalin triumphantly declared, removed a 'blot of shame'.[8]

Yet Stalin was not the last Soviet communist leader to redefine the RSFSR. In 1954 his rising successor, Party First Secretary Nikita Khrushchëv, proposed the transfer of Crimea from the RSFSR to the Ukrainian Soviet Republic. The ostensible motive for this was largely logistical. Crimea's transport links were more convenient to Kiev than to Moscow. It made sense, argued Khrushchëv in the confidential discussions of the Kremlin, to put Ukraine in command of the peninsula.[9]

The emotional echoes of the decision were strong even though public debate was prohibited. Crimea had been conquered by the troops of Catherine the Great in 1735. They had attacked and defeated the Tatars, who had been Russia's enemies for centuries. Generations of educated Russians were taught to regard Crimea as a 'Russian' region bought by Russian soldiers' blood; and the Russian Imperial fleet had been a strong presence at Sevastopol by the Black Sea. Even so, Khrushchëv blithely transferred this region from Russia to Ukraine. His reasoning was probably not confined to geography. Khrushchëv had served as First Secretary of the Communist Party of Ukraine before and after the Second World War; he was therefore acutely aware that Stalin had trampled upon Ukrainian national identity from the 1930s and that this had done much damage to Russo-Ukrainian relations at the popular level. Many of Khrushchëv's political associates either were Ukrainians or had worked in Ukraine. After Stalin's death he began a display of conciliatory gestures to Ukrainians. Educational and cultural controls were relaxed somewhat– and the release of Crimea into the administrative framework of Ukraine was a sign of the Kremlin's goodwill.

This decision, at any rate, was the penultimate alteration of the RSFSR's territory. The very last was taken in 1956 when the Karelo-Finnish Soviet Republic, to the north of Leningrad, was abolished and the region was re-absorbed into the RSFSR as the Karelian Autonomous Soviet Socialist Republic. Among the stimuli was Khrushchëv's wish to put the Stalinist past behind him. Stalin had set up the Karelo-Finnish Soviet Republic with barely disguised expansionist intentions, and its continued existence was an unnecessary complication in the USSR's relations with Finland.

The Soviet Party Politburo left the RSFSR at that, and the 1960s, 1970s and 1980s were decades when territorial adjustments ceased to be made; this inactivity was unprecedented since the October 1917 Revolution. Behind the scenes, in fact, there were still discussions about the Russian frontier. Politburo member Nikolai Podgorny, who became the USSR head of state when Nikita Khrushchëv was ousted in 1964, reopened the cartographical question. It was his case that the transfer of land to Ukraine in 1954 had been niggardly and demanded that Stavropol Region – to the east of Crimea and bordering the Black Sea coast – should also be removed from the RSFSR.[10] The Politburo turned him down. Presumably it was thought too provocative to ethnic Russian opinion. Whereas Crimea was cut off from the RSFSR by Ukraine, Stavropol Region was integrated into the RSFSR's territory and its transfer would have caused more problems than it could have solved. With that, discussions came to an end about redrawing of the map of the RSFSR. There was no further alteration to the boundaries of the

RSFSR through to the USSR's abolition – and things remain like this in the Russian Federation.

Across the period after 1917 the maps told a tale of the changeability and diminution of the RSFSR – and the RSFSR, in the understanding of most people, was 'Russia'. Territorially it would have been more indulgent to Russian nationalist opinion if the entire USSR had been known as the RSFSR – as Stalin had originally proposed in the early 1920s. This would have allowed the Russian people to think of 'Russia' and the entire Soviet state as one and the same thing and to take pride in this as a Russian military and political achievement. Alternatively the Politburo could have permitted Lenin's USSR to stay in place with the RSFSR as the largest Soviet Republic and refrained from cutting away whole regions from the RSFSR. Before the Second World War there were five Soviet Republics – the Uzbek Soviet Republic (1924), the Turkmen Soviet Republic (1924), the Kazakh Soviet Republic (1936), the Kirgiz Soviet Republic (1936) and the Karelo-Finnish Soviet Republic (1940) – formed entirely out of the body of the RSFSR. Altogether this quintet covered an area as big as Western Europe from Portugal through to Germany.

But there are two diametrically opposite ways of interpreting this. The first highlights the fact that the spatial reduction of 'Russia' under successive Soviet leaders was not to the liking of Russians living outside the RSFSR. The second starts from the premise that Russia's recurrent diminution served to boost Russian national pride and prestige. The bigger the colonial possessions, the more glorious the empire. Thus the handing over of large tracts of land from the RSFSR to new Soviet Republics may have indicated not so much an unease in the Politburo about the threat from the non-Russians as a complacent assumption that the Russians were so comfortably in control of the USSR that virtually any amount of territory could be transferred from the RSFSR without permanent loss of Russian political control in the USSR. Personally I feel that both ways of analysis count for something. Russia became a lesser country in the decades after 1917; it also became a greater one. Two contrary forces were simultaneously at work – and operated through to the end of the USSR. Her rulers admired Russia and feared her simultaneously. 'The Russian Question' was never definitively solved in the Soviet period.

This was not just a question of territory. In a constitutional sense, too, the RSFSR had always been an oddity. Although it was the first Soviet Republic to be established, there was no agreed plan for its permanent status. Many leading Bolsheviks expected the RSFSR to engorge the non-Russian regions of the former Russian Empire once the military conflict was over. In 1919–21, as new Soviet Republics were being established, the authority of the RSFSR was paramount. Each Soviet Republic, including the RSFSR, had its own government; and each such government, designated as a Council of People's Commissars (or Sovnarkom), was ostensibly in control of an independent state. Yet the relationships between the RSFSR and the other Soviet Republics were highly unequal. The main ministerial bodies (or people's commissariats) of the RSFSR, including those responsible for the armed forces and foreign policy and the economy, were placed in a position of direct command over their counterparts elsewhere. Lenin and the Politburo were determined to hold on to the levers of central political control. By party decree they prohibited the other Soviet Republics from signing treaties with each other. The only permissible kind of treaty was a bilateral one with the RSFSR – and such a treaty, of course, would be drawn up in Moscow.[11]

Lenin, however, constantly denied that the RSFSR should simply swallow up the 'borderlands' when the Civil War was over. While wanting real power to remain concentrated in Moscow, he also wanted this to be disguised. In 1922 he successfully insisted that the Soviet Republics should acquire equal formal status with a Union of Soviet Socialist Republics (USSR). The constituent bodies would be the RSFSR, the Ukrainian Soviet Republic, the Belorussian Soviet Republic and the Transcaucasian Soviet Federation (which included Georgia, Abkhazia, Armenia and Azerbaijan). All these Republics were to be subordinate to the official authorities of the USSR as a whole. The USSR government had precedence over all the other governments, including the government of the RSFSR.[12]

Yet the RSFSR was already suffering in some ways in comparison with the other Soviet Republics. The USSR was a one-party state and its party staffed, controlled and directed all the Soviet Republics. Each Soviet republic had a parallel communist party taking its orders from the central apparatus of the All-Union Communist Party in Moscow.[13] But whereas there was a Communist Party of Ukraine, there was no equivalent Communist Party of Russia. All the Soviet Republics had communist parties except for the RSFSR. Armenia, Azerbaijan, Belorussia, Georgia and Ukraine had communist parties, and even little Abkhazia had one. But not the RSFSR. The communist organisations in the RSFSR had to submit directly to the All-Union Communist Party without any intermediate tier. This continued to be the case throughout the pre-war decades. The reasons for this can easily be guessed. Russians filled most of the leading posts and the RSFSR itself was massively larger territorially and economically than any other Soviet Republic. If the RSFSR acquired its own communist party, much administrative duplication would have occurred. But also the communist political leadership in Moscow felt the need to prevent a Russian national agency being formed which might one day challenge the integrity and supremacy of the USSR and its institutions. Lenin did not want to have a problem with Russia.

Nor did Stalin. By the late 1920s he was reversing those policies which appeared to give precedence to peoples other than the Russians. Yet he set his face against the foundation of a Russian Communist Party in the sense of a party with a network of organisations covering the RSFSR. Some among his associates, in fact, did not share his thinking on the matter. In the Second World War, several communist leaders discussed the possibility of forming a Russian Communist Party. Most of them were based in Leningrad, where they had survived a siege by the German armed forces lasting 900 days. Under the leadership of Andrei Zhdanov, Politburo member and Stalin's confidant, their morale was high after 1945. But when Zhdanov died in 1948, they lost their principal protector. Stalin, suspicious of Leningrad leaders as constituting a rival political group, had all of them shot. Among the charges laid against them was that they had espoused Russian nationalism and advocated the creation of a Russian Communist Party in the RSFSR in parallel to the communist parties in the other Soviet Republics.[14]

Khrushchëv took a somewhat different approach after Stalin's death. He recognised that the provinces of the RSFSR were disadvantaged in their negotiations with the central party apparatus in Moscow by the ban on any RSFSR-wide party agency. The Communist Party of Ukraine had opportunities denied to the party organisations in Leningrad, Saratov and Magnitogorsk. But Khrushchëv, too, feared the potential of a Russian Communist Party. As a compromise he established a Bureau for the RSFSR (Byuro po RSFSR) in the Secretariat of the Central Committee.[15] The idea was to facilitate control and consultation across the RSFSR; and perhaps, too, he wanted to offer some crumbs of self-esteem to the ethnic Russian party functionaries. It was a minor modification which Khrushchëv's successor Brezhnev thought altogether too risky. After Khrushchëv had been removed in 1964, the Bureau was abolished and this remained the situation through to the Gorbachëv years. The

RSFSR kept its right to having a government, its Council of Ministers; but there was no equivalent party agency. Brezhnev mollified any feelings of resentment by constructing a magnificent high-rise building for the RSFSR by the river Moskva in central Moscow. But derogations from the authority and prestige of the supreme USSR bodies were punished.

The dam burst in 1990. The causes were twofold: first, many communist party functionaries in the RSFSR hated Gorbachëv's reformist objectives; second, they were reacting to Yeltsin's ploy of using the state bodies of the RSFSR as a way of undermining the authority of the institutions of the USSR as a whole. Ivan Polozkov and other conservative-communist politicians foresaw that the result would be the disintegration of the Soviet Union. To avert this they demanded permission should be given for the formation of a Russian Communist Party. The paradox was a delicate one. The original ban on an RSFSR-based communist party derived from the fear that such a party would destabilise the USSR. Polozkov, however, wanted a Russian Communist Party for exactly the opposite purpose: namely to avoid any such destabilisation. The USSR had to be maintained. Gorbachëv, while unsympathetic to the communist conservatism of Polozkov, granted his request. Apart from anything else, Polozkov might prove to be a useful counterweight against Yeltsin. Only a year before the USSR's collapse the central communist leadership, after over seventy years in power, at last sanctioned the creation of a party representing the communists of the largest Soviet Republic, the RSFSR.[16]

By then Yeltsin had ceased to be a communist party member. His election to the RSFSR Presidency in June 1991 testified to the weakness of the Russian Communist Party's appeal to the average Russian citizen. During the attempted coup of August 1991 Polozkov's comrades sided with the coup leaders and fell into temporary disgrace. The situation was convoluted. By the last months of the year Yeltsin, ex-communist and anti-communist, was leading Russia into independence. But the 'Russia' he led remained designated not as Russia nor even as the Russian Federation but as the Russian Soviet Federative Socialist Republic (RSFSR). As such it was prescriptively committed to a socialist social order. Indeed the RSFSR Constitution of 1978, the last to be passed into legal writ, recognised the communist party organisations as the vanguard of the country's political forces. Yeltsin initiated the attack on this heritage. He largely ceased to mention the RSFSR. Instead he referred to 'the Russian Federation' or even simply 'Russia'.[17] Long live Russia! In the final months of the USSR's existence Yeltsin took the stage as a

Russian patriot who would sweep away the communist party and its ideology and allow Russia to flourish as never before.

He implied that this new country had an unquestionable set of boundaries and that the spatial identity of Russia was clear. Indeed, he suggested, if only by omission, that the country was an old and established one. Perhaps he himself believed this. But the historical facts were against such a position. The Russian Federation – as the RSFSR was becoming known – was an entity created in the half-decade after the October 1917 Revolution and subjected to substantial boundary alterations in 1924, 1926, 1936, 1940, 1945, 1954 and 1956.

One of the elementary features of the modern state is its territorial frontier. In previous centuries this was not so. States could be defined by the name of their peoples or even their rulers: King Cnut ruled the Angles, Saxons and Danes, not England and Denmark. Such states occupied whatever space was occupied by the designated peoples. This is no longer the case. Territorial delineation is crucial to statehood in the contemporary world. It is true that the RSFSR's boundaries were clearly known in any given year of the Soviet period. The problem was that those boundaries were changed without reference to the opinions of the inhabitants. The Politburo decided; the press reported; the inhabitants noted. Not once was there a serious explanation of why the central party authorities demarcated the frontier in a particular way. The citizens of the RSFSR were typically told, in a hole-in-the-corner announcement either in *Pravda* or in the USSR's legal gazetteers, that yet another change had been made. Frontiers were discussed in secret and imposed without consultation. Signposts were put up the day after the decisions had been made, and this was how citizens first learned of any changes.

Many other countries have undergone drastic territorial change. The maps of Europe in particular have often been altered. Cartographers were hard at work throughout the twentieth century in consequence of military victory or defeat. Hungary until 1919 sprawled across Central Europe; now it is shorter and slimmer, having lost land to Romania, Slovakia and Poland. It was the price Hungary paid for having been a leading component of the Habsburg monarchy, which fell to the Allies in the First World War. By contrast Italy, which had joined the Allies in 1915, was rewarded by the gift of the Tyrol. Poland in 1919–20 was shaped by two events. The first was the gathering of her lands out of remnants of the empires of the Habsburgs, the Hohenzollerns and the Romanovs; the second was her victory over the rampaging Red Army in summer 1920, which led to the treaty of Riga. Poland was reshaped yet again when Stalin, Churchill and Roosevelt agreed to move both her western and her eastern frontiers westwards. This last agreement involved a reconfiguration of Germany, whose frontiers had already been reduced by the Treaty of Versailles in 1919 and then re-expanded by the Third Reich after 1933. With the defeat of Nazism two separate German states were created: the Federal Republic of Germany and the German Democratic Republic. Not until 1989 were these two states united.

The outcomes of the First and Second World Wars prescribed the boundaries within which all this occurred. No Hungarian, Italian, Pole or German could fail to be aware of why the boundaries of their states had undergone their particular alterations. War, in each case, had been the mother of cartography.

Yet most of the alterations to the RSFSR had been made in peacetime and for reasons which had little to do with the security of the USSR. The setting up of the Karelo-Finnish Republic in 1940 and the incorporation of Königsberg in the RSFSR in 1945 are the exceptions. In the other instances the rationale was the product of the USSR's internal politics. Successively the RSFSR had given up territory to newly created Soviet Republics. All this had occurred as if by the wave of a conjurer's hand. Each time the rabbit – the RSFSR – came out of the hat, it was a different shape. No wonder that the RSFSR had little pull on the imagination of its citizens. At best the alterations did not offend them; at worst they were yet another manifestation of policies being decided without their involvement. Politics was someone else's business. The citizens were alienated in a most basic sense from the entity that before 1991 was their state. This boded ill for the future of the RSFSR as an independent state. Its rulers might call it Russia. They might wrap themselves in the cloak of Russian nationhood. But they had not prepared public opinion for the audacious step they had taken. They had taken an historic gamble with their people.

3. WHO ARE THE RUSSIANS?

We're often accused
Of being cut off from the masses.
But tell me: where are the popular masses
We're meant to doing something good for?

A. Zinoviev, 'My Home'[1]

Boundaries were not the only difficulty. Few states have been created with so little sense of national purpose in common as characterised the citizens of the Russian Federation in 1991. There were 148 million of them at that time, and about 83 per cent were ethnic Russians.[2] This was a high proportion of the population, quite high enough by itself for Russians, if they had wished, to set about turning their country into the kind of place they wanted.

Comparison with other countries is again helpful. When the Germans discussed their nationhood in the late 1940s, they agreed that economic regeneration and social welfare were the prime objectives – and the Western Allies ensured that democratic values were inserted into the debate. When the Poles were working out an answer to their own national question in the early 1990s, their universal aim was to rid themselves of Russian influence and eradicate the Soviet ideological heritage. A core of national purpose existed in Germany and Poland despite all the subsidiary disagreements. The Russians in 1991 had no such unity. They had not been conquered like the Germans at the end of the Second World War; they had not been released from the USSR's political and military domination like the Poles in 1989. Russian citizens were mystified as to why 'their' state – the Soviet Union – had disintegrated. Confusion was the most common emotion. No general viewpoint on the situation prevailed: Russians as a people were divided about their national identity; and even the fact that communist rule had come to an end was not a cause for general rejoicing.

It was not a new thing for the Russians to be confused or divided. There is a myth – and it is a myth believed by many Russians – that the Russian people has always had a clear sense of nationhood and that this national sense has been more or less constant for centuries. The history of the country points to a more complex picture. Russians at the beginning of the twenty-first century are different in important ways from what they were at the end of the nineteenth century. Wars, revolutions, industrialisation, urbanisation and mass literacy have generated transformation – and it is a transformation that continues into the twenty-first century.

Conditions in 1900 were grim for most Russians. There is a widespread but erroneous assumption that they were a privileged nation in the Russian Empire.[3] In fact the huge majority of the Russian people were peasants with a distinctly second-class status in the society ruled by the tsars. Sometimes Russian peasants were treated worse than the peasantry of the empire's other nationalities. The most striking example occurred in 1861, when Emperor Alexander II abolished the right of the landed gentry to own peasants. At his insistence Polish peasants received a distinctly more generous economic settlement than Russian peasants. Alexander II wanted to humble the Polish landlords but was nervous about alienating the landlords of Russian peasants. The general discrimination against peasants – whether or not they were Russian – continued in later decades. Unlike other social 'estates', through to the turn of the century, the peasantry was subject to corporal punishment in the judicial system; and even when this formal discrimination was abolished in 1904, the peasantry was still not fully integrated into the wider political community.[4]

Russian peasants felt more attached to their village and Christian beliefs than to their nationhood. Their concerns were of a national kind mainly when Russia was under attack. They rose against Napoleon's invasion in 1812. They also – or at least thousands of them – volunteered when Russia went to war with the Ottoman Empire in the Balkans in 1877.[5] But they were not always patriotic in an emergency. Their support for Emperor Nicholas I was weak during the Crimean War of 1854–6. Much depended, it seems, on whether the peasantry felt that the war was just: they needed to feel their territory or religion was under threat – and that the government was somehow acting in their interest and not merely in the narrower interest of the social and economic elites. The government had only limited means to alter the situation. Schools were few and literacy was thinly spread. Transport and communications across the empire were frail. Power in Russia was politically centralised but opinion was outside the control of the Kremlin.

The peasantry was in any case a very diverse social group. Although most of them were poor, some households – especially in the southern steppes and in western Siberia – were growing rich as the market economy expanded in the late nineteenth century. Religious organisations and sects were legion. In the seventeenth century a great schism took place in the Russian Orthodox Church when Patriarch Nikon, with Tsar Alexei's complicity, attempted a reform of the liturgy. As a result there was a vast exodus to the borderlands of the Muscovite state by Russians determined to stay loyal to tradition. The refugees became known as the 'Old Believers'. Although they were the largest group of opponents of the official Church, there were plenty of other denominations of Christianity in Russia and the variety increased in the nineteenth century as Baptists, *khlysty*, Seventh-Day Adventists and Tolstoians grew in number. Even the Russian Orthodox Church was an unsatisfactory servant of the secular state at the parochial level. Its priests were proverbially needy, drunken and ignorant; frequently they followed the aspirations of their rural congregations more than the instructions of the bishops. Beneath the surface, 'Holy Russia' was a long way from being homogeneous.

Among the Russian peasants and workers there was hostility to state authority. The 'people' paid taxes and delivered conscripts only under protest. Folk memory of the social system before 1861, when gentry landlords could impose their will arbitrarily on their peasantry, was vivid. The lower social orders, once they had discharged their obligations to government and employers, were left to administer themselves. In the countryside they did this through the village land communes, which pursued a primitive egalitarianism in allocating the land and enforcing customary justice. In the towns the workers organised themselves in a similar fashion through so-called *zemlyachestva*, which were based on the principle of geographical origin.

Sustained patriotism in such a society was mainly an urban and middle-class phenomenon.[6] But the trend was growing for Russians to identify themselves as Russians and not just as people of a particular village or a particular Christian denomination. Through to the twentieth century this growing feeling was associated with reverence for the Emperor. Icons of the incumbent Romanov ruler were kept in peasant huts. Yet it was never a reverence automatically accorded. When Russian peasants were told of legislation they disliked, they craftily decided that the Emperor's advisers had deceived him – and they declined to obey such laws. This occurred after the 1861 Emancipation Edict. The financial terms of the settlement were disadvantageous to most peasants. Some of them allowed themselves to be persuaded that Alexander II's real intention had been to give them all the agricultural land and that the gentry landlords had hidden such a decree from them. It took army units to suppress the subsequent disturbances in the countryside. Allegiance to 'the little father', as the Emperor was known, was unaffected. Patriotism and loyalty to the dynasty were co-extensive.

This situation began to be changed by the events of Bloody Sunday, 9 January 1905, when troops fired upon a procession of civil rights petitioners outside the Winter Palace. The dynasty fell into disrepute and never fully recovered its hold on the people's affections. In the same year there was a rise in national consciousness. Much impetus came from urbanisation and the spread of literacy. As Russians gathered in the towns and read newspapers like *Gazeta-kopeika*, they came to understand that some things bound them together more than just their religion and their village of birth.[7] The presence of other peoples among the migrants to the towns – Ukrainians, Tatars or Finns – served to emphasise the importance of the common language for Russians.

Yet this Russian consciousness was an extremely diverse phenomenon. A chasm in material conditions existed between the propertied elites and the mass of the people, and workers and peasants were treated without thought for their dignity as human beings. The upper classes had long since lost contact with the peasantry. From the early eighteenth century, under Peter the Great, these classes had tried to acquire an education and a culture borrowed from the West. Little of this percolated down to the mass of the people. But the deepening sense of nationhood, despite its variety, was unmistakable. Both aristocrats and peasants had a sharp sense that they were different from other nations and were proud of the contrast. Meanwhile, middle-class groups were also moving toward nationalism. This was the case for influential industrialists in the Moscow region who disliked the competition of European capitalism and sought – in religion, culture and politics – to put forward a 'patriotic' alternative to foreign models. Several among them came from families of Old Believers and had been brought up to admire the customs of the ancient Russian past. In principle they also espoused patriarchal support for their workers even though in reality the conditions of the Russian working class were as bad as anywhere else on the continent.

Other nationalist groups, whilst uninterested in the material conditions of the Russian people, were obsessed by the threat to Tsar and Empire posed by disgruntled non-Russians. One such group was the Union of the Russian People, which objected to the concessions Emperor Nicholas II had been forced to make after the revolutionary tumult in 1905–6. The Union was anti-semitic and generally xenophobic; its belief was that the Russians were the only nation in the Russian Empire on whom the dynasty could safely rely.

Yet most Russians were deaf to the slogans of the political far right. The First World War brought millions of them into the armed forces and the factories, where they were subjected to patriotic propaganda. The government used images of the Imperial family more sparingly than in previous years.[8] Although he had clawed back some prestige after the turmoil of 1905–6, Nicholas II remained unpopular. Rumours proliferated. It was said that the Empress was having an affair with the Siberian 'holy man' Grigori Rasputin and that she was conducting a subversive diplomatic struggle for Russia to sign a separate peace with Germany and Austria-Hungary. Nevertheless most young Russian males were willing to fight in the defence of their country. When leaders of some socialist parties opposed the war effort, they quickly lost the popularity they had. Millions of volunteers enlisted in the Imperial forces in 1914; and when the authorities stirred up feeling against the German invaders, they met with little opposition. By then it was clear that devotion to country and dedication to dynasty had become separate emotions. Russians no longer cared about Nicholas II. They wanted a government that could act efficiently against the wartime enemy.

The test of public opinion came in 1917, when the Romanov monarchy fell in the February Revolution. Strikes and demonstrations against Nicholas II took place in the capital city Petrograd. Soldiers supported the workers and the Emperor abdicated. The Provisional Government, at first under the leadership of liberals, committed itself to territorial defence and extensive civic freedoms. Unfortunately the conditions were unpropitious for the new ministers even after they took the Mensheviks and Socialist-Revolutionaries into coalition. There was military defeat, economic collapse and administrative breakdown. The workers, soldiers, sailors and peasants of the empire became preoccupied by questions of bread, land and popular representation. They also sought an end to the war on terms that would hold the state intact – and they came to believe that the Provisional Government was more interested in a war of annexation than in an honourable peace. Increasingly the Bolsheviks made gains in the elections to soviets, trade unions and factory-workshop committees by arguing that only a transfer of power to a socialist regime would resolve the questions. Carefully they adjusted their vocabulary to the language of the streets. Their popularity rose.[9] Lenin, returning to Petrograd from his hiding place in Helsinki, gained his party's support for the overthrow of the Provisional Government. The Soviet state was founded under his leadership in October 1917.

In many parts of the former Russian Empire the 'national question' was posed ever more sharply. Ukrainians, Finns and Georgians had demanded autonomy between February and October, and forces in their public life began to contemplate secession after the communist seizure of power. But Russians were deaf to attempts to mobilise them as a national group. When General Lavr Kornilov attempted a counter-revolutionary mutiny against the Provisional Government in August, he made a direct appeal to Russian patriotism. Even his troops were unconvinced by him; he was arrested and put into prison at Bykhov.

During the Revolution and Civil War it was hard to persuade most Russians that nationalism would best serve their interests. When they voted in 1917 they did not worry about the nationality of the leaderships of the various parties. Jews, Poles, Latvians and Georgians were prominent in practically all the important political organisations – and not just in the Bolshevik Party. The cities of Russia teemed with refugees from the borderlands in the First World War. Although the influx was composed mainly of non-Russians, there was no popular backlash.[10] At the Constituent Assembly election in November 1917 the overwhelming proportion of voters in the Russian provinces, 85 per cent, opted for socialist parties with a decisively anti-nationalist programme.[11] This indifference to national appeals continued in subsequent years. The pogroms against Jewish communities occurred mainly in Ukraine. The White Armies of Kolchak, Denikin and Yudenich found it difficult to recruit peasant volunteers for patriotic military service against the Red Army. Generally Russians wanted to be left alone. Most of them were frantically trying to survive the disease, malnutrition and economic disruption that were a severe problem everywhere.

This is not to say that national assertiveness did not exist. It would be fanciful to think that Russians, who were the largest element in the Red Army, did not feel that in conquering Ukraine, the Transcaucasus and Central Asia they were to some extent winning back ancestral territory legitimately held by Russia. This was not true of the Bolshevik party leadership's ideology. But it was almost certainly part of the mental baggage of the average conscripted soldier. When war flared up between the Soviet state and Poland in 1920, there were plenty of volunteers ready to fight under the Red banner against Russia's historic enemies.

The next great stage in the development of Russian national consciousness came in the 1930s. Until then the Soviet state authorities had tried to restrict its manifestation. The Orthodox Church was persecuted; peasant customs were ridiculed. But this official hostility to things Russian began to change after the abandonment of the New Economic Policy in 1928. The regime was worried about popular opinion. The sense had been growing among Russians that the October 1917 Revolution had benefited the other peoples of the USSR to a greater extent than the Russian nation. Such support accrued to the Bolsheviks for the establishment of a socialist government had not been a mandate for the systematic assault on the social, cultural and religious traditions undertaken by the communists. The fact that many members of the ascendant party leadership were not Russians began to be a cause of resentment. The 'Russian question' was at least starting to be posed at the popular level. A poster appeared on walls in Saratov depicting two groups of men confronting each other across the river Volga. On one bank stood Trotski, Zinoviev and Kamenev – all Jews; on the other bank were the Georgians Stalin, Yenukidze and Ordzhonikidze. The caption read as follows: 'And the Slavs fell into dispute about who was going to rule in Old Russia.'[12]

An economic transformation took place. Through the First and Second Five-Year Plans, starting in 1928, an industrial society was built. Russians swarmed from the countryside into the cities of Russia and indeed the rest of the USSR. They were educated and trained. They were habituated to new rhythms of work and leisure and to new patterns of life. Although it took until the late 1950s for a majority of the Soviet population to reside in towns, the decisive move towards this was accomplished in the 1930s.

The impact of all this on Russian national consciousness was diverse. Unlike many other nations of the USSR, the Russians faced no impediment to getting educated in their own language; and after they left school, there was no negative consequence for their wishing to speak in their own language. Books by classical Russian authors became available in cheap editions and by the late 1930s nearly all adults below pensionable age had become literate. The history of Russia ancient and modern was propagated by the press and radio. Russians could take open pride in their Russianness. This was not merely a matter of official policy; there was also a demographic trend at work which would have had an impact regardless of the ideological imperatives of Marxism-Leninism. Migrating from villages across the Soviet Union, Russian peasants became ever more aware of their common background. Abruptly the association with a particular hamlet or patch of agricultural land faded. Urbanisation deepened the sense of nationhood. The authorities gave this further stimulus by suggesting, too, that the Russian people was in many ways – culturally and economically – superior to the other peoples of the USSR.

Russians migrated not only from one part of the RSFSR to another but also to other Soviet Republics. Fetching up among Ukrainians in Ukraine or Uzbeks in Uzbekistan, they became more sharply aware of their distinctiveness. There was a massive influx of ethnic Russians into the newly developing areas of industry in the Don Basin and Siberia as they went in search of work – and in flight from the horrors of agricultural collectivisation. This, too, increased the importance of their national identity to them.

Yet there were also many aspects of Russian life which did not change very much. The arrival of peasants in the towns had the unintended result of ruralising the urban areas.[13] The migration was intense and, initially, uncontrolled. The authorities introduced a universal passport system in 1932 so that the police might regulate things. But the urgent need of factories and mines for labour meant that the influx continued. Usually when the migrants reached a town, the amenities were abysmal. Living conditions were grim. Newcomers sought out peasants from the same province in order to settle into the area. The traditional *zemlyachestva* were maintained. Peasants coped with the chaotic environment by applying attitudes which they had picked up in the villages. They were suspicious of all authority. They had always been sceptical about the tsar and government and they were no less sceptical about the communists. They did not expect too much from officialdom and did not receive more than they expected. They stuck together collectively. They kept their mouths shut about politics.[14]

Yet not every aspect of rural life was imported into the towns. Peasants who hastened to the urban areas in search of food and employment were leaving a way of life behind. They had seen their prosperous neighbours arrested, their priests shot, their churches turned into warehouses and their church bells melted down. In the towns they were separated from the sense of natural environment and the seasons that they had taken for granted over the centuries. They faced new, troubling conditions. Often they had lost contact with their families in the great upheavals of the 1930s. When they reached the towns, they were fortunate if they could find lodgings, church or a cafeteria. Life was always hard in the countryside, but the direct and daily oppression by the USSR's administration was still more difficult to bear. The Soviet urban existence wrecked more than could soon be replaced.

Then a foreigner caused even greater destruction. This was Adolf Hitler. Tossing aside the Nazi–Soviet Non-Aggression Pact of 1939, he ordered the preparation of Operation Barbarossa on 22 June 1941. Peasants in Russia were yearning for liberation from the yoke of the collective farms laid upon them by Stalin. Many preferred invasion by Germany if it might mean an end to the communist regime and the reversion to the social customs and religion of the past. The Nazis, however, had a different purpose. Slavs were marked down as *Untermenschen*. Although Russians were not to be exterminated like Jews, Roma and homosexuals, they were marked down as members of an inferior race to be treated with brutality. Their economy was to be ransacked. They were to have no legal rights under German military occupation, and millions of them were transported to Germany as forced labourers in concentration camps. Russians who were communist party members were subject to instant execution. But the Russian people in general were put on notice that they were being persecuted for no other reason than that they were Slavs. The 'Great Fatherland War' pressed national consciousness deep into the psyche of Russians.

With the eventual defeat of Nazi Germany, Russian national pride rose to a peak. Russia had supplied the greatest proportion of soldiers for the Red Army and workers for the armaments factories. Russians rightly regarded themselves as the nation that had decisively contributed to the military victory. The USSR turned into a superpower; but most Russians were living in very unpleasant conditions. Their material situation was poor and no serious effort was made to improve their food supplies until after Stalin's death in 1953.

Yet it felt better to be a Russian than a member of the other nations of the Soviet Union. The Russian people were hymned as the 'leading people' and hostility to certain ethnic groups was fostered. Whole nations had been deported to Kazakhstan in 1944–5 on the charge that they had collaborated with the Nazis. These included the Chechens, Crimean Tatars, Volga Germans and Meshketian Turks.[15] After the Second World

War the Jews, too, were subjected to persecution. The merits of the Russians were simultaneously trumpeted. Russians got accustomed to being treated as if they were an imperial nation. Many of them were sent to Estonia, Latvia and Lithuania to consolidate the Baltic region's annexation by the Soviet Union. Army generals retired to houses on the coast. Workers came to take up employment in the factories. The communist parties of the region – Estonia, Latvia and Lithuania – were led by persons of Russian national origin. As a consequence hardly any Russians bothered to learn the local languages. The same was the case across the USSR. In Bashkiria, for example, 40 per cent of the population were Russian, but only 0.01 per cent could speak Tatar.[16] Russians did not need to exert themselves. For them, the USSR was a kind of expanded Russian homeland.

The basic position of the Russians did not change fundamentally after Stalin's death in 1953. They remained officially the senior nation in the multinational state and other nations had to defer to them. Yet the obeisance before all things Russian was moderated. Outside the RSFSR the titular nation of each Soviet Republic supplied leaders to the republic party and government – previously Russians had occupied the supreme posts nearly everywhere. But still the Russian nation had distinct advantages. Their culture was praised and privileged. Their history, including their conquest of the non-Russian peoples, was approved. Their language was compulsory in all schools. Their migration to each and every region of the USSR continued to be encouraged.

One aspect of the Khrushchëv years, however, deserves further attention. In 1943 Stalin called a halt to the open persecution of the Russian Orthodox Church and allowed the election of a Patriarch and the opening of thousands of churches. He also frowned upon proposals for the existing collective farms to be amalgamated into larger agricultural units. With Khrushchëv's rise to power these policies were reversed. Khrushchëv left only 7,560 churches standing, and most of these were forbidden to function;[17] he also launched a campaign of farm amalgamations. Whole villages were destroyed in an effort to introduce an ideologically acceptable 'urban' culture to the countryside. This had a devastating impact on the old peasant way of life. Stalin, by destroying the village land commune, did not completely eradicate all traces of the old life. Sometimes the new collective farm was based exactly on the land of the commune and so the remaining peasants were able somehow to conserve something from their past. When Khrushchëv came to power in the mid-1950s, the campaign against the village was resumed in earnest. Like Stalin, he praised the Russians more than the other peoples of the Soviet Union. But he also kept Russian nationalism firmly in check.

Russians were brought up with a national identity that mixed 'Russian' and 'Soviet' aspects.[18] By and large, this did not worry them; most of them did not even think about the matter. They were treated as the dominant people of the USSR and regarded the USSR, a larger entity than the RSFSR, as being mainly their own creation. Yet they continued to exist without the trappings of nationhood accorded to the titular nations of the other fourteen Soviet republics. They had no Russian Communist Party whereas the Ukrainians, Georgians and others had had these institutions since the Civil War. Under Khrushchëv a 'Russian (*Rossiiskoe*) Bureau' of the Party Central Bureau was introduced, but Brezhnev got rid of it – evidently it was thought a hostage to nationalist fortune. But this act of abolition was simultaneously a humiliation and a source of pride. Russians needed the trappings; but they could also easily do without them. The Russians knew they were the imperial people of the USSR. To a large extent the Soviet Union belonged to them in so far as any people owned it. This in turn made many of them more relaxed about their national separateness than were some of the other national groups. Ethnically mixed marriages were increasingly commonplace. By 1979, for example, 12 per cent of wedded citizens in the RSFSR had spouses of a different nationality.[19]

Things started to change, however, in the late 1960s when Brezhnev initiated his policy of 'stability of cadres'. This gave the chance to the national elites of the Soviet Republics to run republican affairs without much interference from Moscow on condition that they did not unduly indulge nationalism. There were occasional sackings of leaders who ignored warnings. But the more cautious officials avoided trouble and got on with promoting their own cliques of supporters to posts of importance. The result was a steady movement towards favouring persons of the titular nation of each Soviet Republic. The losers were the Russians.

This tendency was observable not only in the fourteen other Soviet Republics but even in the RSFSR. The reason for this was that the RSFSR contained seventeen autonomous republics as well as various other autonomous regions and areas named after specific national and ethnic groups. Altogether they covered 53 per cent of the territory of the RSFSR.[20] Set up in the Lenin period, they were an attempt to reconcile the national minorities to rule from Moscow. This was a constitutional concession that was abused from the late 1960s. In several republics the national communist elite discriminated against Russians in making appointments to posts. This was the case, for example, in the Bashkir Autonomous Soviet Socialist Republic and the Tatar Autonomous Soviet Socialist Republic. Tatars and Bashkirs automatically stood a better chance of preferment. The process was not as marked as outside the RSFSR, but it was remarkable enough for Russians to feel uneasy. As in the 1920s, the Kremlin was thought to be failing to protect their interests as well as they thought proper. The supposedly imperial nation felt itself treated as a colonial people without rights to appeal to the central political authorities.

The resentment of Russians grew under Gorbachëv when it became possible for the various nations of the USSR to express their grievances. Tatars, Bashkirs and others justifiably complained about the damage done to them under Stalin. First intellectuals and, eventually, communist politicians themselves picked up the theme. By permitting this tirade of criticism, Gorbachëv appeared to be colluding in the besmirching of the Russian reputation. Or at least this is how things seemed to a rising number of Russian people.

Their concern was all the stronger in the light of demography. The point is that the Russians were far from being a tiny minority in the 'ethnic' republics of the RSFSR. Nor were the titular nations of these republics and regions always a large majority or even a majority at all. Thus Russians constituted 72 per cent of the Buryat Autonomous Soviet Socialist Republic as against only 23 per cent for the Buryats themselves. It was a similar situation in the Karelian Autonomous Soviet Socialist Republic, where the Russians had 71 per cent and the Karelians merely 11 per cent.[21] These are the extreme cases. Yet the fact remains that the Chuvash and Tuva Autonomous Soviet Socialist Republics were the only ones where the eponymous nationality constituted a majority. If we look at all republics of this sort in the RSFSR, the Russians made up 43 per cent of their population.[22] By any standard this was a substantial minority, and it was a minority that sensed itself abandoned by the political leadership in the Kremlin. The Russian nationalist intellectuals who had always claimed that Russian nationhood had been damaged by Soviet communism stoked the boiler of resentment; Gorbachëv's political reforms gave them ample chance to speak out at last.

But the Russians also complained too much. Unlike the Azeris or the Uzbeks, they had not been annexed to the Russian Empire and the USSR by military conquest. They had not suffered a national deportation from their ancestral lands like the Chechens, Volga Germans or Crimean Tatars. They had not had to learn a new language as citizens of their state. At the uppermost levels of politics and culture they supplied a larger number of influential figures than any other nation. Moreover, the autonomous 'ethnic' republics contained only a seventh of the population of the RSFSR. Most Russians lived elsewhere. Out of 114 million of them, according to the 1979 census, nearly 105 million resided outside the autonomous republics within the RSFSR.[23]

Not all Russians felt done down. The Russian people had a distinct language and history, but there was also a lot that bound them to the other peoples. The place of residence continued to have an influence in this respect. A Russian household in the mountains of the North Caucasus had much in common with the ethnic groups that had lived there for centuries. Everybody faced the same problems of existence: the mountains, the lack of roads, the climate, the distance from the nearest town. But elsewhere, too, there were similarities between the Russians and other peoples. Soviet life was enormously standardised. It was not just the Russians who dressed and ate in the manner prescribed by the central communist authorities; it was all the nations of the USSR. There was no secret about this. Stalin explained that he and his comrades aimed at a kind of 'modernity' (*sovremennost*) that was different from what was offered by contemporary capitalism. He lauded modest, simple patterns of material provision. For Stalin, communism offered the only possible mode of avoiding the wastefulness inherent in economies run on the principle of private profit. The lifestyle of Russians and other nations followed the demands of a state-directed social template. Their conditions of housing, health-care, diet and dress involved little individual choice.[24]

Standardisation has admittedly been a global trend. In every country the cultural differences between one region and another have been diminished. Local idiosyncrasy has been reduced or eliminated altogether. Soviet communism was doing to the USSR what the world capitalist economy was doing to countries elsewhere – and the influence of American culture on all the other continents became intense in the years after the Second World War. But the USSR and other communist states underwent a cultural homogenisation still more drastic than anything occurring in capitalist states. New towns were built according to the ordination of central politicians – and the rebuilding of the many old towns razed to the ground by the Wehrmacht followed the same pattern. Organised religion, folksongs, handicrafts and other traditions were not quite suppressed, but they were severely reduced in scope. There were few opportunities for social initiative outside the control of the state. Capitalism offers at least a degree of variety through the competition of rival enterprises. Under communism there was a bleak uniformity. The Russians as a nation were pressed into a dispiriting mould throughout the years of the Soviet one-party state.

Because so many Soviet citizens descended from a plurality of national and ethnic groups, there was no easily recognised Russian physiognomy. Industrialisation and urbanisation contributed to the further mixing of cultures. Across the RSFSR, therefore, there was a great deal of similarity in the attitudes and conditions regardless of nationality. Nevertheless surveys of the inhabitants of the large cities indicate that non-Russian migrants held on to their customs more tenaciously than the Russians. Thus the Tatars in Leningrad remained loyal to their extended families before and after the Second World War, and they strove to prevent mothers of youngsters from having to go out to work. They tried, too, to maintain their national cuisine. Russian newcomers to the city abandoned many of their traditions much more quickly.[25]

And so the Russians, as the USSR's days drew to a close, had undergone a complex and diverse experience. They had had a sense of nationhood before 1900, but it had been deepened and sharpened by the history of the twentieth century. The general effects of urbanisation, migration and schooling contributed to this. So too did the Great War, the Civil War and the Second World War. The media reinforced the trend. In the process there was a shaking out of older aspects of Russian nationhood – and the state's role in this was substantial. The importance of Church and peasantry was drastically reduced. This was not a unique phenomenon. What made Russians different was their insulation from the rest of the world to a greater or lesser degree. In the 1930s and 1940s the country was almost totally sealed off from direct foreign influences. The situation eased in subsequent decades, but still the cultural isolation was considerable. This enabled the authorities to cultivate whatever sense of nationhood they wanted; and, like the tsars, the communist party authorities wanted Russian national consciousness to be blended with a supranational identity. The tsars wanted allegiance to the Empire, the commissars aimed at creating a 'Soviet people'. Yet the residual traditions of the country were never fully expunged. Ideas and practices from both the Russian Empire and the USSR were commingled.

The sediment of the various stages of history lay upon the Russian mind. Indeed, there was no single mind. The various social groups had differing pasts and differing expectations of the future. There remained a gap between town and countryside, between professional groups and the working class, between Russians in the 'Russian provinces' and Russians in the ethnic 'borderlands'. There were also varying degrees of intensity in the sense of nationhood. For most Russians, national identity was a given fact of life but not a supreme one. For others the nation was paramount. But for nearly all Russians, too, there were other alliances beyond nationhood. They belonged to families, to social groups, to towns and to regions. Many of them also felt they belonged to the USSR – and some believed that a still wider community was important: the global community of communism or religion or even scholarship. And so Russians were not the same in 1991 as they had been in 1900. They were recognisably the same people, but also a people which had undergone substantial alteration. For this reason alone no reforming regime could expect simply to turn Russia back on to a path of development abandoned in 1917. The task of building a new Russia had to include an endeavour to create new Russians.

4. PUBLIC IMAGES, 1800–1991

Many people today give thought to the peasantry, its past and its present. Not only persons who have a direct relationship with the countryside but indeed everyone who holds the fate of the Fatherland dear.

M. M. Gromyko, *The World of the Russian Countryside* (1991)[1]

Unfortunately the Russian intellectual tradition was not entirely helpful in the task of building a new Russia and creating new Russians. Politicians, thinkers and creative artists before 1991 endlessly debated how to improve life in Russia. Their ideas were highly diverse and have continued to have an impact through to the present day. Discussion was not confined to the topic of nationhood; it also touched economics, sociology, religion, philosophy, painting, music, literature and politics. In Russia it has never been acceptable to demarcate topics in the Anglo-American style. Unfortunately, however, only a very few of the contributors to the debate advocated ideas congruent with the grand reform project of Yeltsin and his supporters at the end of the Soviet period. Advocates of liberal democracy and a market economy have always been thinly represented.

The debates did not take place in a public void. The tsars had always striven to inculcate a sense of patriotic pride among their subjects. It was patriotism of a distinct sort. The Romanovs ruled an empire and wanted all its peoples, not just the Russians, to show loyalty to the dynasty. They therefore refrained from an unambiguous encouragement of Russian nationalism; indeed, by the nineteenth century they had come to fear that Russian national sentiments, if ever they got out of control, might lead to revolution.[2] Nevertheless even the Romanovs needed to identify themselves with the Russians. In 1833 the Minister of Education in Nicholas I's government, Sergei Uvarov, announced principles of Orthodoxy, Autocracy and Populism (*Narodnost'*) and gave instructions for them to be inculcated in schools and universities. This was an attempt to bind the Emperor's subjects in loyalty 'to throne and fatherland'. It was no surprise that Nicholas I stood by the doctrines of the Russian Orthodox Church and the claims of his dynasty. But Populism was a curious term. Uvarov could have chosen Nationality (*Natsional'nost'*), but presumably felt it would come close to a denial of imperial unity of purpose. Populism would have to do instead. When associated with Orthodoxy, it still strongly implied a Russian national preference.[3]

In the late nineteenth century the state ideology was to give still higher status to things Russian. The Russian language was compulsory in schools. The Russian Orthodox Church was allowed privileges at the expense of the other Christian denominations. And when Pëtr Stolypin became Chairman of the Council of Ministers in 1906, explicit approval was given to the idea that 'the Great Russian people' were the backbone of the Russian Empire. Even Stolypin, however, was mindful of the need to avoid excessive annoyance to most other subject peoples of Nicholas II. Thus the tension between imperial and national concerns lasted through to the end of tsarism.[4]

Yet unequivocal Russian nationalism was not absent from the wider public arena in the decades before the First World War. The intelligentsia had been preoccupied with the 'Russian question' since the middle of the nineteenth century. In novels and poetry, in painting, theology and ethnography, even in geography, there was a growing tendency to assert that there was something 'special' about the Russians and that Russia had a unique and virtuous destiny to fulfil. This tendency came out of a centuries-old tradition. After the Ottoman capture of Byzantium in 1453 the Russian Orthodox Church had claimed Moscow as the 'Third Rome' and the new centre of world Christianity. Such an idea lay dormant after the schism in Orthodoxy in Russia in the seventeenth century, but it was never entirely eradicated from the consciousness of many Russians.[5] In the mid-nineteenth century it resurfaced among thinkers such as Ivan Kireevski and Alexei Khomyakov who became known as the Slavophiles. Their case was no longer purely ecclesiastical. The Slavophiles contended that the Russian peasantry's qualities of forbearance, charity, spirituality and collective endeavour made for a system of life superior to anything available in the individualistic and materialist West.[6]

While phrasing themselves carefully so as to obviate problems with the censorship office, Kireevski and Khomyakov were critical of the Imperial state and its military and bureaucratic priorities. They were also reacting against the essayist Pëtr Chaadaev, who insisted that the way to understand Russia was to accept that it was a country without a past. For Chaadaev, his motherland had yet to enter the chronicles of global history. In retrospect we can hardly imagine greater nonsense. But he was followed by others in later decades who were similarly disrespectful towards Russia. Marxists in particular – or at least many of them – maintained that the sooner Russia followed the Western route of capitalist economic development, the better for her and her people. Pëtr Struve and several leading liberals agreed about this with the Marxists but proposed that parliamentary democracy instead of socialist revolution should be the parallel objective in politics.[7]

Liberalism was poorly supported outside the narrow stratum of teachers, lawyers and other members of the professions and was attacked by an ever wider variety of writers and public figures. The Slavophiles did this as Christian reactionary romantics. From the 1850s onwards a secular and socialist version was propagated by leading Russian thinkers. Among the first of these were Alexander Herzen and Nikolai Chernyshevski. Herzen operated from exile in London, Chernyshevski from his places of confinement in Siberia and Saratov. Their most important contributions – unlike those of the Slavophiles – were published illegally. Herzen, Chernyshevski and their successors, who were dubbed the *narodniki* ('populists'), argued that Russia had a singular opportunity to create an egalitarian society. The basic *narodnik* idea was that the traditional land commune, which held together the peasant households of each village, constituted the embryo of socialism. Peasants in such communes engaged in practices involving co-operative labour and redistribution of goods; they also had a concern for the general social welfare of the village. The *narodniki* accepted that the peasantry had its flaws: greed, exploitation and cruelty were also to be found in the countryside. But they blamed this on the oppressive nature of the Imperial political and social order, and suggested that a revolution was needed in order to liberate the great positive potential of peasant customs.

Others had already rejected the idealisation of the peasantry, including several literary figures, starting with the poets Alexander Pushkin and Mikhail Lermontov in the 1830s.[8] So too were ethnographers such as Pëtr Semënov. Enquiries were put in hand throughout the nineteenth century. Several among them had a political axe to grind – and very few were entirely on the side of the Romanov monarchy. It was a fascinating process as intellectuals, brought up in isolation from the mass of the people, sought to correct their ignorance. The peasantry was like a dark forest that needed to be penetrated if Russia was ever to be explained to itself.

Scholarly interest existed also in the interaction of the Russians and the other peoples. Nikolai Karamzin's *History of the Russian State* rehearsed the spread of the Muscovite state from the conversion of Duke Vladimir in 988 onwards. This was one of the great works of Russian letters in the early nineteenth century. Karamzin and his distinguished successors in later decades of the century – Sergei Solovëv and Vasili Klyuchevski – concentrated on the armed struggles between the Russians and their enemies. They had little interest in the cultural amalgamation that resulted from these encounters. Battles, conquest and territorial expansion were the themes that gripped their imagination. There was, however, an exception: the Mongol invasion of the thirteenth century. The Golden Horde of the Mongols did not simply mount an occasional armed threat to the Russians; it swarmed over the Muscovite lands and thrust its way into Poland. The Mongols' military success was complete and their rule over the Russian people lasted until the latter half of the fifteenth century. Before Karamzin this dark period had been known to Russians mainly in their folklore. Karamzin was one of the first to examine the archives and bring his discoveries to public attention.[9]

The question arose of the impact this lengthy subjugation had upon the Russians. The Grand Duke in Moscow had to prostrate himself annually before the Great Khan and deliver an enormous financial tribute, and the collection of the money necessitated a centralised, ruthless control over the Duchy's patrimonial lands. For Karamzin, the Mongols were a plague which, mercifully, was eventually eliminated; he drew the lesson that a strong central state had been needed for this end – and he considered centralism in politics an eternal prerequisite of the Russian historical success. Others retorted that the tradition of sullen, distrustful resignation to the rulers was an enduring feature of the Russian popular psyche. The culture of Russia became the object of recurrent intellectual dispute.

But at the same time there was among Russian intellectuals an appreciation that the Russians – who looked upon the peoples of the Caucasus as 'Orientals', as noble savages or just as savages – were themselves exotic in the eyes of observers in the rest of Europe. Poets and novelists began to take pride in this. The novelists Tolstoi, Dostoevski and Gorki depicted Russians in general – whether they were aristocrats or peasants – as tending to resent those constraints on their behaviour that were considered normal and desirable in Western Europe.

Their novels depicted scenes of long, drunken nights in gypsy encampments or in gambling dens. To be a Russian, therefore, was to reserve an area of one's soul for self-indulgence. Tolstoi's *War and Peace* gave plenty of instances of Russians living life to the full, living it for the pleasures of the moment. As his contemporary Dostoevski stressed, such an attitude could all too easily spill over into self-destructive excess. The lyrical novels of Ivan Goncharov, especially his *Oblomov*, proposed that the polar opposite to Russianness was the Protestant, neat and obsessive Shtolts, a businesslike bailiff of German origin. Still later writers contrasted the Russian – child of emotions – with the Jew, who was represented as a product of human greed and calculation. Contrasts between Russia and 'the West' became the norm.[10]

Musical composers, choreographers and painters increasingly followed this line.[11] For most of them, the Russians as a people had qualities setting them apart from Europeans. After the turn of the century Sergei Diagilev's Ballets Russes took European theatre by storm. Extravagant costumes and gestures were their hallmark; Western spectators adored the performances as outlandish and intuitive. One of Diagilev's composers, Igor Stravinski, composed *The Rite of Spring* in 1912 to celebrate the pre-Christian, the pagan, the paradisial and the untamed. Domesticated Europe (and indeed domesticated Russia) swarmed to the theatres. Writers picked up the theme. In 1918 Alexander Blok published his poem 'Scythians', which welcomed revolutionary upheaval and rejected the values of Enlightenment, Progress, Education and Tolerance. Blok saw the Russians – including the makers of the October 1917 Revolution – as the reincarnation of the Scythian nomads who had devastated the states around the Black Sea in the eighth century BC. The penchant for violence was, according to Blok, the 'music of the times'.[12]

Yet this wild romanticism was no more popular with most intellectuals than the kindly image of the Russians propagated by the populists. Even in the mid-nineteenth century there were writers who stood out against idealisation of 'the people'. Short-story writers such as Gleb Uspenski inveighed against the way that certain intellectuals lost contact with knowable reality when they offered visions of the peasantry. Uspenski himself had once wanted to blame every woe upon the gentry. In practice, he found, peasants oppressed and exploited each other and had little altruism.[13] It has to be said that before the century drew to a close, the populist revolutionary movement had abandoned its early credo that 'the people' simply needed freeing from the Romanov dynasty's rule in order that they might construct a perfect society unaided.[14]

The long-running, vibrant debate on Russia's nature – its 'essence', its 'soul' – had barely reached the minds of most Russians before the October 1917 Revolution. This was mainly because literacy was thinly spread; for the state censorship, although it clamped down on writings hostile to the Romanov dynasty and the political system, never prohibited discussions on the 'Russian Question'. In the educated sections of society the answers were fiercely debated and the altercations continued even during the Great War. The dispute was many-sided and there was no prospect of agreement. The Russian intelligentsia consisted of conservatives and radicals, believers and atheists, nationalists and internationalists, economic materialists and aesthetes, liberals and terrorists, gradualists and revolutionaries. Faith in Russia competed with faith in the West. Confidence in 'the people' was in contest with distrust of the 'dark masses'. In each intellectual grouping, moreover, there were divergences of opinion on the 'Russian Question'; and the fact that the tsars ruled an empire meant that there was perennial dispute about the position of the non-Russian peoples, whose religion and culture as well as nationality marked them off from the Russians.

But then came the October 1917 Revolution. Within months, only one party was free to express opinion on matters of great moment. Lenin's communists had no scruples about monopolising political power and deploying it to carry out ideological indoctrination. From the 1920s the only answer to the 'Russian Question' with any practical importance was the one supplied by Marxist-Leninist intellectuals.

Marxist-Leninists did not rush to answer the question. Lenin and his comrades were internationalists. Ultimately the communist leadership hoped that all 'national questions' would become obsolete as the cultures of the world's nations became fused in a common global culture for humanity. At Lenin's instigation, the Soviet state gave opportunities for national and cultural self-expression in the former empire to those groups which were not Russian. Lenin believed this to be necessary for the attainment of racial, national and ethnic harmony. He also thought it vital for the spread of socialism: people would more readily accept Marxism-Leninism if it were explained to them in their native language.[15] Strict political control was maintained to prevent the process from spinning out of control. It was recognised as a risky policy. And one nation was regarded with particular suspicion: the Russian nation. The communists especially feared the development of Russian nationalism. When Lenin and his comrades addressed the 'Russian Question', it was usually to warn against what they called 'Great Russian chauvinism'.

The slightest sign of Russian national self-assertion was anathematised and punished.[16]

Other individuals and organisations had to use oblique methods if they wished to offer an alternative opinion. Priests did it through their sermons. Despite the persecution of the Russian Orthodox Church – which included the execution of dozens of bishops even after the end of the Civil War – most Russians continued to believe in God and to attend Christian services. The sermons had to be discreet in the way they discussed the onslaught on Russian national traditions and feelings. The Orthodox Church was in any case split by liturgical and organisational controversies of its own. Even without the persecution and interference mounted by the Cheka, the priests would have found it difficult to raise a banner of struggle against communism.[17]

In the arts the resistance was more spirited and effective, but it too was a divided affair. Sergei Diagilev and the Ballets Russes fled abroad. The world-famous bass singer Fëdor Shalyapin, after a brief stay in Russia in 1921, also emigrated. The composers Igor Stravinski and Sergei Prokofiev wanted no part in the official Soviet culture and stayed outside the country.[18] The artist Marc Chagall, who tried his hand at running a painting school for workers in Vitebsk, decamped to Paris in 1922. The Politburo hastened the exodus by deporting the philosopher Nikolai Berdyaev and dozens of other creative writers and thinkers in the same year on a special train to Berlin.[19] The departed individuals included many with strong opinions on the 'Russian Question' who would have caused trouble for the Politburo if they had had the chance. The leaders of the one-party Marxist regime aimed to insulate the country from other ideologies. A powerful censorship body, Glavlit, was set up in June 1922 and the Politburo went on ordering the arrest of intellectuals thought to be recalcitrant dissenters.[20] Meanwhile the communist party commissioned works on Russian Imperial history denouncing tsars and Church, criticised the peasant life and castigated the Imperial conquest of the peoples of the borderlands.[21]

Yet the Politburo could not totally suppress the 'Russian Question' unless it was prepared to lose many of the 'fellow travellers' amidst the intelligentsia whom it was seeking to keep on its side. In the 1920s countless novels and poems were printed that took pride in Russia. The poet Sergei Yesenin and the novelist Leonid Leonov praised the dignity of the 'common people', especially the peasants. There was a degree of sentimentality here. But such writers were also making the basic practical point, however indirectly, that Marxism-Leninism failed to take traditional values into account. This had been a frequent refrain from the Slavophiles to the populists, and it did not die in the decade after the October 1917 Revolution. Yesenin was one of the most famous figures of his day. He married the American dancer Isadora Duncan and frequented the Moscow bars and cafés, playing his guitar and singing his songs – and his volumes of poetry were best-sellers. But his career did not last long. Becoming disillusioned with communism, he wrote a poem, 'Stern October Has Deceived Me', in which he fulminated against the communist dictatorship. A nervous breakdown followed and he died by his own hand in Leningrad in 1925.

Less famous were the figures who pondered the fate of Russia from abroad. One of them was the liberal conservative Nikolai Ustryalov, who had taken refuge across the Chinese border in Harbin and founded the 'Change of Landmarks' émigré group. His main contention was that the communists, having introduced a New Economic Policy in 1921 after the Civil War, were shedding their communist ideology and reverting to Russian national type. Thus they had reconstituted the Russian Empire in the disguised form of the USSR and were bent on turning it into a great industrial and military power. For Ustryalov the attractiveness of Lenin's Russia lay in its willingness to smooth the path of talented professional people to positions of authority regardless of social background. Communism was transforming itself into an instrument of meritocracy. Without the dead weight of the aristocracy and the landed gentry, the country could begin again to compete with other great powers in the world.[22] The Politburo saw Ustryalov's work as useful for rallying support for the regime from among Russian social groups which had been on the opposite side to the Reds in the Civil War, and his ideas were allowed to be debated in public.

Other writers were not handled as gently. Nikolai Trubetskoi, a conservative polymath, argued that even if Ustryalov was right that Russia was re-emerging as a Great Power, it would always be dissimilar to the other ones. Its Christianity came not from Rome but from Byzantium. It had missed the Renaissance and, to a large extent, the Enlightenment. Trubetskoi picked up ideas from the nineteenth-century Slavophiles. But whereas the Slavophiles had suggested that the Russian people were the nation in Europe that was the closest – if only potentially – to the principles of Christianity, Trubetskoi stressed the Asian aspects of the country's history. Russia had a larger portion of her territory in Asia than in Europe. Her traders and generals had always operated in China, Persia and the Ottoman Empire. Trubetskoi argued that the

'Mongol Yoke', lifted by the conquest of Kazan in 1552, left Muscovy with the lasting mark of 'Asiatic' traditions – and he insisted that this was no cause for regret. Instead, he argued that Russia had its own history and culture and should not seek to copy other nations but rather should follow her own unique path. Russia, he urged, was a peculiar hybrid, being neither European nor Asian but 'Eurasian'.[23]

Trubetskoi called attention to the oppressive state machinery, geared more to the extraction of monetary tribute than to a productive economy and social harmony. He pointed to the weakness of social initiative and the democratic impetus in Russia. The people were sullen and resigned to their lot and the rulers ruled by whatever brutal methods they fancied. Russia, despite the occasional efforts at Westernising reform, would never become like Britain, France or the USA. Trubetskoi and his fellow 'Eurasianists' denounced the communists for disregarding the geographical and historical specificity of Russia. What Lenin and his successors were attempting was bound to end in failure, and the country would be sacrificed on the altar of a set of utopian doctrines alien to Russian historic interests.

Nikolai Berdyaev, expelled from the country in 1922, thought Trubetskoi had exaggerated the distance between the communist leadership and Russia's ideological and cultural traditions. Berdyaev was a former Marxist who had converted to Orthodox Christianity but remained an advocate of socialism. He explained this to the appalling head of the Soviet political police (Cheka), Felix Dzierżyński, in the hope that this would save him from persecution. Dzierżyński icily replied that the fact that Berdyaev continued to promote a rival form of socialism was among the reasons why the Cheka was harassing him. Berdyaev's *The Russian Idea* postulated that the communists essentially were continuing the customs of rulership in Russia. They were anti-democratic. Like the tsars and their ministers, the communist party worked against the expression of alternative opinion. They were also 'believers'. The tsars had professed Christianity – and had subjugated the Orthodox Church to their will in the process; the communists were devotees of Marx and Engels. For Berdyaev, Russia could be regenerated only when there were conditions for both democratic self-rule and Christian spiritual development. Like the Slavophiles, he declared that Russian peasants were uniquely responsive to the requirements of the name of the general good. They were accustomed to collective modes of decision and behaviour and were as yet undamaged by the excesses of individualism characteristic of capitalist societies.[24]

Not all Christian thinkers concurred with Berdyaev. Fellow *émigré* Ivan Ilin denounced the communists as godless, anti-national criminals. He was heavily influenced by the nineteenth-century novelist Fëdor Dostoevski, who had said much the same in his novel *The Devils*. Ilin left Russia after the October 1917 Revolution and stayed in the West until his death in 1954.[25]

As the communist regime tightened its grip, however, such ideas were kept in quarantine from Soviet public opinion. Apart from Ustryalov, none of these writers could reach their potential readers except in a small number of smuggled copies. Inside the USSR there were a few fitful attempts by political writers to offer a vision of the future different from the tenets of the ascendant communist leadership. The Socialist-Revolutionaries and Mensheviks, who had been thrown aside by Lenin's party in the October Revolution, kept up their critical campaign against the Politburo; but they had to do this in conditions of clandestinity, establishing little groups and distributing their literature.[26] Unable to contest the elections to public office, they issued newspapers and pamphlets denouncing the general oppressiveness of the Soviet regime. Only in an oblique fashion did they make a contribution to the discussion of the 'Russian Question'. Socialist-Revolutionaries emphasised the plight of the Russian peasantry under communism whereas Mensheviks tended to highlight the punitive campaigns against non-Russian rebels. But a comprehensive direct answer to the question was not forthcoming from them; they were international socialists and a specifically Russian solution to contemporary problems in politics and society did not commend itself to them.

Meanwhile, official communist politicians and historians praised Russian revolutionaries not because they were Russian but because they were revolutionaries. Russians were not told what it was to be a Russian. Russia as a separate category, both territorially and historically, had become a topic to avoid. When the history of the Russian Empire was told, it was always a negative account. The tsars and their generals were depicted as rapacious conquerors.[27] By contrast, friendly accounts appeared of the cultures of those peoples of the USSR who were not Russian. Even large nations such as the Ukrainians were allowed substantial cultural and religious autonomy. They could enjoy this freedom so long as they did not challenge the October 1917 Revolution, the Soviet one-party state or Marxism-Leninism. Smaller peoples, moreover, were given schools in their native languages; and, wherever necessary, they were provided with visiting scholars who could learn their languages and invent an alphabet for them.[28] But for the Russians there was different treatment. Russian peasants were studied in terms of their ownership of land, ploughs and cows, and surveys were published on the size of their households before and after the October Revolution.[29] Officially approved scholars were encouraged to examine the socio-economic determinants of Russian peasant life; the deeper cultural aspects of that same life were put beyond the limits of exploration.

This tendency was reversed at the end of the 1920s when Stalin, while turning economic policy towards forced-rate industrialisation, lifted the clampdown on Russian cultural self-expression. He did this in a characteristically nasty fashion. Initially he increased the official persecution of Russian nationalists. The historian Sergei Platonov, a patriotic conservative, was shot. But at the same time Stalin fostered pride in Russia and personally upbraided *Pravda*'s versifier Demyan Bedny for ridiculing the Russians.[30]

In the mid-1930s there was a further movement in this direction and by then it was rare for Russian intellectuals and former politicians to be arrested for 'bourgeois nationalism'. The empire of the Romanovs was described in ever-warmer terms, especially in regard to the peace and culture supposedly conferred on the various peoples of the 'borderlands'. Until then the dominant interpretation of Russian history had been supplied by the communist writer Mikhail Pokrovski, who portrayed tsarism as the world's most reactionary system of rule.[31] This indeed had been Lenin's opinion. But under Stalin the analysis changed drastically. Even some of the tsars were semi-rehabilitated. Ivan the Terrible was praised for 'gathering the lands' under the aegis of the Muscovite state and Peter the Great's achievement in building up military might, industry and education was applauded. The victorious generals Suvorov and Kutuzov were celebrated. It was still acknowledged – indeed it was repeatedly emphasised – that even the best of the tsars injured the interests of the people and that the landlords, factory-owners and bankers were 'bloodsuckers'; but a definite shift in the official attitude to the past and to Russian nationhood had taken place.

The Russians were fêted in the history textbooks as having supplied the vanguard of a socialist revolution that would inevitably cover the entire world. *Pravda*'s editors put it boldly:[32]

> Russian culture enriches the culture of other peoples. The Russian
> language has become the language of world revolution. Lenin wrote

in Russian. Stalin writes in Russian. Russian culture has become international since it is the most advanced, the most humane.

At the end of the Second World War, indeed, Stalin offered his opinion that it was the Russian people who had made the crucial contribution to the defeat of the Nazi invaders. He said that any other nation, having suffered the disasters of the German Blitzkrieg in 1941, would have abandoned its government. (He omitted to mention that there had been scant chance for anyone in the USSR to be disloyal to the Soviet authorities.) Keenly he offered his plaudits: 'Among all the peoples of our country it is the leading people.'[33]

The Russian aspect of Soviet official identity grew stronger. But it was a carefully controlled and selected aspect. The last thing in Stalin's mind was to permit free discussion and development of national identity – or identities – for Russians. He stamped on any notion that Russian national identity derived from peasant virtues or rural ideals. Likewise he denied that Orthodox Christianity had had a beneficent historical influence. Although he had permitted the Church some relief from persecution since the middle of the the Second World War, he continued to sponsor the defamation of priesthood, liturgy and beliefs. There was similar ruthlessness in the treatment of the arts. Stalin gave approval to some classical authors, composers and artists – Tolstoi, Chaikovski, Glinka, Repin and above all Pushkin – while terminating access to the works of others. The novels of Dostoevski, who had excoriated socialism in all its versions, were no longer printed; Musorgski's opera *Boris Godunov*, whose subject was an individual who swept to the Russian throne by means of murder, remained unperformed: it was too clearly akin to the story of Stalin's own career. Yet even the favoured writers and composers were subject to restrictions. Several poems of Pushkin were withheld from publication. Glinka's opera *A Life for the Tsar* was retitled *Ivan Susanin* and the libretto was overhauled. Tolstoi's overtly Christian pamphlets were banned from publication.[34]

This authoritarian selectivity was a calculated one: Stalin was contriving to control the version of nationhood propagated among Russians. He aimed at acceptance of a Russian national identity characterised by militarism, large-scale organisation and urbanism and by the supremacy of the interests of state over the wants and needs of society. Pride in Russia as a great power and as a permanent star in the world galaxy was asserted. For Stalinists, Russians were a people of unique talent whose potential had been liberated by Lenin's October 1917 Revolution and the industrial and cultural transformation accomplished by Stalin. The Russian people would soon transfer its achievement of a superior social order to the rest of the globe.[35]

Change occurred after Stalin's death in 1953. Nikita Khrushchëv put a stop to the exclusive praise of Russia and the Russians. The other nations of the USSR, especially the Ukrainians and Belorussians as fellow Slavs, were accorded a measure of esteem that had previously been absent. Increased attention was paid to the objective of forming a 'Soviet people' from the various nations of the state. Khrushchëv introduced reforms in agrarian policy and permitted writers to expose deficiencies in the state's treatment of the villages. Writers such as Valentin Ovechkin, Yefim Dorosh and Vladimir Soloukhin described the plight of decent, conscientious collective farmers. Their books supplied harsh implicit criticism of Stalin's policies. They hinted – and this was all they could do if they were to have their works printed – that the 'mass collectivisation' of agriculture from the late 1920s had brought about social and cultural devastation. At first they were willing allies of Khrushchëv, who in 1962 sanctioned publication of a novella on the Gulag in the 1940s: Alexander Solzhenitsyn's *One Day in the Life of Ivan Denisovich*. The main character in the novella, Ivan Denisovich Shukhov, is a convict thrown into a labour camp without having committed a crime, and the chapters calmly and unobtrusively expose the brutal, arbitrary treatment of the inmates.[36]

The problem was that Khrushchëv was as hostile to rural traditions as Stalin had been. He amalgamated collective farms into vast state economic enterprises. He industrialised agriculture with tractors, fertilisers and fashionable crop rotations. He pulled down most of the remaining parish churches. His supreme aim was to turn the USSR into a military and scientific colossus. For him, the hero was the cosmonaut and not the peasant. Russians were enjoined by Khrushchëv to trace a lineage back to Lenin and to act as the bearers of the highest form of supranational political and cultural modernity.

Under Brezhnev, who ousted Khrushchëv in 1964, a further attempt was made at reconciliation with the Russian nationalist writers, mainly because the Soviet communist leadership doubted its own ability to retain the loyalty of Russian citizens. Throughout the 1970s there was an official protection of the 'village prose writers'. They won literary prizes and were granted print-runs that would be envied by Western best-selling authors. Viktor Astafev had 5.4 million copies of his books published in 1983–5 alone.[37] Each such writer commended himself as standing up for centuries-old Russian values of hard work, frugality, social responsibility and personal modesty – and the Politburo welcomed their help in counteracting the attractions of the consumerism and selfishness which were integral to the capitalist culture of the West. The film director Vasili Shukshin joined them, even daring to let his camera lens dwell lovingly upon the cupola domes of Russian churches. The painter Ilya Glazunov took militant pride in the Romanov tsars and Orthodox patriarchs. And Lev Gumilëv – former Gulag prisoner and son of the poets Anna Akhmatova and Nikolai Gumilëv – revived the Eurasianist analysis of the nature of Russia.[38] All agreed that the country's general history made Russians essentially different from peoples elsewhere.

The nationalist intellectuals caused bother to the Politburo, but not as much bother as came from Andrei Sakharov and advocates of liberal ideas who led campaigns for general civic rights and a market economy.[39] The dangers of Russian nationalism were contained by a mixture of stick and carrot. Nationalist writers had moral authority and popularity, but no power. If they wanted to stay out of prison and have large print-runs, they had to avoid criticism of Marxism-Leninism, agricultural collectivisation or atheism.

The relationship between the intelligentsia and the authorities changed at Gorbachëv's accession to power in 1985. His hope was to convince fellow citizens that Marxism-Leninism, suitably reformed, was the best instrument for the regeneration of state and society. It was a risky strategy since it involved freedom for long-standing grievances and aspirations to be expressed. The result was the irruption of the 'Russian Question' into public life. Gorbachëv set the tone by appointing Valentin Rasputin to his consultative Presidential Council. He also put Dmitri Likhachëv in charge of the USSR Cultural Fund. Gradually and not always consciously Gorbachëv was breaking with the whole ideological programme of Marxism-Leninism. In 1987 he hailed the February 1917 Revolution – which Lenin had denounced as having brought advantage only to the country's capitalists – as an event of benefit to the whole people.[40] Gorbachëv even began even to acknowledge that not everything in the tsarist past had been of negative significance. Lenin's period of office was no longer treated as a period of superior attainment. Gorbachëv also ceased to maintain that the USSR was currently in a stage of 'developed socialism'; he accepted that political freedom and economic welfare were too cramped for the regime to be able to make such a claim.[41]

By the late 1980s the nationalist writers, using the freedoms of *glasnost* and *perestroika*, were overtly challenging all this. Communist rule, they declared, had been disastrous for Russia. What had once been implicit in novels was frankly expressed in works such as Vladimir Soloukhin's *Reading Lenin*. Alexander Solzhenitsyn, then living in enforced emigration in the USA, made a similar point in his *Gulag Archipelago* which, after many years on the banned list of Glavlit, was published legally.[42] The campaign to induce a wider and deeper knowledge of 'Russia' was intensified as old historical classics by Nikolai Karamzin, Vasili Klyuchevski and Sergei Solovëv were published. Positive analyses by contemporary authors appeared on Emperor Alexander II, Stolypin and other reformers. This gave a sharp stimulus to debate about Russia past and present. Some contributors were unmistakable extremists. One group, Pamyat ('Memory'), contained anti-semitic members; but the xenophobia of many other writers was remarkable. All of them argued that Russian national interests had been damaged in the Soviet years.

The intellectuals of a nationalist tendency asserted that Russians had a long illustrious history which had been kept secret from them by the Soviet censorship. For them, communist rule had degraded land, faith and people. The damage to the natural environment under Stalin, Khrushchëv and Brezhnev was beyond calculation. Lake Baikal, once an unspoilt wonder of the world, had been turned into a latrine for chemical pollutants. The ruination of the cultural heritage – the churches, agricultural estates, sacred books, literary archives and paintings – had reached an extreme. The consolations and inspirations of Christianity had been suppressed. Russians of every generation had been demoralised by the ideas and practices of militant communism. Alcoholism and hooliganism were one result; the yearning for Western commercial products was another. Even patriotism seemed on the wane. The nationalists appealed to the Russian people to wake up to the nation's jeopardy. Writers Alexander Prokhanov and Valentin Rasputin in July 1991 signed an open letter – 'A Word to the People' – that supplied the intellectual rationale for the coup against Gorbachëv in August. The result was disastrous for the nationalists. The coup's failure produced a situation of benefit not to them but to the politicians and intellectuals around Boris Yeltsin who rejected their blood and soil nationalism.

Yeltsin and his supporters had no agreed idea of Russian identity. They were a disparate group. Until his death in 1989, the physicist and leading former 'dissident' Andrei Sakharov had belonged to this group.

On its fringe were the elderly literary scholar Dmitri Likhachëv and the economist Gavriil Popov. All these figures in their various ways suggested that the way forward for Russia was to secure integration in the global economy. Some wanted a 'patriotic' dimension to this. Likhachëv in particular emphasised that Russians had to stay Russian while reincorporating themselves into the culture of the West. But what was to be done about contemporary Russia? Boris Yeltsin and his group, frustrated by Gorbachëv's politics at the supreme level of the USSR, concentrated their activity on the RSFSR and strove to devise and implement their own policies in 'Russia' regardless of the wishes of the Party Politburo. They spoke with growing fervour of the need for each of the Soviet republics to find its own route towards the reform of state and society. They had no explicit commitment to the destruction of the USSR, but – to put it mildly – several of them were plainly unworried by the possibility.

Others in the Communist Party of the Soviet Union were opponents of not only Yeltsin but also Gorbachëv. They too turned to the institutions of the RSFSR in order to realise their objectives. Their ultimate purpose was to preserve and consolidate the USSR as a unitary state, but they chose to do this by forming a Russian (*Rossiiskaya*) Communist Party in parallel to the communist parties of the other Soviet republics – and from its formation in 1990 this party conducted anti-reform propaganda. Their leader Ivan Polozkov was hardly a theorist of distinction. (Nor, for that matter, was Yeltsin.) But in pursuit of a stronger centralisation of power, the Russian Communist Party formed an alliance with advocates of Russian nationalism amidst the cultural intelligentsia. Behind the scenes, there was also a growing willingness to play the anti-semitic card in political campaigns.

By the start of the 1990s, therefore, the most powerful and prestigious figures in the Soviet Union provided a kaleidoscope of versions of the Russian future. Gorbachëv wanted a social-democratic Russia within a reformed (and social-democratic) USSR. While remaining ambiguous about the constitutional structure and his preferred ideology, Yeltsin had a clear commitment to a rapid introduction of political democracy and the market economy. The Russian Communist Party and its nationalist allies wanted to maintain the USSR in a highly centralised form with respect for the achievements made under the communist regime. Other nationalist groupings would have nothing to do with communism of any kind and urged a return to traditional Russian values; but they had no fixed position on the territory, structure and policies of the state in

Russia. The Russian Orthodox Church avoided politics for the most part and called for spiritual regeneration through a resumption of Christian beliefs among the people. By the time of the attempted coup against Gorbachëv in August 1991, the 'Russian Question' was at the heart of disputes about the country's future. But there was more heat than light. The plurality of standpoints made pitched battle impossible. Each protagonist and his supporters fought in a limited area against all-comers.

No end was in sight to this convoluted, noisy struggle. The 'Russian Question' had been suppressed in the early Soviet period. It had been readmitted to public discourse under Stalin; but this was done in so intolerant and selective a manner that offence was given to many of Russia's old traditions. It remained under discussion after 1953. But the tenets of Marxism-Leninism were superimposed on it until the years of Gorbachëv's rule. Open debate at last became possible in the late 1980s; but the proponents of liberal democracy, universal civil rights and the market economy were no more successful in winning it than they had been before the First World War. And hardly had the various tendencies in the debate been marked out than the USSR collapsed and the 'Russian Question' had to be reformulated for a post-communist future. Continued conflict was inevitable.

5. SOVIET LEGACIES

Two skeletons are having a chat:
'When were you alive?'
'Oh, I lived in the times of Brezhnev.'
'And when did you die?'
'I died in the same period. When, though, were you alive?'
'I lived in the period of "perestroika".'
'And when did you die?'
'What do you mean? I'm still alive!'

Moscow joke, 1993

Ostensibly the attempt at decommunisation in Russia has been completely successful. Nothing is more startling for the seasoned visitor to Russia than the disappearance of Soviet memorabilia. In the old days, slogans were draped across streets proclaiming the superiority of the communist way of life. Posters extolled the wisdom of Lenin and the Communist Party of the USSR. The symbolism of hammer and sickle and of the Red star was ubiquitous. Now things are very different. It is true that statues of Lenin survive and that monuments commemorating the Great Patriotic War have been preserved. But in most respects the transformation has been drastic, and the visual and ideological residues of communism have been uprooted from the soil of Russia.

Yet although Soviet communism as a state ideology was been tossed aside, the personnel who staffed the institutions of the communist order continued to operate freely. The reasons for this were no secret; Yegor Gaidar, Yeltsin's Acting Prime Minister in 1992, argued he had to accept the old elites playing a part in the new Russia if there was to be political stability during the creation of a market economy.[1] Those who had held office in the USSR retained enormous capacity to disrupt the process. Gorbachëv had been chastened by experience. His adversaries had hidden supplies of goods in order to discredit him. In one notorious instance a

vast consignment of sausages was unloaded near Leningrad and buried
by the railway. Such possibilities for the disruption of reforms endured.
Yeltsin had initially tried to restrict the potential for mischief by ban-
ning communist party organisation on the territory of the Russian
Federation after the failed coup of August 1991.[2] This prohibition was
not as definitive as it seemed. He never attempted to prohibit Soviet
public figures from office after the fall of the USSR: his aim had been
solely to crush the organisational structures of the old party. But he was
thwarted even in this objective; for the Constitutional Court in November 1992 ruled the prohibition illegal, and the Communist Party of the
Russian Federation resumed its activity under the leadership of Gennadi
Zyuganov.[3]

In any case, Yeltsin flatly rejected the sterner sort of action witnessed
in Poland, the Czech Republic, Bulgaria, Albania and the former German
Democratic Republic. In Germany several communist leaders were
brought before the courts for abuse of human rights – Erich Honecker
was sentenced to imprisonment for his activity. In Poland there have
been cases at lower administrative levels, but generally the emphasis
was on the method of so-called 'lustration'. This involved the listing
of those posts in communist states which involved the post-holders in
perpetrating acts of oppression. Such persons in both Poland and the
Czech Republic are barred from high public office for several years.
The purpose is to exact a degree of retribution for the abusive rule under
communism as well as to prevent a communist political restoration.[4]

Not only Yeltsin but nearly everyone else in the Russian Federation
blenched at proposals to follow this path, and it is easy to see why.
Amidst wide strata of society in Eastern Europe there had always existed
a deep antagonism to communism, which was perceived as having
assaulted the dignity of nationhood. The contenders for high office after
the elimination of communist dominion over such countries included
many talented men and women who had refused to join the communist
party. In Eastern Europe the communists had come to power only after
the Second World War, usually with the assistance of Stalin's Red Army.
When communism started to crumble in Moscow, by contrast, only the
most elderly pensioners could remember times before Lenin had power.
Practically every citizen had been born and educated under communism.
Russians and the other nations of the former Russian Empire had
established the Soviet communist state after the October 1917 Revolution.
It was not a state introduced by universal suffrage; it was a dictatorship. But it was a dictatorship that no foreign power had imposed upon

Russia. Over subsequent decades millions of Russians staffed the Soviet state and carried out its injunctions.

The authorities of the newly independent Russian Federation in 1992 therefore held back from a general purge of personnel who had served the communist regime. Even notorious miscreants were left alone. Lazar Kaganovich, Stalin's henchman, was still alive and had never been brought to court for his horrific activity in the Great Terror of 1937–8. Those Politburo members who had sanctioned later bouts of repression, through to the 1980s, were also left alone. At the local level the functionaries of party, government, police and army lived quietly on their pensions. Torturers, Gulag camp commandants, prison psychiatrists, security-police deportation officers and party cell secretaries: not one of them needed to tremble about the future. The KGB's millions of confidentially registered informers were untroubled.

Yeltsin and Gaidar had a point: it is genuinely doubtful that the systematic pursuit of the miscreants would have been feasible. There were far too many people who had committed abuses, sometimes abuses of the most awful kind. The courts would have been overwhelmed with such business if a comprehensive judicial campaign had been instigated. What happened instead was that the Yeltsin regime had to satisfy itself with a symbolic trial of the Communist Party of the Soviet Union in summer 1992.[5] Witnesses were called, including Gorbachëv. Prosecuting lawyers adduced the plentiful evidence that abuses of power occurred not only under Lenin and Stalin but also throughout the communist period. TV and radio journalists reported the main points of accusation. But no arrests were made at the end. The purpose was to affect public opinion rather than to set about punishing the guilty. Apart from anything else, some of those who had been complicit in the dictatorship had risen to power under Yeltsin. Indeed Yeltsin himself had been a complacent enforcer of Brezhnev's policies. It was always unlikely that such a ruling group would strive to rid Russian public life of all persons who had collaborated with the Soviet communist regime.

Meanwhile, Yeltsin continued Gorbachëv's policy of 'rehabilitating' individuals condemned on spurious charges in the Soviet period. This was nearly always a posthumous procedure. The press coverage has a bleakness that increases the poignancy. The newspaper *Moskovskaya pravda* simply recorded the names of victims and the jobs they held:[6]

> Gribkov, Stepan Vladimirovich; railtrack man
> Dvorkin, Sergei Vasilevich: vehicle-base watchman

Dubanova, Nadezhda Antonovna; crèche nurse
Kozhurin, Nikita Semënovich; metro shaft-sinker foreman
Komarov, Kuzma Ilich; loader
Lukashin, Dmitri Vasilevich; meat enterprise worker
Pankratov, Alexander Mikhailovich; welder

The jobs are nothing unusual; their ordinariness indicates the demographic depth of the Great Terror. Not just People's Commissars but also nurses, loaders and welders were pinned in the teeth of the NKVD and devoured. In the late 1950s, when Khrushchëv had organised a process of rehabilitation, the relatives benefited materially in as much as they were allowed to claim the pension rights of the victims. Nowadays few widows or widowers survive. It is children and grandchildren who look for the announcement, and they do so mainly for the family's good name.

One person who applied for his father's rehabilitation in 2000 had an extraordinary ancestry. This was Sergo Beria, son of Stalin's feared NKVD chief Lavrenti Beria. The plea to the courts was that Beria was himself really a victim of Stalin and that he had moderated the Stalinist terror whenever he could. This was one rehabilitation too far for the judicial authorities. While it is true that Beria was in favour of reform after Stalin's death, no one could seriously deny the monstrosity of his behaviour in the 1930s and 1940s.

Generally, though, rehabilitations of the dead have been liberally granted and the freedoms of the last living generation of communist office-holders has been protected. The various elites were put in a strong position to survive the 'transition from communism'. There was a shorthand term for them: 'the *nomenklatura*'.[7] The origins go back to the 1920s when the supreme communist party leadership, mindful of the precariousness of its power, drew up an inventory of important official posts. The Party Secretariat in the Kremlin kept this inventory – or *nomenklatura* – for use by party leaders when they needed to fill a vacancy for a particular post. Ostensibly the leading organs of the government, trade unions or armed forces appointed their own personnel. In reality, if the posts belonged to the *nomenklatura*, it would be the Politburo, Orgburo or Secretariat which made the appointment. The system was replicated at the lower levels of the administrative hierarchy: there were hundreds of republican, regional and provincial *nomenklaturas* covering every sector of state and society.[8] To have a post within a *nomenklatura* was to have access to a definite degree of power and privilege. By the 1930s the system had become refined and each post offered a specific salary as well as delineated rights to use particular shops, hospitals and holiday resorts. The administrative stratum had emerged as the ruling group of the USSR.

In the Great Terror of 1937–8 this stratum was picked out for attack and hundreds of thousands of its members were arrested and killed. But those who survived retained a range of privileges and he purges became less widespread. Under Khrushchëv, who frequently resorted to sacking officials, there was a further development: demotion from office no longer carried the risk of individuals being dispatched to the Gulag. Things settled down to a still greater extent when Brezhnev came to power in 1964. So long as post-holders showed no disrespect to the Kremlin leaders and their policies, they could enjoy their privileges in permanence.[9]

As the USSR entered its terminal crisis at the end of the 1980s, the *nomenklaturshchiki* – including those who had opposed the reforms of Gorbachëv – manoeuvred in order to maintain influence and income in the post-Soviet future. They appropriated the assets within their reach. Inside the Kremlin *nomenklatura* of the party and the economic ministries there was opportunity to transfer funds to confidential bank accounts abroad or to new foreign joint-stock companies. Another tactic, as Gorbachëv tentatively expanded the private sector of the economy, was to secure loans on highly advantageous conditions of repayment. Property in land was also easier for members of the elites to obtain. As Gorbachëv extended the elective principle to politics, the *nomenklatura* members manipulated arrangements so as to secure their existing posts. Functionaries at each level of the state hierarchy tried to hold on to privileges in the changing forms of public life. The needs of the vast majority of the population were not merely overlooked: they were trampled in the dust. The elites behaved with the selfishness that had characterised them since the revolutionary period. Sensing that the Soviet Union was on the brink of collapse, they strove to make the gap between themselves and the rest of society permanent as well as deep.[10]

The motives of Yeltsin and his ministers in letting this happen were not only negative ones. The USSR's administrators had much-needed organisational skills. The extirpation of anti-communist individuals and groups had been undertaken with great thoroughness in the Civil War and the Great Terror. The consequence was that most of the practical expertise for the running of society belonged to persons in the *nomen-klatura*. Individuals of administrative talent, except for the tiny group of 'dissidents', joined the official hierarchy. The decommunisation of the USSR was inconceivable without the co-operation of the communist elites.[11]

This is not the same as saying that either Yeltsin or Russian citizens in general liked the indulgence shown to these elites. Yeltsin got over his scruples; indeed, he and his relatives themselves started to help themselves to the material rewards which the *nouveaux riches* were already enjoying.[12] Other Russians were less mutable. They had always known of the privileged life led by their hierarchical superiors. They had no direct acquaintance with it unless they happened to be servants, chauffeurs, nurses or private tutors, but word got about nevertheless. Since the Civil War there had been special restaurants, shops and hospitals for the communist leadership. Through to the end of the USSR there was no sign outside such buildings.[13] From the 1930s this furtiveness was accompanied by a public insistence that for the foreseeable future there would have to be wider pay differentials; the 'levelling down' of material rewards was pronounced an evil. The ascendant party leaders continued to preach adherence to the 'class principle' in politics and economics. Policy highlighted the 'working class' and its requirements. This fooled no one. Inequality of opportunity and circumstance was built into the foundations of the Soviet order.[14]

Resentment existed from the beginning to the end of the USSR. At times the people's urge for justice got out of hand. Most famously, there were anti-government demonstrations in 1962 when Khrushchëv, having promised that the USSR would catch up with the American standard of living by 1970, raised the prices of meat and other staple products. In Novocherkassk, in the Russian south, crowds lynched leading figures in the party and the KGB before the armed forces had time to restore order.[15] When Gorbachëv acceded to power, he put social fairness at the core of his own programme. He succeeded more in rhetoric than in achievement, and in the late 1980s Yeltsin continually piqued him by demanding an end to the communist system of privileges. Disgruntlement at the inequalities between the rulers and the ruled was widespread in the last years of the USSR.

Yet disgruntlement has been balanced by a wide acceptance that bygones should be bygones. The traumas of the Soviet period were many: civil war, repression, famine and invasion. Citizens wanted to avoid any repetition, and a judicial settling of accounts with the perpetrators of past abuses of power would have led to immense instability in politics. The yearning for peace was almost universal after the Second

World War.[16] The recurrent affirmation by Khrushchëv that he sought peaceful co-existence with the USA was strongly approved, and this continued to be true under his successors. Nor were all aspects of the Soviet social and economic order unappealing to citizens. When sociologists interviewed refugees from the USSR after the Second World War, they discovered considerable respect for many basic values supported by Marxism-Leninism. Former Soviet citizens fled from their country still believing in the fundamental need for the welfare state, full employment and social justice. Much as they detested Stalin, they saw virtues in the state ideology.[17] The surveys of popular opinion conducted after Stalin's death (and only recently made available) came up with the same result. Although people wanted greater fairness in society, they shared several of the principles embedded in communism. Attitudes in this aspect had remained remarkably constant.[18]

The organisation of life, too, stayed much the same across the Soviet period. Housing is a case in point. After the October 1917 Revolution the communists ejected the owners from city mansions and gave the rooms to needy workers.[19] Domestic facilities were organised on a communal basis. The hallway, kitchen, toilet and telephone were typically available to the tenants of a group of rooms, and they lived together in cramped conditions that left little opportunity for privacy. When Stalin took up his campaign for housing construction in the 1930s, he instructed architects to plan urban life according to the same scheme. His favoured type of housing was the *kommunalka*. The basic amenities were shared by resident families. It was virtually impossible to have a private life in such circumstances. The *kommunalka* was the sort of dwelling where most Russian citizens lived until Khrushchëv in the late 1950s commissioned separate apartments for each family. The buildings were poorly maintained by the authorities and the overcrowding produced tensions that inevitably led to malice and nosiness. Whereas there is a literature of nostalgia about the peasantry's land commune, no one remembers the *kommunalki* with affection.[20]

Yet this was far from meaning that the USSR as a whole was an egalitarian society. Relations among the various social groups were deeply unequal and hierarchical. Conditions differed in direct dependence on the jobs done by individuals and the personal connections they each enjoyed. Bossiness was pervasive. In the USSR the normal way for individuals to secure advancement in their career or their standard of living was to join the communist party. But this was not enough in itself. Sensible individuals also tried to join a informal group headed by an informal patron. The members of the group acted as his clients. The patron looked after their interests in so far as it lay within his or her power; the clients for their part did whatever the patron asked of them.[21]

This sort of interdependence has existed in many societies around the world to a greater of lesser extent – and of course it was widespread in the Russian Empire before the First World War.[22] But whereas patron–client relationships were of patchy importance in the Russian Empire, they were all-pervasive in the USSR. It had been Stalin's purpose in 1937–8, during the Great Terror, to expunge clientelism. But he found that the Soviet political order would be fatally destabilised if he persisted with his campaign. From then onwards it was tacitly agreed that public leaders should be able to introduce their *protégés* to office.[23] It was not what you knew but who you knew and who you supported that made the difference between a failed career and a successful one. After Stalin's death in 1953, Khrushchëv promoted his supporters in Moscow and Ukraine to the high posts of power. When Khrushchëv fell, Brezhnev notoriously gave preferment to men who had served with him in Dnepropetrovsk. The custom was continued under Andropov and Chernenko, and it was only when Gorbachëv rose to the Party General Secretaryship that this informal principle of selection fell into abeyance.[24] But Gorbachëv was exceptional. When Yeltsin took power, he initially showed remarkable favour to candidates for office who had served with him in the Urals.[25]

It is important to avoid exaggeration. Yeltsin did not turn the clock entirely back to the communist practices: he had no compunction about sacking his early appointees even if they came from his old base in Yekaterinburg.[26] (In fact, sacking people was one of Yeltsin's cherished forms of recreation.) But certainly the communist period hung over the Yeltsin years. Particular cliental networks have collapsed but clientelism as a system has endured as Russian politicians stick to the kind of relationships that worked for them and for their predecessors in earlier generations.[27] When Putin was transferred from St Petersburg politics to his first post in the Kremlin in 1996, a friend tried to dissuade him:[28]

> Look, they're all bosses in Moscow; there are no normal people there – one has an uncle in a ministry, another has a brother and yet another has a son-in-law's father. But you don't have anyone there, so how is it going to be for you?

Once in Moscow, Putin did not fail to appoint some of his St Petersburg friends to help him survive.[29]

Another legacy of the communist order was the continuing importance of the single leader at each level of power. The USSR repeatedly
produced leaders of dynamism and confidence. The wonder was that a
regime that laid stress on ideological uniformity and collectivist restraint
threw up leaders as individualistic as Stalin in the 1930s, Khrushchëv in
the 1950s and Gorbachëv in the 1980s. How did that grey, bureaucratic
monolith of the Soviet Union manage to do this? The explanation is not
a difficult one. The communist order judged its leaders – from the level
of the Kremlin down to the lowest party organisation in the provinces
– by their respective practical achievements. This placed a premium on
the attainment of objectives by any means whatsoever, including illegal
ones. The rule of law was disrespected from Lenin onwards. Leaders
of party and governmental agencies at lower levels of the administrative
hierarchy were put on notice that they simply had to supply the Kremlin
with the political or economic results it demanded. Failure would lead
to disgrace or demotion; under Stalin it could result in execution. It is
hardly surprising that such an environment encouraged the emergence
of persons of exceptional motivation.[30]

The clientelism of Soviet politics facilitated this. The leader could
achieve little on his own: he needed a group of trusted supporters to
help him – and the group needed their leader to operate ruthlessly if
they themselves were to enjoy the fruits of success. There was a bond of
common interest. This was not a phenomenon confined to politics. In
running the Soviet economy, ministers and enterprise directors behaved
in the same fashion. In the arts and sciences it was the same story. The
secret of survival in Soviet public life was that each cliental group had to
acquire an energetic, cunning leader and hope that he or she would
prove dynamic and successful.

The culture of leadership was contagious. Even many individuals
who remained outside such groups showed exceptional self-confidence
and determination. Three examples demonstrate the point. Dmitri Shostakovich, despite having been denounced by Stalin's cultural overseer
Andrei Zhdanov in 1948, went on writing symphonies on his own terms.
Alexander Solzhenitsyn came out of the Gulag in 1953, fought off cancer
and wrote his anti-Stalinist novella *One Day in the Life of Ivan Denisovich*,
which appeared with Khrushchëv's permission in 1962; and when Solzhenitsyn fell out with the state authorities in later years, he refused to
mollify his opinions even though his outspokenness led to his deportation in 1974. Likewise Andrei Sakharov, the nuclear physicist, was willing
to tell Khrushchëv to his face that the government's policies on both

nuclear-weapons science and international relations were flawed. Brezhnev sent Sakharov into internal exile in the city of Gorki (now known again as Nizhni Novgorod) in 1980, but nothing could induce Sakharov to recant his criticisms of Soviet communism.

The *perestroika* years themselves brought plenty of assertive individuals to the foreground of Soviet politics. Nowadays it is modish to depict Gorbachëv as a rather weak-willed character. This is calumny. He was a leader who took on the most uncompromising elements in the Communist Party of the Soviet Union and made political transformation virtually irreversible. With him in the Kremlin were rivals of similar resolution. Yegor Ligachëv was Gorbachëv's deputy in the party and his most dangerous internal critic until his demise in 1989. Gorbachëv's allies Alexander Yakovlev and Eduard Shevardnadze were just as wilful as Ligachëv; and of course the person whose will triumphed in the end was the ebullient Boris Yeltsin.

Dynamic leaders emerged in every sector of Soviet public life. Collective farms, factories and offices; villages, towns and great cities; whole regions and republics: each organisational unit in society had its problems and was accustomed to its leader representing its interests to the higher level of power. As the economy went into steep decline in the late 1980s and the network of administration fell apart, so the reliance of most people on their particular unit deepened. Gorbachëv and his fellow reformers were mystified about this. Their strategy had been premised upon a belief that their measures would quickly 'liberate' society.[31] They assumed that the removal of the carapace of political dictatorship would be enough to induce fellow citizens to participate actively in public affairs. They reckoned without the decades of social conditioning before 1985. People had been habituated to operate within groups based on patronage. The growing emergency in political and economic conditions simply strengthened the incentive to stick with forms of organisation that had helped survival in the past.

People managed as best they could. They continued to put faith in their informal relationships. The entire economy would have juddered to a halt many decades earlier if the authorities had not turned a blind eye to illegal practices. Some deals were conducted by professional criminals on the black market – and in the most notorious cases, large manufacturing enterprises were operated by gangs with the connivance of the police and the local party authorities.[32] Nearly everywhere, goods of high quality were kept off the shelves by the shop staff and sold on the side. Practically everyone got up to this. Respect for the law had

never been wide or deep in the Russia of the tsars. Under communist
rule this trend was reinforced. Lenin, a qualified barrister, despised
legal procedures and his contempt turned into an axiom of Marxism-
Leninism.[33] With Stalin the rejection of due process of law became
extreme and lawlessness became the norm. Although the Great Terror
was brought to an end in 1938, equality before the law and impartiality
of judicial procedure were never achieved either in Stalin's last years or
even after his death. No communist leader until Gorbachëv even had
them as objectives.

Popular distrust of the communist state persisted. The state had
repeatedly instigated terror. The state had wrecked the Church and
ruined agriculture. The state had trampled upon popular traditions;
it had intruded in the private life of people. The state had recruited
and trained officials to carry out instructions at the expense of the rest
of society. Undoubtedly there were exceptions. Respect for the armed
forces, for the Church, for the institutes of science and technology and
for the universities never entirely disappeared; but it was not as strong
as in many other societies.[34] People in Russia were generally suspicious
of officialdom, and this had been true long before the communists came
to power in 1917. 'Ordinary people' had no greater reason to welcome
the attentions of the Imperial bureaucracy of the tsars than to warm to
the Marxist-Leninist commissars who succeeded them.[35]

They distrusted, resented and grumbled. At work they did the
minimum that was officially enforced. They assumed that working
people should stick together and keep the bosses at arm's length.
Contrary to the Western stereotype of the Russian character, however,
they were not devoid of individualism. One way to demonstrate this
point is to look at Russia's popular proverbs. Few of them lay emphasis
on communality or togetherness.[36] Their sayings and quips relate mostly
to individual behaviour, as a selection from a popular anthology shows:[37]

> God takes care of him who takes care of himself.
> If you don't want to get burned, don't play with fire.
> A hen isn't taught by her eggs.
> Trust in God but rely on yourself.
> Any fool can ask more than ten wise men can answer.
> He who laughs last laughs the best.

This is scarcely amazing. When things got tough, Soviet citizens had to
use individual initiative in order to acquire what they needed in life.
They might get support from family, work-group or patron, but in the

ultimate resort they also had to fend for themselves. As the edifice of communism was dismantled, Russians had several qualities essential for survival in the new market economy. They had been trained by adverse circumstance to look after themselves, and many of them were itching to take advantage of the opportunities afforded by the end of the USSR.

This attitude, however, did not extend as far as a wish to get involved in public life. Most Russians seemed glad to see the back of the enforced participation typical of the communist decades. Previously they – or some of them – had joined the party and trade unions because it was helpful in obtaining the perks of the communist order. By the late 1980s there were nearly twenty million members of the Communist Party of the Soviet Union. But already it was evident that Russians preferred to watch their politics on television than to supply the commitment that Gorbachëv rightly judged crucial to his plan for the transforming of society in the USSR. They enjoyed his willingness to embarrass and annoy officials. But most of them liked the spectacle of the new politics without wanting to get actively involved.

Russians in the twentieth century learned from experience that public life could be dangerous. The Great Terror of 1937–8 traumatised an entire society. Scarcely a family existed in the USSR that did not lose a relative to the firing squad or the Gulag, and the memory has been passed down the generations. The Great Terror came after a series of state terror campaigns. In the Civil War mass repression had been applied to the former upper and middle classes. During the First Five-Year Plan there was a resumption of terror when kulaks, private traders, priests and former adherents of long-liquidated political parties were exiled, imprisoned or executed. The process continued in the early 1930s, and although the Great Terror was terminated in November 1938, there was no phasing out of terror as a method of rule. Bloody purges of generals took place in the Second World War. Deportations of whole national groups were also undertaken. Returning POWs were herded into the Gulag camps after 1945. The Leningrad party leadership was purged in 1948–9 and there were indications of plans for the initiation of yet another Great Terror shortly before Stalin died in 1953.

The statistical chance of being repressed was greater for those in a high position in the official hierarchies of party and government. Most members of the Party Central Committee, the Soviet government and the Red Army high command at the beginning of the 1930s were dead by the end of the same decade.[38] A cautious approach to politics became a sensible option. Why participate when the stakes of participation had been piled so high within the memory of the older generation?

Yet the Soviet historical experience was complex. Despite all the traumas, citizens frequently criticised abuses of power at their local level. They could not criticise Party General Secretaries, Marxism-Leninism or the current official policies until Gorbachëv's rise to power. But they were strongly encouraged to speak out on other matters. This happened throughout the communist period. It was one of the means by which the Kremlin leaders could inform themselves accurately about the provinces without having to rely upon data supplied by provincial officials who had a tendency to deceive them.[39] Of course, no sane individual dared openly to raise objection to Stalin and his policies or to question the legitimacy of the Soviet order. Yet even in the darkest days of the Great Terror there were plenty of workers, *kolkhozniki* and office clerks who gave voice to their local grievances. Alternatively they could confide their thoughts to paper and send a letter, anonymously if they preferred, to higher authority. Russians were accustomed to expressing their opinions with moral forcefulness. They kept a strong sense of social fairness and expected the state to take care, even at a minimal level, of its citizens.

They had got used to a measure of state welfare. In fact, the financial provision for the unemployed was scant and jobless persons were liable to be categorised as 'parasites'. Average pay below the level of the central and local *nomenklaturas* was ungenerous. Diet was neither exciting nor diverse. In the mid-1970s, when I lived in Leningrad, it was often hard to devise ways to ring the changes on carrots, beetroot and cabbage. In other cities things were much worse at that time. In Sverdlovsk, where Yeltsin was the communist party chief, food rationing had to be reintroduced. Even so, people could at least fill their stomachs. They also had guaranteed housing. The great apartment blocks constructed after the Second World War were scarcely models of comfort; but they were inexpensive and the governmental subsidy of gas and electricity made fuel so cheap that few citizens bothered to switch off lights and heaters. Soviet hospitals and schools may have been sparsely equipped, but health-care and education were provided without charge. Citizens of the USSR expected such facilities to be permanently available to them. To that extent the regime had achieved a wide consensus.

It had also succeeded in diminishing religious belief in society. Seven decades of Marxist-Leninist propaganda and atheistic repression had

had their effect. A peaceful process of secularisation was already evident before 1917 as industrialisation and urbanisation bit into traditional society. The communists in the Civil War and later in the 1930s conducted a violent campaign against religion. Priests perished in their thousands; buildings for worship were demolished; sacred books were banned from open sale. The physical destruction of churches was resumed by Khrushchëv. Exactly how many people in the Soviet Union still held fast to their religious faith is hard to say. The census of 1937 recorded that 55 per cent continued to believe in God.[40] But the proportion must have been much higher in as much as many people were justifiably scared of stating outright what they thought – and Stalin in the Second World War recognised this by allowing the Russian Orthodox Church to function somewhat more freely. None the less there is no serious doubt that religious faith went into drastic decline in the later years of Soviet rule.[41]

Yet belief in the supernatural did not disappear. While expelling organised religion from the minds of most Russians, the communist regime from Lenin to Brezhnev did not succeed in filling the gap entirely with Marxism-Leninism. Only a minority of the population embraced the Soviet state ideology. There were periods of communist zeal, notably in the Civil War, the First Five-Year Plan and – to a lesser extent – the period of Khrushchëv's supremacy. But there was also widespread, constant antagonism to the ideology of the political leadership. By the 1970s communist journals admitted to the difficulties faced by activists carrying out propaganda.[42] Apathy and cynicism were reported, and Gorbachëv's subsequent efforts to stir up enthusiasm for a 'return to Lenin' came to nought. Into the void left by Christianity entered other beliefs. Russian Orthodox Christianity at the popular level had always been accompanied by folk superstitions. Priests before 1917 had been notorious for blending Christian dogma and age-old customary notions. Most Russians, reared in the countryside, had remained credulous about wood spirits and devils. What has not been appreciated, at least until recently, is that many such superstitions survived into and beyond Soviet communism. Even witchcraft continued to be practised, especially in the rural areas; and official communist prohibition of white and black magic, fortune-telling and astrology did not eradicate people's trust in their efficacy.

And so citizens of the USSR, including those who lived in the cities of the RSFSR, were nowhere near as 'modern' as they are usually conceived.[43] Their traditions lived on with them in the form of proverbs, beliefs and practices which would probably have been eroded if Russia had not undergone the peculiar experience of mono-ideological repression over the seven decades after the October 1917 Revolution.

A conventional way to deal with the pressure of life in the USSR was to adopt a double persona. Thus people affected obeisance to the communist line of the day while thinking entirely differently. I well remember an example of this. In 1987 I went to Moscow for a conference on Soviet history. A fellow participant – a historian from south-eastern Russia – made a trenchant criticism of my account of Lenin's foreign policy at the end of the Civil War. His ideas were typical of the current communist party orthodoxy; his manner of oral assault was innocent of scholarly pleasantry. When, however, we came to the tea-break, we had a more congenial conversation. More than that – and I have never forgotten this – he told me that members of his own family had had a difficult time at the hands of the Reds in the Civil War. Historical simplifications were put aside, and as he abandoned the position he had taken a few minutes earlier, he showed respect for both sides in the armed conflict when he thought about his deceased relatives. At the time I regarded this as intellectual schizophrenia of a bizarre sort.[44]

Now, however, I feel differently, especially since meeting the man again a decade later.[45] What he recently told me convinces me that he had had no notion that what he said in the conference session contradicted what he said in the tea-break. Instead he had two entirely separate mental chambers in his life: the official chamber and the chamber that enclosed the memories within his family. For the former he needed to obey the demands of career; for the second he just kept thinking about what his parents and grandparents had said to him. Both parts were vital for him and he questioned the legitimacy of neither of them. Double-thinking was a way of life. Thus it was for millions of citizens of the USSR.

And so the legacies of the USSR were complex, mutable and contradictory. There were positive as well as negative features which affected the chances of successful reform after 1991. Some could help while others would hinder the creation of a freer and more dynamic kind of society in the Russian Federation. The negative features were stronger than the positive ones; but, contrary to the simplistic analysis given by most Western commentators, the inheritance was far from being monolithic. Although the formal doctrines and organisation of the Leninist state have left their mark, it is the informal – the unofficial, the secret and the illegal – aspects of Soviet communist society that have made the deeper imprint. Russians and other peoples of the USSR had accommodated themselves to the Soviet regime not only in behaviour but also in attitude. They formed groups based on patronage; they coped with shortages in the economy by use of favours, barters and outright fraud. The cliental system pervaded the entire state. At the upper levels it provided a base which enabled those who were already powerful to proceed to exploit the conditions of post-communism. Russian society was left prone to further bouts of oppression after the collapse of Soviet communism. Today's Russia is the child of the USSR.

PART TWO

POWER AND THE KREMLIN

6. THE NEW RUSSIAN STATE

Even in states with stable structures, victorious political leaders inevitably imprint state policies and state institutions with their personalities. In a situation where state structures have not yet crystallised, these structures are even more vulnerable.

A. M. Yakovlev, *Striving for Law in a Lawless Land* (1996)[1]

What made things turn out more for the worse than for the better was the way in which the legacies of the USSR were handled. Even before coming to supreme power, Yeltsin was ignoring many popular sensibilities and constitutional proprieties. The present-day Russian state lacks the aureole of legitimacy. Citizens of Russia were not consulted in advance about Yeltsin's decision to dismantle the USSR in late 1991; and by his own admission he used violence to overturn the constitutional order in 1993.

The ending of the Soviet regime – the one-party state, Marxism-Leninism, arbitrary police power – was a process of historic proportions. Yet all great events have their complications. History never supplies us with images in black and white; there is always some grey in the picture. The British 'Glorious Revolution' of 1688 is celebrated as the inception of an epoch of religious tolerance for all Christian denominations. In fact, although it involved the defeat of a potential Catholic restoration under James II, it involved a worsening of conditions for most of the Protestant sects of the day. The larger truth, however, is undeniable. This is that William of Orange's victory over King James was an event of importance in moulding the present-day British constitution. Similarly, the War of Independence in British America between 1775 and 1777 is commemorated as the unequivocal struggle of a people fighting for universal civic rights. Yet even the most liberal advocates of the American secession either owned slaves or saw no reason to liberate the slaves of others. Nevertheless the example of the young USA in establishing at least the formal principles of personal freedom had a decisive significance not only for North America but also for the world as a whole in the longer term.

The USSR's collapse was equally complex. Conducted in the name of freedom, Russia's independence was attended at birth by blatant impropriety. The USSR Constitution of 1977 permitted the secession of individual Soviet Republics, but the necessary procedures were not spelled out. Lenin, despite insisting on the rights of nations to self-determination, never made clear out how any of them would be able to leave the Union, and Brezhnev's 1977 Constitution was just as opaque. It was only in April 1990, when Gorbachëv introduced a Law on Secession, that a degree of clarity was introduced. It was this legal provision that Yeltsin had entirely ignored.

The Law on Secession had not made things easy for those who wanted to dismantle the USSR. There was meant to be a vote by two-thirds of a Soviet Republic's electorate in favour of seceding, and any such result should have been followed by a transitional period of five years when the other Soviet Republics might make objections. Gorbachëv had also stipulated that a follow-up referendum could be held if one-tenth of the electorate so requested and the USSR Supreme Soviet was empowered to confirm or deny the wish of any Soviet Republic to move out of the USSR.[2] On 17 March 1991, furthermore, Gorbachëv had come forward with a referendum of his own. The question he posed was as follows: 'Do you consider necessary the retention of the Union of Soviet Socialist Republics as a renewed federation of equal sovereign states in which the rights and freedom of people of every nationality shall be guaranteed in full measure?'[3] Nationalists could hardly vote against him, otherwise they might look as if they opposed the granting of the 'rights and freedom' of their own nation – and what was being offered by Gorbachëv was more useful to them than the political status quo. Communist-conservatives would support him on the ground that at least he was proposing the Union's retention.

Gorbachëv won the referendum with a handsome majority. A turnout of 80 per cent of electors occurred,[4] and 76.4 per cent of these replied positively to Gorbachëv's question. In the RSFSR, the USSR President secured the support of 71 per cent of persons who voted.[5] His gamble had paid off. The electorate of the USSR, a state created with a commitment to one-party dictatorship, confirmed its wish for the USSR to be maintained and reformed. When he appeared on television to announce the results, Mikhail Gorbachëv was a visibly happier man than he had seemed for several months. He was justified in stating that people had been invited to affirm support for the Union and, with the exception of those Soviet Republics where voting had not taken place, had resoundingly assented. Although the referendum had no constitutional force, it had a certain political and moral weight. Citizens had been asked voluntarily to back the Union, and had done so; consensus had been obtained. At the very least any subsequent attempt to dissolve the Union would be seen to contradict not only the USSR Constitution but also the freely consulted popular will.

But the August 1991 coup attempt changed the whole situation. Gorbachëv later claimed that the Union would never have been in jeopardy if the plotters had not moved against him. But Yeltsin got an unearned chance. Gorbachëv put this vividly: 'He had it served up to him in bed like fried eggs on a blue-rimmed plate.'[6] Yeltsin seized his opportunity after the overwhelming majority in the Ukrainian referendum in favour of state independence on 1 December. A week later the Presidents of the RSFSR, the Ukrainian Soviet Republic and the Belorussian Soviet Republic declared the USSR unsustainable. Suspending the current negotiations with Gorbachëv, they proposed the creation of a Commonwealth of Independent States.

The Presidents of the three Slavic states had assembled in Belovezhskaya Pushcha outside Minsk without a mandate from their three Supreme Soviets, which were the quasi-parliamentary bodies to which they were theoretically accountable. Yeltsin, Kravchuk and Shushkevich came together without a definite plan. The suddenness of their agreement to meet was such that Kazakhstan President Nursultan Nazarbaev – who had also been invited – had insufficient time to board a plane and attend. There is another possible interpretation of Nazarbaev's absence. This is that Yeltsin and the two Slavic Presidents had only pretended to want to involve Nazarbaev since Kazakhstan was the second largest Soviet Republic. But Nazarbaev was simultaneously the object of their suspicion. He had been among the warmest supporters of the USSR's maintenance earlier in 1991; and he could have been an even more prominent leader at the apex of the Soviet political leadership if Gorbachëv had better appreciated his talents and usefulness. The failure to give Nazarbaev time to fly from Almaty to Minsk may therefore have been a deliberate ploy of Yeltsin, Kravchuk and Shushkevich.

It was the decision of just these three men that brought about the Union's disintegration. They had not consulted their governments or parliaments. Kravchuk, the Ukrainian President, was the only one of them who had consulted his electorate. But there was no USSR-wide referendum on the break-up of the Soviet Union; and the proposed secession of Ukraine, in constitutional terms, did not in itself imply the end of the Union. Several further stages of discussion and decision had yet to be passed if the Law on Secession of 1990 was to be complied with.

Yet politics are politics. The constitutionality of Yeltsin's design was dubious; but he it was who held real power in the RSFSR. Gorbachëv telephoned Yeltsin asking when he planned to come to the Kremlin. Yeltsin, still nervous about what had happened in Belovezhskaya Pushcha, asked: 'But I'm not going to be arrested there, am I?' Gorbachëv, whose whole political strategy had rested on the minimising of force in politics, exclaimed: 'What are you on about? Have you gone off your head?!'[7] When they met, Gorbachëv made one last effort to save the Union by offering to step down from office and give Yeltsin a free run at the Union Presidency: 'Let's talk man to man about this.' Desperately wanting to preserve the Union, he was willing to relegate all their previous disputes to oblivion. Perhaps, he thought, Yeltsin would respond to the friendly tug on the arm. But Gorbachëv misunderstood his rival. Yeltsin still resented what had been done to him in 1987 when Gorbachëv had had him dragged from hospital and shamed at a Moscow Party City Committee plenum. He also fumed at Gorbachëv's condescension. While Yeltsin respectfully used the formal word for 'you' (*vy*) when addressing him, Gorbachëv called him and most other individuals by the familiar *ty*. Now that Yeltsin had a chance to humiliate his perceived tormentor, he would not pass it up.

In December 1991 Gorbachëv had to pack his bags and prepare for retirement. The country's politics and administration were falling apart. The economy was in chaos. Gorbachëv, for all his historic greatness, had presided over this degradation. He had had his chance; another would not come his way. And so he prepared his farewell address to the people of the Soviet Union. The tiredness had gone from his features when he appeared on television on 25 December 1991; but the emotional charge inside him was evident. He read his text calmly. He spoke to 'fellow citizens' without specifying which state's citizenship he had in mind. He made no secret of his disappointment at recent political events.

A Union of some kind was still what Gorbachëv wanted. But he had to admit defeat: 'Events have taken a different path. The dominant line is towards the dismemberment of the country and the disunification of the state, with which I cannot agree.'[8] He recited the achievements made under his leadership. He argued that 'the totalitarian system has been liquidated'; and he added: 'A thrust has been undertaken along the path of democratic reforms. Free elections have become a reality along with freedom of the press, religious freedoms, representative organs of power and a multi-party framework. The rights of man have been recognised as the supreme principle.' The Cold War was over. A mixed economy was being created. Ways had been found to bring harmony among the various peoples of the Union. Gorbachëv acknowledged that conditions for citizens had deteriorated in other ways and that this had caused discontent: 'But I would like yet again to underline: cardinal changes in so huge a country, and with such an inheritance, cannot occur painlessly without difficulties and disturbances.'[9] The question of the validity of the political decision to end the Union continued to bother him, and he declared his conviction 'that decisions of such a scale should have been taken on the basis of the expression of the popular will'.[10]

Yet Gorbachëv was not going to raise a banner of revolt against Yeltsin. 'Nevertheless I will do everything in my capacity,' he commented, 'so that the agreements signed there [in Almaty] might lead to a real agreement in society and might facilitate both an exodus from the crisis and the process of reforms.' But he did not resign. He did not even say that he was retiring on pension. He simply stated: 'Because of the situation that has arisen with the creation of the Commonwealth of Independent States I am ceasing my activity in the post of President of the USSR.'[11] This was a statement of fact. But it was a comment, not an endorsement.

And so Russia became independent by anti-constitutional methods. Yeltsin tried to disguise this and in 1992, fresh from taking over the Kremlin precinct from Gorbachëv, stressed the need for constitutional propriety under his rule. The paradoxes were acute. Yeltsin had brought the USSR to an end primarily on the grounds that it had been a despotic state. But if he was going to abide by the formal procedures of politics in the newly independent Russia, he himself would be compelled to adhere in the first instance to the terms of the RSFSR Constitution. This Constitution, however, had been introduced in 1978, when Brezhnev was still Party General Secretary and while the RSFSR was the largest territorial unit of the despotic state which Yeltsin was later to help to destroy. After dismantling the USSR, Yeltsin ceased referring to the RSFSR other than as 'the Russian Federation' or 'Russia'; but the fact remained that the appurtenances of statehood – including his own post as President – derived from the RSFSR; and all his leading political supporters, now appointed to posts in the government and the central and local administrations, were in the same situation. The regime of independent Russia was born in a communist wedlock.

A further problem was the lack of clarity in the formal inter-relationships of the President, Vice-President and Supreme Soviet Chairman. This became obvious when Yegor Gaidar, Yeltsin's appointee as Acting Prime Minister, tried to implement the programme of economic reform. Yeltsin praised Gaidar as 'a real find', even claiming that his lack of practical experience in economic management was an asset in as much as he came to his job without worries about changing things.[12] But Vice-President Alexander Rutskoi and Supreme Soviet Chairman Ruslan Khasbulatov were uneasy about the government's measures. They were uncomfortable, too, about the consequences of the USSR's collapse in terms of politics and security. They resented Gaidar and Yeltsin's other young appointees; they also hated having to operate in the President's shadow and argued that his powers were too extensive and his manner overweening; and Yeltsin had made a tactical error, when taking over the Presidency in June 1990, by leaving intact his powers as Chairman of the Supreme Soviet for use by his successor Khasbulatov. To Yeltsin's consternation, Khasbulatov proved to be a tireless maker of mischief.[13]

Dispute between the two sides continued through 1992 and 1993 and the Supreme Soviet discussions criticised practically everything done by the Yeltsin-appointed government. In December 1992 Yeltsin had to get Gaidar to stand down because of their joint difficulties in handling the Vice-President and the Supreme Soviet Speaker. The suspicion grew that Yeltsin was no longer determined to come out on top. He visited the Supreme Soviet infrequently and seldom spoke with his previous verve. The claque of opposition parties seemed to have depressed him, especially after the Congress of People's Deputies removed his emergency powers and came within seventy-two votes of impeaching him in March 1993.[14] But Rutskoi and Khasbulatov did not have it all their own way. With his customary deftness Yeltsin asked Vice-President Rutskoi to oversee agrarian reform: this was an effective way of deflecting anyone from trouble-making. It was the regime's task of Sisyphus, the hero who had to roll a massive stone up the hill every day – only to find that as he reached the top, the stone got the better of him and hurtled down to the bottom. As for Khasbulatov, Yeltsin treated him with obvious disdain. He also picked on the Chechen and other Caucasian criminal gangs in Moscow as threats to public order in the city. Chechens were popularly blamed for the capital's street violence. The fact that Khasbulatov was a Chechen did not fail to be noticed by Yeltsin's audiences.

In April 1993 Yeltsin arranged to break the stalemate of his struggle with the Supreme Soviet by holding a referendum on his Presidency. Sixty-four per cent of the Russian Federation's electorate turned out on the day. Of these, 54 per cent expressed confidence in him as President. But slightly fewer, 53 per cent, voted in favour of his economic and social policies. This was hardly an overwhelming endorsement of Yeltsin, but it was good enough for him to say that he retained the support necessary for his programme of reforms. He was also cheered by the fact that 67 per cent cast their ballot for the early holding of fresh elections for an RSFSR Congress of People's Deputies.[15]

Yet he could hardly ignore another aspect of the referendum: namely, that 49 per cent of the turnout voted for early elections to be held for the Russian Presidency.[16] However this was interpreted, it meant that nearly half the voters were uneasy about their current President. Yeltsin had sought to validate his leadership by means of a plebiscite, but had succeeded even less well than Gorbachëv before the continuous political crisis that took place from August 1991. He had little choice but to go back to trying to keep on decent terms with the Supreme Soviet. Associates of the two groups resumed negotiations in an attempt to secure an understanding about how politics should be conducted in the future. Both sides concurred that the existing RSFSR Constitution, inherited from the Soviet period, needed to be replaced. Joint drafting commissions were in constant session over the next few months. Khasbulatov, a trained specialist in jurisprudence, kept a close eye on developments, and it appeared that an agreement would eventually be obtained. In the Supreme Soviet there was fierce open dispute. In private a whispered constitutional compromise was emerging.[17]

By then, however, Yeltsin was contemplating a different scenario. His precise calculations, if he had any such, remain obscure. What is clear is that he worried about the possible consequences of a deal with the Supreme Soviet. As his suspicions of Rutskoi and Khasbulatov increased, he questioned how reasonable they would be in handling any new Constitution. He himself felt cheated by their attitude. He had won a massive victory in the Russian presidential elections of June 1991 at a time when neither Rutskoi nor Khasbulatov had been a figure of great fame or influence. They had soared to prominence by clinging to Yeltsin's coat-tails. The time seemed overdue to cut loose from them and pursue the tasks of reforming Russia by himself. In summer 1993, as he pondered how he might achieve this aim, Yeltsin became increasingly convinced that it would be better to write the Constitution himself than to allow his opponents any contribution to it. This meant in turn that his Constitution would be highly biased in favour of presidential power: Yeltsin did not intend to be bound by compromises with his former 'allies'.

For this purpose he thought it best to be less than straightforward. He developed his plan on the quiet, and the plan involved nothing less than the closure of the Supreme Soviet, the holding of fresh parliamentary elections and the inception of a new Constitution. Even Viktor Chernomyrdin, his Prime Minister from 14 December 1992, was not initiated into it until Minister of Defence Pavel Grachëv and Interior Minister Viktor Yerin had been consulted and had given their assent. The details were then worked out in the strictest secrecy before Chernomyrdin returned to Moscow from a trip to the USA. According to Yeltsin's later account, the plan did not immediately commend itself to governmental ministers. The constitutional talks between the representatives of the President and the Supreme Soviet were steadily narrowing the ground of disagreement. There would inevitably be a furious reaction from most political parties in the Supreme Soviet if the President were to take the offensive in the way he proposed. Chernomyrdin was in any case much less antagonistic than Gaidar had been to those parties in the Supreme Soviet which wished to slow down the introduction of a market economy. But Yeltsin cajoled the lot of them. There would be a new parliament and a new Constitution – and they would be convoked on Yeltsin's terms.

On 22 September 1993 Yeltsin issued Decree No. 1400, announcing his intention of suspending the Supreme Soviet and holding parliamentary elections and a constitutional referendum.[18] He indicated too that presidential elections would be held six months after the parliamentary ones. The gauntlet was thrown down to his opponents. Following his instincts, Yeltsin went back to Gaidar and appointed him as Minister of Economics. Simultaneously he took the Supreme Soviet's property into the possession of the Presidency.

The trouble was that he had neither kept his plan entirely confidential nor worked out what to do if the plan were to become public knowledge. In fact Rutskoi and Khasbulatov, having being forewarned, were determined to resist the President. Their supporters amassed personnel, arms and communication equipment in the White House where the Supreme Soviet was based. There they announced their defiance of

Decree No. 1400. The Supreme Soviet refused to be dispersed, and Rutskoi and Khasbulatov declared that any constitutional and political settlement would require their prior consent. Yeltsin was denounced as a tyrant. The Supreme Soviet, despite having been elected in 1990 when political democracy was still weakly developed, was portrayed by Rutskoi and Khasbulatov as the epitome of popular accountability. Groups which had always denounced the termination of the Soviet Union came to their side in the White House. These included leaders such as Albert Makashov and Viktor Anpilov who had bitterly castigated them in the recent past. Makashov, a former Soviet army general, had stood against Yeltsin and Rutskoi in the 1991 Presidential contest; Anpilov, leader of the Russian Communist Workers' Party, had denounced Gorbachëv, Yeltsin and all those who had sought to introduce the politics and economics of reform since the late 1980s.

Rutskoi and Khasbulatov were encouraged by their arrival and invited crowds to surround the White House in a protective cordon. Rutskoi addressed all of them in elevated mood on 1 October. He had concluded that Yeltsin's days were numbered; the very fact that Yeltsin was keeping troops in a ring around the crowd was a strong sign, in Rutskoi's opinion, that the President was becoming desperate. Rutskoi then made several stupid mistakes. He proclaimed himself Acting President and 'appointed' Makashov, an advocate of the USSR's restoration, as his Minister of Defence. Indeed, he urged his audience to seize the Ostankino television station in the capital and to broadcast an appeal for support for the besieged Supreme Soviet. Rutskoi was, for practical purposes, preaching armed rebellion against a regime he had helped to found.

All this played into Yeltsin's hands. The Russian army, under Grachëv's authority, made things difficult for the inhabitants of the White House. The electricity and water supplies were turned off. The crowd at the Ostankino television station was dispersed by force. On Yeltsin's orders, cannonades were fired at the White House in the early morning of 4 October. As acrid smoke rose from the blown-out windows, TV cameras recorded the stunned exodus of Supreme Soviet deputies, many of them terrified and exhausted. Not all of them were supporters of Rutskoi and Khasbulatov, still less of Makashov and Anpilov. But all had been defeated. Rutskoi and Khasbulatov were arrested. Yeltsin had them locked up in the same Sailors' Rest Prison where the organisers of the attempted coup d'état of 1991 were in detention. Yeltsin's purpose was to identify Rutskoi and Khasbulatov as being as anti-constitutional and dictatorial as Gorbachëv's opponents in August 1991. The public media played up the theme of a democracy saved and enhanced. Parliamentary elections would be held. A Russian Constitution would be introduced and the parliament would not be a Supreme Soviet but a State Duma. Communist institutions, practices, and ideology were to be buried once and for all.

Yeltsin had a reasonable case that the endless political conflict between his supporters and those of Rutskoi and Khasbulatov was damaging the country's interests and that a definitive resolution had to be found. But he also exaggerated the nastiness of their intentions, and by his own actions incited an exaggerated nastiness in them. Whichever side we take in the debate about the events of September and October 1993, however, the main point is that Yeltsin behaved with extreme recklessness. He brought about a crisis by dispersing the Supreme Soviet. It cannot even be excluded that he deliberately leaked his 'plan' so as to get his opponents to take him on in a direct fashion. Perhaps he calculated that in this way he would be able to put himself into the right with the Russian general public. This is not proven, but it cannot be discounted. Nor can it be entirely excluded that the information reaching the defenders of the White House was consciously skewed so as to make Rutskoi assume that he had overwhelming popular support. According to this hypothesis, Yeltsin actually wanted Rutskoi to do something violent so that Yeltsin might justifiably treat him as a traitor to the existing RSFSR Constitution.

The truth will possibly never be known. Yeltsin did a lot by word of mouth either on the telephone or in conversations with his aides, and committed little to paper. But this hardly affects the core of the matter. In his quest for a political settlement, Yeltsin used brutal force. He wrecked the old Constitution by military means. The constitutional, legal and democratic protector of the state had broken constitutional, legal and democratic procedure. Yet another stage in the creation of the new Russia was initiated by an infringement of the very principles in whose name the creation was being undertaken.

Yeltsin appeared on television and urged voters to turn out on 12 December 1993. He pleaded with them to give their consent to the new Constitution and to cast their votes in the elections to the State Duma. The name of the state was to be formally changed from the RSFSR to the 'Russian Federation (Russia)'. Yeltsin made clear that the political party he supported was Russia's Choice, led by Gaidar. For a time it seemed that Yeltsin would announce his membership of the same party, and spokesmen intimated that he would address the Party Congress. In the event he drew back from joining the party. But he stuck to his objective of limiting the participation of the elements of Russian politics which did not accept the end of the USSR. The Communist Party of the Russian Federation, despite his efforts, had been relegalised in November 1992. But any ideas about forming political parties that Rutskoi and Khasbulatov might have had were quashed by their arrest. Yeltsin meanwhile stayed in complete charge of the rules governing access to the TV and radio. Politicians who approved of the draft Constitution found it easy to get air-time; those who disapproved were disabled from conducting a full and open campaign.

The draft Constitution proposed to the electors gave enormous powers to the President. He could issue decrees without having to submit them at a later date to the State Duma; not even Nicholas II had that degree of freedom after 1906. The President could pick the Prime Minister. He could appoint the Chairman of the Constitutional Court. He could declare war. He could be impeached by the Federal Assembly, which consisted of the lower State Duma and the higher Federation Council, only when a majority of two-thirds of both houses had been obtained. And he could in any case disperse the Federal Assembly.

Yeltsin's own rules insisted that half of the active electorate had to vote in favour of the draft Constitution for ratification. The turnout across Russia on a day of wettish snowfall in Moscow was disappointing. According to the official records, slightly less than 55 per cent of the potential electors visited the polling booths. Of these, 58.4 per cent cast their votes for the draft Constitution. This means that only 32 per of the entire potential electorate actually voted for Yeltsin's draft.[19] Yeltsin was disconcerted. In June 1991, when he had stood as candidate for the Russian Presidency, 43 per cent of the RSFSR's total number of adult citizens had both exercised their right to vote and chosen him. If the referendum was a surrogate test of confidence in the Russian President, then undoubtedly his popularity had declined. Things were even worse than they appeared. The authorities handling the referendum were under instructions from the government to ensure that Yeltsin's constitutional draft was ratified – at any cost and by whatever means. The counting of the votes took place in secret and the announcement of the results was quickly followed by the incineration of the ballot papers. Vyacheslav Kostikov, Yeltsin's aide, was sure that gross abuses took place after he noticed that figures in the printed official report on the referendum had been corrected by fountain pen. Quite possibly, too, less than half the electorate had in fact voted and therefore the entire referendum had been invalid in any event.[20]

Out of this dirty business came the fresh institutional configuration of Russia after communism. It was a form quite unlike the Soviet regime in many ways. Russia, established on the territory of the former RSFSR, had been one among fifteen of the Soviet Republics of the USSR. It now had a President with powers to appoint the Prime Minister and to rule by personal decree if the parliament – the Federal Assembly – were to oppose him. The lower house, the State Duma, was announced as a regenerated version of the last parliamentary body under the tsars. The ideology and history of communism was repudiated. The whole future of Russia was declared to involve a rupture with the communist past.

Yeltsin had created and consolidated an order that suited him. He had done this in an improvised manner. There is no sign that his main policies of 1992–3 were already in his mind in 1991. What seems to have happened is that he had set up various advisory groups offering him different kinds of counsel and that he decided in favour of one or another in the light of the current situation. The consequence was that he worked out his route as he proceeded. He was not a strategic visionary. But he trusted his instincts and blustered his way forward. When he encountered resistance, he proved ruthless and imperious. He only initiated the electorate into his developing strategy as considerations of convenience occurred to him at any given time. In 1991 he was trusted and even idolised by most Russians. But they had not known about his exact intentions – nor for that matter did he. They were willing to follow him for a while. But they had not given him a mapmaker's *carte blanche*. All this gave Yeltsin an opportunity which would not be permanently available and the voting pattern on 12 December indicated that his political resources were already fading somewhat.

And in the longer term his methods undermined the chances to build a popular sense of legitimacy for the new Russia. State independence was achieved by anti-constitutional means. Russians in March 1991 had voted for a retained Union; Yeltsin in December 1991 had colluded with the Presidents of Ukraine and Belarus to disband the Union. He broke the Law on Secession. He failed to consult the Supreme Soviet in advance or the electorate afterwards. In 1992 he ruled more by decree than through co-operation with the Supreme Soviet. Detailed constitutional negotiations took place in 1993, but Decree No. 1400 rendered compromise impossible. In the ensuing disorder Yeltsin by his own admission behaved unconstitutionally. He suspended the RSFSR Constitution and directed artillery fire upon the White House. He imposed the new Constitution in December 1993 by methods involving electoral fraud. The birth of new Russia was induced by anti-constitutionality, violence and corruption.

7. POPULAR OPINION

Yes, you've freed us from statehood and history, from work
and wages, from science and culture, from ethics and morality,
from a legal order and from the future of our children, from
friends and relatives ... But when will we be freed from you?

Sovetskaya Rossiya, 1993

The people of Russia had always had their doubts about the desirability
of breaking up the USSR. The legitimacy of the new Russian state was
widely and frequently questioned, and surveys of public opinion caused
deep concern to the authorities long before the violent events of October
1993. The newspaper *Nezavisimaya gazeta*, which generally supported
Yeltsin at the time, reported in May 1992 that 57 per cent of Russian
citizens favoured the slogan 'USSR yes, Commonwealth of Independent
States no!'[1] At roughly the same time another survey found that two-
fifths of the public favoured a Great Russia as their state. The meaning
was not wholly clear except that the respondents definitely preferred that
'Russia' should be reconstituted with larger borders than those of the
Russian Federation.[2] In the previous year there had been an attempt to
examine this conundrum. People were asked about the status of Crimea
and the Don Basin in Ukraine and of North Kazakhstan. In Moscow,
36 per cent of respondents wanted these regions to be reunited with the
Russian state – and in other cities, towns and rural areas the percentage
was as high as 44.[3]

The authorities immediately intensified their propaganda efforts.
Despite this, 74 per cent of the citizens of the Russian Federation in 1995
denied that Russian state independence was a good thing. The USSR was
remembered fondly by them. They saw no reason why Gorbachëv should
have been compelled to accede to the abolition of the Soviet Union.[4]
When the same pollsters returned to the matter in 2000, only 4 per cent

of respondents declared themselves 'totally positive' about the break-up of the USSR.[5]

This was not the same as believing that the leaders of the August 1991 coup had been right and that the USSR should be re-established. When a survey was conducted in spring 1994, only 9 per cent of Russian citizens 'agreed strongly' with the proposal to 'restore the former communist system'; and by 2001 the proportion had tumbled below 4 per cent.[6] For the USSR was not just a territorial phenomenon; it was a whole political, economic, social and cultural entity. Citizens of the Russian Federation might not have positively wanted to terminate communism in the late 1980s; but they were not entirely hostile to such a desire either. They were in a condition of personal and collective flux. They wanted something different. They wished for a better future and held many half-formed ideas they had had since the long years of communism. They were willing to be surprised. They were not hugely unrealistic; they and their immediate ancestors had had enough of promises – utopian promises – made by politicians. But they wanted to believe that betterment would not be too long in coming. They needed to believe this even though they were incapable of thinking through all the complications involved. They were not rebelling. They were not even contemplating rebellion. They were amenable to the politics of radical change – but they would require careful handling.

They got accustomed to being asked their opinion. In the Soviet years, at least until the late 1980s, the gauging of the general public mood occurred mainly through the secret reports of the KGB. Sociology was a suspect academic discipline and its practitioners had to steer clear of matters that the Politburo treated as sensitive.[7] Things changed under Gorbachëv, and the leading sociologist Tatyana Zaslavskaya set up an organisation that is now known as the All-Russia Centre for the Study of Public Opinion. Other opinion-poll bodies were quickly formed, including foreign rivals such as the New Russia Barometer.

A survey by All-Russia Centre for the Study of Public Opinion, published in early 2000, yielded fascinating results.[8] People were asked to evaluate the periods of twentieth-century history. Easily the least favoured were the years after 1991. Sixty-seven per cent expressed a negative attitude to the experience of the Yeltsin regime. Even the years of *glasnost* and *perestroika* scored better, albeit only marginally. Thus Gorbachëv's rule elicited an unfavourable response from 61 per cent in the survey taken.[9] This pointed to a grim verdict on the continuous changes made since 1985. Easily the most popular period of the last century, according to the same survey, was the long rule of Brezhnev. Gorbachëv characterised the years from 1964 under Brezhnev's leadership as a time of disgusting 'stagnation' in Soviet public life; to Yeltsin, they appeared equally unseemly. But 51 per cent of Russian citizens had come to regard that particular period in a positive light (and only 10 per cent in a negative one). Nostalgia for the Brezhnev years, when social conditions were stable and predictable and when the USSR was united and powerful, has continued to grow. No other period comes near it in popularity despite the daily grind of official commentary under Gorbachëv, Yeltsin and Putin.

These are attitudes that developed and ripened after 1985. Indeed, when Brezhnev died in 1982, he and his regime had been held in near universal contempt. There can be little doubt that the popular enthusiasm for Gorbachëv at the inception of his Party General Secretaryship was sincere. It was only in the 1990s that the days of Ol' Man Brezhnev came back into favour.[10] The contrast with other periods was also remarkable. Khrushchëv's rule attracted the approval of 30 per cent. The Revolution gained 28 and Nicholas II's reign 18 per cent. Stalin's despotism did not do at all badly with 26 per cent; but the adverse opinion about it was higher, at 48 per cent. Despite the fondness for Stalinism amongst the older generation, the horror at its memory was greater.[11]

The survey data needs to be handled with care. Like most other peoples in the world, Russians are capable of saying one thing to public-opinion pollsters and thinking entirely another. They can also think entirely contradictory things in the privacy of their minds. The newspaper *Sovetskaya Rossiya* – admittedly not a loyal supporter of the government – took delight in the resultant confusion. In spring 1993 it carried a report on an incident outside the White House:

> For a lark near the House of Soviets of the RSFSR [some individuals] set about collecting signatures of passers-by for an appeal and request to raise B. N. Yeltsin to the throne of the tsars and to give him recognition as a saint. To the astonishment of the pranksters themselves, twelve people signed the form within twenty minutes, and only one person recalled that this was happening on 1 April.[12]

It could of course be that the twelve interviewees knew perfectly well which day it was and that they themselves were quietly having a joke at the expense of the pranksters. But what is clear is that popular opinion is not monolithic, unchanging or coherent in present-day Russia.

One attitude in society has been very widespread for many years; indeed it has existed throughout the decades after the Second World War.[13] This is the feeling that further political tremors, especially those involving violence, must be avoided. Russians have a horror of civil strife – or, as they usually put it, civil war. Still less do they support demands for the retrieval of the territory of the former Soviet Republics. Unease about the 'loss' of these republics is not the same as a desire to drag them back into a unitary state governed from Moscow. There is acceptance, however reluctant, that what has gone has gone. Ukraine, Azerbaijan, Armenia, Georgia, Kazakhstan and the other Soviet Republics are now independent and proud of it. The condition of the armed forces anyway makes resubjugation unfeasible. If Chechnya – which is a part of the Russian Federation – is difficult to pacify, the difficulties in larger regions would be still greater; and few Russians would want to fight in such a campaign of conquest. Russian national pride does not extend to a willingness to die for the cause of empire.

The only feasible way of expanding the territory of the Russian Federation would be by negotiation and peaceful pressure. In fact various bilateral treaties have been signed with other states of the Commonwealth of Independent States and, in April 1996, an agreement was signed approving the eventual reunification of the Russian Federation and Belarus.[14]

But Russian citizens gave all this a mixed reception. Belarus has a standard of living even lower than Russia's. Full reunification would have the likely consequence that the citizens of the Russian Federation would have to bail out the finances of their neighbour. Ukraine, too, has an economy that has plumbed the depths, and Kazakhstan has hardly been a model of agricultural and industrial regeneration. Russians, therefore, have not been thirsting to send their armed forces and civil administration back into the other lands of the former USSR. They do not want to take responsibility for even bigger economic messes than their own; and there are other countries of the Commonwealth of Independent States that are even less attractive than Belarus. Tajikistan has been tormented by civil war and most of the ethnic Russians have fled. In Georgia, too, there has been war. The Georgian armed forces have been tied down in endless conflicts with the Abkhazians, who aspire to statehood and independence. Azerbaijan and Armenia, meanwhile, have fought each other sporadically over the mountainous terrain of Karabagh. Russians fear military entanglement in such countries.[15]

They also have little stomach for moving against those former Soviet

Republics that have made a reasonable start with their economic regeneration. Chief among them are Estonia, Latvia and Lithuania. Although Soviet citizens until 1991 were always told that the Baltic region had been legitimately and permanently incorporated in the USSR in 1944, there is scant desire among Russians for territorial expansion. Popular Russian imperialism is a dog that has yet to bark.

This is at first sight baffling in the light of the fact that twenty-five million ethnic Russians lived outside the Russian Federation in the various other states of the former Soviet Union. Russians in eastern Ukraine, north-western Kazakhstan and eastern Estonia constitute local majorities of the population.[16] From 1991 there was a worry that they might suffer at the hands of the freshly established national governments. Discrimination occurred quite widely against Russians, who found it hard to get registered as citizens and to obtain promotion or employment. Yeltsin and Putin have stressed their wish to guarantee the security of Russians in 'the near abroad', and official warnings have been issued to foreign states that persons of Russian nationality must be treated fairly. Still more alarming was the physical danger confronting Russians in certain zones of the former Soviet Union. The worst case is Tajikistan, where civil war among Tajiks was accompanied by outrages against the Russian population. The result was a frantic exodus of Russians. All this has led to a sense of humiliation among the Russian people. A very few years ago they were the great nation of a superpower and the idea seemed preposterous that other national groups in the USSR might somehow hurt the interests of Russians. But there is little active support for armed interference to restore Russian political and military dominance.

Popular opinion is focused instead upon the situation in the Russian Federation. By the mid-1990s there was scepticism whether the elites were willing or able to act for the public good. When asked which organisations they most distrusted, Russians picked political parties. Not far behind the parties came trade unions and private commercial companies. And in fourth place trailed the government itself.[17] But how should the country be run if the existing elites were so much distrusted? Fifty-four per cent answered that economic policy should be decided not by the government or the Federal Assembly but by a panel of experts. This sort of response was perhaps a sign of despair of any improvement except by magic.

But another response was much less easy to dismiss. This is that 43 per cent believed that a 'strong leader' – rather than parliament and elections – was what the country needed most of all to get it out of its predicament.[18] This is a Russian tradition with a long lineage. The Romanov tsars governed without having to resort to written legislation until Nicholas II sanctioned the Basic Law in 1906 – and even then he insisted on articles that permitted him to issue commands without reference to the State Duma. After the October 1917 Revolution, Russia acquired rulers of strength in Lenin and Stalin. Khrushchëv and Andropov were also dynamic and ruthless; and although Gorbachëv allowed dissent inside and outside the party, he too imposed his decisions with an insistent verve.[19] Russia from time immemorial has had rulers who have governed with 'an iron hand'. While they were in power, many of them were feared and hated. But even the worst of them, including Ivan the Terrible, enjoyed posthumous affection among the people. Folksongs and popular proverbs kept alive the idea of a firm but fair leader being needed to control Russia's vast and diverse society.[20] Even Stalin was regarded in this light by many Soviet citizens after his death, and this attitude has not entirely disappeared from present-day society.[21]

But what sort of strong man did Russians want after the end of communism? There was a degree of open-mindedness about personal features. Only 61 per cent of citizens in the late 1990s felt that the President should be a Russian. Exactly the same percentage were indifferent about the President's set of spiritual beliefs.[22] Moreover, only 55 per cent of citizens stipulated that the President should be a civilian. Obviously the notion persists amidst a minority that it might take a military commander do the job of President effectively. But as usual there are contradictions in the evidence. When asked what style of leadership should be adopted, the largest group of respondents – 43 per cent – laid down that the President, however 'strong' he might be, should use a 'collective' technique.[23] It would seem that Russians want a strong man who acts like a prime minister seeking consensus among his ministers rather than ordering them what to do. Some strong man! Initially President Putin seemed to fulfil the popular longing for 'the firm hand'. His invasion of Chechnya; his clampdown on individual 'oligarchs'; his introduction of control over regional political bosses: all this gave the impression of a strong man in the Kremlin.

In August 2000, when Putin was thought insensitive to the fate of the crew of the ill-fated submarine *Kursk*, popular opinion demanded that he display a more sensitive side to his character. Yet the mood quickly passed and he returned to favour.[24]

From this standpoint the Russians would appear an incorrigible people, never ready for democracy. This is a misunderstanding of a very complex situation. As material conditions worsened for them from the late 1980s, Russians wondered whether an unrestrained single ruler might serve them better than would democratic institutions. Such was their pragmatic response to difficult circumstances. It was, however, not the only response. Not only in the late 1980s but also in the early 1990s they were telling the pollsters that they believed, too, in the positive role to be played in Russia by 'the consolidation of democratic principles'.[25] These were not mere words. The elections to the Presidency and the Federal Assembly have invariably enticed a substantial proportion of the electorate to go out and vote. Even the 2000 Presidential election, in which the victory of Putin was a foregone conclusion, attracted 69 per cent of the potential electorate.[26] There is no longer any compulsion to vote in Russia. But the Russian people feel that it is of importance who is chosen to represent their interests. Russians have mixed attitudes. Many of them want to be governed by an authoritarian leader; at the same time they desire the right to name the one they like.

Nor were they absolutely hostile to the market economy after communism's collapse. Sixty-eight per cent of Russian citizens in 1993 already advocated the private ownership of small manufacturing enterprises as well as shops and cafés. Even more of them – 87 per cent – wanted to see small plots of land transferred to private owners. Most Russians, however, refused to go further in this direction. Enough was enough. Only 21 per cent were willing to endorse the privatisation of large factories and mines (and 24 per cent would accept the denationalisation of large tracts of land).[27]

Although resentment continues to exist against individuals who grew rich by illegal methods, there is not a majority in favour of taking their wealth back from them. Only 45 per cent of respondents in a 1995 survey called for such expropriation.[28] Throughout the rest of the decade the government went on selling off enterprises and most Russians have gained little or no direct personal benefit from this. Their reaction, naturally, is not a positive one: by 2000 only 18 per cent of them were willing to endorse 'the market economy' as the main guiding principle in public life.[29] People under the communist regime were told that the state owned and directed the economy in their collective interest; but they knew that the members of the political, administrative and economic elites in practice derived the greatest material advantages from the system. Now the economy is in private hands – and there is not even a pretence that citizens have benefited on an equal basis from the change.

TV, radio and press are full of stories of the abusive practices whereby the wealthy acquired their fortunes. Nevertheless those political parties which call for a renationalisation of industry, agriculture and commerce have not once commanded an absolute majority in any election to the Presidency or to the Federal Assembly.

So what ideas do Russian citizens live by? The answer has always depended on which kinds of citizen are asked the question. There are differences between generations. In 1998, when they were asked, people aged between fifty-six and sixty-five still felt an attachment to the ideals which were propagated under the communist authority. Half of them thought 'the ideas of Marxism' to be true. Most of them were deeply patriotic. Thus 84 per cent took pride in the military victory in the Second World War; and nearly as many – 81 per cent – admired the achievements of post-war reconstruction and regarded 'the Fatherland' as an important idea. Only half of them were willing to declare that 'the crimes of Stalinism' were unjustified. Years of anti-Stalinist propaganda before and after the fall of the USSR had fallen on deaf ears. The late middle-aged generation in the Russian Federation looked askance at the West. Sixty-three per cent of them thought 'Western democracy, individualism and liberalism' unsuitable for Russians. This is a pretty damning verdict: they were saying not merely that such concepts might not presently be realisable but that they are generally not the right thing for the Russian people. This intensity of conservatism is deeply dispiriting for the reformers in the government.[30]

The picture changed when the younger generation was looked at. Persons aged between sixteen and twenty in the same survey rejected the communist heritage in its entirety. Only 24 per cent of them thought Western democracy, individualism and liberalism unsuitable for Russians and a mere 27 per cent accepted Marxist ideas as 'true'. The young shared with their elders a pride in the Soviet military victory of 1945. But they also gave a still greater positive importance to Russian literature, painting and music. Fifty-five per cent of the late middle-aged generation exulted in this national heritage whereas the proportion for the young was 72 per cent.[31]

Another finding in the late 1990s was that adolescents and young adults were less judgemental than their elders about the Soviet past; history was no longer a vibrant subject for them. The most unpopular leaders for young people were the same as for most other generations: Gorbachëv, Stalin, Yeltsin and Lenin. But in each case the level of unpopularity was lower than that registered among their parents and grandparents.[32] Perhaps this means that the generation which will soon be in control of politics and the economy in Russia carries little ideological baggage on their shoulders. Perhaps the past for them is a dead topic. The absence of bitterness about the past would therefore serve the purpose of enabling them to make a better future. Such is the optimist's interpretation. But there is another way of looking at the matter. It may be the case that younger Russians, with their reluctance to think much about the country's twentieth-century history, may become prey to those politicians who try to persuade them that extreme political solutions are required for national salvation. This does not look likely at the moment, but it cannot be discounted as a possibility.

The further question arises about the feelings of Russians for the new Russian state. They have been taking time to regard themselves as 'citizens of Russia'. In 1996 the percentage was 53; in 2000 it was 67.[33] Not all Russians feel comfortable, years after the collapse of the USSR, with the territory of their present state. The Russian Federation still does not feel like their homeland for many of them. There lingers a sense that the larger territory of the former Soviet Union somehow belonged to them by right.

But there are also contradictory tendencies. Even within the Russian Federation there are places where ethnic Russians have always felt themselves to be alien. This is not true about all the areas where the non-Russians form a majority or have autonomous republics in their own name: Russians in Tatarstan and Bashkortostan do not think the other nationalities have a higher right to reside there. But further south the situation is different. Particularly in the mountains of the Caucasus there is a definite wariness among Russians to claim the location as being 'Russia'.[34] The indigenous peoples of Kalmykia, Dagestan, Chechnya, Ingushetia and Osetia were always depicted in Russian nineteenth-century literature, since Alexander Pushkin, as wild, exotic, oriental and foreign.[35] This tradition persists. When Russians speak of the Caucasus, which lies to the west of the line of longitude of the Russian city Vyatka, they still categorise it as belonging to 'the East'. They do not regard it as part of Europe. In the early 1990s there were some figures in public life, including even Alexander Solzhenitsyn, willing to contemplate surrendering independence to such republics. This readiness was hard to find by the end of the decade, and Solzhenitsyn – not a man often known to change his mind – announced support for the Russian government's second post-communist invasion of Chechnya.

His reasoning lacked his usual moral fervour. Solzhenitsyn simply declared that the process of national humiliation had gone on too long. The Chechens had cocked a snook at Russia. It was time to teach them a lesson. None the less not even Solzhenitsyn argued that Chechnya was Russian in any sense other than in terms of international state frontiers.

Meanwhile, most citizens identify themselves less with the Russian Federation than with the particular individuals and groups with which they come into contact. Eighty per cent feel a sense of commonalty with members of their family. This is by far and away the highest count of self-identification. When asked with whom they feel most comfortable, their usual response is that their close relatives are dearest to them. Next in line come friends with 74 per cent. After friends come people of similar beliefs with 53 per cent.[36] Broader categories then start to be registered. In particular, 45 per cent say that 'nationality' is an important factor in their identity. This could mean two things. One possibility is that nationhood does not matter very much if 55 per cent failed to identify their Russian ancestry as a crucial characteristic for themselves. Another is that the response in most countries would hardly be very different and that it is the 45 per cent highlighting their nationhood who should catch the eye. The basic question is whether the bottle is half full or half empty.

Russians do in fact live harmoniously with most other ethnic groups in the Russian Federation. Attitudes in the more remote areas are instructive. In Karbardino-Balkaria a questionnaire asked people which national group they found congenial. Russians predictably rated Russians most highly: 80 per cent made this choice. But almost as many Russians – 77 per cent – chose the Kabardinians; and 67 per cent of them chose the Balkarians.[37]

Yet there is another side to this. The Russians of the North Caucasus are not very impressive in integrating themselves with the other ethnic groups. Across the Russian Federation, indeed, few Russians bother to pick up the local language. Nearly every Russian is monolingual.[38] This is not resented, however, as much as might be anticipated. Asked whom they found congenial, Kabardinians chose the Russians first, the English second and the Balkarians third. As for Balkarians, they chose Balkarians first, Kabardinians second, Japanese third and Russians only fourth. A similar survey undertaken in North Osetia found that Osetians by a long way disliked the Ingushes most of all. Then, in order of dislike, came the Chechens, the Roma and the Germans. Russians in North Osetia pinpointed the Chechens as their most disliked group, followed by Latvians, Roma and Tatars.[39] Yet the Russian inhabitants do not have a general hostility to their fellow inhabitants of the mountains. The exception is Chechnya, where life long ago became intolerable, and the younger and better-off Russians took flight. Elsewhere in the North Caucasus, though, Russians have been reluctant to move away. The mountains are their home.

Nevertheless, there is rising unease among Russians living in many of the 'national' republics and regions of the Russian Federation. The leadership of such republics tend to be dominated by persons of the titular nationality of the republic. Russians dislike this. Tatarstan illustrates the point. Whereas two-fifths of urban Tatars have confidence in their respective republican leadership, only a fifth of their Russian neighbours do.[40] But the Russians of Tatarstan have even less confidence in the political leadership in the Kremlin. Whilst they might be unhappy about politics in their republic, they are even more distrustful towards Moscow – and the rural Russian inhabitants are especially sceptical about the idea that the government in the capital might ease their plight.[41] The results of such surveys must be treated with caution; but it is reasonable to assume that most Russians, whatever their prejudices, feel that their destiny lies with the area where they presently live. In so far as they retain hope for improvement in social and material condition, they look for action to be initiated within the same area and not in distant Moscow.

Yet Russians do not lack hostile prejudices about other ethnic groups. They dislike on a grand scale, and their attitudes have more than a trace of imperial condescension. Antagonism is strong towards certain peoples of the North Caucasus and the Transcaucasus, an antagonism strengthened by Chechen terrorism and the wars started in Chechnya in 1994 and 1999. One survey suggests that 6 per cent of Russians fear persons of Azeri nationality and that 38 per cent feel either irritated by them or mistrustful towards them.[42]

The concentration of hostility on Azeris and Chechens may come as a surprise in the West, where it is widely supposed that Russians – nearly all of them – are rabid anti-Semites. This is a stereotype repeated in newspaper after newspaper. If there is one image that stuck to the Russian people through the twentieth century, it is that they were viscerally hostile to Jews. There is indeed much anti-Semitism in Russia, and under Nicholas II and Joseph Stalin it was given direct official encouragement – and today it is being fostered by the Russian nationalist politicians.[43] Jews themselves feel uncomfortable in both Russia and Ukraine. The emigration of hundreds of thousands of them to Israel

1. Boris Yeltsin, Russian President, 1991 to 1999.

2. Ceremonial meeting of Yeltsin with Belarusian President Alyaksandar Lukashenka and Russian Orthodox Church Patriarch Alexi II.

3. Vladimir Putin, Russian President from 2000.

4. Presidential Crest of the Russian Federation.

5. New Gate to Red Square.

6. Statue of Marshal Georgi Zhukov, erected in 1994.

7. *Left.* Zurab Tsereteli's Peter the Great Ensemble by the Moscow River.

8. *Above.* Newly built underground supermarket complex on the Manège in central Moscow.

9. Advert for cigarettes named after Peter the Great.

10. Russian spoof version of James Bond with Andrei Fëdorov saying: 'The name's Bond. Vasili Bond!' (*Sem' dnei*, 6–12 May 2002)

and the USA testifies to their severe concerns. Yet most present-day anti-Semitism among Russians is of the casual kind encountered in Western societies in the first half of the twentieth century. When asked about their attitude to Jews, Russians rarely express fear of them. In the same survey only 2 per cent said so; and only 14 per cent have professed irritation with or mistrust of Jews. Although this is hardly consoling from a liberal viewpoint, it is not as disturbing as the misleadingly extreme image of the Russian people that is conventional.[44]

Inter-ethnic relations are therefore complicated. Russians have hostility to certain other peoples, but they also have friendly prejudices. In areas where they constitute a minority, moreover, they make for peaceful, tolerant neighbours and are appreciated for this. They are not devoid of nationalist notions wherever they live in the Russian Federation, but this is not the focus of their thinking.

But when they ponder the future, Russians have had more sombre thoughts. Pessimism spread fast. Three-quarters of respondents to questions about the future agreed that 'Russia is entering a dead-end'. Things, they concurred, were going to the bad. At the same time three-fifths of respondents affirmed that personal happiness is more important than 'national salvation'. Most citizens of the Russian Federation stopped expecting their country to climb to the sunny uplands of human achievement and contentment in the near future. What is more, they came to have a very mixed set of feelings about what happened to the USSR and what they want out of life in the Russian Federation of today. There grew up much nostalgia for the Brezhnev years. There was regret about the USSR's collapse. Pride remained in the Soviet military victory in the Second World War. Yet at the same time the citizens of the Russian Federation criticised the lack of political freedom and economic fairness in the USSR. They appeared to wish for communism's provision of a welfare state without accepting the attending political and administrative authoritarianism. Countries such as Sweden continued to enjoy a high rating with the Russian public. But there was a final contradiction here that requires attention. This is that most Russians now contend that foreign models of development are inappropriate for Russia. And so the popular belief grew stronger that the country must follow its own path to reform in state and society.

Consequently the Russian people were confused. They were not seeking to overturn the order established by Yeltsin, but they declined to give it an enthusiastic sanction. Although they can hardly be blamed for their equivocations, their position makes it difficult to imagine that political and economic conditions are quickly going to improve. Popular scepticism about the designs of its rulers is profound. Such scepticism is not ineradicable. But this would have been an easier task in the early 1990s than it has subsequently become.

8. MASTERS OF RED SQUARE

And then I said to Putin: 'I'm a cellist, I play the cello. I could never be a surgeon. But I'm a good cellist. But what's your profession? I know you're an intelligence officer. I don't know what that means. Who are you? What can you do?'

And he said to me: 'I'm a specialist in relations with people.'

Sergei Roldugin, 2000[1]

It would have helped if other politicians had ruled from the Kremlin after 1991. Yeltsin had discharged an indispensable task as a leader willing and able to break through the political impasse which had trapped Gorbachëv. The need for radical measures had become acute, and Yeltsin and his team had provided the necessary energy and vision. Unfortunately, however, too much depended on him as an individual. His style of leadership had become erratic and corrupt. His authorised image was sullied not only by memoirs and rumours but also by his own observable behaviour. The political capital he had accumulated in the years of struggle against Gorbachëv and the communist establishment was recklessly dissipated.

The personal decline was gradual, but soon his inadequacies put his positive qualities in the shade. On good days, when he appeared on television, he was a serene performer – and his ease amid crowds and his aura as the tribune of the Russian people in 1991 stood him in good stead. He made an effort to enhance his country's name abroad. He dressed in a smart, sober suit during the day and at banquets he and his associates donned smoking jackets.[2] He called President Bush his 'friend George' and took Helmut Kohl for manly saunas and for swims in Lake Baikal. When travelling abroad, he lived up to local expectations. He refitted the Presidential jet so that he could travel in style. He sequestered decorations and furniture kept in the state dacha previously used by the

Gorbachëvs. In his early life, he had been a good volleyball player and on entering the Kremlin, he set up a Presidential Club with a tennis court and gymnasium.[3] Yeltsin was aspiring to acceptance as a ruler with a 'modern' outlook; and when he spoke on TV and radio in his own country, he avoided lecturing about his policies. He consciously eschewed the habit of communist leaders of laying down exactly what people ought to think.

His charisma remained with him into the mid-1990s. With his thick, silvery hair and his long physical frame there was something of the mature film star about him. He continued to emphasise how in his youth he had shared the sufferings of the Russian people. In his second volume of autobiography, published in 1994, he wrote of his father who had been arrested for loose talk in the 1930s. He recalled, too, how the hungry Yeltsin family grew potatoes on disused land in the famine years immediately after the Second World War. As one of his associates put it, he was a quintessential 'Russian person'.[4] Another emphasised that the President 'liked to see the expression of characteristics of a purely Russian kind: breadth, openness and perhaps even a certain recklessness'.[5]

But was he really any longer a man for the people? Even before taking power in the Russian Federation, he had stopped arriving at work by public transport. His long-suffering wife Naina no longer had to queue up for food and medicine; instead she had them delivered. Yeltsin bought himself a Mercedes in 1995.[6] The Yeltsin family made plenty of money whenever the opportunity arose or could be made to arise. The President's daughter Tatyana Dyachenko forged links with the multimillionaire financier (and ex-academic) Boris Berezovski.[7] Her son, named Boris in honour of his grandfather, was sent to Millfield School in Somerset to be turned into a proper English gentleman. The President did not seem personally engaged in fraud, but there were suspicions even on this: his former bodyguard leader Alexander Korzhakov has mentioned that an inexplicably large sum of money accrued to Yeltsin's account in royalties for the second volume of his autobiography. Berezovski, according to Korzhakov, put the ill-gotten gains into Yeltsin's purse.[8] In September 1999 a scandal broke out over Dyachenko's use of her credit card in Switzerland. Her extravagance became the object of press scrutiny and the question was asked how on earth a person who had no well-paying job could afford a lifestyle of such opulence. Yeltsin's defence of his daughter served only to attract accusations of corruption to himself as well as to Tatyana.[9]

Then there was the scandal of the President's physical condition. Efforts were made to disguise his problems in a manner reminiscent of the subterfuges used about Lenin, Brezhnev and Andropov. When he had to stay in the Barvikha Clinic outside Moscow, it was usually said he had influenza. If ever he needed to appear in public, the cameramen were given instruction about the angles from which he could be filmed; and when he gave addresses on television, his aides prepared the text on laminated pages so that no one might notice his pathetic fumbling. (Another problem was that he refused to wear his spectacles in public.)[10] The entourage raised his spirits when he was down. He often got nervous before speaking to the Federal Assembly, and had to be nagged into attending it.[11] On one occasion a Presidential aide cheered him up by making the sign of the cross over his head before he went on to the platform. Yeltsin, despite his lack of unequivocal religious faith, was deeply grateful.[12]

Notoriously he took to the bottle in Berlin in August 1994 and, despite being accompanied by German Chancellor Helmut Kohl, grabbed the baton of a military band conductor and set about giving a raucous rendition of the Russian folksong 'Kalinka'. On a flight back from the USA, on another occasion, his plane stopped over at Shannon airport near Dublin. His chief bodyguard Korzhakov in his memoirs denied that it was the drink that kept Yeltsin from meeting the Taoiseach on the airport apron. In reality, apparently, the Russian President had had a heart attack in the toilet of the plane and his wife, together with Korzhakov, had to drag him out on to a seat for treatment.[13] The judgement was made that it was better for Yeltsin to be rumoured to be tipsy than for it to be admitted that his cardiac problems were chronic. Korzhakov also suggested that Yeltsin had mental problems even when his heart was not troubling him. He was prone to depression and supposedly had tried several times to commit suicide.[14] In 1996, moreover, he had to undergo a quintuple heart bypass operation. It could not be said that the Russian Presidency was in calm and steady hands.

Yeltsin misbehaved just as badly in Russia. One day in the Kremlin a TV cameraman caught him passing behind the desk of a secretary and pinching her bottom. On another occasion he flattered some waitresses about their physical appearance. When they looked disconcerted, he shouted: 'Well, why is it you're staying silent? Am I really so fearsome? Look, I'm your President!' With that he grabbed one of them round the waist and pressed a kiss on her lips.[15]

The Kremlin was run like a court, but it was not a court such as the tsars had maintained. Anyone displeasing him had to humble himself. His aide Vyacheslav Kostikov described the ambience:[16]

> On not a few occasions the thought entered one's head to go and talk with the President, even to express repentance. Yeltsin, feeling himself within his team as being like the father of an extended family, showed a familial sort of love when someone asked him for forgiveness, more often than not on some trivial charge of bureaucratic misdemeanour. Just after I joined the group of Presidential aides, the experienced and cunning head of chancellery Valeri Semenchenko gave me instructions on this theme: to ask the forgiveness of 'Daddy'.

Another of his little tricks was to take out a pair of spoons and start playing them on the head of one or other of his aides (on one occasion President Akaev of Kyrgyzstan was a victim).[17] Although this was done in a jocular fashion, it was pretty painful. The unfortunate aide had to grin and bear it, and hope that it would be somebody else's turn next. Such rituals degraded the victims; Yeltsin's need for the self-abasement of his associates was repellent.

The Russian President had always behaved a bit like this. As Sverdlovsk Province Party Committee Secretary, he used to gather his aides together in the forest upon his return from trips. Each of them had to report directly to him how well or how badly his instructions had been fulfilled during his absence. Sitting on tree stumps, they would sink tumblers of vodka in the process. There was method in this. It enabled Yeltsin to bond his team around him and subject them to his will.[18] His waywardness intensified in Moscow, where he was Party City Committee Secretary from 1985. Any infringement of his will was met with instant dismissal and the personnel of party and soviet posts was changed with giddying rapidity. Once he had become President of Russia, Yeltsin's imperious demeanour knew no bounds. The violent dispersal of the Supreme Soviet in October 1993 was an extreme case that gave a clear signal that he would allow nothing to stand in his way. Implicit obedience was required of his subordinates. Any refusal to submit would be crushed, and even his loyal followers had to put up with intermittent humiliation.

Few subordinates could stand up to him for long. Oleg Poptsov, chairman of the state-owned TV channel ORT, refused to stop his reporters from investigating scandals involving Yeltsin's relatives and friends. Yeltsin summoned a meeting of media editors and harangued

Poptsov. But Poptsov surprised Yeltsin by retorting: 'You can't proclaim principles of open politics and simultaneously protect the authorities from the presence of journalists.'[19] Poptsov's liberal commitment did him no good in the end. In January 1995 he was sacked without ceremony.[20] Like a Canadian Mountie, Yeltsin always got his man.

Yet increasingly he let his ministers and aides run affairs. The inner core of his associates included Viktor Chernomyrdin, Sergei Filatov, Alexander Korzhakov, Valentin Yumashev, Anatoli Chubais and Boris Berezovski. They were a diverse bunch. Chernomyrdin, a former USSR Gas Industry Minister, was Prime Minister. Filatov was Chief of the Presidential Administration while Korzhakov was Chief of Presidential Security. Yumashev started as Yeltsin's press adviser, eventually being appointed Presidential Administration Chief. Chubais was initially in charge of the State Committee for the Management of State Property, but later occupied other ministries. Berezovski was a wealthy business-man and financial counsellor to the Yeltsin family; in 1998 he was made Secretary of the Commonwealth of Independent States. This was the group that dominated the politics of the Kremlin during the lengthening periods when Yeltsin was either ill or apathetic. They had to be wary. At any time he might reassert himself and punish any of them for disobedience. But increasingly a mutual bond developed between the President and his associates. He needed them as much as they needed him.[21]

When Gaidar had been Prime Minister, ordinary citizens thought they were being ruled by a government that was wet behind the ears. Under Chernomyrdin they thought differently. No longer did it feel like being governed by overgrown adolescents. It was more like being bossed and exploited by veteran crooks.

Before the USSR's collapse no one – least of all Chernomyrdin himself – foresaw Chernomyrdin as someone to supervise a transition to capitalism. But he was a steady administrator and initially had a rapport with most factions in the State Duma, including the Communist Party. He was no ideologue. He was also proud of his past career in the USSR government; he knew the gas and oil industry from the inside and was generally 'patriotic' and 'state-minded'. But this did not stop him looking after himself and his family in a lavish fashion, and he was slow to reprimand colleagues for dipping their hands into the till. In tempera-ment and demeanour he was like Brezhnev without the vanity. Unflap-pable, he wanted a comfortable life and a minimum of disputes, and he lasted as Prime Minister for longer than any of his rivals. For over five years from December 1992 he was Yeltsin's right-hand man. This was quite a feat. Yeltsin hinted that if ever he had a chance, he would restore Gaidar to the post of Prime Minister. Snide criticisms were aimed at Chernomyrdin whenever Yeltsin needed someone to blame for his own failures or – as sometimes happened – Chernomyrdin's ratings in the polls rose higher than his own. But Yeltsin and Chernomyrdin got along reasonably well for all that.

The State Duma elections in December 1993 killed Gaidar's last hopes. Russia's Choice – led by Gaidar – won only seventy of the 450 seats. Zhirinovski's Liberal-Democratic Party came tantalisingly near to this with sixty-four and the Communist Party attained forty-eight. The Communist Party's close allies, the Agrarian Party and the Women of Russia, took another fifty-six between them.[22] The scale of the government's failure was understated by the official voting returns. Television coverage had hugely favoured Gaidar and behind the scenes there was much infringement of the legal procedures. Yet still Russia's Choice did poorly. Even with his enhanced powers under the new Constitution, Yeltsin knew he had to relent. He did not need to pick his Prime Minister from the largest political party in the Duma.[23] But he could not govern without a degree of informal consent – or at least he could not do so without risking trouble in the Duma and on the streets.

Press commentators, as they scrutinised the emerging political system,[24] put forward the idea that power had fallen out of the hands of one section of the Soviet *nomenklatura* and been grabbed by another. Yeltsin, the former Sverdlovsk party First Secretary, was said to have installed a Sverdlovsk clique in power just as Brezhnev had had his clique from Dnepropetrovsk. There truly were individuals from the Urals in Yeltsin's entourage. Burbulis was an example. But generally Yeltsin resisted the temptation to select post-holders mainly from those who had served alongside him in his native locality. The studies that have been done to tease out the truth make for interesting reading. Sixty-five per cent of Yeltsin's ministers and administrative associates had served in the Soviet *nomenklatura* and only 31 per cent of the top businessmen had belonged to it.[25] These are pretty low figures in relation to the need to attract talented organisers to the regime's support. The transition from communist state and society was already well under way.

What disturbed even their well-wishers was the tendency of Kremlin post-holders to take corrupt advantage of their position. The fact that Chernomyrdin had recently headed the Gazprom company and, as Prime

Minister, provided the company with tax exemptions was taken as proof that he retained a financial interest in the business. Worse still were allegations that Defence Minister Grachëv procured the assassination of the journalist Dmitri Kholodov, who exposed the illegal sale of the army's equipment both to foreign states and to Chechen guerrillas. Supposedly Grachëv sanctioned the killing to prevent his own role becoming public knowledge. Another case involved Interior Minister Barannikov, who interceded with Yeltsin on behalf of the businessman Boris Birshtein when a campaign for Birshtein's arrest was started in the press.[26] And then there were figures such as Berezovski, one of the financial 'oligarchs', who was appointed Executive Secretary of the Commonwealth of Independent States in 1998–9. His shady dealings from the time when he engaged in private enterprise in 1989 were notorious. The fact that Yeltsin gave him so responsible a post was taken badly by the general public: it appeared to confirm that the whole political elite was hand in glove with the magnates of Russian finance.

The personal evolution of Chubais, one of the almost messianic reformers of 1991–2, confirmed the stereotype. Chubais headed the state privatisation project in 1992 and performed several crucial political tasks for Yeltsin. In spring 1997 he took over the Presidential Administration. Whenever Yeltsin needed a vigorous political operator to sort out a problem, he called in Chubais.[27] But Chubais was no altruist in public service. He made himself rich in power, adding the role of businessman to his normal official duties.

Yeltsin had few genuine intimates in his entourage. He remained fond of Gaidar, who was almost like the son he and his wife had never produced. Gaidar was brash and daring and Yeltsin admired these qualities; perhaps the younger man also appealed to him as a political kamikaze willing to sacrifice himself for the greater good.[28] The nearest substitute was his bodyguard chief Korzhakov. They drank together. They and their families spent summer weekends together. Korzhakov had worked for Yeltsin from 1987, when Yeltsin's career had been at its nadir, and he had come to depend on this gruff former KGB colonel for political advice. He asked Korzhakov to set up 'a personal mini-KGB' and allowed him to act independently of Chernomyrdin even in matters of public policy.[29] Such rivalries of entourage were one of the ailing Yeltsin's few remaining means of maintaining control over high politics. But still Yeltsin felt frustrated. He wanted someone like Gaidar not merely for personal reasons but also because he aimed to accelerate and deepen the process of economic reform. Chernomyrdin would do as he was told, but was not a reformer at heart. Whenever Yeltsin travelled abroad, it was made clear to him that foreign governments, bankers and investors were looking for a reversion to the more radical capitalist vision of Gaidar.

December 1995 brought further problems when Duma elections were held. Again the pro-government political parties had greater financial resources than the parties of opposition. Again the media showed a distinct bias in favour of the establishment. Again there was reasonable suspicion of much electoral fraud. Yet Chernomyrdin, who had recently formed Our Home Is Russia so as to establish a party unequivocally supportive of the government, still did poorly. Our Home Is Russia took fifty-five seats out of 450. The Communist Party was easily the largest party, with 157 seats, and the Liberal-Democratic Party, despite doing worse than in 1993, obtained fifty-one. By allying itself with the Agrarian Party, the Women of Russia and other sympathetic parties, the Communist Party was about to hold a strong position in the State Duma even without an absolute majority for itself. Chernomyrdin had been humiliated. He had not run a dynamic electoral campaign and his speeches had been delivered in a leaden fashion. But the main objection to him lay with his policies. The electorate, having already spat out the half-dose of 'shock therapy' by Gaidar, rejected its more moderate application by Chernomyrdin. The more traditional liberal parties, Grigori Yavlinski's Yabloko and Russia's Democratic Choice under Yegor Gaidar, won only forty-five and nine seats respectively.

Nevertheless Yeltsin kept Chernomyrdin as Prime Minister, and Our Home Is Russia became the governing party even though it held only a ninth of the Duma places. The lack of accountability in the Russian political system was severe. The Constitution allowed the President to go on ruling the country almost as if the elections had not happened.[30]

Yeltsin, persuaded by his family, decided to stand again as a candidate in the Presidential election projected for summer 1996.[31] Victory for him was not a foregone conclusion. At that time the economy was in a poor condition and the war that Yeltsin had started in Chechnya in 1994 had not been brought to a close. His popularity had plummeted. Sample surveys of popular opinion in January suggested that only 3 per cent of the electorate felt positively about him. Gennadi Zyuganov, about to be confirmed as the candidate of the political block led by the Communist Party of the Russian Federation, scored much higher. Yeltsin was frightened. A former communist functionary himself, he knew how effective the communists could be in issuing propaganda and organising meetings. He was aware that the Communist Party of the Russian Federation had a much greater number of members, half a million strong, than any other party in the country. Having tried to ban it from operating, he had been jolted in November 1992 by the Constitutional Court's decision to revoke his decree. He expected grim times ahead both for Russia and for himself personally if Zyuganov were to gain the Presidency. In March 1996 the State Duma passed a motion sponsored by the communists condemning the December 1991 decision to break up the Soviet Union.

What could be done to retrieve this situation? Support could be mobilised by financial inducements to local elites. The Electoral Commission could be selected on the basis of the loyalty of its members to Yeltsin and their antagonism to Zyuganov. Votes could be counted unfairly. Funds could be gathered from the large-scale entrepreneurs who had made their fortunes in the private economy since 1991. But there could be no guarantee that this would be achieved without serious disturbance to the politics of the Russian Federation. One alternative was for the Yeltsin team to put up another candidate. For a while it was seriously considered that Prime Minister Chernomyrdin might make a more popular candidate with voters. But Chernomyrdin, as the pollsters quickly discovered, was only a little more favoured by the electorate than Yeltsin. A crude alternative was advanced by Alexander Korzhakov: this was simply to call off the election and prolong Yeltsin's Presidency. A state of emergency could be declared. The Russian Communist Party would object, but could be banned if it resisted the emergency decree. Indeed, it could be banned even if it stayed quiescent. Korzhakov put things brutally to his President: 'It's senseless to struggle when you have a three per cent poll rating, Boris Nikolaevich. If we lose time with all these electoral games, then what?'[32]

Yeltsin welcomed Korzhakov's proposition. Although his rating was improving a little, he was worried: 'It's late – too late. It will take too long to make all these changes.'[33] Yeltsin was always inclined to action: 'It had always seemed to me that chopping the Gordian knot was easier than spending years untying it.'[34] He ordered the preparation of a decree calling off the election, dispersing the Duma and outlawing the Communist Party. Chernomyrdin did not assent to Yeltsin's plan, but it held a majority among those ministers he consulted. Anatoli Kulikov, Interior Minister, asked for time to think out his position and eventually advised against calling off the election;[35] and Anatoli Chubais agreed with Kulikov. Chubais had been appointed as Yeltsin's electoral campaign manager and told the President:[36]

> Boris Nikolaevich, this is not 1993. The difference between that moment and now is that now, whoever goes outside the Constitution will be the first to fail. It doesn't matter that the communists were the ones to go out of bounds back in 1993. It's a crazy idea to get rid of the communists in this way. Communist ideology is in people's heads. A Presidential decree can't put new heads on people. When we build a normal, strong, wealthy country, only then will we put an end to communism. The election cannot be postponed.

After an hour of angry disagreement Yeltsin gave way, and the Presidential election went ahead.

The main candidates were Yeltsin, Zyuganov and the former military commander Alexander Lebed. By fair means and foul, Yeltsin hauled himself back into serious contention. He had the press and broadcasting media almost entirely on his side, and he disbursed money, promises – and threats – to local political leaderships in order to secure victory. Boosted by prescription drugs, he managed to sustain a vigorous electoral campaign until the final days.

Yeltsin and Zyuganov emerged as the two leading contenders in the first round on 16 June 1996 and Lebed was eliminated. Lebed had spoken strongly about the need for peace in Chechnya, for a restoration of Russian national honour and a sound Russian state and for an end to corruption in government. There was a danger that those who had voted for this outspoken general might transfer their allegiance in the second round to Zyuganov. A deal was done between Yeltsin and Lebed – it may even have been secretly in place before the election. In return for being appointed Secretary of the Security Council, Lebed would support Yeltsin's Presidential candidature and would urge his own supporters to do the same; and he would be given important political tasks once the election was over and Yeltsin had been installed as President. Lebed would conduct the vital negotiations over Chechnya. If he were to prove successful in this role, he would obviously be in a fine position to become Yeltsin's successor as President. With this deal in his pocket, Yeltsin went forward to the second round on 3 July 1996 and won a resounding victory with 54 per cent of the votes cast. Zyuganov went down to defeat; and although there were the usual reports of electoral malpractice, there is little doubt that a majority of the electorate preferred Yeltsin.

Politics subsequently reverted to the pattern established since 1993. The war in Chechnya was brought to an end through the offices of Lebed; and once he had performed his task, he was unceremoniously sacked by Yeltsin for arrogant conduct towards other ministers. Lebed was doubtless an awkward colleague; he was also nakedly ambitious. But the main motive for his dismissal was Yeltsin's unwillingness to let others rival him in prestige. Chernomyrdin was kept on as Prime Minister. The Duma elections of December 1995 had produced results too embarrassing for Yeltsin to try to promote a radical economic reformer to that office.

Not until March 1998 did Yeltsin think it practicable to do so. The problem by then was who to choose as Chernomyrdin's replacement. Gaidar was still very unpopular with the State Duma and popular opinion, and Yeltsin's choice fell upon Sergei Kirienko. He took office in March 1998. Kirienko was in his mid-thirties and had experience in political and commercial circles in Nizhni Novgorod. He was dapper and boyish-looking. He had met Yeltsin only a couple of times before being appointed,[37] and always looked like a ventriloquist's doll when he appeared alongside the President. But Yeltsin, proclaiming his faith in the younger political generation, treated Kirienko with unusual respect: he refrained from giving him the kind of public dressing-down that had often been received by Chernomyrdin. Kirienko was charged with the completion of Gaidar's task of organising the transition to a capitalist economy. The reintroduction of radicalism annoyed the Duma and fresh impetus was given to the campaign of criticism of President and government. In May 1998 a motion of impeachment was passed against Yeltsin. By a vote of 241 to seventy-seven in the Duma he was found guilty of nothing less than state treason.[38] Yeltsin survived because he could not be removed unless the Council of the Federation also voted by a two-thirds majority against him; but the political atmosphere was extremely heavy.

Kirienko coped surprisingly calmly with these difficulties. But he was an unlucky Prime Minister. The troubles in the world economy, especially in the Far East, had repercussions on Russia and in August 1998 the Russian financial system suddenly collapsed. Kirienko, after speedily making arrangements for a drastic devaluation of the ruble and a repudiation of the country's debt-repayment schedule, had to step down as Prime Minister.

His place was taken by Yevgeni Primakov. At first Yeltsin had hoped to bring back the dour Chernomyrdin; but by then the Duma had a deep distaste for the man they held almost as much responsible as Gaidar for the economic and social difficulties in Russia. Primakov by contrast commended himself to the Duma for his willingness to work with nearly all political shadings of opinion. He had an academic background and had earned political promotion under Gorbachëv. He also had served as Director of the Central Intelligence Service of the USSR in the last months of 1991 and gone on to head Russia's Foreign Intelligence Service. From 1996 he had been Foreign Minister. No one in the Kremlin could match his experience and expertise in high politics; and Yeltsin said: 'Primakov is one of the few persons from [the old] Politburo not to have got up to dirty business against me.'[39]

Primakov steadied ministers' nerves in the winter of 1998–9. But he and Yeltsin were wary of each other: Primakov was Prime Minister only because he was the least unacceptable politician to Yeltsin at a time when a degree of support from factions in the Duma was essential. Yeltsin quickly grew annoyed. Primakov clearly wanted a less radical economic policy than his President and was inclined to do legislative deals in the Duma, even with the Communist Party of the Russian Federation. Moreover, Primakov refused to try to stop Yuri Skuratov, the Procurator-General, from investigating financial scandals involving members of the President's family and entourage. There also started to be plausible talk of Primakov's likely candidature in the Presidential election of 2000. It was therefore only a matter of time before Yeltsin retaliated. In May 1999 he abruptly sacked Primakov and introduced Sergei Stepashin as Prime Minister. Stepashin had served as Minister of Internal Affairs. Like Primakov, he had links to the intelligence services. He was forty-seven years old and a capable administrator. Quickly there was speculation that Stepashin might eventually succeed Yeltsin as President, speculation that Yeltsin did not discourage. The two men seemed to work together amicably – and Stepashin succeeded in hastening the pace of economic reform in a fashion that was agreed between them.

Then in August 1999 Stepashin too was fired for no very obvious reason. Quite possibly he had annoyed Yeltsin by refusing to give an assurance that the Yeltsin family would have immunity from prosecution in the event of Stepashin becoming President. This was a topic of vital importance for Yeltsin, whose relatives had accumulated great wealth in a distinctly dubious fashion since 1991.

Stepashin's replacement was Vladimir Putin. It was a choice that astonished Russia, Putin being no less surprised than the rest of the country. Spotted by the Yeltsin team as a talented organiser in Leningrad, he had been transferred to the Presidential Administration. Yeltsin took to him, and promoted him to successively higher state posts. Although Putin was unknown to the Russian public, his ministers soon learned he meant business. His ruthless streak was revealed in October, when he resumed the war in Chechnya. This won widespread popular praise. Already by November he had the approval of 36 per cent of the public (and this rose to 45 per cent in the following month).[40] Yeltsin announced Putin as his favoured candidate at the forthcoming Presidential election. Elections to the State Duma were held in December 1999, and Putin's supporters rapidly formed a party called Unity. The results were pleasing for the government. Unity, whose centrist ideas were little different from those of the defunct Our Home Is Russia, obtained eighty-three seats. Although the Communist Party of the Russian Federation got eighty-nine seats, Putin did not need to worry since the other large centrist party – Fatherland-All Russia – took forty-six seats. For the first time the government could expect to work with a co-operative Duma.[41]

On 31 December 1999 Yeltsin went further. In a speech that was astounding even by his standards he announced his resignation from the Presidency.[42] The Constitution entailed that the Prime Minister should become the Acting President, and it was from this position of strength that Putin put himself up for election in March 2000. He barely needed to campaign. He made few public statements; he travelled little. He issued no programme of projected policies. On television, Zyuganov and the other candidates railed against the abuses of power that had scarred the Yeltsin years. But Putin was unflustered. Riding a wave of popularity, he coasted to a huge triumph in the election.

At the ceremony of inauguration on 7 May 2000 he enjoyed his triumph. Diminutive in stature, he processed alone into the Great Kremlin Palace along a red carpet hundreds of metres long. It was reminiscent of the scene in Sergei Eizenshtein's film *Ivan the Terrible* when Tsar Ivan enters the Uspenski Cathedral and scrutinises the assembled congregation of nobility, merchants and clergy as he makes his way towards the altar. Tsar Ivan had vengeance on his mind, being about to retaliate violently against those he knew to be his enemies. Putin had no reason to be vengeful; the opposition to him in the country was a negligible force. But his gestures indicated a man who was not only confident but also very impatient. He was raring to get on with the Presidential job. Since his appointment as Prime Minister he had barely concealed his sense of frustration. Whenever the television carried pictures of him with Yeltsin, Putin – almost half Yeltsin's size – had had to exude respect for the President. When they sat in public at the same table, Putin's duty had been to carry a pen and notepad and act as the great man's amanuensis. But this changed at the inauguration ceremony. Yeltsin stood with the new President on the platform at the end of the hall and, frail and mumbling, delivered a brief homily as the Russian Federation fell into the hands of his anointed successor.

Putin's speech was a concise one.[43] The main theme was his intention to restore the power and honour of the Russian state and to bring order to society. There was no surprise in any of this. Since entering high office, he had condemned the chaos both in the Kremlin and elsewhere. There had been young Prime Ministers before him: Gaidar, Kirienko and Stepashin. But none had had the same restless menace as Putin. His comportment reinforced this impression. Putin had been a Leningrad city champion at judo in the 1970s and had kept up his physical exercises. As a man of action he had flown to Chechnya from Moscow in a two-person plane. He came over as a man without a fixed ideology but with a determination to revive national pride and rebuild Russian economic, military and political might. He wanted change, and he wanted it fast.[44]

Putin's earlier life explained a lot about him in office. At the tender age of fifteen he had applied in person to the KGB for employment. Such initiatives were not welcomed: the Soviet security services had a rule prohibiting the recruitment of volunteers. But when he entered Leningrad State University as a student of law, the KGB came back to him and trained him as an expert in 'counter-intelligence' work. The pursuit of dissidents was among his functions before he was redeployed to the German Democratic Republic. Quite what he did in Dresden is not yet clear, but probably he ran agents engaged in operations to conduct industrial espionage in West Germany. As a result he saw hardly anything of the USSR during Gorbachëv's *perestroika*. When the Berlin Wall was pulled down in 1989, there was nothing to keep him abroad any longer. He returned to a different country. No food on the shelves. Nothing but disorder in the economy, administration and politics. No sense of direction from the Kremlin. He was horrified. According to his account, he had been a Soviet patriot and a bit of a romantic when joining the KGB. (Supposedly he had given no thought to the events of the Great Terror and the year 1937 meant nothing to him.) The official regime had been good to him and he wondered, as the USSR crumbled, what the purpose of his life had been.

Returning to Leningrad, he joined the administrative team of Mayor

Anatoli Sobchak. During the anti-Gorbachëv attempted coup in August 1991, they sided with Yeltsin. From that point Putin's extraordinary rise to prominence began and he became Sobchak's adviser. In 1996 came the move to the Presidential Administration in Moscow. Yeltsin quickly made him head of the Federal Security Service (which was the successor organisation to the KGB) and then, in August 1999, Prime Minister. It was a meteoric rise from political obscurity.

Putin surrounded himself with friends from his native St Petersburg and distanced himself from those of Yeltsin's ministers who had not been popular. Anatoli Chubais (who ironically came from St Petersburg) was among them.[45] Putin wanted to emphasise that he was his own man. He had already criticised Chubais before being elected President. Subsequently he went after other leading supporters of Yeltsin such as the wealthy businessmen Boris Berezovski and Vladimir Gusinski. He was not hostile to business as such or to all Yeltsin's ministers; he even retained the last Chief of the Presidential Administration, Alexander Voloshin. But Berezovski and Gusinski were a different matter. Berezovski had bragged once too often about his influence over Yeltsin and had acknowledged the financial favours he had showered upon the Yeltsin family. As for Gusinski, his television station – NTV – had mocked Yeltsin and Putin in its weekly satirical puppet programme *Kukly* ('Dolls').[46] Police enquiries into the affairs of Berezovski and Gusinski were initiated. Implausibly Putin disclaimed any role in this. Gusinski was arrested in June 2000 and was released only after an international outcry about freedom of political expression. But by summer in the same year both Berezovski and Gusinski had sought refuge abroad, and Berezovski had resigned his seat as Duma deputy.

Unlike Yeltsin, Putin did not need extraordinary financial subventions in order to gain the Presidency. He won the election in the first round without need for a second one, and appeared to assert the primacy of politics over sleazy finances. The nests of corruption in at the apex of public life seemed about to be unravelled.

But appearances deceived. When Yeltsin stood down from the Presidency, Putin granted legal immunity to the former President for anything done by him in his period of rule. Ambiguity remained about the fate of Yeltsin's family. Tatyana Dyachenko, Yeltsin's daughter and personal adviser, was widely assumed to have engaged in fraudulent activity. There seemed a possibility of her arrest, especially when the Swiss authorities began investigating the dealings of persons known to have been close to her. But Putin refused to take matters further. His own financial affairs began to come under scrutiny. This was a tricky task for journalists after the open pressure placed upon Gusinski and NTV. But enough appeared in print to reveal that Putin, whose job in St Petersburg had once involved the licensing of foreign commercial companies, was not as pure as the driven snow. The fact that he promoted Mikhail Kasyanov, a former associate of the disgraced Berczovski, as Prime Minister strengthened the popular notion that Putin's zeal to root out fraud and deception from the Kremlin was not unconditional.

In fact Putin had already broken Berezovski politically and Kasyanov did not try to rehabilitate his former patron. Putin and Kasyanov worked together efficiently. Whereas Yeltsin's attentiveness to detail had diminished after 1991, Putin educated himself across the whole range of governmental policy – and on matters of internal security and foreign relations it was always he rather than Kasyanov who was in charge.

His tactic remained to tower above the various contending political groupings and unite them under his leadership – or at least secure their acquiescence in it. With this in mind he refrained from open criticism of the Russian Communist Party, Yeltsin's perennial *bête noire*.[47] He supported the communist Gennadi Seleznëv's reselection as Speaker of the State Duma. He even held a meeting with Vladimir Kryuchkov, who had headed the KGB and had been one of the leaders of the August 1991 coup. Kryuchkov had sat in one of Yeltsin's prisons till his release by order of the Constitutional Court in 1994. As well as Kryuchkov, Putin met Alexander Prokhanov – one of the fiercest cultural critics of both Gorbachëv and Yeltsin. And yet Putin also took care to balance these meetings. He continued to express respect for his predecessor Yeltsin. He held a conversation with Gorbachëv. Most strikingly he requested and was granted an audience with Alexander Solzhenitsyn despite his contempt for the entire political order. Solzhenitsyn stated that areas of disagreement existed in their discussions but that generally he was positively impressed by the young President. From communists to anti-communists, Putin courted support from the widest range of supporters.

His behaviour as President was businesslike but also rather authoritarian. He liked to give orders. This bossiness was displayed even with army commanders when the war in Chechnya seemed to him to be conducted inadequately. The man in the Kremlin brooked no challenge. He admitted that Russia's regeneration, politically as well as economically, would take many years. He did not anticipate being able to discharge the task within a single Presidency. Obviously he expected to remain the country's leader for a long time.

9. ECONOMISING ON REFORM

Viktor Stepanovich [Chernomyrdin] after a few months of his premiership began to propose to the President: 'Why are you deciding all this? Let me get engaged with this question; don't heap so many matters on your shoulders.' The more frequently such conversations took place, the more acutely Yeltsin reacted: if he handed over his duties, he'd be handing over power.

Alexander Korzhakov, *Boris Yeltsin: From Dawn to Dusk* (1997)[1]

The pressures of political struggle after 1991 indisputably contributed to the implosion of the grand reform project. But they were not the only factor. Also of primary importance was the attitude taken to the project – from the start – by some of the reformers themselves. Yeltsin and several members of his entourage were not dedicated democrats – far from it. Gennadi Burbulis, First Deputy Prime Minister in 1991–2, even expressed praise for Chile's authoritarian General Pinochet;[2] and Alexander Korzhakov barely disguised his doubts about the need for elections.[3] Yeltsin aggravated he problem by insisting on appointing Yuri Petrov, who had been his successor as Sverdlovsk communist party leader and had never belonged to 'the democratic movement', to head the Presidential Administration. Worse still, Yuri Skokov was made Chairman of the Security Council. This was a man widely known to be suspicious of radical reform in general.[4]

The best that could be said for such choices of personnel was that Yeltsin could not afford to annoy the Supreme Soviet by appointing exclusively radical reformers. But even the radical reformers in the government had their failings as democrats. They wanted democracy. But the desire for it among most of them was not as fervent as the wish for other things. Chief of these was the liberalisation of the economy. The 'market' counted as a higher priority for the reformers than the reinforcement of reforms in the political, cultural and national sectors. The advocates of a radical agenda in such sectors were influential figures. Valeri Tishkov, Chairman of the State Committee for National Policy, argued that all national and ethnic groups should enjoy equal treatment; Andrei Kozyrev, Minister of Foreign Affairs, sought to enhance harmony in Russia's relations with Western democratic governments; and Yeltsin himself rejected calls for restrictions on the freedom of cultural expression. Tishkov, however, was compelled to resign early on, in October 1992, and Kozyrev stood down in December 1995.[5] And under Putin there was pressure on those organs of the broadcast media which criticised governmental policy.[6]

The movement away from the grand project was lubricated by the fact that Yeltsin and his associates had never defined it closely. They had put it together as they went along. They had spoken – and this was especially true of Yeltsin – about objectives: democracy, the market economy, a law-governed state, human rights, cultural freedom, social peace and a 'normal life'.[7] These objectives were slogans that had yet to be turned into policies. And within governing circles there was no preparatory agreement about how to co-ordinate the achievement of the objectives; the sequence of measures needed to attain them both individually and as a group had yet to be elaborated. Each minister had his own predilections – and not all of them felt comfortable with the project as a whole. In such circumstances there was bound to be conflict and disappointment.

The decision on the sequence of steps was taken even before the USSR's collapse, when Yeltsin opted to give priority to economic changes. Instead of calling fresh parliamentary elections and securing a clear mandate for his emergent policies, he opted to push ahead instantly with measures for the transformation of the economy. The choice was finely balanced. The Supreme Soviet had been elected in 1989 and had a majority of members hostile to fundamental economic reform. New elections, while Yeltsin's popularity was high, would have helped his cause. But this would have taken time, and meanwhile the industrial, agricultural and commercial difficulties were becoming catastrophic. The USSR's net material production in the last three months of 1991 alone had fallen by a fifth, and the decline seemed about to become a free fall.[8] There was no guarantee that the electorate would always vote for rapid transition to a market economy. Yeltsin and Gaidar therefore hoped that when they started to get the economy into shape, they would be more easily able to achieve the other objectives of the reform project. At times the reformers seemed economic determinists. But whereas Lenin's communist theories had been the economic determinism of the political Left, the new Russian regime was decidedly on the Right. A reformed economy, they suggested, would pull along a reformed politics and a reformed society in its trail.[9]

With Yeltsin's support, Gaidar threw himself into this campaign. On 2 January 1992, the second day of Russia's independent existence, he removed state controls on the prices in shops. The predicted result was rapid inflation. Within twelve months the ruble was under 4 per cent of its value at the beginning of the year.[10] Wage levels in state enterprises were raised to ease the social pain, but huge popular resentment existed. The value of deposits in the Savings Bank (Sberbank) collapsed. The government's ministers tried to explain that things would get better and that price liberalisation would lead to an increase in trade. In the last years of Gorbachëv's rule there had been a shortage of nearly all goods in the shops. Private holdings of rubles had been virtually valueless. I well remember going into a dairy supermarket in December 1990 where a dozen shop assistants stood behind counters with absolutely not a half-litre of milk, a lump of cheese or a carton of yoghurt for sale. A lot of hoarding had been practised by enterprises, and Gaidar's measures released goods into the shops. As he had anticipated, the market in food and other products became livelier. Although they moaned about the prices, many consumers nevertheless could go out shopping again.

There were prophecies of trouble on the streets. Commentators compared the situation with the circumstances of Russia in 1917, when food shortages and currency inflation led to the overthrow of the Romanov monarchy in February and the Provisional Government in October. It was also suggested that Gaidar's economic prognosis was flawed and that widespread starvation would occur before the year was out.

Yeltsin and Gaidar acquired the reputation for applying 'shock therapy' to the Russian economy.[11] Their credo embraced a commitment to radical privatisation, and if Gaidar had thought it practicable, he would have demolished virtually the entire state-owned sector overnight. Yet both he and Yeltsin were concerned about adverse popular opinion and took precautions to alleviate poverty and minimise unemployment. Enterprises were given tax incentives to retain large workforces. Apparently the government gave precedence, for social reasons, to keeping a high level of employment over accelerating the drive for higher productivity.[12] The regime also preserved cheap charges for utilities. Gas, electricity, telephone calls and transport continued to enjoy a massive state subsidy and, at least until the mid-1990s, the government maintained agricultural subsidies to secure low food prices.[13] Credits were also advanced to industrial firms on 'soft' terms enabling them to stay in business even if they hardly produced anything useful.[14] Gaidar's policies, abrupt though they were, did not administer anything like the shock to the ailing body of the economy his critics liked to claim.

These precautions allowed the radical economic reformers to be bolder in other ways. Quickly they issued instructions for the state's withdrawal from involvement in the business of imports and exports. Pëtr Aven, one of Gaidar's closest associates in government, cut down the number and size of customs duties.[15] The unfortunate result, however, was that goods came flooding into the country and crowded out Russian domestic production. Although consumers were able to buy what they wanted so long as they had the money, the effect upon Russia's industry was disastrous. Output fell with few remissions in the decade after 1991. The state's withdrawal also had a deleterious impact upon governmental revenues: income from tariffs fell by 40 per cent in 1992–3 alone.[16]

In July the government approved its 'Programme for the Deepening of Economic Reforms in Russia'. Nearly all state enterprises across industrial, agricultural, commercial and service sectors of the economy were to be privatised. The aim was to produce a balanced budget as the state ran down its obligations in expenditure. By lowering the commitment to the military sector, ministers aimed to create 'a competitive market environment'.[17] In August 1992, President Yeltsin signed the enabling decree on privatisation. The method was peculiar. Each adult was to receive vouchers worth 10,000 rubles which could be used to buy shares in the enterprise where he or she worked. Alternatively the vouchers could be traded in the auctions arranged to sell off state property. Yeltsin explained his thinking in a TV address on the first anniversary of the abortive 1991 coup: 'What we need is millions of property-owners, not merely a handful of millionaires.' The voucher, he claimed, was

> a sort of ticket for each of us to the free economy. The more property-owners and business people there are in Russia for whom concrete activity is more important than futile discussion, the sooner Russia will become prosperous and the sooner its future will be in safe hands.[18]

Yeltsin was promoting popular capitalism.

Something very different arose in reality. The original paper value of the vouchers massively underestimated the worth of the enterprises being privatised. Financiers and managers understood this better than ordinary employees and persuaded most of them to sell off their vouchers. The result was that huge profits were made without effort. The gas company Gazprom was a striking example: its declared worth at the time of privatisation was US $250 million but already by 1997 it was being valued on the Russian stock market at over $40 billion.[19]

Another important aspect of the economic programme was the decision to concentrate on the export of oil and gas rather than to regenerate industry. Revenues from this source had been crucial to budgetary stability under Brezhnev, and undoubtedly it was a dependable way of getting income for the government. The energy sector's importance was emphasised by the choice of Chernomyrdin to succeed Gaidar as Prime Minister, and little attempt was made to slow down the decline of manufacturing. The thinking behind this was that factories and mines were incapable of acting as the motor of economic recovery but would act as a drain on the government's exiguous resources. Industrial reconstruction would take a very long time and would require foreign capital investment as well as new technology. The government also calculated that energy exports by a small number of huge privatised companies would be easily supervised and that the collection of revenues would be a convenient process – and indeed in the 1990s oil and gas usually supplied almost a half of central revenues.[20] The policy was not explained to the public in these blatant terms, but financiers understood immediately what was going on and scrambled to get shares in firms that specialised in the gathering of Russia's natural resources for shipment abroad.

In such a situation Gaidar needed support in the provinces. He found a kindred spirit in Nizhni Novgorod's Boris Nemtsov, who volunteered his city as an experimental base for any scheme of privatisation of enterprises. Nizhni Novgorod was aflame with dispute. Seeing that Nemtsov might benefit from help, Gaidar and Chubais flew out to support him on the day of the first big auction. They were disconcerted by what they found. On arrival in the city, Gaidar was heckled and jostled. He kept calm amidst a menacing crowd. Chubais, however, saw red and thumped the nearest objector before rejoining Gaidar.[21]

This was not the only policy that Russia might have followed.[22] The Communist Party of the Russian Federation wanted state subsidies for former Soviet enterprises to be maintained and demanded a halt to the schemes for privatisation. Economic regeneration, argued party leader Zyuganov, should be attempted by means of high tariff walls that would foster the growth of manufacturing industry. He scolded the government for its apparent indifference to the plight of those working in mines and factories; and he also tried to capture electoral support among white-collar workers, especially clerks, doctors and teachers. Zyuganov's nostalgia for the Soviet years embraced a fondness for the mixture of political authoritarianism and economic liberalisation attempted by the communist leadership in the People's Republic of China. He abandoned his opposition to private enterprise and most fellow communist party members to a greater or lesser extent agreed. The Chinese model had a distinct appeal to the Communist Party of the Russian Federation. The obvious exploitation of vouchers by the old *nomenklatura* and by the commercial newcomers for personal self-aggrandisement made this case more widely attractive outside the party than it would otherwise have been. *Privatizatsiya* became known popularly as *prikhvatizatsiya*, not privatisation but expropriation.

Another possibility, raised by Grigori Yavlinski and his Yabloko Party, was to privatise much more gradually, starting with the shops, restaurants and small workshops. Then the government could have moved on to denationalise light-industrial enterprises. Meanwhile the great export sectors – oil, gas, diamonds, gold and timber – could have been retained by the state.[23]

Privatisation did not quickly involve the entire economy. Yeltsin and his cabinet clearly wished to introduce a new Land Code and to set up a class of small-holding individual farmers; but there were problems in taking the collective farms out of governmental ownership. Most farms were badly run, poorly equipped, physically inaccessible and chronically unprofitable. This was bad enough. But a further difficulty lay with social demography. Reformers had to deal with the fact that a disproportionate segment of the less industrious, less able-bodied and less enthusiastic citizens was engaged in agriculture. This was an unpromising base from which to launch agrarian capitalism – and the government's political opposition did not fail to point this out. The Communist Party of the Russian Federation and the Agrarian Party raised a hue and cry about the damage about to be done to the interests of collective farmers. They also stirred up hostility to the prospect of foreigners buying up Russian land. Consequently Yeltsin and his ministers trod very cautiously. Most collective farms were turned into co-operatives, keeping their original chairmen and workforces. Only a quarter of a million individual freeholders succeeded in breaking free from association with the other families on their collective farms.[24]

The bursts of economic reform were increasingly difficult for the government to sustain. Only preliminary measures had been undertaken. The currency had yet to be stabilised. Industry needed to be regenerated. Foreign capital investment remained at negligible levels. Rules on corporate governance were constantly ignored. The re-training of employees in practically every economic sector had scarcely been initiated. Subsidies to bankrupt or unprofitable enterprises had yet to be entirely withdrawn. Collection of direct and indirect taxes always fell below the government's projections.

Several agreements aimed at stabilising the ruble were made after meetings of the G8 group of nations. In 1992 a fund was gathered from abroad to the value of $24 billion. A further enormous tranche was promised in 1993: $43 billion. At the same time the government obtained relief on the repayment of debts inherited by the Russian Federation from the USSR. Nevertheless the funds reaching the country were not always used constructively; many were diverted into private accounts. No sooner had the Ministry of Finance negotiated loans on behalf of the state than ways were found by high-ranking officials to appropriate the money and, as often as not, transfer it to banks abroad. Cyprus became notorious as a centre for the 'laundering' of such funds coming from Russia. Swiss banks, too, were lax in querying the provenance of deposits made with them by Russian financiers. Nor did Chernomyrdin's cabinet, while borrowing astronomical sums, feel bound to repay its debts exactly as demanded by the terms of each loan. It had learned, as Count Witte discovered as Nicholas II's Finance Minister in the 1890s, that huge debts permit the debtor to exercise leverage over the creditor. Russia's integration in the world economy was a murky and complex business.

Yet the advisers from the International Monetary Fund (IMF) and the World Bank were not entirely unhappy. Evidently Russia in its rough and ready fashion was adopting some basic principles of capitalist economy and wished to remain a member of the global commercial system; and the fact that Russia remained a nuclear military power meant that the USA and its allies were unwilling to treat it as Brazil and Mexico would have been handled in a similar situation.

Ministers had always felt politically vulnerable. One of the reasons they prioritised economic liberalisation rather than democratisation was that they saw how unpopular they were in society – and Sergei Stankevich sent a confidential memorandum to Yeltsin warning him that 'the social base' of support for radical reform had become dangerously narrow.[25] The many voters who experienced a deterioration of living standards or working conditions were unlikely to show gratitude to them – and this was evident even before the Duma elections of 1993 and 1995. Yet the advocates of reform held their nerve, feeling that history would treat them more kindly. They believed that the invisible hand of 'the market' would have an irresistible force of its own and that the political, ethnic, social and cultural resistance to the grand reform project would steadily fade. They had an economic theory borrowed from abroad and their heroes were Friedrich Hayek and Milton Friedman. They had not rejected communism for social democracy. They advocated the maximum freedom for private enterprise unfettered by state ownership or regulation. In time, they assumed, their policies would prove successful. Russia would rise from the ashes. Until this happened they relied on Yeltsin's crucial ability to keep and consolidate his personal power, and they trusted that his violent suppression of the Supreme Soviet in October 1993 would prove a turning point.

They hoped that political opposition to the speed and depth of the officially sponsored changes would be definitively trounced. With Rutskoi and Khasbulatov under lock and key in the Sailors' Rest Prison, this did not seem an unreasonable expectation. The main worry was the re-establishment of the Russian Communist Party. Banned immediately after the August 1991 coup, it had been relegalised by a ruling of the Constitutional Court in November 1992. Under its leader Gennadi Zyuganov it restored its organisational network and claimed to have half a million members. Some groups were even more vituperative than the Russian Communist Party in denouncing Yeltsin's cabinet. A flavour of this critique is conveyed by a section of the front page of the weekly newspaper *Den'* ('Day'):[26]

> Yeltsin, *give back* the stolen Soviet Union
> Yeltsin, *where* are the savings we earned by our work?
> Yeltsin, the children of Russia *curse* you!
> Yeltsin, war veterans *spit* on your back!
> Yeltsin, *go now*!

Den' referred to itself as the 'organ of the spiritual opposition'. The question was irresistible: if this newspaper stood for spirituality, what on earth were the less uplifting organs of the opposition like?

Publications such as *Den'* were suppressed by Presidential decree along with others in the political emergency of September 1993. Yeltsin hoped finally to bury them for ever as political forces and to secure victory for his supporters in the State Duma election in December. But *Den'* soon resumed publication under the name *Zavtra* ('Tomorrow'). Much more importantly, Gaidar's Russia's Choice performed poorly at the polls and Yeltsin had to re-think strategy. Zhirinovski and Zyuganov had done too well for comfort. Yeltsin decided not only to retain Chernomyrdin as Prime Minister but also to alter the contents and tone of his policies. In particular, he bulked up the Russian national ingredient in his project of reform.[27] This was not done consistently, and the previous commitment to the equality of prestige of all national and ethnic groups in the Russian Federation was still asserted. But a shift had definitely occurred.

There was little economic improvement in the following two years, and in October 1994 there had to be a 27 per cent devaluation of the ruble. The subsequent disappointing result for Chernomyrdin and his party – Our Home Is Russia – in the Duma elections of December 1995 strengthened Yeltsin's conviction that a further movement away from the grand reform project of 1991–2 had to take place.[28] The project was not abandoned. Not entirely. But economic policy was prioritised to an even greater extent than before. Judicial and administrative reform proceeded slowly and criminality flourished. Local elections were conducted with blatant fraudulence. Shocked by the results of the Duma polls in 1993 and 1995, Yeltsin moderated his dismissive rhetoric about the Soviet past and sharpened his attentiveness to the place of ethnic Russians in the Russian Federation. Civic nationhood was not dropped from view; the preamble to the Constitution defining Russia as a 'multinational people' remained in place.[29] But Yeltsin gave less emphasis to this commitment than earlier. Relations with several former Soviet Republics became tenser. There were diplomatic crises with Estonia, Latvia and Lithuania. The amicable ties with the 'West' began to be loosened, and the need for Russia to assert its distinct interest in global politics became official doctrine.[30]

Economic policy itself changed somewhat. Yeltsin badly needed additional funds in order to stand a chance in the 1996 Presidential election. These could come only from the country's wealthiest financiers, and any deal had to be done very confidentially. In deepest secrecy the businessman Anatoli Chubais brought together a group of business-men who became known as the 'oligarchs'. They included Roman Abramovich, Pëtr Aven, Boris Berezovski, Mikhail Fridman, Vladimir Gusinski, Mikhail Khodorkovski and Vladimir Potanin. Although the legal spending limit for Presidential candidates was $3 million, Yeltsin's campaign team probably had as much as $500 million at their disposal.[31] Yeltsin could offer financial inducements to politicians and administrators who could influence the results of the election in his favour.

But there was a price to pay. As part of the deal, the 'oligarchs' were given temporary ownership of the controlling shares in the chief companies working in lucrative mining areas. The nickel industrial sector was a particular attraction.[32] These acquisitions became permanent when the government predictably proved unable to pay off the loans on time. Thus the 'oligarchs', while rescuing Yeltsin, piled up the mountains of their wealth still higher and reinforced the dependence of the political establishment upon their favour. The process of privatisation, which had always been corrupt, sank to unprecedented depths. The government's scope for economic manoeuvre was severely reduced. The 'loans for shares' scheme put the final nail into the coffin of the hopes for popular capitalism. The revenues that might have helped the government in future years fell into the hands of a few clever financiers who had no concern for the public good. Nor did Yeltsin and Chubais have much excuse. The 'oligarchs' needed Yeltsin to win the election as much as he did. The possibility of a return to power of the communists under Gennadi Zyuganov threatened their wealth and perhaps their liberty. Yeltsin got the worse side of the deal, and Chubais – his main adviser here – increasingly lined his own pockets as he moved between the two sides.[33]

The only other shift in policy occurred about Chechnya. The war was unpopular with Russians if only because it was being prosecuted unsuccessfully; and Yeltsin made peace overtures in spring 1996 in order to win the Presidential election in summer. His Security Council Secretary, Alexander Lebed, made a deal with the Chechen rebel leadership in autumn and an uneasy quiet descended over the Caucasus.[34]

Politics otherwise moved along the groove cut since 1993. Between the Presidential election of summer 1996 and Putin's appointment as Prime Minister in August 1999, efforts were directed at completing the privatisation of the economy. This was largely accomplished in industry and commerce. In agriculture the government continued to encounter social resistance. No serious attempt was made to change the status quo in the judicial and administrative sectors of public life. The freedom of the media to criticise the government was left untouched. The persisting struggles over policy were largely about the details. Yeltsin and Chernomyrdin were wary of pushing change too hard. The Presidential electoral campaign of 1996 had indicated, especially in its early weeks, that popular unease about Yeltsin and his policies was widespread. Distaste for Zyuganov did not mean that the electorate was fond of Yeltsin any longer. Always, too, the Duma was able to offer acute criticism. The annual debate on the budget recurrently involved drawn-out dispute. By careful compromise, Chernomyrdin was usually able to get his way. Yeltsin's right to issue decrees independently was also important. And stealthily the government succeeded in spreading the net of the market economy.

Having secured election, Yeltsin tried still harder to identify himself with the ethnic Russians and called for a search for a new 'Russian idea'.[35] But he did not do anything to facilitate the search for such an idea; he left this to Prime Minister Chernomyrdin, who was not a leader noted for his interest in intellectual questions. Chernomyrdin's reaction was an administrative one: he released funds for an open competition to define 'The Idea of Russia'.[36]

In August 1998 came the financial crash. Among its causes were the general tremors in the world economy, especially in the Far East, that started in the previous year. But the Russian government also bore some responsibility: it had become over-reliant on its borrowing facilities at home and abroad and state debts had become mountainous. By May 1998, indeed, the government owed $140 billion in hard currency and a further $60 billion in domestically traded rubles. The practice had grown for the Ministry of Finance to trade its maturing bonds by issuing new ones. But it was becoming ever more expensive to raise fresh finance as the risk of default appeared to increase. The high interest rate made everything worse. In such circumstances it might have been better to carry out a financial devaluation; but this, as the IMF pointed out, would threaten the degree of currency stabilisation which had been achieved. Chubais went on a mission to secure a further loan from the IMF. But at this point the 'oligarchs', who were worried that they might lose everything in the gathering economic crisis, turned against the Kirienko cabinet. The snag was that public knowledge about the bailing out of Russia damaged the confidence of investors. The consequence was a run on the ruble and Kirienko's decision to make a unilateral announcement of a rescheduling of governmental debts.[37]

When Primakov replaced Kirienko, he altered foreign policy and made the West into an object of overt official suspicion. Primakov also made a point of constructing a better relationship with the State Duma and of including members of the Communist Party of the Russian Federation in his cabinet. But there was little change in basic economic policy, and anyway the financial collapse had the unexpected positive effect of inducing greater domestic industrial growth because of the increased cost of buying goods abroad. In 1999, the value of imports fell by a half.[38] Primakov was anyhow sacked in May 1999 and his successor Sergei Stepashin restored the line of policies developed under Chernomyrdin. Quietly, too, Stepashin initiated the planning necessary for the reconquest of Chechnya.[39] Yeltsin had neither forgotten nor forgiven the humiliation of the Russian army in 1994–6.

Thus Vladimir Putin's appointment as Prime Minister in August 1999 made a bigger difference to Russian politics, in content as well as in style, than anyone had forecast. Immediately he gave urgency to the existing preparations for a military strike at Chechnya and an invasion was started in October. He also pursued central administrative control and made menacing noises about the disorder and corruption in the provinces. Most strikingly, he introduced a new administrative tier to the hierarchy of territorial units of power. Such an idea was not new: it had been canvassed in Yeltsin's time. But it was Putin, its persistent advocate, who implemented it. Seven super-districts were established across the Russian Federation. All but two of them were headed initially by individuals who had worked as either army commanders or security officers – and indeed the districts themselves covered the same areas as the districts covered by the Russian armed forces. The task set by Putin for his new representatives was to secure the loyalty and obedience of the various republics and provinces under their control.[40] The President seemed to mean business since he himself had not been afraid to challenge and defeat the two leading 'oligarchs', Berezovski and Gusinski. His determination in this respect increased his popularity among most sections of the electorate.[41]

His confidence was shaken, however, by an event over which he had no control. In August 2000 the nuclear submarine *Kursk* suffered a massive explosion in the Arctic Ocean. Putin was on holiday at the time and was assured by the Ministry of Defence that everything possible was being done to rescue the vessel and its crew. Steadily the incompetence of the Ministry became evident, and a belated appeal went out for foreign technical assistance. A Norwegian specialist vessel and crew was dispatched. But when the *Kursk* was finally reached, it was found that the entire crew had perished. Putin's failure to visit the vicinity above where the submarine lay was criticised in the Russian press.

Hurriedly an attempt was made to recover his reputation. The Presidential Administration recognised that the impression had been given that Russia under Putin was no more attentive to the plight of individuals than the USSR had been under a succession of General Secretaries. Newspapers and TV stations interviewed the relatives of the crew before it became certain that all on board had perished. Distraught mothers, wives and fiancées chided high state officials in person, and Putin decided to hear their complaints in private. This followed an incident involving a woman who became so agitated while haranguing a minister that medical staff stabbed her with a syringe and injected her with a sedative. Putin's popularity temporarily dipped. He no longer appeared the invincible statesman that he had seemed to be during the Presidential electoral campaign. He admitted that the rescue effort had been mishandled, and compelled the Ministry of Defence to apologise for its actions and to reform its methods. It was gradually becoming plain that Putin, who had made his name as a friend of the armed forces, would have to carry through a vast reform in the culture of the army and navy.

The President also sought a constitutional adjustment. At the time of his accession the norm was for executive heads of administration in provinces and republics to have seats in the Federation Council. This gave them legislative influence. It also provided them with legal immunity from arrest; but Putin overturned this convention, insisting that the Federation Council should become elective. As a sop to the incumbents he founded a State Council to which the existing members of the Federation Council could belong, and he steadily persuaded individuals that it would be in their interest to comply with his request. At the same time he moved against local politicians who annoyed him. Even Alexander Rutskoi, who had been released from prison in 1994 and was one of his apparent supporters in Kursk province, fell foul of him. It was an interesting little spat. Putin had irritated Rutskoi by failing to support him in a political dispute in Kursk province. Rutskoi, who was not only a former Vice-President of the Russian Federation but also an airforce commander in the war in Afghanistan, retaliated by making a very public visit to a group of families which had lost relatives in the explosion that destroyed the nuclear submarine *Kursk*. The President was unforgiving. Pretexts were easily found. Rutskoi was declared corrupt and was disallowed from standing as gubernatorial candidate in Kursk province.[42]

At the same time there was movement away from the strident anti-communist line that had characterised the utterances of Boris Yeltsin.

Putin decided to moderate antagonism towards the Soviet past. Whereas Yeltsin had dropped the USSR into the black hole of history, Putin wanted to restore respect for the country's achievements under Lenin and Stalin. But this was not a drive towards recommunisation. Putin was nostalgic but pragmatic. Not for nothing had Yeltsin chosen him as his successor. The objective for Putin was to manage the aspirations of elites and the feelings of the general public while re-establishing the Russian Federation in a position of influence and esteem in the world. Although the criticism of the Soviet past was diminished, this was done in a deft way: communism itself was not rehabilitated and Putin refrained from endorsing or indulging the Russian Communist Party. Indeed, he repeatedly mentioned that the political extremism of the Soviet period had got the country into a frightful mess. At no point did he espouse the restoration of the USSR, Marxism-Leninism or the communist political and economic order. More than anything, he wanted the country to get on with the present-day tasks of national regeneration.

With this in mind he did not rush to finalise the contents of economic policy. His popularity benefited from the economy's quick recovery from the August 1998 financial collapse. This had little to do with him and his ministers. One reason was the rise in the world oil price; another was the opportunity for Russian industry and agriculture to sell their goods at a time when imports had become too expensive. Prime Minister Mikhail Kasyanov paid off some of the arrears in wages and pensions while aiming to complete the movement towards a market economy. Industry and commerce had already largely been privatised; but agriculture was suspended in a condition of semi-reform. Yet even in those sectors where private enterprise was in the ascendant, problems persisted. Local economic laws frequently contradicted the Constitution as well as the laws of the Russian Federation. Uniformity and consistency were prime goals for Putin.

But what did all this amount to? Despite the variations in policy and personnel since Yeltsin's resignation, much remained unaltered. A decisive shift away from state ownership had taken place. About this even the Communist Party of the Russian Federation and the Liberal-Democratic Party more or less agreed at last. No large political organisation any longer tried to bring back the system of commerce, industry and agriculture that prevailed in the seven decades before 1991. Communism as propounded and imposed by Lenin, Stalin, Khrushchëv and Brezhnev was dead, and there was no serious prospect of its resurrection. Communists and their sympathisers still talked nostalgically. Yet most people recognised that the rupture with the Soviet past was permanent. Future politics were inevitably going to be centred upon debate about what kind of market economy was desirable. President Putin and his ministers had yet to make things work more efficiently and fairly in the country. That they really wanted to make such a change was in doubt. The desire for order was obvious; there was no similarly evident commitment to introducing the rule of law. And the brutal invasion of Chechnya in 1999 showed a preference for tackling problems by force.

Nevertheless it appeared to be accepted by most political parties that electoral politics are essential to Russia's future. Yeltsin notoriously wavered on this in 1996. Putin was no more dedicated to democratic procedures in principle and it remained to be seen how he might react if his political popularity fell precipitately. Yeltsin and Putin at best favoured guided democracy. While promising to foster a 'civil society', in practice they tried to control those many non-governmental associations and groupings which had emerged. At a meeting with their representatives on 12 June 2001 Putin declared that they 'must be admitted to the working out' of decisions taken by the government. He admitted that Russia still had too few associations; it was not, according to him, 'to the credit' of the country. An agreement was made to set up a Civic Forum for all of them. But already there was reasonable scepticism about his intentions: by bringing 'civil society' together under a single formal body, he was surely going to have a direct means of supervision. If there was going to be democracy, it was to be a heavily guided democracy.[43]

Quite what the rest of the world might do if even this limited kind of 'democracy' were to be suspended is unclear. The struggles of Russian public life were nowhere near as febrile in 2001 as they had been in the early 1990s. But the possibilities for outbreaks of political violence had not been eliminated.

10. BLOODBATH IN CHECHNYA

'Thou shalt not kill (except persons of the Caucasian nationalities).'

Kukly NTV satirical programme, 2000

Russia since 1991 cannot be understood without consideration of the wars in Chechnya, and this in turn requires attention to the long history of armed conflict between the peoples of the Caucasus mountain chain. The encounter of the Imperial armies with the groups who lived there led to decades of armed struggle in the nineteenth century, and conflict seldom faded even after the Russians completed their conquest. The men of the mountains lost territory and had to swear allegiance to the Romanov dynasty. Yet no sooner had they done this than they rose up in revolt.

The Caucasian peoples were extraordinarily diverse: Dagestan alone contained enough ethnic and religious groups for an entire empire. The Russians never quite knew what to do about any of them. They had difficulty not only with the Moslem majority but also with the Christian nations – the Georgians and Armenians – who lived to the south of the highest mountains. The whole area was a zone of trouble. Several great Russian writers – Pushkin, Lermontov and Tolstoi – wrote on this theme and offered an analysis more complex than anything in the reports delivered by the Imperial high command. All these writers had served in regiments of the Imperial army in the Caucasus and, on the whole, were admirers of their fellow military men. They described the officers as intelligent and cultured. The ordinary soldiers might be uneducated, but they too appeared in poems and novels as well-intentioned, uncomplaining and enduring. Pushkin, Lermontov and Tolstoi, at least in his early work, assumed that Russia's territorial expansion was in the nature of things. They seldom questioned directly whether the Russians had the right to conquer and dominate the mountains.[1]

About the local inhabitants, though, they had confused feelings.

Russian authors portrayed them as wild, unpredictable and ruthless. Caucasian customs, to the Russian mind, seemed uncivilised. Most people in the region stayed impervious to Russian cultural influence. Their vengefulness was notorious. Once subjugated by the Russians, they refused to lie down even when war was unfeasible. They went on taking Russian women into captivity and forcing them into marriage. They continued to seize stray Russian soldiers and hold them to ransom. Supposedly their word was unreliable. And yet many writers simultaneously conceded there was something magnificent about them. They were unspoilt by urban living. They could walk through forests without rustling a leaf. Russian nineteenth-century literature described the Caucasians as children of nature existing almost in a state of divine grace. Indeed it seemed that the 'civilisation' brought to them by Russia had a corrupting aspect. The Caucasians might be rough and ready, but they had their own codes of honour and conduct – and seldom did they break them. The way they stuck to family, faith and tradition impressed those very authors who were famous for questioning everything about Russian life and human existence in general.[2]

And so the idea of what it was to be a Russian was predicated upon the encounter of the Russians with Dagestanis, Chechens, Osetians and other ethnic groups in the Caucasus. Contact with the conquered peoples had the effect of sharpening the Russian sense of identity. First there had come the 'little peoples' of Siberia. Then there were the Poles and the Jews after the partitions of Poland at the end of the eighteenth century.[3] Afterwards, in the nineteenth century, came the Georgians. And in the twentieth century a growing contrast was sensed between Russians and other Slavic peoples such as the Ukrainians and Belorussians.[4] There were also more distant nations which pushed the Russians into clarifying what made them different. This happened most brutally in 1941–5 when the German SS and Wehrmacht treated the Slavs as *Untermenschen*. The difference between a German and a Russian became a matter of life and death.[5] Then after the Second World War there arose the competition between the USSR and the USA as military superpowers in the Cold War. *Pravda* constantly compared the Soviet and American 'ways of life' and sought to demonstrate that Russians had more to be proud of. Russians were never short of other peoples with whom to compare themselves.[6]

Yet it is the Chechens, the tiny nation inhabiting the northern slopes of the eastern Caucasus mountain chain, who have tried and tested Russian national identity most frequently in the last two centuries.

Russia's armed forces had been establishing themselves in the mountains and valleys of the North Caucasus since the sixteenth century. But rudimentary conquest did not take place until the early nineteenth century. It was a bloody campaign. General Alexei Yermolov, the Russian commander from 1817, understood it was not enough to defeat the mountain peoples in battle. He therefore set up a military blockade of the region to prevent Chechen fighters from returning to their villages. He hacked down routes through forests to enable rapid movement of troops; he also settled garrisons at strategic points and forcibly transplanted the warlike inhabitants of the mountains into the valleys where Russia's forces could keep them pacified.[7]

But peace was not the result. Yermolov and his successors – Paskevich, Rozen, Golovin and Neidgardt – had simply assumed that the mountain peoples would accept that further resistance was futile. But sporadic attacks on Russian settlements and garrisons continued. Indigenous inhabitants, especially the Chechens and the Dagestanis, refused to accept their subjugation. Determined to hold on to the region and to secure the routes across the Caucasus mountain range into Georgia and Armenia, the government in St Petersburg expropriated farming land for loyal Cossacks and helped them build fortified villages. This failed to quell the Chechens and neighbouring ethnic groups. It was in the late 1820s that the banner of Islamic revolt was raised by Imam Shamil, who caused several Imperial regiments to operate in the mountains until his capture in 1859. The building of Cossack villages and military garrisons was accelerated, but the outward tranquillity was illusory. In 1905, when Russia was inflamed by revolutionary crisis, the mountain peoples seized the chance to challenge the political order. Nicholas II reintroduced the post of governor-general to bring the North Caucasus to his heel.

Then in 1917, when Russia was caught in another tornado of revolution, the inhabitants of Chechnya and the nearby region reasserted themselves. A Mountain Republic survived until the end of the Civil War when the Red Army incorporated the Chechens into the RSFSR. At first the Chechens were treated better than under the tsars. As proof of their good intentions, Lenin and Stalin decided to dispossess the Cossacks of their land and hand it back to the Chechens.[8]

But then in the 1930s came the violence of agricultural collectivisation and the purges. The Chechens suffered as badly as any other people in the USSR. Their secular and religious leaders were treated savagely. Still worse was to follow in the Second World War. Once the Red Army had expelled the Wehrmacht occupiers from the Caucasus, Stalin wreaked revenge on those national and ethnic groups which were alleged to have contained many collaborators to the Nazi cause. In 1944 he instructed Beria to oversee the deportation of every Chechen and Ingush, man, woman or child, to Kazakhstan. Nearly half a million of them were rounded up and crammed in cattle-trucks with inadequate food, clothing and sanitation. In Kazakhstan the survivors were abandoned and ordered to set up collective farms without the equipment for the task. This was not genocide in the absolute sense: not all the deportees died. But it was horribly close to it. The Chechens had supplied dozens of Heroes of the Soviet Union in the Great Patriotic War and yet they were treated as Nazi collaborationist scum and dumped in the most inhospitable areas of Central Asia.[9] They could no longer read newspapers in their language. They could not send their children to Chechen-language schools. They had no mosques for their worship. Their nation was treated as a collective pariah.

Somehow they found the tenacity to survive. Love for their religion, land and tradition proved ineradicable and hatred of Russians grew more intense. Chechens went on thinking rebellious thoughts long after the other ethnic groups had given up. A barbarous injustice had been done to them and they did not forgive or forget. When Khrushchëv denounced Stalin in 1956, he exposed the near-genocide of the Chechen people. The order for the deportation was revoked and the Chechens were allowed to return to most of their ancestral lands in a newly created republic of Checheno-Ingushetia. There in their mountains they retrieved a sense of dignity even though the financial resources available from Moscow were ungenerous. They could express resentment against Russians only in private and among themselves. But their resentment did not fade with the passage of years. The Chechens were determined to get back what had been brutally taken from them: their land, homes, mosques and graveyards. Many Russian residents in Checheno-Ingushetia felt so intimidated that they abandoned their houses and moved elsewhere in the Soviet Union.

The fact that the Kremlin insisted on the Chechens sharing a republic with the Ingushes was the sign of a lingering worry that the Chechens might cause trouble. They were kept under surveillance by the Soviet central authorities and forced to compromise locally with the Ingushes. At first the policy appeared to work and by 1980 it even seemed safe to promote a Chechen officer, a certain Djokar Dudaev, to the command of the prestigious Heavy Artillery Aviation Regiment in the Soviet armed forces.[10] The communist establishment had concluded that the age-old problems of the North Caucasus had been solved.

It was in this mood of complacency about 'the national question' that Gorbachëv initiated his campaign for political and economic reform in the USSR. Immediately there were disturbances in the North Caucasus as various peoples, especially the Chechens, used their freedom to denounce Moscow. An Islamic revival also began. The investigation of abuses against the Chechen people under Stalin was resumed both in Grozny and in Moscow, and several Chechen leaders began to make overt demands for national independence. In October 1991 Djokar Dudaev became President of the Chechen Republic (which, to the satisfaction of both Chechens and Ingushes, separated itself from Ingushetia in 1992). He had made a name for himself when stationed in Estonia by refusing to let his troops oppose the Estonian moves towards independence. He was no ordinary politician: in fact he was not a politician at all. He was a general and a trained wrestler. He was fit, lean and photogenic – and he could speak on television without sounding mealy-mouthed. By the time he had returned to Chechnya, in 1990, he was a declared Chechen nationalist – and, apart from Ruslan Khasbulatov, no Chechen was more famous.

This was the Chechnya with which Yeltsin had to deal throughout his time in power. Of all the republican presidents of the Russian Federation it was Djokar Dudaev who proved the most intransigent towards the Kremlin. Meanwhile Chechen groups acquired notoriety for running criminal gangs in Moscow and other large Russian cities. They were also involved in organised crime in Chechnya itself. Gun-running, drug-smuggling and kidnapping for ransom were local specialities. Dudaev's Chechen regime was a disgrace to minimal standards of political decency.

Such was not the image that Chechnya had abroad. Dudaev and his supporters were regarded by the rest of the world as plucky democrats fighting against the imperialist demands of an illiberal state. Propaganda was masterminded by Dudaev, who claimed he had always been committed to democracy, the rule of law and national freedom. Chechens themselves came to know a very different leader. Dudaev had never been universally accepted as father of their nation, and had not made a serious effort to unify the Chechens. His priority was to strengthen his personal supremacy and enrich himself. He did private deals with some clans at the expense of others and left the criminal gangs alone so long as he and his relatives got a financial cut. Dudaev also went to the length of imposing Shariat law. The Russians and the many non-religious Chechens in the republic were not consulted: Dudaev and his ruling group unilaterally declared that the Koran was to be the basis of governance and justice. There was an irony in this in as much as Chechnya had not been known as a centre of unusual religious devotion in the nineteenth century. But in the 1990s Dudaev, aiming to emphasise Chechnya's separateness from Russia, saw the advantage of playing the Islamic card. He was a flagrant opportunist.

He had little awareness, until the last moment, of the risks he was running; he quite underestimated the Russian government's resolve to strike back at him. The provocations were endless. A kidnapping mission was undertaken by Chechen fighters in the little town of Mineralnye Vody from May to July 1994. The purpose was criminal. Buses of innocent Russians were hijacked and millions of dollars were demanded as a ransom. The exploit failed and the hijackers were killed, arrested or forced to flee back into Chechnya. But the effect on Russian public opinion was sharp. Mineralnye Vody is one of those spa towns described by nineteenth-century writers. It is a Russian town, built to the north of the newly conquered Caucasus. The attack on it was one affront too many to Russians exasperated by the government's apparent unwillingness to take steps to restore order and security.

The popular outrage across Russia constituted a major reason why the Kremlin decided in August 1994 that enough was enough and that Dudaev's regime had to be overturned. Dudaev had thumbed his nose at Yeltsin since October 1991. By declaring state independence for Chechnya, he threatened the territorial integrity of the Russian Federation; and by introducing Shariat law to Chechnya, he flouted the Federal Constitution introduced in December 1993.[11] All this had been bad enough. But Dudaev's transparent reluctance to prevent the training and equipment of anti-Russian terrorists was no longer sufferable. The other charges against him were also grievous. There was much evidence that foreign Islamic groups were becoming involved in armed struggle on the territory of the Russian Federation. From both Afghanistan and Saudi Arabia there came finance. Volunteers arrived, too, to strengthen the military campaign against Russia and to spread the revolt across other republics in the region. It is easy to see why ministers in Moscow thought Chechnya was turning into a base for a *jihad* that would, if no counter-measures were taken, destabilise international relations as Iran had in the late 1970s and Afghanistan in the early 1990s.

Economic considerations also came into the reckoning for the Kremlin leadership. The oil pipeline from the Azerbaijani capital Baku on the Caspian coast across to the Russian city of Novorossiisk by the Black Sea ran through Chechnya. It was a large source of revenue and, with the discovery of oil reserves under the Caspian Sea, had increased financial potential. Chechen criminals were regularly siphoning off quantities of oil from the pipeline; this was a problem that would inevitably have been aggravated if Chechnya ever managed to secede from Russia. The rise of Turkey's influence in the region was also worrisome. Russian ministers, especially Sergei Shakhrai (who succeeded Valeri Tishkov as Minister of Nationality Affairs in 1992), urged the need for ruthless action before the Chechen boiler-house exploded.[12]

It is customary in the West to overlook the arguments made by the Russian government. Or at least Western journalism neglects them. Ruling politicians in the West have been more indulgent, especially British Prime Minister Tony Blair. Presidents Yeltsin and Putin maintained that the frontiers of all European states should remain intact. Once the sanctity of territorial boundaries is challenged in any single country, it was argued, the rest of the continent will be shaken by secessionist armed struggles. By holding on to Chechnya, Russia was depicted by her government as bolstering the foundations of international peace and order. There is something in this. Until now the boundaries of most of the former communist states have been held in place; and where this is not true, as in Yugoslavia, there has been terrible trouble: the 'ethnic cleansing' in Croatia, Bosnia and Serbia is notorious. Russia's insistence upon preserving its existing frontier was therefore presented as a roadblock against potential trouble. Putin went further than this. At a joint TV press conference with Mr Blair he declared that Western governments should be grateful to the Russians for cauterising the bacillus of Islamic fundamentalism before it got out of control and became a threat not just to Russia but to other countries in Europe.

The decision on the first invasion in 1994, when Yeltsin was still President and Chernomyrdin his Prime Minister, had been taken in defiance of advice from the Federal Intelligence Service and the army's Chief Intelligence Administration (GRU). These agencies knew of the ill-preparedness of Russian military forces and the dangers awaiting them in Chechnya. But their arguments were ignored. Minister of Defence

Pavel Grachëv and Minister of the Interior Mikhail Barsukov, confident of easy victory, persuaded Yeltsin that it could be achieved chiefly through the efforts of Chechen troops equipped by Moscow.[13] The Russian government declared Dudaev a usurper and a tyrant and officially recognised the self-styled Chechen Provisional Council under Umar Avturkhanov; the Chechen Ruslan Labazanov was entrusted by Grachëv with the initial assault on Grozny.

The effect in Chechnya was immense. Dudaev's great rivals Shamil Basaev and Aslan Maskhadov rallied to him and internal disputes among most Chechens ceased; and there were no groups of Russian residents able to give serious assistance to the invaders. The Chechen republic was up in arms. What further helped its cause was the extraordinary incompetence of the Russian campaign. Grachëv had believed his own rhetoric. The thought had not occurred to him that ill-armed Chechen guerrillas might be resourceful foes. Nor did he consider that Russia's army of demoralised officers and reluctant conscripts might not be in a suitable condition to undertake the task. Grachëv mobilised not only the Russian army but also the forces of the Ministry of the Interior; but this made little difference. The invading troops were simply not convinced that Chechnya was 'their' native land. They feared the wildness of the Chechens. They were aware of the ill discipline and corruption in their own forces. Not infrequently they actually sold equipment to Chechen rebels even though it might soon be used against them. The 1994 invasion was doomed. Estimates vary, but certainly tens of thousands died on both sides.

Russian forces were worn down by the wintry conditions on the mountains. Chechen irregulars made counterattacks whenever and wherever they sensed weakness. Helicopter gunships and landmines did not scare them. The Chechens, who had been told by their mullahs that death in battle would be a passport to heavenly paradise, fought fearlessly. It was a stand-off: the Russians could not win but the Chechens refused to lose. Even when they were in difficulty in Chechnya, the Chechens could hugely disturb the Russians. In June 1995 Shamil Basaev infiltrated Budënnovsk, a town in Stavropol Region, where he captured a busload of Russian civilians. A shoot-out followed at the municipal hospital. Basaev withdrew only after protracted negotiations: yet again Russian armed might had been mocked.[14]

An angry Grachëv replaced one commander with another. Yeltsin criticised Grachëv. The press criticised Yeltsin, Chernomyrdin and Grachëv. Public opinion concluded that no serious preparation had been made for the campaign: Russians did not want an invasion if it was going to be incompetently led. What to do about this was another matter. Yeltsin recognised his mistake, but could not withdraw without looking foolish. In the Presidential election campaign of 1996 he announced his willingness to compromise and this bought him political respite – and again he looked like a peacemaker. A meeting took place between him and the Chechen commander Zelimkhan Yandarbiev. Then, after the successful election, Yeltsin appointed Alexander Lebed, one of his former rivals for the Presidency, as his representative in negotiations. Lebed had a record for bringing civil war to a close in Moldova. He was no mild-mannered figure; indeed, his ferocity in the Afghan War had been extraordinary. A swaggering bear of a man, he was said to have communicated with his troops across the valleys of Afghanistan merely by use of his booming bass voice. But he disliked the deployment of Russian forces as the instrument of internal political order. This was how he saw the Chechen War. The campaign had been botched. Political and diplomatic instrumentalities had been overlooked or mishandled. As far as Lebed could see, the aspirations of Chechens ought to be accommodated to some considerable degree.

Yeltsin wanted an end to the war on honourable terms for himself, but had no interest in Lebed gathering all the glory. At the first opportunity he sacked him on the grounds, largely justified, that he disdained to work amicably with government ministers. Nevertheless he benefited from Lebed's conciliatory work in Chechnya. Lebed had produced an armistice. Under its terms the Russian army would be withdrawn from active operations and the Chechen government would be allowed to resume its duties, and the Kremlin promised to hold a referendum on Chechnya's political status inside or outside the Russian Federation in 2001.[15]

The Russian public was relieved at this outcome. The losses had been enormous and the fighting morale of the troops was lower than in any military campaign since 1917. The protests of mothers of conscripts also had an impact; and although the government controlled the content of its own television and radio stations, it could not get NTV to desist from reporting on the horrors.[16] In any case a growing number of citizens had access to foreign television and radio. Yeltsin came near to publicly regretting that he had sponsored the invasion. Beneath the surface, however, offence had been given to Russian national self-esteem. The might of the armed forces had been repulsed by ill-trained rebels on an obscure southern fringe of the Russian Federation. What had happened to the Great Power which had defeated Nazi Germany in 1945 and competed with the USA in the ensuing Cold War? The situation was worsened by the knowledge that no truce would guarantee an end to hostilities initiated from the Chechen side. Terrorism would still be a menace. There might also be an increase in instability in the other Moslem-inhabited republics in Russia. The deal negotiated by Lebed left many concerns unresolved.

These worries grew. President Dudaev had been killed by Russian forces on 31 April 1996; he had been traced when using his satellite phone, and special units had launched a missile at the place he stood. For a while the Chechen media denied that Dudaev had died and public life fell still further into a mess. But a presidential campaign was held in January 1997 and the result was victory for Aslan Maskhadov. His authority was no greater than Dudaev's had been. Clan-based violence intensified. Hostage-taking of Russians and Western technical specialists and aid workers grew more frequent – and some of them were butchered. Terrorist activity in Dagestan continued and the Federal Security Bureau gathered information on the influx of money and human volunteers from Afghan and Saudi sources. Chechnya became ever more lawless.

The resumption of Chechen terrorism outside Chechnya, in Russian cities, increased government support for rapid retaliation. In 1997 two Chechen women were arrested for detonating a bomb that killed civilians. This was just one spectacular incident among several. Meanwhile, the Russian military campaign of 1994–6 as well as the disorder among the Chechens themselves led to a massive exodus of refugees from Chechnya. The administrative frontiers were lightly protected. The rise in criminality was immense and the authorities claimed that kidnappings were the work of Chechen gangs. The result was that the ethnic Russians were reluctant to accept even the Chechen refugees, however innocent they might claim to be. Alexander Chernogorov, governor of nearby Stavropol, routinely refused permits of residence and employment to newcomers from Chechnya even though he was acting outside his constitutional authority. All this in turn prodded them into illegal activity in order to subsist. The exacerbation of national hostilities was constant.[17]

Under Stepashin, Prime Minister from May to August 1999, plans were got ready for a resumption of war at an early opportunity. Stepashin had been Minister of Internal Affairs when a general in his ministry had been kidnapped by terrorists at Grozny airport while carrying out a mission for Yeltsin. The planners worked out a scheme to bomb terrorist training camps and to undertake the military occupation of the entire northern zone of Chechnya.[18] The main immediate task was to prepare Russian public opinion for such a campaign: the lesson had been learned that success would depend on the amount of popular support that could be sustained.

Russian TV carried reports on every outrage elsewhere in the Russian Federation, and often the blame was put on the peoples of the Caucasus even where there was not the slightest evidence. Already in 1993 Yeltsin, despite his protestations about wishing to create a state where all nationalities might live in harmony, had issued a decree permitting the Ministry of the Interior to deport undesirables from Moscow. Implicit sanction was being given for the police to stop and search passers-by with a swarthy complexion and, if they turned out to be from the Caucasus, expel them from the capital.[19] Chechens were anathematised as especially suspect. There were indeed several large Chechen criminal gangs in Moscow, but the condemnation of Chechens passed all reasonable limits. When Moscow apartment blocks were ripped apart by three bombs in September 1999, it was not difficult for the Russian government to pin the responsibility on Chechen terrorism.[20] A few journalists raised awkward questions. But the public was easily persuaded that at last the government, rough and ready though its methods might be, was doing something about an acute problem of security.

In August 1999, furthermore, Chechen armed groups led by Shamil Basaev had moved into Dagestan. This attempt to spread the insurrectionary contagion into other regions of the Russian Federation and to unite Moslems in armed struggle was bound to provoke a reaction from Moscow (and indeed from the Dagestan administration). The possibility of an Islamic secessionist movement was growing. By then Chechnya had become a base for international Moslem militants, especially those who followed the Arab Mujahedinn leader Ibn-ul-Khattab. Funds were also made available by the Taleban in Afghanistan.[21] Russian politicians were intensely worried lest the situation might get out of hand. It was no longer merely a question of Chechnya's rebellion. The loss of southern regions, one by one, had been added to the agenda of official and popular concerns.[22] After Valeri Tishkov left the government in October 1992, no minister had a detailed knowledge of the Caucasus; indeed, none of them had sophisticated acquaintance with Imperial and Soviet history. Nevertheless a misty awareness of the campaign led by Imam Shamil in Dagestan and Chechnya was widespread, and Soviet history textbooks had also mentioned that attempts had been made in the 1920s to unite the Moslem peoples against the authorities in Moscow. Moreover, the foreign precedent of Moslem fundamentalist uprisings in Iran and Afghanistan in the 1970s was terrifying to Russian officialdom.

Chechen public figures held back from absolute disapproval of the terrorist bombings in Moscow. Shamil Basaev made his position clear:

> I denounce terrorism, including state terrorism used by the Russian empire. The latest explosion in Moscow is not our work but the work of Dagestanis. Russia has been openly terrorising Dagestan . . . For the whole week, united in a single fist, the Army and Ministry of the Interior units have been pounding three small villages . . . What is the difference between someone letting off a bomb in the centre of Moscow and injuring ten to twenty children and the Russians dropping bombs from their aeroplanes over Karamachi and killing ten to twenty children?[23]

In October 1999 Vladimir Putin, Prime Minister as from August, advised President Yeltsin that the time had arrived to crush the Chechen rebellion. Commanders were told that the entire government was determined to erase the military humiliation of 1994–6. The terrorist explosions in Moscow were fresh in the memory. It was easy to convince Russians, whose TV stations had shown them pictures of the NATO air bombardment of Serbian towns in the Kosovo international crisis between March and June 1999, that their own forces should restore Moscow's control over Chechnya by whatever means came to hand. Chechnya itself remained in disarray under the divisive presidency of Aslan Maskhadov. Putin could hardly have chosen a more propitious moment to attack. And he had learned the lesson that war was most effectively prosecuted when journalists were kept out of the way. Putin put Chechnya into quarantine while the massed might of the Russian army went to work; he also ensured that NTV, which had criticised government and army in the war of 1994–6, would treat the resumed military campaign differently.[24] He identified himself vigorously with his policy. In 1994 Yeltsin and Chernomyrdin had sometimes given the impression that they had nothing to do with the invasion of Chechnya. Putin by contrast said unequivocally that the military campaign would be carried through to a victorious end.[25]

Crossing the Chechen administrative frontier, the Russians made a furious air assault. As planned, a strict censorship was imposed: Russian and foreign television crews were kept out of Chechnya and the government supplied the media with stories of its armed forces' unimpeded success. Putin's popularity in Russia rose enormously, to such an extent that he hardly bothered to campaign for election as President in March 2000.[26] When the military campaign looked like wilting, moreover, he flew to Chechnya and chided the generals. Grozny had to be overrun. The Russian army dropped leaflets over the city urging civilians to flee before the bombardment commenced. Then the slaughter started. By the last days of 2000, Grozny looked like Stalingrad at the end of the Second World War.

By then a quarter of a million people were living in tents on the borders of Chechnya; they were refugees too terrified to return home after the Russian army's victory. Stories from the official detention camps described torture, malnutrition and casual killings. When Chechen armed groups struck back with attacks on garrisons, the Russian army took retribution against the prisoners already in their hands. Agriculture, the main economic activity of the republic apart from oil refining, was shattered. The remaining residents of the Chechen towns became dependent on food parcels from foreign charity organisations. Putin talked about the desirability of Moscow's direct rule over Chechnya. He seldom referred to the restoration of refugees. His priority was to restore public order within a secured territory and the rights of Chechens no longer counted for much with ministers. Putin had risen to popularity and power through a commitment to rebuilding Russian national pride. He had told foreign powers to stay out of Russia's domestic affairs; and apart from the occasional criticism by leaders in the USA and France, nothing serious was done to impede him. The electorate of the Russian Federation applauded Putin. In the Presidential elections of March 2000 he stood as the anticipated conqueror of Chechnya and was awarded a majority of the votes.

Yet there could hardly have been a more disastrous outcome for the already damaged general project for reform in Russia. The military campaigns of 1994–6 and 1999 onwards left a blot of shame. There are those who contend that Russian politics – the zigzags of policy, the factional in-fighting, the institutional rivalry and the extra-parliamentary polemics – follow their course regardless of the situation in Chechnya. Certainly it would be difficult to show that particular events in Moscow have been shaped mainly by the military campaigns. But this is to miss the general point that the project for reform in Russia requires a transformation of the fundamental assumptions in public life. Since 1991 the Chechnya syndrome has brought plague upon Russian state and society. It has infected every aspect of political, administrative, military, economic and social affairs.

Throwing off restraint, Putin used all available force. Although he declared that the inhabitants of Chechnya were owed the care and protection of the state, Grozny was blasted by missiles, tanks and helicopter gun-ships and its residents were slaughtered in thousands. The 'filtration camps', where Russian armed forces decided which fleeing inhabitant was a fighter and which a genuine refugee, were sites of gross acts of inhumanity. Russian troops and security personnel behaved appallingly behind the screen erected by Putin against surveillance by journalists. The news blackout during the campaign could not be complete, however, and Russian TV and newspapers began to report on the butchery; and occasionally individual miscreants started to be brought to book.[27] Chechen towns are now like the landscape of a barren planet. It is doubtful whether the government in Moscow will release adequate funds for reconstruction. Grozny in Russian means terrible or awesome; it is a fitting name for a city that is infamous for Russia's brutality to a people it still claims as its own. The message has been leached into the body politic that crude force has been restored as a favoured tool of government.

Yeltsin and Putin were not the first rulers of Russia to deal with rebels in such a fashion. In the centuries before 1917 there were plenty of uprisings that were crushed with exemplary violence. In 1773–5 Yemelyan Pugachëv led a peasant insurrection. The Poles revolted in 1863. The whole country seemed on the brink of overthrowing Nicholas II in 1905. In each case no mercy was given to the rebels when the Imperial army reasserted state order. The Soviet communist leadership was equally ferocious in crushing its enemies in the Civil War after the October 1917 Revolution. Under Stalin from the late 1920s through to his death in 1953 it applied ruthless terror against not only self-declared opponents of the regime but also potential opponents in their millions.

Yet no Emperor before 1917 or General Secretary until Gorbachëv seriously aimed to build a democratic state order. By contrast both Yeltsin and Putin pinned the badge of democracy to their chests. In reality they have behaved in Chechnya as badly as any of their predecessors in the Kremlin. The continuity with centuries of rulership before 1991 is discernible in several basic problems of Russian statehood. Most obviously, there exists the problem of the use of military violence to tackle difficulties of a mainly civilian character. There is the problem of relations between 'the centre and the localities'. There is the problem of arbitrary, secret decisions taken at the centre. There is the problem of non-Russians being trampled by a government in Moscow seeking to assert a kind of imperial dominion. All these problems were meant to be solved through the implementation of the general reform project. Instead Yeltsin sanctioned two wars in Chechnya. Little thought was given as to how a lasting political settlement would be engineered. The Russian government had some legitimate reasons for intervening in Chechen affairs, but it did not discharge its duty to limit the savagery on its own side and plan its campaign in such a way as to make a permanent peace possible.

A Russian military victory was proclaimed in 2000, but armed resistance by Chechens did not really cease and terrorism recurred. Putin steadily moved towards making overtures to the rebels. Even so, he continued to affirm that stability had been secured. He stood in a line of political and military figures holding the same complacent vision. From Army General Yermolov in 1817 to Party Secretary Stalin in 1944, the belief was frequently favoured that the Chechens could be tamed by a short, brutal campaign of conquest. It did not work, and it never will. The Chechens were already a very special people before they confronted the might of the Imperial army. The vicious violence they suffered before and after 1917 served to confirm their sense of uniqueness and mission. Trouble has not disappeared from the mountains of the Caucasus, and the name of Chechnya stands as Russia's shame and reform's disaster.

11. RUSSIA IN THE WORLD

There's no need to go searching, everything's already found. This is the path of democratic development. Of course, Russia is an unusually diverse country, but we are part of West European culture. And our value lies in this. Wherever our people live, whether in the Far East or in the South, we are Europeans.

Vladimir Putin, 2000

Russia's changing position among the powers of the world added to the difficulties of reform. The transformation of global politics had been tremendous. The USSR had been a military colossus laden with advanced nuclear weaponry; it had been treated as the second industrial power on earth. Its leaders conferred at summits with American presidents. Global politics were dominated by the rivalry between the Soviet Union and the USA, and Russians were brought up to assume that this was in the permanent natural order of things.

The shocks were registered in 1989, when the Soviet Bloc in Eastern Europe suddenly crumbled. Country after country seized the chance offered inadvertently by Mikhail Gorbachëv to assert their independence and abandon communism. Poland, Czechoslovakia, Hungary, the German Democratic Republic and Bulgaria had belonged to the 'outer empire' of the USSR. Even communist states which had been hostile to the USSR – Albania, Romania and Yugoslavia – underwent anticommunist transformations. The map of Europe was redrawn. The garrisons of the Soviet Army were repatriated to the USSR. It was a wholly unexpected process. Until it happened, nobody could be absolutely certain that Gorbachëv would stick by his word and refuse to intervene militarily on the side of the beleaguered communist regimes. But he had meant what he said. He was himself disconcerted by the revealed frailty of communism even in its reformed condition in Eastern saw clearly that if he were to use troops, he would wreck his cEurope; but he redibility at home as a peaceful reformer. He could not afford to do as Khrushchëv had done in Hungary in 1956 and Brezhnev in Czechoslovakia in 1968. Eastern Europe had made its choice and Gorbachëv stood aside.[1]

What Gorbachëv would not contemplate was the disintegration of the USSR. He struggled for a reformed Union and the territorial wholeness of the state was axiomatic for him: he hated the idea of Estonia, Latvia and Lithuania (which had been annexed in 1940 and again in 1944) breaking away even though he himself had introduced a Law on Secession in 1990. In the last months of 1991, however, the long-feared disintegration occurred after Kravchuk and Shushkevich met in Belovezhskaya Pushcha and decided to break up the Union, regardless of Gorbachëv's plans, and set up a Commonwealth of Independent States combining all the Soviet Republics except Estonia, Latvia, Lithuania and Georgia. The Commonwealth itself would be a very loose association and each of its members would have full rights of independence. By 1992, therefore, the 'inner empire' too had been lost. It was a giddy process of de-imperialisation. In the histories of empires there has been nothing like it for swiftness and casualness.

Yeltsin had hoped that the USSR's break-up would be followed by a resealing of voluntary ties among the former Soviet republics. He had never been a principled advocate of disintegration. In 1991 he had waited on events; as often as not, he had plotted strategy by recourse to whatever opportunities came his way to supplant Gorbachëv. After the Ukrainian referendum in favour of independence, he expected the Union to break into its constituent states while he prepared the conditions for a recombination to take place. In 1992 he assumed that the Commonwealth of Independent States would provide the necessary instrument for reintegration. He and Gaidar also expected to exploit the enormous economic might at the disposal of the Russian Federation. Several states of the Commonwealth depended heavily upon cheap energy supplied by Russia and this gave Moscow a powerful tool in diplomatic negotiations. Furthermore, not all the states had the capacity to defend themselves against aggression, either internal or external, without Russian military assistance. President Yeltsin therefore continued to regard the area covered by the former USSR as falling entirely within Russia's zone of control. He remained a great optimist.

His first decisions were in line with American President George Bush's sketch of 'a new world order'. Yeltsin declared that Russian nuclear weapons would no longer be targeted upon the USA; indeed he announced unilateral reductions in the stockpile of such weapons and conventional arms too.[2] Talks between Yeltsin and Bush proceeded amicably in June 1992 when the Russian President visited Washington. After Bill Clinton occupied the American White House in 1993, the friendliness continued, and Clinton confirmed his goodwill towards Russia by offering financial aid during the economic transition from communism. The Group of Seven promised to supply assistance to the value of $43 billion. In the early years of Yeltsin's rule the emphasis lay upon improving international relations around the globe and enhancing Russia's integration into the world economy. Russian Foreign Affairs Minister Andrei Kozyrev was a convinced 'Atlanticist': it was his belief that the ties between Russia and the USA should be the cardinal relationship to which all other dimensions of foreign policy should be subordinated. This did not discourage Yeltsin from making overtures to several leading statesmen, particularly Helmut Kohl in Germany. Yeltsin and Kohl got on very well personally. But it was the association with 'my friend Bill' that counted for most in the Kremlin.

Kozyrev was a professional diplomat. He had come to Yeltsin's attention in 1990 while working in the RSFSR Foreign Affairs Ministry. At the time it had not been an influential posting. But when the USSR collapsed, Yeltsin was reluctant to appoint anyone associated with Gorbachëv, and so Kozyrev – to his own surprise – got the chance to head a real ministry. Yeltsin liked his initiative, intelligence and coolness under fire.[3]

Yet the compound of the early foreign policy of Yeltsin and Kozyrev was quickly dissolved. President Bush's concept of a 'new world order' had always been more rhetorical than realistic. As things turned out, the elimination of communism in Russia and Eastern Europe caused as many problems as it solved. Many difficulties of an ethnic, social and cultural order had been held on ice during the long period of the USSR's hegemony. The sharpest example was provided by Yugoslavia. Civil war broke out in Bosnia. Croatia expelled its Serb citizens. Serbia intensified its persecution of Albanians, especially in the enclave of Kosovo. Russian diplomats in the early twentieth century had traditionally supported Serbia against the government of Austria-Hungary. Yeltsin resumed the custom of favouring the Serbs and defended them in their troubles with the USA and the European Union. His main motive is unlikely to have involved genuine sympathy for the Serbian plight. Instead he was probably exercised by a wish that Russia should no longer be a mere spectator in the contests of international relations. He wanted power and prestige for his country again.

This was, to some extent, a reaction to criticism in both the Supreme Soviet (until its forcible closure in 1993) and the State Duma that Yeltsin and his successive Prime Ministers were failing to stand up for the country's interests – and that the West was duping him. There was reason for Russian politicians to feel troubled. The countries of NATO, old enemies of the Warsaw Pact, aimed to extend their defensive shield to several countries in East-Central and Eastern Europe; and in 1994 they announced that Poland, Hungary and the Czech Republic would eventually be given membership of the organisation. Stalin's achievement of a buffer zone between West Germany and the Soviet Union was reversed. The Russian Ministry of Foreign Affairs made objections and the Ministry of Defence issued dark threats, but unless Russia was willing to risk losing financial assistance from the West, there was little that could be done to thwart American intentions. The USA also held discussions with Ukraine and Georgia about future military co-operation. Russia's humiliation in the wider world was becoming manifest. Although President Yeltsin continued to attend meetings of the world's wealthiest powers, the G8 group, the basic reality was that the Russian state was incapable of resisting the demands of the NATO states.

There was no serious proposal for Russia itself to join NATO despite occasional overtures from Moscow. Other organisations, however, welcomed Russia. Thus Russia joined the World Bank, the International Monetary Fund and the European Bank for Reconstruction and Development. These were the main financial bodies. Russia also secured entry to the Council of Europe and the Organisation for Security and Co-operation in Europe and committed itself to the European Convention on Human Rights, which it duly ratified in early 1996. By no means, therefore, was Russia excluded from membership of international bodies in the wider world.

In spring 1993 Yeltsin gave approval to a draft Foreign Policy Concept of the Russian Federation. The document clarified ideas that had previously been left vague or unspoken. Russia, according to the Concept, should aim to remain a Great Power. It also retained a special duty to stabilise its relations with the other states of the former USSR. If armed conflicts broke out on its frontiers, the Russian army would be deployed. More widely it remained the objective to reintegrate the old Soviet Republics politically and economically. As for Eastern Europe, it was to be treated as belonging to Russia's 'historical sphere of interest'.

The prognosis was that these ends could be achieved in co-operation with the USA. Both governments, it was asserted, were equally committed to the prevention of regional military conflicts and the proliferation of nuclear weapons. But the preoccupation with Russo-American relations was beginning to give way to consideration of relations with other powerful countries. The Concept urged the establishment of 'balanced and stable relations' with countries in the East, especially China, Japan and India. It was stated that the objective interests of the Russian Federation did not always coincide with those of the West.

Kozyrev himself shifted ground. The Russian military invasion of Chechnya in December 1994 provoked a storm of American criticism. The abuses of human rights were flagrant. Kozyrev replied that the untroubled links with the USA were 'coming to an end' and that he personally supported armed action against the Chechen fighters.[4] He also asserted that Russia ought to be ready to send troops across its borders to protect its 'compatriots abroad'. Here he was referring to ethnic Russian minorities living in the former Soviet Republics. There had been official discrimination against Russians in Estonia, Latvia and Lithuania. Citizenship qualifications had been made hard for Russians to obtain, and the linguistic and cultural tests were especially severe in Estonia. The Russian government successfully argued it was outrageous to expect would-be citizens of the largely Russian-inhabited city of Narva to know the names of long-dead Estonian operatic divas.[5] Kozyrev himself felt obliged to leave the Russia's Choice Party, which vigorously opposed the Chechen war. But he did not move far enough to save himself from the continuing criticism in the Duma and the nationalist press. In December 1995, worn down by the attacks on him, he resigned.

It was not just the lowering of Russia's diplomatic prestige that had annoyed Kozyrev's opponents. It was also the influx of foreign industrial and agricultural products that competed with domestic Russian enterprises. Another galling phenomenon was the influence of international financial institutions upon the Russian government. Sensing the political mood, Yeltsin got rid of Kozyrev and in January 1996 replaced him with Primakov, who had been put in charge of foreign intelligence for the USSR after the August 1991 coup and believed that Russia should break free of the American embrace. Throughout Russian public life there were stirrings of unease. It had become plain that, despite the several summit meetings of Clinton and Yeltsin, only one superpower remained in the world. When they disagreed, it was nearly always Yeltsin who had to give way. Although the Russian President referred to Clinton as 'my friend Bill', nothing could disguise his subordination. Russian financial power was negligible. Its military pretension was exposed as pathetic in the Chechnya War of 1994–6. Although Russia retained its nuclear weapons, it could hardly use them as a serious bargaining counter at the summit meetings: the Cold War was over. Yeltsin was in no position to resist whenever the USA wished to pursue a particular line of policy.

Primakov in the Russian Foreign Ministry made the best of this bad situation. He was regarded by the Communist Party of the Russian Federation as preferable by far to Kozyrev; and he immediately proposed that the 'military-industrial complex' should sell arms to whichever states it wished regardless of the wishes of the USA. Primakov believed that the Iraqi dictator Saddam Hussein should be enabled to purchase arms from Russia even though Iraq was still subject to sanctions agreed by the United Nations Organisation after the Gulf War of 1990–91.

But of all the complications in international relations the most severe arose over the former Yugoslavia. Communist power had started to collapse there after Tito's death in 1980. Nationalist politicians, including ones who had held communist party office, came to the fore in most of the Yugoslav successor states. In Russia there was sympathy for the Serbian government under Slobodan Milošević as it struggled to defend the interests of the Serbs living outside Serbia. Milošević sent troops into Croatia. The resultant war was a disaster for Croatia's Serbs; a quarter of a million of them had to seek permanent refuge in Serbia. In Bosnia, civil war broke out between the Moslems and the Serbs. Milošević encouraged the Bosnian Serbs to believe that the amalgamation of large tracts of Bosnia with Serbia was a realistic objective. The Russian government, supported by most political parties in the State Duma, took the Serbian side. Much was said in favour of supporting an old ally. In the nineteenth century the tsars had given diplomatic succour to the Slavs of the Balkans in their struggle against Ottoman imperial dominion, and it was Russia's support for independent Serbia against an Austrian ultimatum in summer 1914 that lit the tinderbox of the First World War. Quietly forgotten was the massive rupture in relations between the USSR and Yugoslavia during Stalin's last years. Throughout the 1990s, especially after Kozyrev's departure from the Foreign Ministry, Russia paraded itself as the permanent sympathiser of the Serbian cause.

The USA and the European Union put pressure on Yeltsin to cease indulging Milošević. Indeed, Yeltsin was asked to get the Serbian President to constrain the Bosnian Serbs to make peace with the Moslems and give up hope of integration with Serbia. Yeltsin, seeing a chance to enhance his personal prestige, went along with this; and eventually Milošević gave way. It was an international coup for President Yeltsin, and Bill Clinton praised his role.

Unfortunately Russia did not have long to bask in glory because Serbia itself had difficulties in its Kosovo province. Kosovo was inhabited mainly by Albanians. The Serb minority in the province had long felt menaced by them. As his militancy in Croatia and Bosnia ran into difficulty, Milošević turned his eyes to Kosovo. Police became more brutal and army units were transferred into the province. Under pressure from NATO, talks between Milošević's government and the Albanians of Kosovo were held outside Paris. There were signs that the USA had already decided to present Belgrade with terms of settlement that were bound to be unacceptable to Milošević – he had baited the Western powers once too often. The talks were abandoned when Milošević refused to give way. Conflict in Kosovo intensified and by December 1998 the Albanian majority were leaving the province for neighbouring countries. The exodus of refugees took place in distressing circumstances and the NATO countries, equipped with a United Nations resolution, indicated a readiness to bomb Serbia into submission. Russia protested at the military build-up on Serbian frontiers; it also denied that the United Nations had given proper sanction to what the USA and its allies intended. But aerial bombing commenced in March 1999. Some weeks later the Serbian government withdrew its forces from Kosovo: the rout was complete.

Russian ineffectuality had been exposed. Yeltsin had sent former Prime Minister Chernomyrdin as his special representative to get Milošević to back down before it was too late. Milošević ignored the appeal. Yeltsin had criticised the bombing campaign throughout its duration. NATO, however, brushed him aside. All that Yeltsin could obtain was an agreement that Russia should have a share in the military occupation of Kosovo until such time as inter-ethnic harmony had been guaranteed. Yeltsin blustered away, demanding a large area for the Russian army to administer. A contingent of his forces, under the leadership of Lieutenant General Zavarzin, raced from Bosnia to Pristina, Kosovo's capital, and seized control of the nearby airport. It was a bold move. Yeltsin promoted Zavarzin to Colonel-General and awarded him a military medal. But the Russians had to content themselves with the administration of a small area, and they were obliged to leave Pristina. In October 2000, furthermore, Milošević fell from power in Belgrade and

Russia's last friend in Eastern Europe disappeared from the political scene. By July 2001 he was on trial in The Hague for war crimes.

Another priority for Primakov and Yeltsin was to forge closer ties with the Slavic states of the former Soviet Union. The original idea of the Commonwealth of Independent States had been to create 'a single economic space'. Some of the newly independent states, especially those in Central Asia, wished to keep their linkage with Russia. But not all states in the Commonwealth shared this attitude. Ukraine suspected that Yeltsin aspired to hegemony in relations between itself and Russia; it had not broken free from the USSR only to resubmit itself to domination by Moscow. Nor was Russia the sole source of difficulty. War between Azerbaijan and Armenia continued at varying degrees of intensity in Nagorny Karabakh. In Tajikistan there was civil war and Uzbekistan was recurrently tempted to intervene militarily. Georgia was shaken by Abkhazia's armed bid for independence as well as by its own internal violence. Even in those states which were free of military conflict there were uncongenial developments for Yeltsin's Russia. Several states simply confirmed the previous communist leaders in power after a formal renunciation of communism. Russian reformers worried that Russia's campaign for political and economic transformation might be compromised by too close an association with governments which were not equally eager to introduce changes deeply and quickly.

Furthermore, twenty million ethnic Russians formed a diaspora in the former Soviet republics. They were strongly clustered on Russia's borders with eastern Estonia, north-western Kazakhstan, eastern Ukraine and eastern Moldova. It was impossible for any Russian government to ignore the interests of such 'compatriots'. There was also the problem of Crimea. It was there, at Sevastopol, that the Soviet Black Sea Fleet had been based, and Yeltsin was reluctant to give up the port to exclusive Ukrainian control.

Only one country in the Commonwealth of Independent States was keen on reunification with Russia. This was Belarus. From summer 1994 Belarus was ruled by President Alyaksandar Lukashenka, who supported reunification with Russia. Lukashenka was averse to democratic procedures and systematically persecuted his political opponents. Yet he had much popular support. Most ethnic Belarussians felt uncomfortable about the USSR's disintegration. Lukashenka was hostile to the kind of economic reforms being undertaken by Yeltsin's government. It was pretty clear too that Lukashenka, given half a chance, would bid for the Presidency of any future Russo-Belarussian state. This was not a prospect to Yeltsin's liking, and the Russian news media highlighted the shenanigans of Lukashenka and his ministers in Minsk. But as Yeltsin's ratings in the opinion polls fell, his need to show himself as someone who could expand Russian influence rose. Yeltsin and Lukashenka signed a Treaty of Friendship and Co-operation in February 1995. A customs union was also agreed. In April 1996, after years of discussions between the two governments, a deal was struck whereby the Russian and Belarussian leaders agreed to share their military infrastructure, their gas and electricity facilities and, in due course, their currency; and in December 1999 a Union State Treaty was solemnised involving a commitment to the future total fusion of the two states.[6]

Other states were also drawn into the process. In March 1996 a 'Treaty of the Four' was signed by Russia, Belarus, Kazakhstan and Kyrgyzstan, calling for not only a single economic space but also a single foreign policy. The treaty described the states as having been 'joined by a common historical destiny'. Always Belarus wished to press things further and faster. The other signatories of the 'Treaty of the Four' were less enthusiastic about Russia. Kazakhstan resented the Kremlin meddling in the commercial deal completed between the government in Almaty and the American oil company Chevron. Russia obstructed Kazakhstan's plans to bypass the use of Russian pipelines in exporting its energy. There was also trouble about the oil reserves beneath the Caspian Sea. Azerbaijan, Kazakhstan, Turkmenistan and Russia laid competing claims for the right to exploit the reserves, and the Russian government indicated it would disrupt all extractive activity unless Russian companies were given a substantial part of the business. Obviously the Commonwealth of Independent States was no longer seen by Russia as an association of political and economic equals.

Russia's assertiveness in international relations continued to increase under Putin. The President himself was in good health and travelled around the world on frequent occasions, visiting the USA, Japan, India, China, Germany, the United Kingdom, North Korea and several other countries. The Russo-American relationship, so important to Yeltsin, became less prominent in official statements; Russian diplomats stressed that the world was characterised by a 'multipolar' division of power. Putin was welcomed by the leaders of the G8 nations. Even before Putin's victory in the 2000 Presidential elections – while the war in Chechnya still raged – British Prime Minister Tony Blair was willing to visit in the Kremlin, and in November 2000 he repeated the trip and was filmed drinking a glass of vodka with his Russian fellow leader. This was helpful to Putin, whose awareness of Russia's current economic plight was accompanied by a determination to raise his country's prestige. The foreign contacts were a means to this end. So too was the readiness to search out friends among those who had been allies in the Soviet period. Ignoring American hostility, his government made friendly overtures to Iraq, North Korea and Libya to gain greater latitude for Russian diplomacy.

The National Security Concept adopted in January 2000 expressed a desire for co-operation with 'all the leading states of the world'. Unlike the earlier version, however, it picked out the foreign policy of the USA for censure. The American struggle for supremacy in world affairs was roundly condemned and the need for Russia to rebuild its armed forces was affirmed.[7] The Military Doctrine agreed in the same year strengthened this orientation. It emphasised the permissibility of using the armed forces to keep order and maintain peace in the Russian Federation. This was to be expected at a time when military units were fighting in Chechnya. More surprising was the Doctrine's restoration of approval – at least in principle – of the use of nuclear weapons in wars that might be fought by Russia outside its borders.

But the opportunities for increasing influence around the globe remained small while the Russian gross domestic product languished below 0.5 per cent of the world's annual output. Influence needs to rest upon a strong economic foundation. While the Russian economy continued to contract and there was no sign of industrial regeneration, little change could be anticipated. The armed forces continued to be underfunded for anything but limited campaigns either inside Russia or in a few countries of the Commonwealth of Independent States. Escape from the impasse was possible in several ways. One would have involved the reduction of the commitment to nuclear weaponry and the transfer of funds to the conventional armed forces. For this reason it made sense for Russia to seal a deal with the USA for bilateral cuts in the allowable number of nuclear missiles. But all this required patient negotiation – and from January 2001 the Americans under President George W. Bush made this difficult by suggesting that they might begin research on a new anti-missile defence system even at the expense of treaties signed with the USSR and Russia. In such circumstances there was little prospect of Russia resuming the position of the second superpower.

Meanwhile Putin, with his origins in the European city of St Petersburg and his working experience in Germany, stressed his interest in improving relations with the European Union. Many in Moscow saw a Russo-European axis as the most effective policy to restore the country's dignity and influence. There was something in this. While trade with neighbouring states to the south could help with economic stabilisation, it was unlikely to act as the motor of regeneration. For this purpose there was a need for direct financial investment, and – in the absence of Japanese and American long-range enthusiasm – Europe was the most realistic possibility.

Already at the EU–Russia summit held in Helsinki in October 1999 Putin was ready to present a 'Medium-Term Strategy for the Development of Relations between the Russian Federation and the European Union'. It was the first statement of its kind since the fall of the USSR. Putin's main objective was the forging of 'a strategic partnership'.[8] In particular he called for security in Europe to be ensured 'by the Europeans themselves'. The instrument for action preferred by the Russians was the Organisation for Security and Co-operation in Europe (OSCE) and it was clearly the Russian purpose to loosen the relationship of the Atlantic powers even though Putin has professed the wish to avoid isolating the USA. Yeltsin had sought to do this by offering Germany and France a special relationship with Russia, and Putin has added Britain to the list. The Strategy envisaged Russia's integration into 'a common economic and social area' within a decade. Putin also aspired to supervise the general relationship of the Commonwealth of Independent States with the European Union. The Commonwealth in itself had hardly any significance. Presumably Putin's underlying objective was to prevent Ukraine or any other country of the Commonwealth from negotiating separate terms of association.

The European Union was therefore a rival as well as a partner for Russia; and whereas Russian power was declining, the European Union was undertaking both internal integration and territorial expansion. Indeed there was talk of the potential emergence of a new superpower: the European Union had fifteen members at the beginning of the twenty-first century and was planning to increase this number to twenty-six. Thus the Union was set to expand its area by a third and its population by 29 per cent. It would include most of the former allies of the USSR in the Warsaw Pact. The buffer zone between Russia and 'the West' would definitively be removed. Finland, whose frontiers abut the Russian north, had entered the European Union in 1995. Some countries of the former USSR itself joined the queue for membership. Estonia, Latvia and Lithuania were among them, and there was little doubt that their request would eventually be granted. Meanwhile the European Union's economic penetration of Eastern Europe was relentless. Germany had a large stake in the Polish and Czech economies by the early 1990s and began to extend its activity into Russia, including Kaliningrad Province. Lying outside the main territory of the Russian Federation and needing to rely upon Lithuania for its transport links to Moscow, Kaliningrad politicians welcomed closer ties with Germany.[9]

If the expansion of NATO was to be rendered less threatening to the Russian Federation, some kind of co-operation with the European Union was desirable. So was a friendlier relationship with Japan and China. The fact that Russia refused to return any of Japan's former Northern Territories had a cooling effect on moves towards a closer relationship. Exchanges of visits by Russian and Japanese rulers have been friendly and President Yeltsin was poised, in the mid-1990s, to restore the disputed islands to Japan. But this did not happen. The disagreement has remained an obstacle to an improved commercial relationship.

With China there were fewer immediate problems. The Sino-Soviet border dispute of the 1960s was settled; and although China remains under communist rule, its economy is increasingly dominated by capitalism and trade between Russia and China has been continually growing. The Russian Federation made a point of supplying Beijing with the arms it has been unable to obtain from the USA. But worries persisted. The Chinese economy was expanding in the very years when Russia experienced decline. Traders from China regularly came over the frontier into Siberia with cheap goods. The vibrancy of Chinese entrepreneurship was such that the question has arisen whether, in the longer term, Siberia as a whole might fall under China's influence. The Siberian population is thinly spread and the frontiers are easy to breach. China by contrast is over-populated. The fact that China, which is also a nuclear power, is likely to gain in political and military authority in future years is hardly reassuring to policy-makers in Moscow. But for the moment there is calm, and Russia derives benefit from its growing commercial ties. At the moment it is too poor to be fussy about its partners in the wider world.

The part played by Russia in successive political emergencies in Bosnia and Kosovo was not remembered with uniform enthusiasm. Too often it appeared to Western governments that Yeltsin and Putin had been making mischief, and the USA and the European Union usually saw little point in binding Russia automatically behind its diplomatic initiatives. But this Western posture changed abruptly on 11 September 2001 when suicide-terrorists devastated the World Trade Center in New

York and damaged the Pentagon in Washington. The NATO countries sought support from abroad. As suspicion grew that the massacre had been organised by the Saudi Islamic fighter Osama bin Laden, who was based in Afghanistan, the necessity for overtures to President Putin became acute. Russia had close relations with former Soviet republics bordering Afghanistan; it had troops stationed in Tajikistan who patrolled the Afghan–Tajikistani border and controlled garrisons and airfields. American military planners, while putting Pakistan under pressure to co-operate in efforts to eliminate bin Laden and undermine the Afghan government, needed access to Uzbekistan and Tajikistan to start a military offensive. President George W. Bush asked urgently for Russian acquiescence. For the first time since the fall of the USSR the world's sole remaining superpower had to plead with Moscow.

Putin's first reaction was to express sympathy with the victims of the terrorist outrage in New York and to offer his practical assistance.[10] For him, the events confirmed his earlier contention that the West had regularly underestimated the menace constituted by 'Islamic fundamentalism'. He repeated that the Russian military actions in Chechnya had been aimed at eradicating international terrorism and political extremism from the soil of the Russian Federation; and, in a spirit of co-operation that had not emanated from the Kremlin since the first years of Yeltsin's Presidency, he offered logistical facilities to the forces of the USA. Putin saw the global political crisis as an opportunity to justify Russian official behaviour and enhance Russia's status and influence. In return for his support the USA ceased to criticise Russia's military activity in Chechnya.

Thus a further blow was delivered at the small lingering prospect of further reform in Russia. So long as Russia's rulers continued to justify the war in Chechnya, there could hardly be a reversion to a less authoritarian order in politics and the economy. This did not mean that Putin's foreign policy was welcomed even by those who agreed with him about Chechnya. Zyuganov disliked his co-operation with American military objectives; but it was not only the communists who offered criticisms. Putin was castigated for conniving in the USA's global domination at the expense of Russian national interests. A danger existed of damage to growing commercial ties with Iraq and other Islamic states. Actions by international terrorist groups might be undertaken in Moscow, and Russia's own Moslems might become more widely involved. Instability in Tajikistan and Uzbekistan, spreading from any conflict in Afghanistan, would inevitably cause tremors across Russia – and it had taken until 1997 for the civil war in Tajikistan to be brought to an end with Russian military and diplomatic assistance. Russian politicians and journalists remembered the quagmire that enveloped the Soviet army after it invaded Afghanistan in 1979.[11] Inside the Kremlin, including both the Foreign Ministry and the Defence Ministry, the same points were made.

And so the results of the first decade of de-communised government have been depressing. By the late 1980s even the USSR had tumbled from its peak of might and was no longer a superpower. Further years of political and economic disarray have reduced the Russian Leviathan to a museum piece of former glory. And those early hopes of a New World Order led by liberal democracies, including Russia, have been disappointed. Foreign loans to Russia have been creamed off by its prime businessmen. De-industrialisation has continued as the world economy has penetrated the country. Like many a Third World economy, Russia relies crucially upon its energy-fuel exports in order to keep its budget even half-balanced. Russia's power and prestige are lower than at any time since the Civil War. Russian foreign policy and domestic politics are entwined in a baleful knot. The situation is painful for those who advocate a return to the grand reform project of the early 1990s; and the single event which partially restored Russia's importance in world affairs – the terrorist action in New York on 11 September 2001 – served to aggravate the basic problems.

PART THREE

PERSUADING RUSSIA

12. OFFICIAL TRANSMISSION

When we had the old curricula, many of us used to grumble that Moscow did not give us any latitude in deciding what to teach and how to teach it. But I don't think we really anticipated just how difficult it would be to adapt to deciding such matters on our own.

Geography teacher, 1995[1]

The setbacks to the grand reform project were not simply the result of mistakes in practical policy. Although politics and economics counted for much, there was also a wider dimension of failure. This involved the entire way that people – 'ordinary' people as well as politicians and businessmen – felt about the project. Societies need to feel comfortable about the purposes of their rulers. People do not live by bread, steel or guns alone. Unfortunately the Russian government in the 1990s did not succeed in supplying citizens with a persuasive vision of life superior to life as it had been lived under Soviet communism.

The rulers themselves slipped into a quandary. This became starkly obvious in July 1996 when Prime Minister Chernomyrdin started a competition in the newspaper of the Russian government, *Rossiiskaya gazeta*. He did this at the instigation of Yeltsin who recognised that the electorate continued to feel uneasy about him and his policies and called for a search for a new 'Russian idea'. The regime was at an impasse. Having fallen short in formulating popular concepts of its own, it was turning to society for help and support; and Chernomyrdin dutifully organised the work. The competition set a concise subject for readers of the newspaper to write about: 'The Idea of Russia'. The winner would receive a prize of 5 million rubles. Equivalent to nearly $1,000, it was a sum more than a manual worker or office clerk would earn over two years. Each entry had to stay below five to seven typed pages. (This was a Russian peculiarity: why couldn't Chernomyrdin just specify either five or seven?) There was no prescription of content except that competitors were to be people 'believing in a resurrected Russia, in the talent, hard work and patriotism of Russian citizens (*rossiyane*)'.[2]

The newspaper's front page reprinted the oil painting *Eternal Russia* by the Russian nationalist Ilya Glazunov. There were also excerpts from the writings of 'prophets in their own country'. The prophets were all Russians famous for criticising socialism: the nineteenth-century philosopher Vladimir Solovëv, the early twentieth-century thinker Ivan Ilin and the late twentieth-century writers Alexander Solzhenitsyn and Andrei Sakharov.[3] The unmistakable implication was that competitors defending the former Soviet regime were unlikely to win – or even to get their entries printed.

The entries appeared weekly in the newspaper through to the end of the year. The themes were predictable. Patriotism was repeatedly on display. Pride in the military victory in the war and in the moral and social values of the Russian people over several centuries was to the fore. There was also confidence in Russia's science, technology and culture. Pleasure was taken in her natural environment, the rivers, forests and steppes. Contributors lauded the tolerance, endurance and intelligence of Russians. They added that Russians had contributed more to the world's highest achievements in literature and music than any other nation in the twentieth century. Some expressed regret at the decline in Russia's military and economic prowess, others at the fall in living standards. Many contributors identified a rise in national morale as the key to the country's recovery. The point that practically everyone accentuated was the need for citizens to rally behind whatever efforts might be made by the government to make progress, however such progress might be defined, and restore popular confidence. A lot of competitors emphasised that Russia, having tackled problems of incalculable difficulty in the previous decades, could surmount any obstacle.

The winner, announced on 31 December 1996, was a certain Guri Sudakov from Vologda in the Russian North. Sudakov was a fifty-six-year-old philologist who had entered local politics. Interested in 'the Russian soul', he had always asked himself: 'Who are we? Where are we going?'[4] His winning entry, entitled 'The Six Principles of Russianness', allowed that Russians had their faults while stressing their virtues. Russians were described as unusually tolerant towards the people of other nations who lived among them. They were also, he claimed, very alien to materialism and individualism:

Summing up, let us define the difference between the Russian and the West European in a single word: non-marketeer. The Russian national character was not formed on the basis of market activity. From this derives the essential distinction in the spiritual make-up. For the European, social significance lies in business, craftsmanship and wealth. This is the source of the leading values of freedom and law. For the Russian, greater importance is attached to society, Motherland, glory and power.[5]

Sudakov suggested that the uniqueness of the Russian people was eternal. Indeed, his ideas were a hotchpotch of clichés, but he was proud of his country and although he did not oppose reform, he harboured a suspicion of the economics of unfettered markets; this chimed well with Chernomyrdin's prejudices and facilitated his victory.

Until the 'Idea of Russia' competition, the government had employed more traditional methods to propagate its vision of the country. There was systematic use of television, radio and the schools. Of the media it was television that had the greatest impact. Radio was the Cinderella of Russian politics. The state broadcasting stations had twenty-five million regular listeners in the mid-1990s, but it was rare for political leaders to take time on radio.[6] They wanted to give speeches and interviews on prime-time TV. Yeltsin was an exception in as much as he gave Presidential talks to radio listeners; but even he gave priority to appearances in the visual medium.

Yet the television network was no longer what it had been in the communist period. Russian state TV came into existence only in spring 1991. (Previously it was assumed that the viewers of the RSFSR did not need a set of channels different from those of the USSR.) When the Soviet Union collapsed at the end of the year, Yeltsin decided at first to maintain a couple of stations for the state while the rest were to be sold to private broadcasting companies. But the operating costs were enormous and the government was unable to subsidise its own stations. By late 1993, apparently, they received less than a quarter of the amount they needed.[7] Thus the state was increasingly dependent on the financial contributions of wealthy businessmen not known for their commitment to journalism free from their own influence. Furthermore, Yeltsin and his associates were met with popular distrust. In surveys conducted in 1994–6 only 14 per cent of respondents said they relied on governmental sources of information (whereas 40 per cent turned to private TV channels). State television has an influence but it is one that is nowhere near as strong as ministers would like.

The schools and universities were another focus of attention. The USSR had a highly centralised educational system and its teachers had to comply with a very specific curriculum. Textbooks were written under the supervision of the Ministry of Education, which in turn was supervised by the Ideological Department of the Secretariat of the Party Central Committee. In literature there was a single stipulated list of authors, including Lenin. In history and politics there was the *History of the Communist Party of the Soviet Union*. For every subject the Ministry of Education nominated books which were the only ones to be used in teaching the youth of the country. This degree of control had begun to be loosened in the late 1980s, when Gorbachëv allowed greater freedom of discussion in society as a whole and in universities and schools in particular. Yet the result was rather chaotic. Funding for education was inadequate and teachers were perplexed by the rapidly changing content of public debate. They were at a loss about what they should say to their pupils in class and lecture hall. Gorbachëv had his own ideas, but the nature of his reforms meant that he was unable to impose them on others.

Yeltsin did not grant total freedom to schools to develop their own curricula. Certainly he permitted private schooling; he also refrained from prescribing curricula for state schools – by far the greatest proportion of educational establishments across the Russian Federation. The Ministry of Education stuck to the goal of cultural pluralism. Both compulsory textbooks and a uniform curriculum were treated as typical of the communist monolithism that the new Russia must avoid. The fact that liberal democracies such as France practise precisely such monolithism was ignored. The point was to overturn recent Soviet practice.

Not that the state stopped trying to supervise what was taught in schools. In 1992 the government instructed the Ministry of Education to encourage the introduction of fresh methods and texts of instruction, and a list of officially recommended books was produced for each subject. The Ministry also issued a 'basic teaching plan' specifying the main themes to be covered by teachers in each school year. It did not specify a political interpretation, but the selection of themes was such as to promote the government's anti-communist objectives. A visit to any Russian bookshop, especially at the start of the school year, revealed an explosion of authorial activity. Competing textbooks were produced for every grade of pupil. Some had the Ministry of Education's approval, others did not. The writers, in contrast with the growing practice in the

West, are not specialist educationists but prominent scholars in their own right. They have taken up such work not just out of a sense of civic duty but also for more mundane reasons. Textbook sales can mean the difference between a meagre lifestyle on an academic salary and a degree of comfort subsidised by royalties.

Whether the Ministry, through its Expert Council on General Education, vetted the textbooks in an open-minded fashion is an open question. The system was as follows. Authors or publishers submitted a work to the Expert Council, which would hand it on to one of its thirty-one Sections. Each Section had between fifteen and twenty specialist members who would take their decision on the basis of reports submitted by two or three reviewers.[8] A positive recommendation would predictably lead to large sales for any work. The snag was that the Sections contained specialists whose impartiality could not be guaranteed: some of them were themselves textbook writers. Not surprisingly the works gaining the Ministry's approval have shown a distinct preference for authors who are citizens of the Russian Federation – and indeed citizens who reside in Moscow. Perhaps the expense of translating existing Western texts is a disincentive; but some of these texts were rendered into Russian and are on sale. Another explanation may be that the books produced by Russian scholars are better attuned to the kind of material presently needed by schools. But probably a degree of intellectual protectionism is also at work. At a time when Russians are fed up with the consequences of Western advice, especially in the economic and diplomatic fields, such a reaction would not be surprising.

The most sensitive subjects have been Russian history and Russian literature. Ministers wished youngsters to grow up committed to the reformed politics and economics of post-communist Russia. The last school curriculum approved under Brezhnev, who died in 1982, had signs of a Russian national orientation. Boys and girls had to read a number of works of stirring patriotism. In particular, in school year five (ten-year-olds) they were required to study Lev Tolstoi's *Prisoner of the Caucasus*. This bloodcurdling tale describes the fate of an Imperial army officer called Zhilin who was taken captive by a certain Abdul and put up for ransom. Zhilin escapes but is recaptured and hurled into a pit. The inhabitants of the Moslem village are described as Tatars and are depicted as deceitful, unpredictable and wild. The Russian officer by comparison appears as honourable and reliable. The Tatars feature as people of villages and mountains, of customary allegiances, of religious constancy whereas the Russian characters come across as the representatives of European civilisation. In some of his other works Tolstoi was kinder about the peoples conquered by the Russians. But it was *Prisoner of the Caucasus* that was chosen for Soviet adolescents to imbibe. From Stalin onwards, the Communist Party of the Soviet Union wished to encourage Russian national pride.

Another short story on the Soviet curriculum was Alexei Tolstoi's *The Russian Character* (read by twelve-year-olds). Alexei Tolstoi, nephew of Lev Tolstoi, identified himself with the October 1917 Revolution; indeed his lengthy historical novels were supportive of the regime of Joseph Stalin. In the Second World War, Alexei Tolstoi's nationalism was allowed free rein. In *The Russian Character* he never refers to Marxist-Leninism, not even once.

The story is a romance set in the war between Nazi Germany and the USSR. Its plot is very simple: tank commander Yegor Drëmov, decorated many times for valour and adored by the men under his command, is badly wounded in battle. His feat had been to take on and destroy a whole unit of the Wehrmacht. But his face is horribly disfigured; the work of the field doctors permits him to survive only with physical features that leave him unrecognisable even to his parents and fiancée. On a brief return home, he is convinced that a normal life is no longer within his power. He talks with his relatives without revealing his identity. Then he returns to the army and successfully pleads to be re-enlisted despite his wounds. He retains the body of a great athlete. He is remembered as someone who had fought on instinct as well as with the courage of a hero. Then at the very end of the story, as he trains to go into military action again, his mother and girlfriend turn up at the military camp. They have worked out who the stranger was. They want him to know that even with his changed appearance he remains the man they love.

The Russian Character is a sentimental piece, and Alexei Tolstoi plays on every chord to enhance the feeling that Russians are different and – with their modesty, simplicity and courage – superior to every other people. The Germans may have advanced technology and ideological zeal, but they are stupid and even comic when it comes to a hand-to-hand conflict in a little village.[9]

And so it went on. The first poem by the nineteenth-century poet Mikhail Lermontov to be learned by schoolchildren was his 'Borodino', written in commemoration of the Russian victory over the invading forces of Napoleon in 1812. One of the stanzas ran as follows:

And so light glowered. All were ready
To fight another fight till morning
And stand until the end!
And so the drums were rattling –
And the invading robbers retreated.
Then it was we started to count our wounds,
Counting our comrades.[10]

Other works included stirring stories by the openly nationalist writer Valentin Rasputin. Pride in Russian achievements on the fields of battle and in social and cultural virtue was meant to be instilled into every schoolchild, regardless of national background. The stress was always on the positive side; the less laudatory reflections on Russian national characteristics of any age were ignored. This is not an unusual phenomenon in state educational curricula elsewhere. But what is significant is that Russian patriotism was inculcated into pupils decades before the inauguration of an independent Russian state.[11]

Yet the changes after 1991 were substantial, especially in the teaching of literature and history. The communist element was urgently removed. For example, the story by Alexander Tvardovski about *Lenin and the Stovemaker* was no longer recommended for schoolchildren to study in literature classes. Nor were the most obviously pro-Soviet novels and poems. Similarly, there was no provision or encouragement of the study of Marxism-Leninism in history classes; and although the October 1917 Revolution remained a topic of instruction, there was no insistence – quite the opposite was the case – that Lenin and the communists brought benefit to the country by their actions.

Yet the teaching of literature otherwise did not need to be changed very much. The reason for this is that non-communist, pro-national works had been part of the Soviet curriculum. 'Village prose writers' such as Valentin Rasputin had already been included. After 1991 there was no longer a prescribed list of poems and novels to be studied in schools and universities: instead the Ministry of Education simply recommended dozens of introductory textbooks offering their own selection of works for study. The choices in the textbooks tended to be roughly the same as before 1991,[12] but there were also important additions. Even in the Soviet period it had been possible to read the classic authors Fëdor Dostoevski and Lev Tolstoi despite the fact that Lenin had condemned them for spreading the opium of religion among the people; after 1991, however, the attention to such writers was increased. Previously banned authors, too, began to be studied with official encouragement. Notable among them was the philosopher and historian of ideas Nikolai Berdyaev, who had been deported from the USSR in 1922. Evidently the government wished schools to provide a complete antidote to Marxist-Leninist prescriptions for literature.

History teaching also underwent change. Decommunisation, as originally envisaged, involved the facilitation of a plurality of standpoints; but in the Russian Federation certain standpoints are anti-constitutional, especially those which are dictatorial or racist. The Ministry of Education did not ban works, but it at least sought to provide some with the imprimatur of official endorsement.[13]

What initially happened was more a mirror-image reversal of the interpretation than a change in the contents. Lenin, once the idol, was turned into the villain. The communist party and Marxism-Leninism became the plagues of the twentieth century. Simultaneously the last years of the Romanov monarchy acquired an aura of positive possibility. The reputation of Pëtr Stolypin, Nicholas II's vigorous Chairman of the Council of Ministers from 1906 to 1911, soared. Church, peasantry and rural customs were re-envisaged as having had much potential to aid social progress. As to the Soviet period, the White Armies – previously dismissed as a pestilence – were rehabilitated as patriotic forces seeking to destroy the communist terror-regime. Doubts were cast upon the educational and economic achievements of the Five-Year Plans.[14] Only a few episodes in the history of the USSR attracted praise: the victory in the 'Great Patriotic War'; the scientific discoveries and technological breakthroughs of the 1960s; the cultural splendour of Dmitri Shostakovich, Boris Pasternak and Andrei Platonov; the endurance and resourcefulness of the Russian people. Otherwise the Soviet decades were painted in dark colours.

But bit by bit a more equivocal analysis started to appear in several textbooks. Nearly all were written by professional historians, mostly Russian citizens and nearly all of them based in the Academy of Sciences or Moscow State University.[15] In the Gorbachëv years it was admitted by historians themselves that the reading public continued to distrust them as the regime's intellectual hacks. But steadily the confidence of these scholars returned. They held the levers of power in the state's educational institutions. They sat on editorial boards of publishing houses. They had the authority to promote or balk the careers of young scholars. In any case, the historical profession offered few material incentives to postgraduates. Historians were ill paid. Archives were starved of resources; in

1998 the former Central Party Archive (now known as the Russian State Archive for Socio-Political History) could no longer afford to turn on its heating on a daily basis. Libraries can hardly afford new books. Bright youngsters were likelier to go into commerce than into the scholarly community. So the ageing cohort of professional historians – not all of whom were even private critics of Brezhnev – was still marshalled as the instrument whereby a sense of Russian history is transmitted to students in schools and universities.

The textbooks were written very quickly, but the results were not unimpressive. Among the most detailed works was the two-volume *Soviet Society*, edited by Yuri Afanasev. This is a man who came to prominence in the years of Gorbachëv. His previous career was as a historian specialising in 'the criticism of bourgeois falsification'. Under Gorbachëv he revealed a different side. He became so radical in his reform proposals that he offended even Gorbachëv after condemning the USSR Supreme Soviet as 'Stalinist-Brezhnevite'.[16] In the early 1990s he was a prominent ally of Boris Yeltsin. He appeared on television – a handsome middle-aged man with brown hair and a distinctly flamboyant style in front of camera – to explain why the communist regime had been flawed from start to finish. Like many intellectuals, however, he did not flourish in the politics of the new Russia, and to general surprise he buried himself in the University of Humanitarian Studies, devoting himself to the editing of scholarly books. A noble cause it is: the delineation of the Russian past without the political interference that prevailed in the Imperial and Soviet periods.

Not only Afanasev but also most historians have altered their opinions. Few have failed to perform an intellectual somersault. Little of a positive nature is said now about Lenin, the communist regime or Marxist-Leninism, and nowadays it is rare for new textbooks to fail to discern some virtue or other in nearly every tsar who ruled Russia before 1917.

A notable example in 2000 was the university-level work produced by scholars belonging to the Institute of Russian History in the Academy of Sciences. The introduction was written by V. P. Dmitrenko. Instead of laying out a set of guidelines, he posed several fundamental questions:

> Why must Russia pay so heavy a price for historical progress? Perhaps the people carries within itself its own gene for destruction, unbridled passions and aspirations, risk-taking and romanticism? Or has the country because of the specificity of recent times fallen

into some immense mill-stones of a global movement which, heavily turning, are ceaselessly shattering, imagining, forming and re-making into some shape known only to them the nature and character of a Russian society which nevertheless still tries to preserve the face of the nation?[17]

The rest of the book continued to set more problems than it answered. Western as well as Russian scholarship was adduced, and measured argument rather than closed-off assertion prevailed. Despite being officially recommended,[18] it held back from directly sanctioning the black-and-white interpretation of Soviet history put forward by Yeltsin. At the same time it avoided eulogising the USSR and its past.

Evidently it was no longer easy to impose the image of Russia desired by the President and government. The media could no longer simply be instructed. Until April 1998 the Presidency had its own newspaper, *Rossiiskie vesti*.[19] But this was given up by Yeltsin because, apart from anything else, it was barely read by citizens; and although the government retains a newspaper, *Rossiiskaya gazeta*, the readership is small.

State-controlled TV still exists, and has not been slow to show films that expose the horrors of the communist period. There had been plenty of this under Gorbachëv. Two programmes stood out. One was *Risk*, which examined the global dangers of the Cold War and the USSR's part in them. *Risk* traced a line of political and ideological continuity from Stalin through to Brezhnev. The other such film was *Vlast' solovetskaya*, whose title was a pun on 'Soviet power'. Solovki was the Orthodox Church monastery-island turned into a forced-labour prison camp in the 1920s. The film gave an account how a place of torment was represented to the world as a model of social rehabilitation for convicts. The abuses carried out by the Cheka and the camp guards were described in harrowing detail: the violent interrogations; the miserably low rations; the punishment for the slightest acts of disobedience. To his shame, the world-famous Russian writer Maxim Gorki had allowed himself to be filmed visiting the island and indicating his approval of the methods of incarceration. Both *Risk* and *Vlast' solovetskaya* were shown frequently after 1991, especially in weeks preceding elections. Yeltsin and his ministers wished to rid the country of any lingering nostalgia for communism.

Unlike Gorbachëv, moreover, Yeltsin aimed to add Lenin to the list of Russia's oppressors. Many secret files were declassified. Lenin's primary role in starting and continuing the Red Terror had long been obvious from published material; but the newly released documentation broke ground by demonstrating the personal relish he took in ordering repression. A telegram he sent to the Penza communists in August 1918 was particularly shocking:

> Comrades! The insurrection of five kulak districts should be *pitilessly* suppressed. The interests of the *whole* revolution require this because 'the last decisive battle' with the kulaks is now under way *everywhere*. An example must be demonstrated.
>
> 1. Hang (and make sure that the hanging takes place *in full view of the people*) *no fewer than one hundred* known kulaks, rich men, bloodsuckers.
> 2. Publish their names.
> 3. Seize *all* their grain from them.
> 4. Designate hostages in accordance with yesterday's telegram. *Do it in such a fashion that for hundreds of kilometres around the people might see, tremble, know, shout:* they are strangling *and will strangle to death the bloodsucking kulaks.*
>
> *Telegraph* receipt and implementation.
> Yours, Lenin.
> Find some truly hard people.[20]

Television programmes gave prominence to such revelations to corroborate the government's arguments about the Soviet past.

They were not always successful, and the difficulty was not confined to the continuing popularity of Lenin. Just before the December 1993 State Duma elections, a programme denouncing Vladimir Zhirinovski was shown. Confidential opinion polls had indicated that Liberal-Democratic Party leader Zhirinovski was likely to do well against Yeltsin's favourite politician, Yegor Gaidar. The programme suggested, plausibly enough, that Zhirinovski had no objection to the dictatorial methods previously used by the communists. But Zhirinovski proceeded to do better in the elections than Gaidar – proof, perhaps, that there is no such thing as bad publicity. The government's 'spin doctors' learned a lesson from this, anyway. In the State Duma elections of 1995 and 1999 and the Presidential elections of 1996 and 2000 the *ad hominem* technique was abandoned. By then the main threat to Yeltsin came not from Zhirinovski but from Communist Party of the Russian Federation leader Gennadi Zyuganov. Instead of an overt personal attack, the state-owned TV stations – and indeed the private ones too – confined themselves to documentaries on Soviet history and went little further than asking viewers whether they wished to take a gamble on Zyuganov's promise to adhere to democratic methods.

Yeltsin's general policy was otherwise to encourage and guide the media rather than to prescribe the exact contents of what they printed or broadcast. Schools, universities, press and TV stations were not left to their own devices: ministries clearly indicated the direction they preferred. But nothing was directly banned unless it infringed the Constitution (and, even so, extremist political literature – including fascist leaflets – was readily available on the streets). Yeltsin was proud of having abolished the censorship office (Glavlit), and having endorsed cultural pluralism, he was willing to abide by its consequences. Yet he was no absolute liberal. Far from it: he sacked Oleg Poptsov from the chairmanship of one of the state-owned TV stations for showing programmes about financial corruption in the Kremlin.[21] Yeltsin also disliked being the butt of TV satire. The long-running satirical puppet show *Kukly* ('Dolls') on the private television station NTV annoyed him. The character Boriska, obviously based on him, irritated him so much that the General Procurator subjected the main script-writer to an aggressive interview. But that is as far as it went, and *Kukly* survived.[22] This was the litmus test of freedom of expression and Yeltsin passed it.

Vladimir Putin did not. He resented the sniping in the media at the many achievements of the Soviet state, and intended to bring an end to it. The official change in approach was evident soon after he became Prime Minister. The government's newspaper, *Rossiiskaya gazeta*, led the way with an article appearing the day before the October 1917 Revolution anniversary in 1999:

> Let's stop humbling the overthrown shadows of the past. Let's call things by their real names. And for a start let's stop feeling ashamed and referring to what happened eighty-two years ago in the city on the river Neva as 'the October coup'. Coups last for days, weeks or months. Yet we lived under the sign of that event for almost a century. This was not just an event for us in our own country: the entire world was genuinely shaken to its foundations by the Russian Revolution. And this defines its greatness, whether we like it or not.[23]

This was almost a call for a positive historical re-evaluation of the seizure and consolidation of power by Lenin and the communists. Nothing like it had been heard from a government minister since the inception of Yeltsin's Presidency.

Putin continued his campaign after becoming President. Rejecting Yeltsin's repudiation of the Soviet historical legacy, he aimed to make a bridge between the pre-communist and post-communist periods but to lay a road through all Russian history: pre-communist, communist and post-communist. He wanted to put an end to what he saw as the denigration of the USSR's achievements. Interviewed by journalists, he put all this in personal terms: 'My impressions of the KGB arose on the basis of romantic stories of the work of intelligence agents. Without any exaggeration I could be considered the successful product of a Soviet person's patriotic education.'[24] This did not mean that he denied that dictatorship and terror had occurred after 1917: he accepted that Stalin's rule had been abusive and that the Soviet Union had been 'a totalitarian state'.[25] But he wanted a balance to be struck between light and dark:

And is there nothing good to remember about the Soviet period of our country? Was there nothing but Stalin's prison camps and repression? In that case what are we going to do about Dunaevski, Sholokhov, Shostakovich, Korolëv and our achievements in space? What are we going to do about Yuri Gagarin's [space] flight?[26]

Continuity, not rupture, was to become the guiding principle in official ideas about the history of Russia.

Quite how he might set about this was not immediately clear to anyone, including probably Putin himself. Initially he limited himself to changing some of the state symbolism introduced by Yeltsin.[27] In practical terms he ordered that compulsory military training should be re-instituted in the school curriculum for boys between the ages of fifteen and sixteen. Pride in the state was not enough. Putin wanted every young male to have the capacity to fight in the armed forces if and when the need should arise.

But there followed no drastic revision of the contents of schooling, the governmental press or TV stations. The literary and historical works published under Yeltsin remained available in the schools and universities; and the critique of the Soviet order in the media owned by the government continued to be robust. The publicly transmitted values were not much different from those espoused by the government since 1991. Behind the scenes, especially in the Ministry of Education, there were discussions and it became clear that the teaching of national history was the object of Putin's hostility. In August 2001 the matter at last came into the open when Prime Minister Kasyanov declared at a cabinet meeting that he 'found so much that was astonishing' in various textbooks.[28] Particular mistakes were discussed. Even the solid work edited by V. P. Dmitrenko was subjected to criticism; and the suspicion grew that the underlying cause for the government's ire was that Dmitrenko's book barely mentioned Putin and entirely overlooked Kasyanov.[29] Two of the country's most influential historians were called to give account at a cabinet meeting chaired by Kasyanov. These were Professors Andrei Sakharov (not the deceased nuclear physicist and dissident) and Alexander Chubaryan. They attended as Directors of the Institute of Russian History and the Institute of World History respectively. Both were themselves prolific writers and editors of textbooks. The meeting charged them to help in setting up a competition for the preparation of fresh works for use in schools and universities.[30]

The evident intention was that such material would be more congruent with the 'patriotic' orientation announced by Putin since 1999. A tightening of state regulation of schooling was in prospect. It was doubtful whether it would be instantly implemented. Professors Sakharov and Chubaryan, under pressure from the government, promised that the winning textbooks would be available by September 2002.[31] Gorbachëv had made similar demands on textbook writers in 1987; he had even laid down that certain historians should be instructed to sit in certain libraries and write their books to a prescribed schedule.[32] But the result was disappointing, as it was bound to be: books take longer to write than poems or newspaper articles. The same fate may await the competition of 2001. All that is clear is that the government was moving further down the path of exerting control. The project for the transformation of Russia had always been in the hands of a few politicians, and Putin made that grip ever tighter. For many citizens the reversion to a less negative interpretation of the Soviet decades was a pleasant change.[33] But generally the attempt to reshape popular consciousness was not a conspicuous success. The government remained dissatisfied. The crucial threshold had yet to be crossed: most people still did not feel that what had happened in Russia since 1991 was for the good of most people.

13. SYMBOLS FOR RUSSIA

Glory to our free Fatherland,
Age-old union of brotherly peoples,
Popular wisdom handed down by our ancestors!
Glory to you, our country. In you we take pride!

Refrain of 'The Hymn of Russia'

In trying to transform opinion, Yeltsin and his associates had less control over television, radio and academic institutions than over state symbolism. One of their first actions had been to remove the old insignia. The name of the state – the USSR – vanished at midnight on 31 December 1991. With it went the state flag with the golden hammer and sickle in the top left-hand corner. Also into history, at least for some years, went the national anthem (or 'state hymn'). Heraldry too was altered. Until 1992 the state emblem had consisted of a pair of workers reaching towards each other across a globe of the world; underneath was inscribed the motto: 'Proletarians of the world, unite!' The uniforms of state officialdom, including those of the armed forces, were changed at this time. Monuments too came tumbling down. Already in autumn 1991 the statue of Felix Dzierżyński – the dreaded founder of the secret police under Lenin – had been removed from Lubyanka Square outside the granite premises of the former KGB, and the statue of Lenin within the courtyard of the KGB itself was pulled down.[1] Across the Russian Federation statues, busts and bas-reliefs of Lenin himself were being removed in the winter of 1991–2.

Soviet symbolism was being attacked on a wide front and many citizens took an active part. Piles of statuary were gathered in parks and courtyards of the principal cities. There was a purging of the public spirit. Language was cleansed. The iconoclastic spirit was rampant.

But it quickly exhausted itself. There was much about the symbols of the Soviet Union that was close to people's hearts. The USSR anthem, introduced in 1943 as the winning entry in a competition judged by Stalin, evoked heated emotions. Alexander Alexandrov had composed its rousing melody and words were added by Sergei Mikhalkov and Garold El-Registan. Even foreigners found it moving; there are few national anthems – France's 'Marseillaise' is an example – that stand comparison. The original words became an embarrassment in 1956 when Nikita Khrushchëv made his posthumous attack on Stalin. The second stanza had run as follows:

> Through the storm the sun of freedom shone on us
> And the great Lenin lit up the way for us:
> Stalin brought us up – he inspired us towards loyalty to the people,
> Towards labour and towards heroic feats!

Stalin's name was expunged. Nevertheless the melody and most of the words were left intact since they belonged to the core of official ideology and contemporary Russian national identity. The authorities had issued the text of the anthem as a free postcard for troops to send home from the front in the Second World War. The Soviet military victory in 1945 was a unifying myth. Indeed, by the 1990s it was the sole myth that bound Russians together. The abandonment of anthem as well as flag, heraldic badge and motto was not going to be something that citizens of the Russian Federation would like.

Yet the success of the Russian Federation as a new and separate state required the rapid substitution of such symbolism. The government understood this and its ministers had sought ways to legitimate their rule even before the USSR's collapse. But what could they do? They decided to act without consulting public opinion. They wanted to mould it before it could otherwise be formed. They wanted to take charge of events.

Their instinctive reaction was to ferret around in the archives of musicologists to find a song that was tuneful, patriotic and popular. There was no repetition of the competitions that had typified the Stalinist period. Yeltsin's ministers opted to discover a potential anthem among existing melodies. This had been done by the Provisional Government after the February 1917 Revolution. Among the tsarist anthems had been the song composed by A. F. Lvov and V. A. Zhukovski, 'God, Save the Tsar!', and after Nicholas II's abdication the words were changed to 'God, Save the People!' Yeltsin might have gone back to this anthem with suitable verbal adjustments as the cellist Mstislav Rostropovich advised.[2] But Yeltsin took a different approach, opting for a composition known since the Second World War as 'The Patriotic Song'. It was played as an anthem for the first time at the Supreme Soviet of the RSFSR on 23 November 1990 and was quickly it adopted as the melody representing the Russian state against the claims of the USSR. 'The Patriotic Song' was based on a sketch found posthumously in the papers of the nineteenth-century classical composer Mikhail Glinka. This stirring melody had the advantage of being the work of someone who by no stretch of the imagination was a Soviet cultural figure. Glinka had been a Russian and a patriot.[3]

Yet 'The Patriotic Song' had uncompromising critics. The Russian Communist Party objected, demanding the restoration of the USSR anthem even after the abolition of the USSR at the end of 1991. Debates were held in the State Duma after 1993 and each time the government failed to get Glinka's melody accepted. The Constitution was no help: article 70 merely stated that the 'state hymn [is] established by federal constitutional law'. The official authorities continued to recoil from commissioning a text to accompany the melody or even conferring legal status on the melody. There was not much chance to engender civic cohesion in Russia if an elementary decision such as the choice of a national anthem was beyond the authority of the politicians to resolve.

The state flag and the state emblem presented difficulties. The choice fell upon a white-red-and-blue tricolour to replace the red banner with its hammer and sickle. Controversy immediately ensued and again it was the communists who were the main critics. The white-red-and-blue tricolour that enraged communists had been one of the state flags – as distinct from the dynastic flag – used until 1917. Admittedly it was not the flag of the House of the Romanovs, which was a tricolour of black, yellow and blue. But the white-red-and-blue tricolour had been used officially in the tsarist period, and that was quite bad enough from the standpoint of present-day communism. Worse still, General Kornilov had flown it after the fall of the Romanovs in the February 1917 Revolution. Kornilov led a counter-revolutionary mutiny against the Provisional Government in August 1917 and proceeded to raise a White Army to fight the communists in 1918.[4] The tricolour was an unmistakable symbol of anti-communism. In the Second World War it was the banner chosen by Lieutenant-General Andrei Vlasov. This fact was especially divisive. Vlasov, in a desperate effort to overthrow Joseph Stalin, formed regiments from Soviet prisoners-of-war held by the

Germans. He had been captured by the Red Army in 1945 and hanged in Moscow. For most contemporary Russians, Vlasov remains an ignominious historical figure, a traitor to his country who threw in his lot with Adolf Hitler.

The state emblem is not much more congenial. Heraldic officials devised for the Russian Federation a set of insignia not very different from that of the Romanovs. The double-headed eagle has returned and St George appears on official crests. After 1917, of course, the communists strove to eradicate religion and its images from the popular mind; the cult of Lenin was militantly secular in content (even though it was an ersatz religion in form). Now the images of the double-headed eagle and St George are nearly as common on Russian poster-boards – and indeed on cigarette packets and vodka bottles – as once, before 1991, were hammers, sickles, red stars and images of Lenin.

This was never going to be sufficient to make the citizens of Russia quickly comfortable with the state – the Russian Federation – in which they lived. President Yeltsin strove to give the new symbolism a chance to root itself by tearing down further symbols of the Soviet past. Lenin's birthday, routinely celebrated in official pomp on 23 April, ceased to be noted by television and radio. Yeltsin also wanted to remove the embalmed corpse of Lenin from the Mausoleum on Red Square and give it an overdue burial – on 6 June 1997 he went so far as to suggest the need for a referendum to settle the matter definitively. There was talk in the national newspapers that Lenin had expressed the wish to be interred next to his mother's grave in St Petersburg. This was a figment of Yuri Karyakin's imagination in a speech to the USSR Congress of People's Deputies in 1989. Archivists in the former Central Party Archive searched in the files of the Ulyanov family – Ulyanov was Lenin's real surname – to discover documentary evidence. But in vain. Lenin loved his mother; one of the first things he did on returning to Russia in April 1917 was to visit her grave. But he expressed no wish for his coffin to be laid beside hers in the Volkovo Cemetery; he did not care what happened to his corpse.

Yet there was a problem. Despite hoping to close the Mausoleum and bury Lenin as a symbolic interment of Soviet communism, Yeltsin confessed that, as a person born and bred in the USSR, he felt uneasy about it. He had been schooled to venerate the maker of the October 1917 Revolution and recognised the offence he might give to many people. His tactic was to test opinion by recurrently raising the question of a funeral for Lenin. When he did this in 1997, a protest demonstration was organised by communist sympathisers on Red Square. I was in Moscow at the time and witnessed the noisy scene. A BBC camera team employed a Lenin impersonator to walk about on Red Square. Predictably the demonstrators were outraged. The impersonator, heavily caked with facial make-up, was lucky not to be beaten up, and his wife complained that foreign media teams were jeopardising her family life. She implored him to get 'a proper job'.[5]

And so Lenin's corpse still rests in the Mausoleum and President Putin, whose grandfather was one of Lenin's cooks at the rural mansion where Lenin died in 1924, is unlikely to arrange an interment in St Petersburg. It is also notable that, despite the burst of iconoclasm in 1991–2, plenty of statues of him remain in Russian cities. While the other former Soviet republics in the USSR have pulled him down from pedestals, he stands proud on October Square in Moscow and elsewhere in Russia, including the 'ethnic' parts, to this day. Lenin Prospekt, one of the widest and longest of the capital's thoroughfares, has kept its name. This is appropriate in its own way. Dozens of streets in old Moscow were destroyed in the making of Lenin Prospekt; the topographical layout is now so different that it would be impossible to revert to the original designations. In south-east Russia, the authorities in Ulyanovsk – which was Simbirsk until the Politburo renamed it after Lenin – have not sought to change the city's name back to Simbirsk. The emotional linkage to seven communist decades had not entirely faded. Fond images of Lenin remain. He was the object of official idolatry until 1991. Gorbachëv, although objectively he de-Leninised the ideology and institutions of the USSR, continued to admire Lenin; and Russian citizens, who in the Soviet period were taught virtually to worship him, have not yet rejected the Lenin cult. Not entirely, anyway.

The lesson here is that it is easier to change flags, emblems and postage stamps than to alter popular mentality. Belatedly the government recognised the danger of forcing things too hard, but the process of change was sustained, at least until Putin's accession to power. Among the ways this has been done is by altering nomenclature. Yeltsin, formerly party boss in the Urals capital of Sverdlovsk, approved the reversion to its pre-revolutionary name Yekaterinburg. Other cities, too, were renamed. Gorki, the great Volga city named after the USSR's officially favoured writer Maxim Gorki, was changed back to Nizhni Novgorod. The city of Kirov again became Vyatka. Even some places with linkages to Lenin were affected. Most strikingly, Leningrad was given back the name it had at its foundation by Peter the Great, St Petersburg.

Leningrad was one of the 'hero-cities' of the Great Fatherland War; the memory of the 900-day siege was imprinted on the consciousness of all who had endured the travails of 1941–5. Nevertheless the change was confirmed. It had been instigated by a popular referendum held in Leningrad itself and perhaps it was the fact of this local initiative that restricted the protest.[6]

St Petersburg was also the vivid scene of anti-communist symbolism on 17 July 1998. On Yeltsin's orders, the remains of the last Emperor, his wife, son and daughters were buried in a solemn ceremony in the St Catherine Chapel of the Peter and Paul Cathedral. Nothing so clearly signalled the rupture with the Soviet past. From all the ends of the earth there arrived those members of the Romanov family whose parents and grandparents had escaped death by fleeing abroad. They had become resigned to permanent emigration. Their dynasty had been a term of abuse in the mouths of official spokesmen in the USSR. As the latest generations of Romanovs arrived in St Petersburg, the Russian public tried to discern any physical likeness between them and the ill-fated tsar and his close relatives. A particular favourite was Prince Michael of Kent, who bore a quite uncanny physical resemblance to Nicholas II at the time of death. (It is a resemblance, enhanced by hairstyling and beard-trim, that has helped his commercial interests in Russia.) Attention intensified with the arrival of the coffins at Pulkovo Airport after their transportation from Yekaterinburg. A stately motorcade was organised in the direction of St Petersburg on 16 July. The burial service began at noon on the following day. No Russian religious ceremony has attracted so much foreign attention.

The execution of the Romanovs had been shrouded in mystery. At the time, in 1918, the Soviet authorities denied that the Tsar's relatives had been killed. The question has never been definitively solved whether all the Romanov prisoners in Yekaterinburg really died – it is just possible that some escaped. More recently, furthermore, there has been controversy about the human remains found in the earth near Yekaterinburg. It has been questioned whether they are genuinely those of Nicholas II and his immediate family. The doubts were increased by the growing feelings, first among scientists that DNA tests were not completely reliable, and then among historians that perhaps the tests carried out on persons biologically related to the Romanovs may not in fact have had a totally clear-cut genealogy.[7] Alexi II, Patriarch of the Russian Orthodox Church, was pressed by some of his bishops to stand aside from the funeral since no one could be sure that the bone fragments, corroded by both acid and by time, were those of the Imperial family. Patriarch Alexi had already decided to canonise Nicholas II as a martyr of the Church at the hands of communism. But he rebutted Yeltsin's plea to him to conduct the funeral in the absence of incontrovertible identification of the physical remains. Yeltsin had to turn to a more compliant cleric in St Petersburg to carry out the ceremony.

Many Russian citizens were moved, but not to the point of condoling with the long-dead Romanovs. Nikolai II had been widely detested during his reign and his image was subjected to posthumous vilification by the communists through to 1991. Other tsars enjoy a higher degree of popular favour, especially Peter the Great. Yeltsin understood this. When asked to name the character from history he most admired, the Russian President took Peter as his hero.[8]

Stalin, while criticising all the tsars, acknowledged that Peter had overseen a spurt of industrial and cultural transformation and military success that could not be entirely outweighed by his oppression of the peasantry. Peter the Great, according to the communist history textbooks from the mid-1930s, was a national hero, a flawed hero but nevertheless a hero even for the USSR. Nearly every leading politician, both before and since Yeltsin's retirement, has expressed admiration for Peter. The Mayor of Moscow, Yuri Luzhkov, commissioned a statue from a friend of his schooldays Zurab Tsereteli. The favouring of Tsereteli is a bit of a scandal since his talent lies at the Walt Disney end of the artistic range. His statue of Peter the Great standing aboard a sailing ship did not even start out as the representation of the Russian tsar. Originally Tsereteli made it for an American patron who had wanted a 'Christopher Columbus' for the celebration of the quincentenary of his voyage to the Americas in 1492. But the commission was withdrawn and Tsereteli, finding himself with a massive piece of statuary, persuaded Mayor Luzhkov to install it in Moscow. The ship was of the early-modern period and had sails; the ship's captain was heroically large. The monument would therefore do just as well for a memorial to Peter the Great and the foundation of the Russian Imperial fleet. Thus it came about that the man sent by Ferdinand and Isabella to discover a westerly marine route to the Indies became the symbol of the naval power of eighteenth-century Russia.

Tsereteli's skills were used elsewhere in the capital. In the Sparrow Hills a massive tower was erected representing St George and the Dragon. Nearby there is a vast complex commemorating the victims of the Gulag in the form of hundreds of drooping figures. Alongside there is also a

building housing a panoramic staging of scenes from the Great Fatherland War.

It would be churlish to dwell on Tsereteli's inadequacies as a
sculptor; and at least he cheers up Muscovites, if only by stirring them
to laughter. Perhaps the greatest architectural success, then, is not a new
work of art at all but a restored ecclesiastical masterpiece. This is the
Church of Christ the Saviour. The symbolism at work here is intense.
The Church of Christ the Saviour was built to celebrate the defeat of the
Napoleonic invasion of 1812. It was knocked down late at night in 1934
as part of Stalin's preparation for a massive ensemble of avenues and
parks. At the centre there was meant to be a Palace of Soviets with a
huge statue of Lenin on top. The grandiose project came to nothing. Air
transport experts pointed out that the Lenin statue, while making the
Palace of Soviets the highest building in the world, would present a
hazard to aircraft approaching Moscow. It was left to Khrushchëv in the
1950s to use the site for an enormous public swimming pool. Even this
was problematic. No matter what the architects and surveyors contrived,
nothing stopped the leakage of murky water into the pool. People said
that God was punishing communist hubris. Funds were released by the
Russian government after 1991 to rebuild the Church of Christ the
Saviour in an attempt to seal the bonds of continuity with the regime of
the tsars.

Moscow's tsarist topography was never going to be brought back in
its entirety; but wherever possible, Mayor Luzhkov sanctioned restoration. The return of the old street names required a very large set
of alterations. Nowhere was this more evident than in the centre of
Moscow. To the north of the Kremlin stretched not Gorki Street but
Tver Street. The parade at the bottom of Gorki Street resumed its old
name, Okhotny Ryad (Hunters' Row). Streets bearing the names of
communist heroes were steadily changed to something else.

Russians are accustomed to such a process of redesignation. Lenin's
Sovnarkom regularly changed street names; and when Lenin died in
1924, it altered the name of Petrograd (which had been St Petersburg
until 1915) to Leningrad. Under Stalin in the 1930s a number of past and
existing heroes were consigned to the bench of knaves and street names
were altered again. When, one by one, Stalin's surviving confederates
displeased him, he not only arrested them but also redesignated the
places that had briefly carried their names. His successor Khrushchëv
did the same to Stalin. Thus Stalingrad became Volgograd; it is difficult
to exaggerate the egregiousness of the decision: Stalingrad was one of the

crucial symbols of the Great Fatherland War regardless of Stalin's abuses of power. Along with Stalingrad there disappeared Stalin Prizes, the Stalinist *Short Course* in the history of the Soviet communist party and Stalin Boulevards. When Gorbachëv came to power, the re-naming game began again. First he took away the place names that honoured Brezhnev. Then he moved against the communists who were exposed as having carried out terrible crimes in the early Soviet Union – and not just the Stalinists. Consequently there was nothing unusual in the changing of street names.

The pace of alteration was so fast that maps, however new, were useless. Strangers to Moscow in the mid-1990s had difficulty in getting guidance round the city. Streets, Metro stations and districts were being altered so often that the local residents themselves were bewildered. They coped only with the aid of glossaries appended to the back of atlases; and to some extent they welcomed the changes especially when they brought the comfort of restoring the names of the ancient past. A few novelties also appeared. Academician Sakharov Avenue was introduced in honour of the deceased campaigner for civil rights. But in general the priority was to restore the pre-communist past rather than to commemorate the recent victory over communism – and as yet Gorbachëv is not thought worthy of celebration.

Many people, indeed, sensed that minds were being manipulated by the politicians. It was the federal and local authorities that were deciding which names were appropriate. There was seldom any consultation. The poet Boris Slutsky noted the syndrome many years before 1991:

> But when any name was altered,
> it meant that someone had fallen.
> And a name in the least bit dodgy
> no school could possibly own
> With a roaring noise, like a landslide
> coming down a mountain valley,
> from the wall above the street corner
> the nameplate would tumble down.
>
> The nameplate would roar and tumble,
> but wouldn't soon be forgotten,
> although to forget it – and sharpish –
> is what the law told us we ought.
> In our memories, it went on ringing,
> an echo of ancient quarrels,

and who could ever be certain
that this was the end or not?[9]

The calendar of state celebrations was altered in the same imperious
fashion. Cunning was also used. Thus instead of blatantly suppressing
the October 1917 Revolution festival on 7 November, Yeltsin reduced
financial support for it and tried to neutralise it by giving it the new
name of Accord and Reconciliation Day.[10] May Day, too, was problematic for Yeltsin and his pro-capitalist ministers since the occasion was
associated with the labour movement. The authorities tried to divert the
festival away from politics by sanctioning the setting up of street markets.
But not everyone would comply. In Samara there was a particularly
chaotic situation:

> For us any holiday is an excuse for attracting the attention of people
> to our slogans and ideas. May Day is a very good holiday. Firstly
> it's a holiday for workers, secondly it's the traditional day of the
> witches' sabbath. There's a legend that the workers' holiday derived
> from nothing less than the celebration by dark forces.[11]

In fact the October 1917 Revolution festival also continues to be marked
by mass meetings and demonstrations held by the Communist Party of
the Russian Federation. (As far as I know, there has been no suggestion
that the Devil is involved in this instance.) The reform of the calendar
has been more complicated than the reformers expected.

Yeltsin also added new festivals: he definitely did not want to be seen
as a killjoy. In deference to Christianity he restored the Russian Orthodox
Church's Christmas Day, 7 January, as an official holiday – and he
himself sometimes attended services of worship on Easter Sunday. He
also introduced a celebration of Independence Day on 12 June.

His two prime commitments were to the 9 May commemoration
of the military victory in Europe in 1945 and to the 12 June festival of
Russian state independence. The first of these was already a highpoint of
the Soviet calendar. On that day there would always be a parade on Red
Square; tanks and missiles would be trundled over the vast cobbled area
in front of the Kremlin Wall while members of the Politburo looked
down from the top of the Lenin Mausoleum. Aeroplanes flew overhead.
The crowds were enormous. The USSR's triumph over Nazism was
celebrated not only by veterans but also by younger generations with a
gusto without parallel in the other countries of the Grand Alliance.
Every year the message was repeated on television and radio that the

USSR had broken the spine of the most powerful army ever to have attacked another European country. This tradition was strongly supported by the new administration after 1991, and President Yeltsin regularly gave a speech on the anniversary. It was not an uncomplicated task. The ceremonies of 9 May had traditionally involved the Soviet national anthem and the commemoration of the Red Army. Until 1988 even Gorbachëv had been politically unable to deny that Stalin had played a role of positive importance. Thereafter he tried to praise the Communist Party, the Red Army and the people of the Soviet Union while denouncing every aspect of Stalin's career.

The task for Yeltsin was trickier. He had come to power as an anti-communist and as an advocate of Russian interests. And yet it was undeniable that communists had fought against Hitler and that the other nations of the USSR as well as the Russians had made a decisive contribution. This had been the official version of history since 1945. Somehow Yeltsin had to Russify the commemoration. This he tried to do, to the accompaniment of a new flag and a new anthem, by stressing that the war had been won by the Russian people despite the murderous interference of Joseph Stalin. Yeltsin contrived to downplay the Soviet dimensions of the military triumph by simply ignoring it.[12]

In order to corroborate this new historical version he sanctioned what amounted to an official cult of Marshal Zhukov. He had already introduced an Order of Zhukov in 1994. The holders of this rare and coveted award for military valour in defence of the Russian Federation were given a badge in the shape of a cross and a medallion with a bust of Zhukov.[13] Newspapers and television devoted laudatory items to him in 1994–5. His crude manner with subordinates and his ruthless use of troops as cannon fodder were overlooked. What was stressed was his personal bravery in the battles of the war. He was also acclaimed for arguing about strategy with Stalin, who could have consigned him to the Gulag for his audacity. The 1945 newsreel of him riding across Red Square on a white horse at the head of the victory parade was shown frequently on TV, and the pathos of his subsequent demotion first by Stalin and again by Khrushchëv was highlighted. Zhukov the peasant lad. Zhukov the worthy successor to Mikhail Kutuzov, Napoleon's conqueror. Zhukov the defender of the armed forces against persecution by the communist security police. Zhukov the unrepentant pensioner who refused to bow his head before Brezhnev's Politburo. Zhukov the most Russian of Russians and the commander who was equal to the other military leaders of the Grand Alliance.

An equestrian statue of him was commissioned in 1994 and quickly produced. Yeltsin had intended to situate it on Red Square. His defence adviser Dmitri Volkogonov sensibly counselled him against this on the grounds that it would irreparably destroy 'a setting composed over centuries for Russia's most famous place'. (Volkogonov did not mention that the Lenin Mausoleum had already had such an effect.) Nor did Volkogonov see the point of introducing an Order of Zhukov when the country was trying to build a reputation for peacefulness in foreign policy.[14] He lost the argument on the Order but got his way with the Zhukov statue, which was erected more discreetly on the Manège below the north side of the Kremlin. It is in any case not a very impressive monument: Zhukov looks too youthful and carefree and his steed too much like a horse taking part in a dressage competition. The whole effect is bland. No sense of the Marshal's ferocity, cunning and endurance is conveyed. Neither Zhukov nor, for that matter, Stalin would have sanctioned such a monument.

Yet the cult has an echo in popular consciousness and Georgi Zhukov is likely to endure as an attractive figure for most citizens of the Russian Federation. The same is not true of the other festival given priority by President Yeltsin and his government: Independence Day on 12 June.

This was the date chosen to celebrate the state independence of the Russian Federation. An attempted deception was at work here: 12 June is really the anniversary of Yeltsin's election to the RSFSR Presidency in 1991. In both constitutional and practical terms Russia did not gain independence until New Year's Day 1992 even though Yeltsin had frequently claimed independent status for Russia in the previous year. The choice of date is politically motivated. The advantage of 12 June for Yeltsin was that this was a day of personal triumph, the day when 57 per cent of those who voted were on his side and against the candidate favoured by Mikhail Gorbachëv. In the USSR, Constitution Day had always been 5 December. By replacing the old Constitution Day with Independence Day in the Russian Federation, Yeltsin put himself forward as a kind of national liberator. Yet the festival resonated faintly in the minds of Russian citizens. While welcoming a day off work, they did not turn out joyously on the streets or do anything unusual in celebration even at home. Independence Day has turned out to be a damp squib. The point is that the USSR's disintegration was not widely approved by the electorate at the time or afterwards.[15]

Another attempt to bind people together in the new Russia has been the invention of awards and titles. The Order of Zhukov is one of these, but there are already dozens of others. Several of them simply replace their Soviet equivalents. For instance, the Order of Friendship – which is conferred on Russian citizens and foreigners for strengthening of international co-operation in science, culture, economy and peace – was introduced in 1994 as substitute for the USSR Order of the Friendship of Nations. Medals, too, have been struck. One of these, the Defender of Free Russia Medal, was introduced in 1992 for persons who had displayed valour in resisting the August 1991 *putsch*, particularly those who helped to defend the Russian White House. But yet others are really new versions of old medals. Under Stalin, pre-revolutionary Russian commanders were installed as heroes. The Suvorov Medal and the Ushakov Medal were named after two of the Russian Empire's most famous military leaders, the first being a general and the second an admiral. Thus Yeltsin contrived to maintain an honours system that, with just a few modifications, is reminiscent of what prevailed before 1991.

Titles, too, have undergone only slight adjustment. In politics the shift towards Western-style names had started before the fall of the Soviet Union, notably when Gorbachëv introduced the post of USSR President. Until then the holders of supreme political office had been Chairmen or General Secretaries. Gorbachëv's redesignation was welcomed by Yeltsin as well as by all the other heads of republics in the RSFSR. There was an epidemic of presidential inaugurations across the country. When Yeltsin became President of the RSFSR, moreover, he lobbied for Ruslan Khasbulatov to become Chairman of the Supreme Soviet in his place and for Khasbulatov to manage the business of the Supreme Soviet. The newspapers decided that Khasbulatov's title was too wordy. Instead they referred to him as the Speaker (*spiker* in Russian).

But this proved an Americanism too far. The Chairmen of the State Duma and the Council of the Federation have occasionally been called Speakers since the introduction of the new Constitution in December 1993, but this has been mainly a shorthand usage among foreigners. Yeltsin himself confirmed the policy of using honorific titles used in social and cultural affairs in the Soviet period. Stalin himself had developed the nomenclature. Among the most coveted titles had been People's Artist of the USSR. This was an award for those deemed the greatest novelists and poets of the day. The holders enjoyed privileges such as dachas, foreign travel and large pensions; and when a holder returned from a trip abroad, he did not need to queue with others at the passport control posts. Similarly prestigious and profitable was the title of Academician. Anyone elected to the USSR Academy of Sciences was allowed perks that were the envy of fellow scholars. An Academician had a chauffeur-driven car at his disposal around the clock and some of them used it even to do the shopping. Such was the prestige of the title that when the dissident Andrei Sakharov challenged the communist party leadership, his privileges were left untouched until the Politburo banished him to the closed city of Gorki in 1980.

The Soviet system of titles has been retained, and existing holders of USSR titles were redesignated with analogous titles for the Russian Federation. The privileges are diminished. People's Artists and Academicians no longer have large pensions or material perks as the state has run down its financial subsidies in general terms. But the prestige and hierarchy of the titles has been preserved. Just as once it was possible to become a Meritorious Scientist, a Culture Worker or even a Drainage Engineer of the USSR and to pin the appropriate badge on one's lapel, so now a similar badge can be worn by the holder in the Russian Federation. Only the wording of the badges have altered.

Changes in the modes of address in daily life have also changed less than was originally expected. In the Soviet Union, everyone could be addressed in the same way, at least from 1936 when Stalin's Constitution stipulated that the old class and social discriminations should be abandoned. Thereafter each Soviet citizen – male or female, young or old, Russian or otherwise – was a 'comrade'. If in doubt, everyone referred to strangers as such. Stalin referred to his subordinates in these terms, and these subordinates, even more strikingly, referred to him – who could easily have thrown any one of them into prison and prescribed whatever torments he fancied – as 'Comrade Stalin'. This nomenclature was among the reasons why visitors to the USSR were fooled into thinking that the USSR was a genuinely egalitarian state order. But with the demise of the USSR, what was to become of comrades? Officials no longer wanted to use the word. But custom had so imprinted it in the Russian vocabulary that few Russians, whether they are politicians or ordinary citizens, have entirely eliminated it from their speech. It crops up when the speakers least expect it. It has entered popular consciousness and probably will take years to fade, if indeed it ever does.

The problem is partly that no alternative term of relationship is widely congenial. 'I'd like to call the beggars mister,' someone scoffed, 'but it doesn't sound very comradely.'[16] On buses and trains there are warnings against taking a ride without buying a ticket. The message is addressed, however, to 'citizens', and this is one way to replace the use of 'comrades'. As yet 'ladies and gentlemen' is a phrase that is used only on those special occasions when important foreign guests are present. But 'citizens' does not roll comfortably off the tongue. It was often the term used in the Soviet years when reference was made to persons who were not regarded as proper comrades, and it retains a pejorative connotation. The politicians prefer to avoid embarrassment altogether by opening speeches with a reference to fellow Russians (*rossiyane*). In short, there is no congenial term that offers more than formal respect – and Russians are simply not accustomed to this.

And so there has been a settling back into compromise. Putin set the pace. He had never been happy with the outright rejection of the Soviet past. Yeltsin had tried to break the link with the heritage of communism; and whenever he relented, he kept the communist ingredients to a minimum. Putin was different. While agreeing that the new Russia should accept continuity with the Russia of the tsars, he also aimed to restore a linkage with the USSR. On becoming President, Putin put this into effect. The immediate stimulus was a complaint from the Russian members of the Sydney Olympics squad. Some of these argued that their athletic performance had been undermined by the absence of a rousing anthem. Even for those (like myself) who feel this was unfair to Glinka's melody, the fact remained that the melody had no agreed set of words and that the USSR anthem retained huge popular affection in Russia even amongst the younger generation. In October 2000 Putin announced the need for a definitive decision on state symbolism. His own stated preference was to keep the tricolour as the flag and the double-headed eagle as the emblem, but to bring back the USSR anthem with suitably revised words. He also proposed that the Red Army should be given back its red flag with a golden star.

Unlike Yeltsin, Putin encouraged public debate, and several individuals immediately criticised his plans. Mstislav Rostropovich, arguing that the USSR anthem was a symbol for totalitarianism, announced that he would refuse to stand whenever the revised USSR anthem was performed. In the State Duma, Grigori Yavlinski was equally critical. Yeltsin, too, spoke out against the idea.[17] As expected, however, the State Council supported Putin as did the State Duma and the Council of the Federation. Putin had already encouraged the co-writer of the original words of the USSR anthem – the octogenarian Sergei Mikhalkov – to offer a fresh version. Mikhalkov's first verbal draft was rejected as inadequate. But his second managed to avoid so much disfavour. Its opening verse runs as follows:

> Russia, our sacred land of might,
> Russia, our beloved country,
> Your powerful will and your great glory
> Are your possession for all time.[18]

Mikhalkov, despite his Stalinist past, now even included a reference to the deity. At last the debate was over. Putin's proposal was signed into decree on 3 January 2001 and, apart from a brief spate of objections from retired President Yeltsin, the question of state symbolism was laid to rest.[19]

It has been a trying experience for Russian Presidents and their governments. They have attempted to provide Russians with a new way of feeling about their country. Flags, heraldry and anthem have been changed and then changed again. Street names, even the names of cities and republics, have gone and been replaced. The calendar of holidays and celebration is transformed. Official badges and honours have been invented. The tsar has been buried in a Christian ceremony.

Unfortunately the rulers came to the task without prior preparation. Yeltsin and his team took the definitive political decision to break up the USSR only in late 1991. Their attempt to re-create a sense of statehood and nationhood was a rushed one. Few of them had specialist knowledge of the theoretical literature.[20] They were unconcerned about this. They lived in a country where the manipulation of national identity was part and parcel of rulership. Lenin, by spreading doctrines of global socialist revolution, aspired to the fusion of all nationhoods into a single human identity. In this negative fashion he strove to affect the way in which the Russians – as well as the other peoples – thought of themselves. Stalin from the mid-1930s invented a version of Russian national identity. Pride in Russia as well as in the USSR was promoted. Simultaneously Stalin restricted the expression of nationhood among the non-Russians. In subsequent decades the communist leadership reconsidered the framework for the official blend of Marxist-Leninist doctrine and Russian nationhood – and the various intellectual and political groupings outside the party inserted their different ideas into the discussion. Under Gorbachëv there was vibrant debate on what it was to be a Russian and what needed to be done to give the Russians the life they deserved. Yeltsin took up the matter with similar confidence.

But his symbols for Russian statehood and nationhood were imposed without consultation and the old ones were brusquely tossed aside. It was a hamfisted process. Offence was given to national nostalgia, especially in the matter of the anthem. Yeltsin failed to move with the grain of popular feelings. Putin learned from this mistake. His restoration of respect for some aspects of the Soviet historical experience was widely acclaimed – and his willingness to hold a public debate was welcomed. But there remain doubts about the rest of the symbolism. Russians are still perplexed about the events of 1991 and about the political and economic order that supplanted Soviet communism. It will be years before their loyalties can be counted upon as their rulers would like.

14. UNDERSTATING THE CASE

You can't proclaim principles of open politics and simultaneously protect the authorities from the presence of
journalists.

Responsibility for the impasse does not lie solely with Presidents Yeltsin
and Putin and their governments. Other bodies might have been
expected to deepen the process of reform and make it more attractive to
the rest of society. Among these were the religious, military, academic
and media bodies. In the communist decades they had been kept under
the party's heel, and had had to spread whatever message was demanded
by the authorities. Each of them contained individuals annoyed and
frustrated by such an environment. It seemed reasonable to anticipate
that support for a radical reform agenda would be widespread and strong
among them. This expectation has proved rather illusory.

The state authorities were quick to mend relations with the Russian
Orthodox Church, and Patriarch Alexi II, appointed in June 1990,
relished the opportunity. For centuries – ever since the abolition of the
Patriarchate by Peter the Great in 1721, the Orthodox Church had been
subject to strict state control. The tsars appointed a lay Over-Procurator
to govern the Church; the communist leaders did the same through a
Council of Religious Affairs. The Patriarchate had been re-established in
1917 only to be put into abeyance at Patriarch Tikhon's death in 1925.
Although Stalin had permitted the appointment of Patriarch Sergei in
1943, the Orthodox Church remained servile to the communist regime.
Only with Gorbachëv's *perestroika* did a different relationship emerge.
Benefiting from the religious freedom, priests and bishops called openly
for a Christian renaissance in Russia. Inexpensive copies of the Bible,
which had been printed in only small editions in previous years,
appeared on bookstalls in hundreds of thousands of copies. Cathedrals

and monasteries attracted inquisitive Russian youths. Old ladies on Red Square prayed for the health of Mikhail Gorbachëv who had broken the fetters on the Church. Orthodox believers could practise the faith without fear a few years before the USSR's demise.

With Gorbachëv's consent, 1988 had been designated as the millennial anniversary of Russia's conversion to Christianity. He himself was an avowed atheist. On coming to power, however, he showed respect for religion. By 1990, he was admitting that the world's religions embodied philosophical values that contemporary communism should incorporate.[2]

Patriarch Alexi pushed himself forward in August 1991 during the attempted coup d'état against Gorbachëv, offering the Church as a mediator and urging the need for everyone to avoid violence. The same happened in October 1993 when violence broke out between Yeltsin and the Supreme Soviet. Again the Patriarch called for a peaceful resolution of the emergency, and he entered the White House to plead with Alexander Rutskoi to come to terms with Yeltsin. Alexi and Yeltsin got on well at the personal level[3] and reached a working compromise on reform. Yeltsin restored the surviving Church buildings to the Patriarch's control while Alexei for his part refrained from demanding the restitution of the lands owned by the Russian Orthodox Church before Lenin expropriated them in October 1917.[4] Unlike Gorbachëv, Yeltsin declined to call himself an atheist. He attended church services and liked to be seen in the company of the Patriarch. He was proud he had been baptised as a baby.[5] Yet Alexi's support for Yeltsin was not total. It was a matter of particular annoyance to the President that the Patriarch refused to attend the funeral service for the Imperial family on 17 July 1998.[6]

The days were over when the Church dreaded giving the smallest offence to ruling circles and the spat shows a definite confidence on the part of the Church leaders. In summer 2000, at the start of Putin's Presidency, the Church at last published its 'Social Doctrine'. The document contained more than a trace of monarchist ideas – not a tendency that head of state Putin was likely to welcome. The absence of an unequivocal endorsement of electoral politics was another reason for official concern.[7]

Nevertheless the Church cannot afford to be complacent. Priests cannot legally teach the Christian gospel in normal schooltime (although they have secured TV airtime for both Sunday services and phone-in programmes involving the clergy). And there is surely no more imaginative instrument of spreading Orthodox doctrines than the Church-funded train which left for a tour of the Russian North in October 2000. The diesel engine and its carriages were reconstructed to carry a beautiful replica of a church building. The gold leaf alone cost over US$30,000. The train had stained-glass windows and one carriage was turned into a miniature monastery with twenty travelling monks. First attempted by the Orthodox Church in the reign of Nicholas II, the use of the railway as an instrument of propaganda was copied in the Civil War by the communist authorities with the famous Trotski Train (which, of course, spread atheistic as well as political ideas). Patriarch Alexi had high hopes for the new venture. Accompanied by the Minister for Railways, he sprinkled consecrated water on the train on the day of its first trip.[8]

A Russian opinion poll in late 2000 indicated that 39 per cent of people felt they could trust the Russian Orthodox Church; no other institution, apart from the army with 35 per cent, came near to this.[9] But neither body – Church or army – has a majority on its side. A residual distrust is widespread. Dissident priests in the Brezhnev years felt let down and manipulated by the hierarchy of bishops. The Patriarchate remained silent when Father Gleb Yakunin was arrested and dispatched to the Gulag in 1979. Alexander Solzhenitsyn added to the list of charges. The Church spoke up for Soviet foreign policy. Bishops travelled to the West claiming that religious freedom was substantial in the Soviet Union. Patriarch Alexi himself has a murky past. As Bishop of Estonia, he wrote secret reports for the KGB and was a regular informer. Dozens of bishops did the same and yet they still hold their bishoprics. The only changes in the Church hierarchy have merely been the result of the death of incumbents. There has been no removal of the informers. Such a religious leadership, argued Solzhenitsyn, has betrayed its vocation; and when he returned from emigration, he did not rush to be seen in the company of Russian Orthodox Church leaders.

The Russian army too has had problems with its reputation. Until the USSR's invasion of Afghanistan the country's armed forces benefited from the popular memory of the Soviet victory in the Second World War; and trust in the army continues to exist in the younger generation as well as among the veterans.[10] But increasingly the army has let people see how divided and chaotic it had become from the late 1980s. Under Gorbachëv, several high-ranking officers had opposed his reforms and demanded the retention of the USSR in its pre-1985 form. While the August 1991 *putsch* was going on, however, several leading commanders gave support to Yeltsin. But others again were unsure whether the armed forces should be drawn into struggles among politicians; commanders such as Pavel Grachëv and Alexander Lebed, despite their eventual declaration of support for Yeltsin, had vacillated at times. And between these poles there were plenty of officers who disliked any involvement in public affairs. They wanted armed forces that were well trained and well equipped; their priority was the defence of the country, whether it was the USSR, the Russian Federation or even the Commonwealth of Independent States.

Unfortunately the state budget steadily reduced the resources available to the Russian army and, with thousands of troops still living in appalling conditions after their withdrawal from the German Democratic Republic, the discontent was extreme. Pavel Grachëv, made Minister of Defence as a reward for coming over – rather cautiously – to Yeltsin in August 1991, declared the need for a radical reform of the armed forces. Yeltsin's bargaining position seemed to weaken when he had to call on Grachëv's troops to storm the White House in 1993.

But the Russian army squandered its popularity. When the war against Chechnya was launched in December 1994, there was expectation that military formations that had confronted the Americans in divided Germany would easily crush the Chechen 'bandits'. The subsequent military impasse was humiliating. Already before the war, army and navy officers had taken to arriving at work in civilian overcoats. Their prestige had been battered by the revelations of *perestroika*. It had been admitted that a shambles had engulfed the Soviet invasion of Afghanistan in 1979. Another shock came with accounts of the nuclear radiation released into the atmosphere by the H-bomb tests since the 1950s. The price of the USSR's emergence as a global power began to be understood. Magazines such as *Moscow News* and *Ogonëk* had also exposed the appalling conditions in which the Soviet army conscripts served. Physical bullying was normal. Dangerous rites of 'initiation' were performed upon them by the older soldiers and NCOs, and the officers did nothing to prevent this. The rate of suicides was grievous. Often there was an ethnic element to the persecution; young men from Central Asia and the Caucasus were brutally treated. But no one had a decent time in the armed forces. The barbarity was pervasive.[11]

Organisations of mothers protested to the late Soviet regime about the sending of their boys to Afghanistan, and have been active in complaining about the war in Chechnya. None of these women has become famous; they are genuine heroines none the less. The continuing disgrace is the lack of positive response in the Ministry of Defence and the General Staff. The authorities have spoken about the need for reform in the armed forces and for a smaller and more efficient fighting force, but concrete specific proposals have been few. At the same time there have been scandals. Pavel Grachëv was said to be implicated in illegal sales of military equipment to foreign buyers. Troops in Chechnya were definitely selling their weapons, often even to Chechen rebels. Journalists who tried to expose the scams put their own lives in jeopardy. One of them, Dmitri Kholodov, perished at the hands of a gunman – and suspicion turned in the direction of Grachëv, whose business dealings he had been uncovering. It is hardly surprising that the Russian army lacks the prestige which might rally opinion around the national project of Yeltsin and Putin.

On Victory Day, 9 May, the commemoration remains solemn. Loyal military men try to link the feats of the 'Great Patriotic War' with the later wars fought by Soviet and Russian soldiers. In the magazine *Soldat udachi* ('Soldier of Fortune'), the editor Dmitri Shiryaev wrote:

> As regards myself personally, I send congratulations on the forth-coming Victory Day to those of my fighting comrades with whom I spent time at the crucial spot of the Ishcherskaya settlement and in the October District of Grozny. I remember the commander and still have the notebook which he gave me as a present. I remember the jovial Staff Leader Mikhail, Captains Sergei and Yevgeni as well as Major Alexander who sang wonderful songs to guitar accompaniment while bandits' grenade-launchers were banging. And I wish them luck in finishing off the Chechnya affair and returning unharmed to their families.[12]

But this is a sentiment increasingly rare among Russians. They admire the blood, sweat and tears of 1941–5. They profess respect for the Russian army as the protector of national interests; but the intensity of devotion has gone, perhaps for ever.

Another institution that used to enjoy much popular respect is the Academy of Sciences. Under the tsars it enjoyed a degree of autonomy recognised as being necessary if the Russian Empire wished to produce the scholars in the sciences, arts and pedagogy that its status as a great power required. Not that Academicians were likely to be revolutionaries; they acceded to the authority of state even when they objected to the regime and its policies.

The result was that the communists, when they took power in 1917, were suspicious of the Academy. But Lenin and Stalin also wanted to promote scholarship. As would-be industrialisers they understood the importance of the universities. But how to control the Academy? Their solution was to set up rival institutions such as the Institute of Red Professors. They also arrested those academicians whom they deemed politically uncongenial. Only extraordinary individuals such as the world-renowned psychologist Ivan Pavlov dared to complain of these persecutions to the Politburo. But the communist regime itself, after Stalin's death, recognised that the repression had been taken too far. Steadily they allowed the Academy of Sciences of the USSR a certain freedom. When the physicist Andrei Sakharov started to object to Soviet nuclear policy and, in due course, to the political structure of the USSR, he was deprived of many privileges but was never sacked from the Academy. In 1982 he was exiled to the city of Gorki while retaining his status as an Academician. Through to the end of the USSR, the members of the Academy wore a special badge, passed through customs at borders by the diplomatic channel, received generous facilities for research and had a twenty-four-hour-a-day chauffeur service at their disposal.

Economic reform was catastrophic for the Academy. Its members had coped nonchalantly with the Soviet Union's abolition by simply declaring members of the Academy of Sciences of the USSR to be automatic members of the Academy of Sciences of the RSFSR (and then of the Russian Federation) if they lived in Russia. They also announced their commitment to the new order. In most cases this required no reorganisation. The exceptions were those institutes of the Academy that had been closely linked to the political ideology of Marxism-Leninism. Within the Institute of History, for example, one of the major departments was dedicated to the 'History of the Communist Party of the Soviet Union'. Such a department was no longer appropriate and several new departments were established to indicate the Institute's adherence to decommunisation.

Similar alterations happened elsewhere in the scholarly community. Already under Gorbachëv the Central Party Archive, which had possession of the holdings of communist party records going back to Lenin, had been redesignated as the Institute of the History and Theory of Socialism. But this did not suit the regime of Boris Yeltsin and the archive and library was re-named as the Russian Centre for the Conservation and Study of Documents of Contemporary History (and thereafter as the Russian State Archive for Socio-Political History). At the same time there was change in the universities. Yuri Afanasev, the former radical critic of Gorbachëv, founded the University of Humanitarian

Sciences and became its first rector. Also in Moscow a European University was created. In other major cities of the Russian Federation – at least wherever the finances could be assembled – scholars from the old state universities strove to set up private institutions of tertiary education. As often as not they were based in buildings that had previously housed scholarly bodies of the USSR. Under pressure of circumstances, then, the higher echelons of national education reformed themselves. In 1992, at the inception of the new Russian order, hopes were high among scholars.

But the Academy of Sciences and the broader network of universities did not have the access to citizens that had recently been normal. Under communism, public pronouncements by a novelist or a scientist were made with respect to the state authorities. With decommunisation, many scholars assumed that their impact on popular opinion would increase. This has not occurred. Freedom of scholarly expression is one thing, but it is a freedom that depends heavily upon ability to earn a salary. University finance is in crisis. Lecturers are grievously under-funded. Moonlighting is a pervasive phenomenon and as the older scholars retire, there is no longer a queue of younger ones waiting to replace them.

It is bad enough in Moscow, where – for example – the Director of the former Central Party Archive had to ration the use of electricity and get the agreement of his staff to work (and therefore get paid for) fewer days per week. Things are still worse, much, much worse in the provinces. In Siberia, where the city of Akademgorodok began to be built in the late 1950s, there were plenty of impoverished scientists by the 1990s. The decline from optimism and prestige had been abrupt. Akademgorodok had been a pet scheme of Nikita Khrushchëv. Appealing to the pioneering spirit of the Russians, he had situated this city of science nearly 1,800 miles from Moscow by the river Ob. Finance had been directed to research into subjects of global importance. Institutes had proliferated. Not only nuclear physics and mathematics but also geology, automation and forestry were given the state's support and the directors of the investigative teams were allowed to get on with their work with the minimum of interference. Akademgorodok was associated with initiative and hope, and even though its funds were restricted after Khrushchëv's fall, the dream remained. To the end of the USSR tens of thousands of scientists, administrators and their families constituted a proud part of its population.

Over the years much important scientific work originated in Aka-demgorodok. Alongside discoveries in the natural sciences there were

several ideas that had a political connotation. Akademgorodok research-
ers were among the supporters of the project to turn the great rivers of
Siberia – the Ob and the Yenisei – southwards. Instead of flowing into
the Arctic Ocean they were to be re-directed towards Central Asia.
Another project supported by the most powerful of the Akademgorodok
leaders, was to warm up the Siberian permafrost and alter the regional
climate. Such ideas, if ever they had been realised, would have created
havoc with the natural environment not only in Siberia and the adjacent
countries but indeed across the Eurasian landmass and beyond. Thinking
big, the scientists did not always produce sensible projects (and Valentin
Rasputin and nationalist *littérateurs* had to exert their cultural and moral
authority in the Gorbachëv years to obtain the abandonment of the two
projects).[13] Other Siberian scholars, especially those based at the nearby
city of Novosibirsk, had a more benign effect on the policy-makers.
Chief among these was Tatyana Zaslavskaya, who in the early 1980s
produced a radical critique of the problems of the Soviet political and
economic order. Zaslavskaya, a sociologist, argued that for decades
official communist policies had ignored 'the human factor' in society. It
was partly under her influence that Gorbachëv initiated his reforms on
acceding to power in 1985.[14]

The influence of Akademgorodok and Novosibirsk on the Kremlin
for good or evil has faded. The condition of the institutes is pitiful. One
of the erstwhile academic barons of the area put the matter succinctly:

> I don't know what policy drives our government, or even if it has
> one! Science is now as cut off from the state as the Church used to
> be. As far as I can see, everything's run by the mafia! . . . The future?
> When we have a government that realises no country can exist
> without science, Akademgorodok will flourish again.'[15]

It is a painful situation. There are many opportunities for Church,
army and Academy to address 'the people' in today's Russia. They know
what they want. Their emotions are different: the Church is confident,
the army is angry and the Academy is demoralised. Their leaders appear
on television. They say what is troubling them and they make every
possible appeal to the citizens of the Russian Federation. Yet somehow
they do not manage to evoke popular sympathy. Freed from the shackles
of the communist regime, they remain weakened by their past subordination. They were not just prisoners of communism. They were also its
defenders. They were outside as well as inside the prison and stoutly
endorsed the policies of successive General Secretaries. They allowed

themselves to be appointed to the various ceremonial offices of state. They belonged to the Soviet Peace Committee. They enjoyed privileges, to a greater or lesser extent. They were members of the USSR's establishment, subordinate members but members nevertheless. It is hardly surprising that Russian citizens have declined to accord them the implicit confidence they wish to receive.

Meanwhile, other religious leaders have become prominent. Especially impressive are the Chief Rabbi of Moscow and the Supreme Mufti for Russia and the European countries of the Commonwealth of Independent States. Both have benefited from the religious tolerance accorded since the late 1980s. Rabbi Pinchas Goldschmidt says that his job is not only to rally the Jewish faithful to the synagogues but also to teach uninformed Jews about the rudimentary beliefs of the Torah. He has the advantage of coming from abroad. Rabbi Goldschmidt gets financial support in the West for the building of synagogues and the propagation of the Jewish faith. He is also enterprising in his search for assistance in Russia. Several prominent businessmen – Boris Berezovski, Vladimir Gusinski and Roman Abramovich – are of Jewish parentage. They have not advertised this: each is both secular and Russified. But the Chief Rabbi argues that history teaches that all Jews, however secular, ought to support organisations for their defence in an emergency. He persuaded Gusinski to act as the unofficial lay leader of Jews in Russia. He was unsuccessful with Berezovski, who declared his allegiance to the Russian Orthodox Church; and it was in any case unrealistic to expect Berezovski and Gusinski, bitter rivals, to work alongside each other.

Gusinski himself was a victim of Putin in 2000.[16] But Rabbi Goldschmidt has been indefatigable and raised sufficient funds to have a synagogue built on Poklonnaya Gora where Mayor Yuri Luzhkov has already erected several monuments and places of worship commemorating the end of communism in Russia. Rabbi Goldschmidt admits that few Jews will attend that particular synagogue. Its real use will be to act as a rallying symbol for Judaism.[17] The point for him is to seek a secure and congenial base for the propagation of his ancestral faith in Russia and the rest of the CIS. He is grateful to the state authorities for providing legal safeguards even though problems of popular anti-semitism and of its exploitation by politicians persist. He has needed to build a Jewish religious community virtually from scratch in many places. The books, buildings and even the culinary regulations of Judaism were unknown to most citizens who identified themselves as Jewish in their passports. Those Jews wishing to live a traditional life inside their faith had tended, whenever Brezhnev allowed them and especially after Gorbachëv abandoned controls over emigration, to leave for Israel. This exodus has continued. Perhaps a million of them have not waited around in Russia and Ukraine to discover whether the Chief Rabbi's opinion is realistic, and have emigrated.[18]

The Chief Rabbi's attitude is shared by the Supreme Mufti, Talgat Tadjuddin. His wish is to get Moslems the maximum freedom of worship and organisation; and when asked about Shariat Law, he insists that any campaign for its introduction in the Russian Federation would cause problems for Islam. The Chechen War in 1994 was a disaster for his followers. He deplored the separatist struggle of Djokar Dudaev and the Islamisation of public law in that republic. He also spoke out against interference by foreign Islamic states in the struggles of Moslems in the Russian Federation. Resplendent in his green ceremonial robes, glittering jewellery and high-decked headwear, the Supreme Mufti expresses the wish for continued religious tolerance and travels the country – even as far as Norilsk in eastern Siberia – to attend to the needs of fellow believers. He and his fellow mullahs have sometimes been given the opportunity to explain their faith on television. In the mid-1990s a Saturday morning programme was devoted to exactly this purpose. It is as if the Russian state authorities and the media establishment think that any religion whatever is better than no religion at all.

The claims of Judaism and Islam are made upon a minority of citizens of the Russian Federation. Most ethnic Russians do not turn to them. Such religion as attracts them is usually Christian. American and European proselytisers descended upon Russia in the early 1990s. Clandestine denominations of Christianity re-emerged. The Russian Orthodox Church was far from pleased about this. As before 1917, it strove to limit the competition from rival forms of Christianity. By and large the state acceded to its pleas. In 1997 the State Duma passed a Law on Freedom of Conscience and Religious Organisations, which prevented foreign-based Churches from operating on Russian soil. But this privilege has not yet led to a mass conversion of Russians to the faith of their ancestors. The Orthodox Church remains the object of some suspicion.

Yet it is far from clear that any other public organisation inspires greater trust. Most television and radio stations were owned by the great economic barons who typically have interests in the energy sector, manufacturing and the press. This in itself places limits on the extent of criticism of the government. Few barons want to offend President and Prime Minister. Vladimir Gusinski was an exception. His television station NTV criticised aspects of the 1994–6 Chechen War; it also sponsored the satirical puppet show *Kukly*, which subjected both Yeltsin and Putin to hilarious abuse. But in the end Gusinski was reined back. Gusinski had over-extended his business operation and was hugely in debt to Gazprom, a company with close links to the government.[19] When the second war in Chechnya began in 1999, NTV was successfully put under financial pressure to avoid criticism of the military campaign.[20] But the *Kukly* show continued to be broadcast and Gusinski rejected demands for its withdrawal. He underestimated the danger he was in. A police raid was ordered on the offices of the Media-Most company, which was largely owned by Gusinski, on the grounds that it had been engaged in phone-tapping. Although Putin claimed to have had nothing to do with the raid, he was not widely believed. The net was closing on Gusinski.

What happened to NTV was no minor matter. Russian journalists were given to understand that, whatever Gusinski's misdemeanours might have been, Putin wished to restrict freedom of expression. Seemingly no TV or radio station could expect to be able to renew its licence unless Putin was satisfied it was loyal to the main line of his domestic and foreign policies.

But Gusinski held out against Putin. It had become known that Putin was personally offended by the sinister, lugubrious puppet which represented him; and on 28 May 2000 it seemed that the scriptwriter Viktor Shenderovich had agreed to the request to stop ridiculing the President. The offending puppet failed to appear for the first time in months. According to the NTV announcer, this was at the behest of the Kremlin. Otherwise, he explained, the show would not be left 'in peace'. Avoiding Putin, the scriptwriters made Alexander Voloshin, chief of the Presidential Administration, the main character. The stage-set was a desert. The theme was the wandering of the Israelites, and Voloshin appeared as Moses brandishing the tablets of the Ten Commandments given to him by the invisible 'God'. Obviously 'God' was meant to be Putin: Shenderovich was still up to his playful tricks. Among the commandments enunciated by the Voloshin puppet was: 'Thou shalt not kill (except persons of the Caucasian nationalities).' Another stated: 'Thou shalt not steal.'[21] When the Voloshin puppet said this, there was panic among the state functionaries who were listening to him and who had evidently lined their own pockets in service of the state. *Kukly* remained a biting satire.[22]

The show occasionally strayed over the boundary of social taste acceptable in most contemporary countries. In one memorable perform-ance the Putin puppet was found in a brothel inspecting a line of unbecoming whores before making a choice for the night. The whores were all recognisable as politicians seeking office under the new Russian President.

Unsurprisingly, the pursuit of Gusinski continued. On 13 December 2000 he was arrested on charges of corruption. His financial assets were threatened before the police reluctantly released him in reaction to criticism at home and abroad. Gusinski fled abroad, but his troubles were not over. In April 2001 his creditors, including Gazprom, called in the debt. Gusinski could not pay. The Gazprom media manager, Alfred Kokh, would accept no further postponement and, accompanied by the police, took over the ownership and running of NTV. For some days there were protests by the station's employees and the following message appeared constantly on the screen: 'NTV journalists protest against the TV company's seizure'.[23] Yabloko leader Grigori Yavlinski spoke at a mass protest meeting and his personal popularity rose for a while.[24] But it was not a clear-cut matter. For Kokh had a point when he claimed that Gusinski had failed to pay his way.[25] But it was also hard to believe that Gusinski had been given much chance to put his financial affairs in order. In any case, Putin had won the contest. Furthermore, Gusinski's demise had served the larger purpose of indicating to the privately owned media at the national level that any ridiculing of the President would incur retaliation.

Yet this tension needs to be put into perspective. There was much agreement between the government and the privately owned media. No TV station owner advocated a return to communism. Indeed all of them in general terms supported the political and economic changes of 1991–2; and Gusinski, who until 2000 had personally benefited from the corrupt form of capitalism constructed in Russia, had never called for a reversion to the fine reform objectives announced by Yeltsin in 1992. Gusinski, too, had connived in the corruption of Russian public life.

The hope survived that newspapers would continue to inform and enliven the discussion of the great questions of the day in a responsible fashion. But this, too, was only partially achieved. At the far ends of the political spectrum, Left and Right, there appeared publications that were disgraceful by almost any standards of reportage. A prime example was the newspaper *Den'* ('Day'). Its chief editor was none other than Alexander Prokhanov, one of the signatories of the 'Word to the People' in July 1991 which had provided the ideological rationale for the coup attempted against Mikhail Gorbachëv in August. After the collapse of the USSR, Prokhanov's language became ever more demagogic. *Den*"s intemperance was expressed in virulent anti-Semitism and eventually, in the political emergency of September 1993, the government closed it down. But it re-emerged within weeks with the same format under a different name: *Zavtra* ('Tomorrow'). Israel, Jews, Freemasons, the USA and the 'traitorous' political 'gangs' of Gorbachëv and Yeltsin were regularly castigated. Yeltsin, together with economic reformer Gaidar, was accused of organising a Jewish conspiracy against the Russian people. There was often a homophobic innuendo. For example, the newspaper claimed that 'Gaidar plucks his eyebrows and uses lipstick'.[26]

Several other newspapers were not much cleaner. The publications of Vladimir Zhirinovski's Liberal-Democratic Party used the same rhetoric of political betrayal and dirty sexuality – and the fact that Zhirinovski, who once gave an interview to the American soft-porn magazine *Playboy*, boasts of his heterosexual prowess adds to the effect. The novelty of the Liberal-Democratic Party's reportage lies in the emphasis on astrology. Zhirinovski insists that the signs of the zodiac as well as ordinary factual reports are essential for the understanding of contemporary Russian politics. He describes himself as occupying a position to the right of the political centre. To Zhirinovski's own right, far out on the outermost extreme, lay the Russian National Movement of Alexander Barkashov. Not to put too fine a point on it, Barkashov is a fascist. His opinions about the Russian nation are unequivocally racist and, from a constitutional standpoint, ought to see him arrested. Barkashov's newspapers, like those of Zhirinovski, use the language of the gutter.

Thankfully such newspapers are not the most widely sold in the Russian Federation. After 1991, many editors tried hard to sustain a campaign of measured, informed and fair reportage. Steadily through the Gorbachëv years the press had been allowed to emancipate itself from the communist insistence on purveying a uniform orthodoxy of opinion. There had been interruptions to the process. In May 1989 Gorbachëv had called the main editors to his office in the Kremlin in order to complain about their treatment of him. He threatened to have Vladislav Starkov sacked from *Argumenty i fakty* ('Arguments and Facts') for suggesting, on the basis of readers' letters, that Gorbachëv's popularity had plummeted. But Gorbachëv stepped back from such action and the freedom of the press continued to be expanded.[27] Under Yeltsin it grew still wider even though both he and his ministers sometimes worried lest things were getting out of hand. Measures were contemplated to introduce a control over the moral content of publications. This was clearly a menace to press freedom that potentially might be applied in political matters unrelated to morality. In the event Yeltsin restrained himself and the newspapers were allowed to develop themselves without governmental interference.

Even so, the independence of journalists was probably greater in the last years of Gorbachëv than under Yeltsin and Putin. One problem is the pattern of newspaper ownership. Enormously wealthy businessmen such as Boris Berezovski and Vladimir Gusinski, having made their fortunes in the financial and energy-export sectors of the economy, bought up Moscow dailies and influenced their contents. Opinions at variance with the interests of the owners were cut out. Another difficulty is of a technical nature. The manufacturers of paper pulp have acceded to political pressures to supply those newspapers which have been friendly to the government. Few 'national' newspapers in any case find it easy to maintain a high circulation across the entire country.

The rising cost of newspapers has also led to a fall in sales at a time when most people have to be careful with every ruble. Privatisation of the press has put an end to the huge official subsidies of the Soviet period. But even persons who pay their annual subscription of their favourite newspaper or who go out to buy their copy on a daily basis can no longer depend on a regular service. A recent letter to *Dochki-Materi* illustrates this:

> I very much like your newspaper but was compelled to stop subscribing this year. It wasn't even because it doubled in price (I was willing to reconcile myself to this) but because newspapers are being thieved from post-boxes in our district. Why should I have to pay for someone else's pleasure out of my own pocket? So I started buying *Dochki-Materi* from the kiosk. But since the beginning of March it's simply not been available. What's happened? And how can I get hold of it?[28]

Gone are days when newspapers such as *Pravda*, *Izvestiya* and *Argumenty i fakty* were sold in tens of millions of copies every issue and rivalled the politicians in the formation of public opinion.

Popular consciousness is therefore influenced in a changing fashion. At crucial moments in the past decade it would seem that TV programmes have had the greatest influence. Nothing else – religious organisations, armed forces, academy institutes, radio or newspapers – comes near to the power of television. But a caveat needs to be entered.

This is that Russians, according to most survey polls, watch TV mainly for entertainment and cultural self-enhancement; and the daily news bulletins are treated with a considerable amount of discrimination. This is the consequence of decades of communist rule. Soviet citizens, if they wished to understand what was going on politically, knew that they had to take any official statement with a pinch of salt. The trick had been to read *Pravda* while sifting out the propaganda from the grains of possible truth. Almost regardless of educational background, people learned how to pick and choose. They ignored the bombast; they knew the objectives of the party and took this into account whenever a piece of 'news' was made available. They were expert at detecting discrepancies between one official statement and another. The citizens of the USSR were impressive 'Kremlinologists' before ever that dark art was developed in the West.

Opinion in society remains very diverse and Russians retain a suspicion of institutions seeking to mould their minds. The result is that a unifying rudimentary consensus about many matters – political, economic, social, cultural and spiritual – has yet to be attained. Perhaps the outcome would have been different if Church, army, Academy and media had agreed on a radical agenda and had tried to hold the government to it. But this is not how things turned out. It is not hard to see why the case for reform was understated by the leaders of such bodies. Usually their self-interest held them back. But their calculation had the baleful effect of stunting the growth of desirable reforms.

15. THE POLITICS OF IDEAS

Pondering the future, we must always take counsel with those
who thought about these problems before us.

Gennadi Zyuganov, *Russia and the Contemporary World* (1995)[1]

Opposition politicians have deepened the problem. In a democracy it is
their function to criticise the government and hold it to account; but in
Russia many have gone much further by challenging the very principles
underpinning the new Russian state. The rationale for the USSR's
abolition continues to be disputed. Even politicians who approve of what
happened in 1991–2 offer intemperate judgements on the course of public
life after the demise of Soviet communism. Polemics abound.[2]

Among the peculiarities of this situation is the tendency for the
leading politicians, instead of just arguing with each other on television
or giving interviews outside the State Duma, to compete to write books.
Their books are of a content that would be rejected by publishers in
foreign countries. The 'Russian Question' is the basic theme. Communist
Party leader Gennadi Zyuganov has written *Russia is My Motherland*
and dozens of pamphlets with Russia in the title (see above). Vladimir
Zhirinovski, founder of the Liberal-Democratic Party, has published a
stream of booklets, including a survey of Russian history from Muscovy
to the present day. Yegor Gaidar has written *The State and Evolution*,
a work setting out the case for a liberal market economy in the light
of Russia's twentieth-century communist history. Alexander Lebed, the
former commander of XI Army, has brought out an autobiography in
the form of an historical survey. Grigori Yavlinski, leader of the Yabloko
Party and prominent economist, has pushed *The Crisis in Russia*. Indeed,
Boris Yeltsin, Viktor Chernomyrdin and Vladimir Putin are unusual
among political leaders in refraining from offering a personal panorama
of Russia past and present; and even they have regularly offered opinions

on the course of Russian history and politics – and Yeltsin has published three volumes of autobiography.[3]

This is not a sign that the uppermost layer of the Russian political elite is hugely intellectual. Only Gaidar, Yavlinski and, to a lesser extent, Zyuganov were notable as public commentators before 1991. The rest are notoriously dull. Not that this has stopped Alexander Lebed, the bluff soldier with the booming bass voice, from trying to show off his cultural baggage. On the bicentenary of Pushkin's birthday, in 1999, he was filmed reciting the first stanza of a poem. But to much amusement he could not successfully get past the second line. And the prolific author Vladimir Zhirinovski has been exposed by disgruntled former associates for having to use ghost-writers.

The pursuit of intellectual recognition requires a word of explanation. Soviet political leaders from Lenin right down to Gorbachëv issued programmatic statements; and succession struggles reinforced the tendency of leaders to expatiate about current policy. Each new General Secretary liked to make his mark soon after his accession. Stalin did this by claiming to be the most loyal follower of Lenin. Khrushchëv took the opposite tack by denouncing his predecessor Stalin. Then Brezhnev turned Khrushchëv into a non-person, prohibiting public mention of him. Andropov quietly distanced himself from Brezhnev. Chernenko had no time for Andropov. Gorbachëv went on to castigate all his predecessors except Lenin, Khrushchëv and Andropov. This tradition did not fade after the collapse of the Soviet Union. Whereas Western leaders write memoirs in retirement, Russian ones bring out works on history before they get power. Funds that elsewhere would be channelled into televised political broadcasts or billboard advertisements are put into publications by party leaders. The booklets have bright covers and are cheap. The language is accessible to the general public. In short much money and imagination have been dedicated to the production of material on the past, present and future of the country.

This is not just a matter of following in the footsteps of communist General Secretaries. Russian political leaders are also responding to a particular current problem. Every survey of public opinion indicates that the electorate is sceptical about politics and politicians, although there have been moments of euphoria. When Gorbachëv was embarrassing and irritating conservative communist leaders in the late 1980s, there was hardly a Soviet citizen who did not watch the Congress of People's Deputies on television. They often took a day off work for the purpose. The popular preoccupation with politics was equally intense during the

August 1991 attempted coup. People have continued to turn out in substantial numbers for national elections – to the State Duma in 1993, 1995 and 1999 and to the Presidency in 1996 and 2000 – even after allowance is made for the authorities exaggerating the turnouts. But at other times – which is to say most of the time – the citizens of Russia can hardly bring themselves to think about politics. They watch few programmes about public affairs. They do not attend demonstrations. They do not join political parties. Consequently the politicians have no way of gaining support except by trying to persuade people that their respective programme of action would better their lives and make sense of them.

Thus it came about that when the Soviet ideocracy collapsed, ideas remained a vital component of politics in Russia. Even the least intellectual of politicians needs to appear as someone who has worked out his or her vision of the Russian national past, present and future. The leaders of the parties are not especially bookish. But whether they like it or not, most of them feel compelled to write books.

Even Gaidar is not an intellectual colossus but a graduate in Marxist political economy who moved to the position of a free marketeer. In *The State and Evolution* he tried to explain his purposes. For Gaidar, the painful problems of Russian history were the product of the fanatical pursuit of Revolution. The title of his book was a snub to Marxism-Leninism. Lenin had written *The State and Revolution* shortly before the October 1917 Revolution; he was so proud of its arguments for violent revolution and class dictatorship that he asked his associate Lev Kamenev to ensure that if perchance the enemies of communism were to 'do me in', the book should be published as his masterpiece. Gaidar's grandfather Timur was one of Lenin's early readers as well as a Red hero in the Civil War. Yegor Gaidar, with a not inconsiderable degree of intellectual immodesty, decided that Marxism-Leninism had to be attacked at source – and *The State and Revolution* was the bible of Lenin and the communists. Gaidar went into details of ideological discourse eschewed by Yeltsin in an effort to turn gradualism into an explicit virtue. Generations of Soviet citizens had been taught that a humane modern society had to be constructed by revolutionary means. According to Gaidar, all this had to be unlearned if Russia was to become a civilised member of 'the community of nations'.[4]

Beyond that, Gaidar had little to say. Like his foreign mentors, he regarded 'marketisation' and monetarist policies as the crucial motor of fundamental reform in Russia. About the national question he had almost nothing to say. Economics are the engine of everything he writes. Gaidarism is inverted vulgar Marxism. The basic message is that the government needs only to impose an appropriate financial framework and the political, social and cultural changes will occur by themselves. It is not a programme of intellectual distinction.

Grigori Yavlinski, who became Russia's leading liberal politician after Gaidar's electoral humiliation in December 1993, has always resented that it was Gaidar whom Yeltsin originally favoured. Yavlinski was involved in the last discussions about economic regeneration under Gorbachëv, and his foreign contacts rated him highly. Like Gaidar, he had studied Marxist-Leninist economics and then moved on to adopt Western liberal ideas. Yavlinski did not favour the breaking up of the USSR, but has subsequently accepted the fact. Ever since 1991, he has urged that a reforming government needs to introduce universal civil rights and political democracy as equal priorities with marketisation: he criticised Gaidar's decision to put economics before everything else. As Yeltsin moved away from the agenda of reform he had proposed in 1991–2, it was Yavlinski who was left to make the case for it. He has bemoaned the consolidation of a 'corporative oligarchical state' and called for truly 'democratic institutions' and a truly 'competitive economy'. His *Crisis in Russia: The End of the System?* asked whether the moment has arrived when such reforms have become feasible. Although he tried to give a positive answer, his descriptions of contemporary Russian reality pointed to more depressing conclusions.[5]

Gennadi Zyuganov also started as a student of Marxism-Leninism; but, unlike Gaidar and Yavlinski, he stuck to its doctrines when he worked in the Ideological Department of the Secretariat of the Soviet Communist Party's Central Committee. In 1990 he helped to form the Russian Communist Party in semi-open opposition to Gorbachëv. Zyuganov was one of the few to continue fighting for communism after 23 August 1991, when Yeltsin prohibited the operation of communist organisations in the RSFSR. When others deserted the communist cause, Zyuganov held on and campaigned for the Communist Party of the Russian Federation to regain legal status. Steadily, after dozens of meetings and demonstrations, he clawed his way back into politics. On 30 November 1992 the Constitutional Court revoked the ban on the party and Zyuganov's persistence made him the natural choice as the party's leader. Throughout the 1990s he published books and articles to propagate the new version of communist ideology he upheld. He was prolific though far from being a scintillating thinker. But at least he was able to arrange his political thoughts in a more or less readable sequence.

Zyuganov argues that the regime started to run downhill when, in 1985, Gorbachëv took over. Yet he is the first Marxist-Leninist of the twentieth century who has little time for Lenin; he barely mentions Marx and Engels either. Zyuganov applauds the October 1917 Revolution, the formation of the USSR and the Soviet military victory in the Second World War. But unlike his former colleagues in the Ideological Department of the Secretariat, Zyuganov does not tie this to the genius of Lenin.

It is Zyuganov's claim that the world is far more complex than Marx and Engels imagined. He does not expressly reject Marxism-Leninism but he formulates ideas in a very different fashion. He insists that class struggle, which Marxists have always put at the centre of his recommendations, is much less important than what he calls geopolitics. Zyuganov wastes no time on the October 1917 Revolution as a historical topic or on the specific needs of the working class in the present. For Zyuganov, Russia is a civilisation in itself, a civilisation that has clashed with other great civilisations to the west and the east. As his intellectual influences he cites two foreign thinkers, Oswald Spengler and Arnold Toynbee, who have taken a similar approach to world history. Both Spengler and Toynbee rejected visions of humanity premised upon the superiority of Western Europe and North America, and Spengler's *The Decline of the West*, published in Germany in 1918–22, predicted that the liberal democracies had entered a final decadent phase. Zyuganov has also picked up more recent theoretical literature, in particular he cites the American commentators Samuel Huntingdon and Francis Fukuyama, who see the world as facing a period of instability as clashes occur among the world's great regional cultures.[6]

This way of looking at global change is hardly new. It had deep roots in Russian intellectual life before 1917. The nineteenth-century Slavophiles Nikolai Danilevski and Konstantin Leontev, who draw enthusiasm from Zyuganov, contended that Russian traditions and interests would always mark their country off from the rest of Europe. Zyuganov also admires thinkers who wrote in the period of the October Revolution, notably Nikolai Berdyaev, Sergei Bulgakov and Ivan Ilin. Among recent Russian theorists he names Lev Gumilëv as a favourite author.

This is a bizarre list for any self-proclaimed Marxist. Practically all of these thinkers were Orthodox Christians who put their religion at the core of their analyses of Russia. Those of them who lived under the communist order were also its victims. The Cheka shot Lev Gumilëv's poet father Nikolai as a counter-revolutionary in 1920; his mother, the poet Anna Akhmatova, lived in fear of the same fate after Stalin's associate Andrei Zhdanov denounced her as a 'harlot nun' in 1946. Berdyaev, Bulgakov and Ilin had themselves been pushed into foreign exile in the 1920s. And yet Zyuganov has never castigated the abuses carried out by the communist leadership from 1917. He vaguely criticises the 'command system' in politics and the economy as well as the privileges of the *nomenklatura*. But basically he tries to protect the history of the USSR from being besmirched. Only minor blemishes can be admitted; the technique is one of supreme evasiveness. Zyuganov's aim is to maintain a sense of unity between the epochs of tsarism and Marxism-Leninism. Russia, for him, is to be seen as eternal, unique and unrivalled. Somehow Nicholas II, killed by Lenin's communists, has to be represented as handing on a legacy voluntarily to the Soviet state.

It is presumably for this reason that Zyuganov chooses Russian intellectual heroes who are all dead. Alexander Solzhenitsyn, who stands in a line of succession from Ivan Ilin on many matters, would strenuously object if ever the Communist Party of the Russian Federation claimed him as an influence. Zyuganov has surely been wise to avoid embroiling himself with the country's most famous and indefatigable anti-communist.

Yet he frequently jumps from the bizarre to the brazen. He argues that the Communist Party of the Soviet Union embodied the spiritual traditions of the Russian peasantry. Following Danilevski, Leontev and Berdyaev, he suggests that Russians, especially the 'common people', have a propensity to think and act collectively and to eschew individual selfishness. The word in Russian for 'togetherness' is *sobornost'*, and *sobor* is also the word for 'cathedral'. Outrageously Zyuganov maintains that the Communist Party of the Soviet Union was a kind of cathedral for the Russian people in the period from 1917 to 1991; he ignores the fact that the communists were militant atheists and that his words might therefore give offence to Christian believers. He is proud of the Imperial expansion undertaken by the more dynamic of the tsars; it seems only a matter of time before Ivan the Terrible or Peter the Great replaces Lenin as the man claimed to have founded the communist order in Russia. Zyuganov's work is such a hotchpotch that one hesitates to describe it too lengthily. Suffice it to say that Danilevski and Leontev never admired either of these tsars and that Berdyaev was hostile to tsarism in general.

These three thinkers are being exploited as a means of enhancing Zyuganov's standing among those citizens who would not normally endorse the Communist Party of the Russian Federation. His avowed intention is to appeal across the boundaries of classes, professions, generations and nationalities. He recognises that immediately after 1991 the communists were attractive mainly to persons aged at least sixty. They had become a party of war veterans and pensioners, and this was never going to be enough to win them elections. Somehow, too, he had to gain support not only from Russians but also from other ethnic groups; he also had to reach out to occupational groups beyond the industrial working class. For this reason he has stressed – against much empirical evidence – that the Soviet Union offered an opportunity for people from various national and social backgrounds to live in harmony. There are, however, exceptions to Zyuganov's inclusiveness. He urged that Christianity, Islam and Buddhism should be recognised as the country's traditional state religions. Judaism is noticeably absent from the list. As if this hint of anti-Semitism were not enough, Zyuganov has given the names of those whom he regards as traitors to Russia. Prominent among them are Jews such as Lev Trotski. At the same time Zyuganov makes favourable references to the wartime leadership of Joseph Stalin. Soviet military victory remains at the heart of the communist endeavour to entice the electorate.[7]

This ideological confection is an historical and moral idiocy. But in a practical way it has elements that play effectively upon Russian sentiment. It appeals to national pride. It blames problems on Jews and foreigners. It demands a larger state, a state more like the old Soviet Union, for Russians. It points to the comforts supposedly available until Gorbachëv came along. It suggests that once upon a time it was possible for those with talent – and not just with an eye to the financial main chance in a market economy – to get on in society.

It is no longer possible to categorise the Communist Party of the Russian Federation unequivocally as a political organisation of the Left. Zyuganov has stolen clothes from the traditional Right. The entire spectrum of public life in Russia displays similar contradictions, and nowhere is this more obvious than in the case of the Liberal-Democratic Party (LDP), led by Vladimir Zhirinovski. The LDP is ostensibly on the Right. Many of its ideas have a fascist resonance. But there has always been confusion about the party's stance. Its name suggests some kind of commitment to the Western democratic tradition. When Zhirinovski announced the party's foundation in 1990, he attracted foreigners to Moscow who were staggered to encounter a ranting demagogue more like Mussolini than Abraham Lincoln. Zhirinovski made declarations of a militarist and xenophobic nature. Like Zyuganov, he resented the dismemberment in 1991 of the state established by the Russian Empire and renewed as the Soviet Union. Zhirinovski has an expansionist purpose, suggesting that if he were to become Russian President, the armed forces would be instructed to conquer lands even further-flung than the southernmost frontier of the Soviet Union. In his comical but menacing phrase, Russian soldiers would 'wash their feet' in the warm waters of the Indian Ocean.

Within the Russian Federation he calls for drastic administrative reorganisation. Zhirinovski rails against the disobedience to the Kremlin by the other regions of the country. He would sweep away the 'national' republics that exist across the Russian Federation. Zhirinovski proposes a reversion to a uniform system of provinces (*gubernii*). Tatarstan would cease to exist and, by implication, Tatar political dominance over the local Russians would be eliminated. Russian national interests would be reasserted at last. The armed forces would be used to expand Russia beyond its present boundaries back to the territory held by the Soviet Union. But there would be no discrete republics such as Ukraine. The federalist constitution would be abolished and one of Lenin's worst mistakes would at last be rectified by the LDP. Zhirinovski is urging a reversion to the administrative divisions characteristic of the Russian Empire. He calls for strict central control and for Moscow to be in firm possession of the levers of power. It is hard to miss the hint that Zhirinovski wishes to provide the Russians with a higher status in the state than any other people. There is a distinct trace of nationalism of the extreme kind.

Zhirinovski has always behaved with outrageous contempt for democratic procedures. His party is run on the Führer principle. Its programme in 1994 laid down that his post of supreme leader should be secure until the year 2004; he has taken the precaution of registering the party formally with the soubriquet of 'the Party of Zhirinovski'. Dominant inside his party, he has no time for democratic politics outside it. His contempt for the State Duma has been constant. When Yeltsin introduced his highly Presidentialist new constitution in 1993,

Zhirinovski commended him. Zhirinovski has repeatedly maintained the need for Russia to be ruled with a firm hand.

In these ways the LDP is a typical party of the Right. This was probably why Mikhail Gorbachëv decided that, as the multiparty political system started to emerge in the Soviet Union in 1990, the LDP should be the first to gain a legal licence. Gorbachëv presumably thought that Zhirinovski's right-wing nastiness would put his own Communist Party of the Soviet Union in a good light. Another possible official calculation – and this may have been the KGB's calculation rather than Gorbachev's – was that the LDP might one day be a useful political instrument for the communist *nomenklatura* if ever the Communist Party of the Soviet Union failed to maintain its supremacy. Zhirinovski certainly benefited from the indulgence of the Soviet authorities. It came as a terrible shock to Gorbachëv in June 1991 when Zhirinovski turned out to be a very effective political campaigner. Although Yeltsin easily won the RSFSR Presidential election, Zhirinovski performed brilliantly, both on the platform at open meetings and on television. He had a knack of expressing himself punchily. He was never bothered about criticism by 'respectable' politicians. Zhirinovski loved to be outrageous and public life gave him plenty of suitable opportunities for this.

He declared, for instance, that the communist regime had brought the country to near-disaster. But otherwise he had a strange disinclination to castigate certain Soviet leaders. In particular, he exhibits a nostalgia for the days of Stalinism. Those were days, according to Zhirinovski, of a modest, temperate life for most people. They were days of certainty. People knew what they believed and did not expect too much to come to them without effort. The virtues of Russians had been abused by the rest of the world. Russia's allies exploited her both economically and militarily in the First World War; and the Soviet Union, in saving humanity from perdition in the Second World War, brought herself to utter prostration. For Zhirinovski, Russia had suffered martyrdom in the twentieth century. All this was not so very far from the present standpoint of Gennadi Zyuganov: Zhirinovski the noisy anti-communist has a lot of the communist about him.

But the story does not end there. While he blends fascism with communism, he also adds ingredients from liberal democracy. Zhirinovski claims to respect constitution, law and parliamentary elections and to want Russia to exist peacefully side by side with other states. Occasionally he also includes astonishing concessions to social tolerance.

For example, he has advocated the legalisation of male homosexual marriages on the model (wholly fictitious, at least at the time of writing) of official practices in North London. At the same time he urges a return to the cultural values of the past. He rails against decadence, corruption and fraud. For Zhirinovski, the social modesties of the Stalin years should not be sneered at. He writes: 'Admittedly we were a closed country under [Stalin's] regime. This was positive to a certain degree. For example, inasmuch as we were almost completely free from venereal diseases. Yes, on the whole morality was on a high plane.'[8] This advocacy of the moral fibre of Russians during the Great Terror is not borne out by historical accounts – and indeed syphilis was rampant in the first decades of the twentieth century. But Zhirinovski is out to create a comfortable myth for Russians and scholarly exactitude is the last thing he aspires to.

The blame for Russia's misfortunes, he maintains, has always come from abroad. Unusually among Russian political leaders he does not greatly admire Peter the Great:

> Tsar Peter I was great in his victories, but there were many sacrifices offered on the altar of those victories. Because the extremely rapid Europeanisation of Russia had not only positive but also negative effects. The destruction of the traditions of the patriarchal Russian family also had negative effects. Undoubtedly it was those Petrine times that led to the drunkenness and the drinking bouts. And to smoking and other features of European life. Because Europe brought a disintegrative element as well as civilisation to Russia.[9]

The image of the Russians as a quiet, peace-loving people is recurrent with Zhirinovski, and it is frequently accompanied by xenophobia. Occasionally he has made veiled threats about the Jews even though his father was Jewish. He has also excoriated the West in general and the Americans and Germans in particular. Nor has he held back from making menacing remarks about the possible use of nuclear weapons against the Baltic countries. But no country is more detested by him than Turkey. Why he should have singled out the Turks is not wholly clear. It has been suggested that his ferocity stems from his unfortunate experience in that country in 1969: apparently he was arrested while bungling a mission on behalf of the KGB.[10] Another possibility is that his anti-Turkism is the counterpart of his long-term pro-Iraqism. Be that as it may, there is an unmistakable contrast between the image of Russians as modest, quiet and peaceable and their putative role as continental conquerors.

On the 'national question' in Russia herself, Zhirinovski has frequently expressed support for peoples to be enabled to live freely within their traditional cultures. He rejects calls for Russification. On this he is quite lyrical: 'All peoples are talented. Some husband livestock, some cultivate flowers, some are skilled at catching fish.'[11] At his party's fifth congress he went near to ditching his multiculturalism when he mentioned the specific needs of the ethnic Russians. But he balanced this with a plea for the non-Russians in the following exclamation: 'Russia for the Russians [russkikh] and for all Russia's citizens [rossiyan]. Russia is the fatherland for those who want to live here with us in our common land, for all who respect our history.'[12]

There is of course an ambiguity in these words. What does he mean by respect for Russian history? As usual he is trying to have things both ways. On the one hand he strives to maximise the votes obtained from ethnic Russians; on the other he does not wish to alienate the non-Russians. Zhirinovski has trodden this narrow, twisting path since his entry into national politics in 1989. He has repeatedly given out signals both menacing and reassuring, fascistic and democratic, ethno-nationalist and multiculturalist. It is a confusion that has irritated many on the political far right. Eduard Limonov is among them. Until the early 1990s he was a loyal member of Zhirinovski's LDP. The point of departure for Limonov was his leader's refusal to sanction unequivocal Russian ethno-nationalism. Limonov has claimed that Zhirinovski is taking this position not out of principle or even electoral pragmatism but because his absentee father had been Jewish. Zhirinovski's ideology is said to be a personal convenience – and of course many have gone further still and argued that Zhirinovski has calculated his policies not just in relation to his parentage but also in response to money. To put it mildly, it is strange that he often fulminated against President and government in the Duma only to vote at a later stage in their favour.

Zhirinovski's rivals on the right are a motley group. Limonov himself, who now heads the National-Bolshevik Party, is as odd as they come. He secured permission to emigrate under Brezhnev and in New York he wrote a novel of unashamed pornography, *Hello, It's Me, Eddie*. Slim, dark-haired, Limonov is a restless individual. His position is crude. He wants Russia for the Russians, Russia to cover the whole of the former Soviet Union and the Russian state to act as protector of the interests of all the Slavs against interference by the West. Limonov likes to wear dark sunglasses, to dress up in black leather and to bristle with weaponry. If this were all, he would be the butt of mere ridicule. But Limonov has been sufficiently firm of purpose to lead a group of Russian volunteers to aid the Serbian cause in Bosnia during the wars of the Yugoslav succession. At home he struts around as a demagogic nationalist. Like Zhirinovski, he is extraordinarily vain. Even his newspaper is in his own name, *Limonovka*. It is his belief that the Russian ethnic cause is a time-bomb ticking away beneath the Kremlin.

Not even Limonov has developed the most extreme variant of nationalism. The prize in such a contest goes to Alexander Barkashov. This is yet another man who has broken away from an existing extremist organisation on the grounds of insufficient extremism. Barkashov originally belonged to the Pamyat ('Memory') group which sprang up in the late 1980s ostensibly to defend the Russian architectural heritage. Pamyat quickly became a haven for all manner of nationalists. Along with hostility to the Soviet political order went a deep prejudice against the smaller nations of Russia, especially the Jews. For Barkashov, Pamyat was too much of a talking shop. In September 1990 he founded his own Russian National Unity Movement. The basic ideology was fascist. Barkashov aims to do away with parliamentary politics, cultural pluralism and inter-ethnic harmony. His organisational approach is based upon interwar European fascism. His followers wear a uniform of black shirt, trousers and jacket. They appear in public with armbands depicting a flash of lightning: the influence of the swastika is unmistakable. They sometimes swagger around with loaded guns, making no secret of the fact that they are training paramilitary units for use when a propitious political opportunity arises. Hatred of foreigners is the unifying creed.

The National Unity Movement – which was banned in April 1999 but has resurfaced under different names – is at least as incoherent as other forms of fascism. Barkashov expresses admiration for Hitler despite everything that the Nazis did to Russians in the Second World War. But the National Unity Movement focused its attention not upon the Russian past but on the politics of today. The nation's regeneration, they insist, requires the unlimited assertion of national values and national interests. There is nothing new about their ideological position. In the 1930s there were fascist groups in Russian *émigré* communities. The largest of these existed in Harbin in Manchuria, where Konstantin Rodzaevski led a Russian Fascist Party which drew financial support from the Japanese military authorities. The Russian Fascist Party, despite sporadic attempts, had no following in the USSR and came to an end in a violent fashion.

In 1945 Rodzaevski wrote to Stalin explaining that after years of denouncing Stalinism, he had come to recognise that Stalin himself was really a fascist and had transmuted the internationalist ideology of Lenin into a set of ideas that were distinctly fascist.[13] For this reason Rodzaevski pleaded to be allowed to be repatriated to Russia. Permission was granted. But as soon as he reached Moscow, he was arrested, interrogated and shot.

This odd relationship between fascism and communism exemplifies how much the various ideologies of opposition overlap each other. Even though their leading proponents have little immediate prospect of power, they undoubtedly have influence. The watering-down of the comprehensive official project of reform enunciated in 1991–2 is in no small measure the result of the critiques offered by those parties asserting ethnic Russian interests and demanding a slowdown in the transformation of state and society. Zyuganov and Zhirinovski may not have become President, but their parties have done well enough in State Duma elections from 1993 onwards for Yeltsin and Putin to incorporate some of their ideas in policy.

Yet the threat to the Kremlin's ascendant leadership from politicians of the opposition has proved containable. In particular, such politicians have failed to ignite enthusiasm in the general public. In January 1996, at the outset of the Presidential electoral campaign, not a single candidate could muster a percentage rate of popular approval in double figures. Anger and contempt were commingled. People assumed that the typical politician was corrupt. There was also a feeling that words were ceasing to have meaning. Politicians said one thing, but did another. Debate in the Duma sometimes descended into a brawl. On one occasion, indeed, Zhirinovski physically attacked a female Duma deputy. Russian citizens have naturally recoiled in horror. Whereas the Congress of People's Deputies' debate might draw audiences of tens of millions at critical political conjunctures, the State Duma and the Council of the Federation could never justify a prime-time slot on television. Nor do most people want to join political parties. Zyuganov's Communist Party of the Russian Federation is the largest with a claimed half a million members; but there must be doubt whether most of them even pay their membership dues. The other parties have far fewer members.

Yet people are not only politically apathetic: they are also confused. The overlap between the competing ideologies makes for obfuscation of ideas. Great metaphysical assertions are piled higher and higher. The politicians are more interested in increasing electoral support than in offering philosophical clarity. Language itself is an object of struggle. Some words have near-universal approval. Politicians love to identify themselves with 'Russia', 'the Motherland' (or 'the Fatherland'), 'the Great Fatherland War', 'Peace', 'Science', 'Regeneration' and 'Renaissance'. There is a sameness about the rhetoric across the parties.

Beyond this point there is dispute. Each political party defines 'Russia' in its own fashion. 'Russia' can be tradition or novelty. It can be menace and terror or the incarnation of peacefulness, social harmony or severe authoritarianism, a country for its people or a leader's plaything. Polemics are endless. Barkashov is no democrat and does not pretend to be one. But most political leaders would be offended if they were accused of anti-democratic leanings. This includes both the Communist Party of the Russian Federation and the LDP, which since Zyuganov and Zhirinovski claim to be democratic. There is therefore a struggle over terminology. Yeltsin and Putin have castigated their opponents as anti-democratic. Meanwhile their opponents have referred to Yeltsin, Gaidar, Burbulis and Chubais as 'false democrats' (*lzhe-demokraty*). Increasingly they finessed this. While describing themselves as democrats, they have spat on the Yeltsinites as 'democrats': the contempt was expressed in the inverted commas. The contortions of the public discourse are extraordinary. Politics again entered a linguistic maelstrom in the 1990s. Words elide across conventional divisions and are manipulated for cynical purposes. Leaders argue fiercely while obfuscating what is under dispute. It is the politics of the bear-pit. It cannot go on like this for ever, but it could well go on for a very long time.

16. CULTURE FOR THE NATION

My Russia, in the sense of belonging to it but also in the sense of my personal perception of it as, let's say: My Pushkin! My Lenin! There's really nothing special in my impression of her.

Dmitri Prigov, 1994[1]

In the past when Russia's politicians failed to meet the national needs of the moment, intellectuals filled the void. In the words of the nineteenth-century literary critic Vissarion Belinski, they became the 'alternative government'. Admittedly this was an over-statement since novelists, painters and musical composers did not usually aspire to wield actual power. But they certainly exercised much influence despite being subject to tight censorship.[2] The periods of broad cultural freedom in 1917 and in the years since the late 1980s were few and far between. Throughout the years of hardship, however, brave intellectuals existed who took a stand against the regime and spoke out in favour of a better way of life. When Yeltsin took power in late 1991, many people expected that the cultural intelligentsia would be a united force for the creation of a liberal civic community in a reformed Russia.

This was never likely to happen if only because the intelligentsia was deeply divided and many contemporary intellectuals were hostile to liberal politics, capitalism and social modernity. There was also a vogue among publishers for authors whose works which had been banned or, at the very least, restricted in their circulation before Gorbachëv's rule: Nikolai Berdyaev, Fëdor Dostoevski, Lev Gumilëv, Ivan Ilin and Nikolai Karamzin; and the contents of these works too jarred against the purposes of the grand reform project of 1991–2.[3] The 'Russian Question' was widely debated.[4] One nationalist writer, Alexander Solzhenitsyn, had long since given up deferring to the authorities. Deported from the USSR in 1974 at the Politburo's command, he had condemned the political and moral order of the day. Eventually he settled in Vermont in the USA, where he lived frugally in a large, rambling house sheltered from prying eyes by a high fence. He worked in a hut at the bottom of his garden. It was from there that he issued anti-communist pamphlets warning the West against making concessions to the Soviet regime and excoriating the West for its own materialism and godlessness. Gorbachëv permitted his novels to be published, and invited Solzhenitsyn to return to Moscow; but the author refused: he would not come back until it had been formally acknowledged that the charges leading to his deportation had been spurious.

He did not change this stance after the fall of the USSR, and under Yeltsin he disdained to return immediately. The fresh reason he offered for postponing his journey was the need to complete work on his multivolume novel *The Red Wheel*. Only in 1995 did he relent and come back. He did this in a manner designed to cause the maximum of embarrassment to the authorities. Arriving in Vladivostok, he took the Trans-Siberian railway to Moscow, stopping off at cities and villages on the way and holding impromptu meetings with residents.[5] Solzhenitsyn railed against the degradation of political, economic, social and spiritual conditions in his native land. When he reached the capital, he was invited by Yeltsin to address the upper and lower houses of the Federal Assembly. Characteristically he used the occasion to fulminate against the government's botched and corrupt policies. He was no more a friend to Yeltsin than he had been to Brezhnev or Gorbachëv.

His fury was supposed to be explained in *The Red Wheel*, but Solzhenitsyn had not completed it before leaving America and he found his time in Russia taken up by civic activity. His prestige allowed him to front a weekly chat show on a state-owned TV channel. His basic ideas were constant. Russia, he suggested, had been hurled from its path of gradual improvement by the revolutionary turmoil of 1917. His animus against Lenin and the communists was just part of the matter. Solzhenitsyn hated not only communists but also socialists, liberals and even many conservatives in his country's twentieth-century history. For Solzhenitsyn, the first step on the road to the national Calvary had been the overthrow of the Romanov dynasty in 1917. He laid responsibility on the shoulders of the liberals and conservative leaders in the Fourth State Duma who declined to restrain the crowds of workers and sailors. The Emperor Nicholas II was not his hero. Solzhenitsyn suggested that Nicholas, out of foolishness and vanity, had undermined the position of Russia's last great conservative statesman, Pëtr Stolypin, who

was Chairman of the Council of Ministers from 1906 until his assassination in 1911. The result had been the trapping of the Russian people
under the moving wheels of inhumane, anti-national and godless
Revolution.[6]

The best sections of *The Red Wheel* are the passages on the travail of
the Russian armed forces in the First World War; but none of them is a
patch on Solzhenitsyn's great previous novels.[7] In any case the necessary
labours on the multivolume epic proved beyond him at his age, and he
announced his intention to abandon it unfinished and devote himself
to commenting on Russian public affairs. He discovered, though, that
his opinions were often received unfavourably. His TV chat show was
usually more a monologue than a conversation and the authorities, citing
the need for political impartiality before the 1995 Duma elections, took
it off the air. The prophet was no longer revered in his own land.

Several of his fellow nationalist writers fared little better. Notable
among these was Vladimir Soloukhin, who published *In the Light of Day*
in 1992 (and died in 1998).[8] The book was not a novel but an historical
study of the origins of communism in Russia. Soloukhin carried it off by
means of an enquiry into the ethnic ancestry of Lenin. Using recently
accessible material, he highlighted the Jewish and Kalmyk elements in
Lenin's family and contended that this explained the hostility of communists to the traditional Russian style of life. In earlier years such a
book would have been a best-selling sensation. In fact it was another
author whose work on Lenin made the greater impact. This was Dmitri
Volkogonov. He was an ebullient figure: in Brezhnev's time he had been
Deputy Head of the Main Political Directorate of the Soviet Army, but
became a radical reformer under Gorbachëv and Yeltsin. He was a
prolific writer who, using his position as an adviser to Yeltsin on defence
matters, got access to classified archival material. In particular, he pulled
Lenin's confidential decrees on the Red Terror out of the Presidential
Archive. Volkogonov agreed with Soloukhin that Lenin had disliked the
Russians and their culture; but he simultaneously insisted that contemporary democracy rather than antiquated nationalism should be the way
out of its troubles for Russia; and Volkogonov's biography remained a
popular account after his death in 1995.[9]

A more widely admired nationalist is the painter Ilya Glazunov. His
pictorial themes have always been stoical peasants, decent mothers and
glorious tsars and warriors. Glazunov accentuates the tragedy of Russia's
past, and his picture *Eternal Russia* is shown not infrequently on
television. Leading historical personages swarm across the canvas. In

the foreground are saints of the Orthodox Church – Glazunov's heroes. Tsarist statesmen and writers are crammed together in a motley throng to the left-hand side. Just a few other individuals are picked out. One is the novelist and pacifist Lev Tolstoi, a placard with the words 'Non-Violence' hanging around his shoulders. But in the centre of the picture is a hurtling chariot carrying Stalin in his Generalissimus tunic. Behind him, represented not as an enemy but as a companion, is Trotski; and behind the two of them is Lenin with his fist clenched, his arm raised and his mouth proclaiming Revolution. The sky is red and menacing. To the front of the chariot is a grey space populated with the bodies of the persecuted Russian dead.[10]

Yet perhaps the most moving cultural artefact by a nationalist is Viktor Astafev's novel about the Second World War, *The Cursed and the Killed*, which won the Russian Booker prize in 1994.[11] It is nothing like any other book on 1941–5 by a Russian author. Instead of describing warfare on the Eastern front, Astafev portrays a Red Army regiment under training in mid-Siberia. The conditions of conscripts are appalling. They are poorly fed, ill equipped and regularly abused by their commanders. The soldiers of the USSR are shown to have no greater opportunity to assert their rights than the nearby forced-labour inmates of the Gulag, and Astafev implies that they got hardly better treatment from Stalin's regime than they could expect from Hitler's Third Reich if they became prisoners-of-war in a German concentration camp. Not only Stalin but also regimental officers behaved brutally to ordinary Russians. The message is that nothing in history is uncomplicated. The country's military personnel covered themselves with glory in the Second World War, but they did not always behave well towards each other off the battlefield. Astafev, unlike Solzhenitsyn and Soloukhin, disdains to exaggerate the essential virtues of the Russian nation. Improvement of life today, he suggests, will come only with further immense effort.

One writer who stood out against unthinking nationalism in its less pleasant manifestations was Dmitri Likhachëv. An expert on the Old Church Slavonic language and medieval Russian literature, he had been arrested as a young man and sent to the Solovki prison island. On release he worked quietly as a scholar, but in the Second World War he was caught in Leningrad and imprisoned for the duration of the siege of 1941–3. After Stalin's death, despite recurrent difficulties, he courageously campaigned for the conservation of religious buildings when Khrushchëv renewed the state offensive against the Orthodox Church; and during Gorbachëv's *perestroika*, he was appointed chairman of the USSR Cultural Fund. Among the anti-communists only Solzhenitsyn and Sakharov came near to him in public esteem.

His ideas had been developed over several decades and had a remarkable consistency. He took pride in the fact that Russians are descended from a mixture of various peoples in Eastern Europe and Asia.[12] Also important for Likhachëv was the belief that Russia in the Middle Ages was far from being a 'backward' country. He emphasised that contacts with Europe had been close and that cultural influences had flowed in both directions. Likhachëv argued that the level of literacy had been high by contemporary standards and that national self-consciousness persisted in the folklore, the proverbs, popular songs and religious rituals.[13] 'Modernising' tsars such as Peter the Great, he insisted, had damaged traditions and destroyed values even before the communist regime had brought ruin upon the Russian nation. Recovery would be successful only if older national customs were restored. But Likhachëv shuddered at most of the recommendations of Solzhenitsyn, Soloukhin, Glazunov or even Astafev. Instead he called for the cultivation of peaceful, liberal principles: 'Nationalism is the expression of the weakness of a nation and not its strength.'[14]

Likhachëv retained the broad respect of the intelligentsia for his personal integrity but his ideas were not widely shared; and since the death of the civil-rights campaigner Andrei Sakharov in 1989 he had cut a rather solitary figure. But as a medievalist he took a long view of progress to a better future: he remained optimistic. Russian folk traditions had survived in a subterranean manner despite the onslaughts of tsars and commissars, and these traditions could be renourished and enhanced. The country had to re-enter the stream of 'world civilisation'. Although Russia was unique, it could not fulfil its potential by following the prescriptions of nationalists who wanted to insulate society from foreign influences. Likhachëv felt strongly about every aspect, large or small, of cultural recovery. A frail but vigorous old man, he appeared regularly on TV and radio in the Gorbachëv years. In 1989 he agreed to make a short speech on a variety-entertainment show. Following the acts of comedians and conjurors, he stepped through the curtains to deliver a brief homily on the need for people to improve their behaviour on the streets. Spitting, he asserted, was uncultured. It was a splendid, uplifting performance.

Another writer who has called for civilised standards in daily life, including inter-ethnic tolerance, is the novelist Semën Lipkin. His *Notes of an Inhabitant* is a panoramic treatment of Revolution from the former

Russian Empire to the USSR in the Second World War. Lipkin, a Jew, emphasises the extraordinary ethnic variety of his native Odessa in Ukraine. Unlike writers in Soviet times, he is free to indicate the cultural differences between one nationality and another; he shows no preference for any single national group and is not averse to describing episodes of xenophobia by local Russian mobs. Lipkin's purpose is to engender approval for a softening of social mores in a contemporary setting. Tolerance in his eyes is the key civic virtue and a knowledge of past horrors is the prerequisite for it to flourish.[15]

For all their differences, Solzhenitsyn and Likhachëv were united in their acceptance of the artist's duty to be didactic. They also held in common a deep patriotic commitment, and the origins of their thought lie in the decades they spent under communist rule. Younger writers are less haunted by experience of communism and are more influenced by the kind of literature that appears in the West. An example is Vladimir Makanin. The title of his novella, *The Caucasian Captive*, echoes the title of Lev Tolstoi's *Prisoner of the Caucasus*. The novella is also set in the Caucasus mountains and focused on a recent conflict between Russian military forces and the local inhabitants. But but Makanin deliberately gives a different thematic treatment. Whereas Tolstoi had Russian officers as the captives, Makanin has a Chechen adolescent. Makanin spares the reader no detail of the degraded conditions of towns and villages in the vicinity. Both Chechens and Russians are depicted as grubbing out a squalid life in the beautiful surroundings of the Caucasus. Filthy language and uncouth behaviour is normal. The contrast with Tolstoi's spare, elegant prose is stark.

At the core of the novella are the feelings developing inside Officer Rubakhin as he drags and then carries his hapless young captive through the woods and over streams to escape Chechen armed patrols.

> The youth did not resist Rubakhin. Hugging him round the shoulder, Rubakhin turned him to himself – and the youth (he was lower down) had himself already moved towards him, digging his lips into the artery of his neck below his unshaved chin. The youth shivered uncomprehendingly. 'N-n . . .', he sighed weakly, just like a woman saying 'No,' like a weakness rather than as a real refusal while [Rubakhin] kept an eye on him and waited.[16]

The homosexual undertones are unmistakable. For Makanin, the 'Russian Question' counts less than questions of sexuality, tenderness and love.

Another person inspired by Tolstoi has been the film director Sergei

Bodrov, whose movie *Prisoner of the Caucasus* is still closer to Tolstoi's plot. Bodrov too has Russian officers as the captives. Even their names are the same. Like Tolstoi's characters, they try to escape but are recaptured and thrown into a pit by their captor Abdul. Bodrov, too, is eager to indicate the majesties of nature in the mountains of the Caucasus; and in the final sequence he follows Tolstoi in showing one of the two Russian officers – Zhilin – gaining his freedom. But in other ways Bodrov's film of contemporary Chechnya diverges from Tolstoi's account. The Chechen way of life is depicted as being guided by traditions of faith, custom and decency; and Chechen armed guerrillas are seen as extraneous to the village. The cleanliness of the village is contrasted with the dirtiness and low morale of the neighbouring Russian-inhabited town. Old Abdul emerges as a man of great dignity. In the end he simply lets Zhilin go free even though his own innocent son, a schoolteacher, has been murdered by the Russian army. The closing sequence is tragic. As Zhilin walks by himself down from the Chechen village, a squadron of helicopter gunships flies overhead. It is heading for the village. As Zhilin shouts in vain, an annihilating fusillade is directed at the defenceless Chechens.[17]

Prisoner of the Caucasus is one of the few cultural artefacts to answer the 'Russian Question' in terms uncongenial to Russian national pride. Other films have been less critical. *Burnt by the Sun*, directed by Nikita Mikhalkov and set in the Great Terror in the 1930s, asserts the continuity of Russian spiritual values. The main character is a veteran communist leader and friend of Stalin. Living with his extended family in a vast old country house, he behaves like a paternalist nineteenth-century landlord. Tsarist culture and communist ideology are positively combined in him. Eventually the terror apparatus catches up with him and he is arrested. But he cannot believe that his innocence will not be accepted. He threatens to write to Stalin; and while being transported to prison he attacks the guards who arrested him. The car is halted and one of the guards calmly beats him in the face until he sobs. His left eye is turned into a bloody mess.[18]

Nikita Mikhalkov – son of Sergei Mikhalkov, who co-wrote the words of the national anthem first for Stalin and then for Putin[19] – takes history very seriously. But his ideas grossly misrepresent the course of history. It is incredible that terror did not start in the USSR until Stalin's despotism or that communist leaders were careful protectors of Russian cultural traditions. But the historical facts of the case are hardly the point. In both the films of Mikhalkov and the novels of writers such as

Alexander Prokhanov there exists an urge to restore popular pride in Russia's past as a great and beneficent power even under terrible supreme rulers such as Stalin. (Putin is similarly motivated.) In another film, *Urga*, Mikhalkov explores the daily life of a Mongolian shepherd deep in inner Mongolia. Gombo the shepherd gives shelter to a Russian contract worker whose vehicle breaks down and cannot quickly be repaired. Mongolian and Russian form an instant friendship. At times it seems that the two have a lot in common, and to that extent there are traces of Eurasianism in the movie: Mikhalkov's preference for 'the East' over 'the West' is a robust one.

The 'Eastern' theme surfaces also in director Vladimir Khotinenko's film *The Moslem*. He and his scriptwriter Valeri Zalotukha are preoccupied by the 'Russian Question'. The hero of the film is a former Soviet soldier, Kolya Ivanov, who returns from captivity in Afghanistan to his home village. The scene seems set for a nationalist elegy to the Russian spirit. But Kolya, extremely unusually, has converted to Islam. Living with his mother and his vodka-sodden criminal brother Fedya, he has difficulty being accepted by fellow villagers. He cannot practise his religion freely; his brother violently attacks him, pushing his face into an Orthodox icon. The depressing conditions of rural life are highlighted. Ivanov, unlike his neighbours, refuses to steal, blaspheme, drink alcohol or sleep with a woman outside marriage. Towards the end of the film a corrupt local politician accidentally drops a caseful of dollars into the river. The following day the dollars are seen floating in the water and all the villagers except for Kolya rush to grab their illicit share. Thus Khotinenko condemns both Western materialism and Russian susceptibilities in the past and present; and if there is a fundamental lesson in the film, it is that community cannot be constructed in the absence of an uplifting consensus tolerant of heterodox opinions.[20]

Yet *The Moslem* gives no more specific indication about how Russianness should develop. Several poets felt similarly diffident even before the fall of the USSR. Alexander Kushner expressed his exasperation:

> History doesn't give lessons,
> But as the historian said – and there is
> No reason not to believe him – our ignorance
> Is punished by history.[21]

And Dmitri Prigov, challenging the didactic role conventionally ascribed to Russian intellectuals, lamented:

So here I am, let's suppose, an ordinary poet
And the thing is that by the whim of a Russian fate
I'm meant to be the conscience of the nation
But how to be just that if no conscience exists
Poems, perhaps, exist, but conscience – no
So, how to be?[22]

He offers no answer to the question in the rest of the poem.

Some novelists have dealt comically with such problems. Mark Shatunovski's *The Discrete Continuity of Love* starts with a woman dreaming that she is talking to persons alive at the time of the First World War and the Revolution. As the plot becomes more convoluted, Shatunovski suggests that the fate of Russia in 1917 was sealed not by the machinations of Lenin and Trotski but by a series of petty incidents after the breakdown of an affair between two obscure lovers:

And the presentiment of some important discovery gripped her in her dream. Something to do with history. That there is no history. That the costumes and decorations change, but all the historical events are a vain masquerade performed by their participants. That the most grandiose turning-points in history change nothing except fashion.[23]

This extreme reductionism is balanced by the heightened importance attached by Shatunovski to emotional relationships. The novel contains steamy episodes of lust. The heroine, waking up on a moving train, is grasped by an army officer travelling in the same carriage. At first she resists, but then, almost against her wishes, finds herself enjoying an experience which ends in sexual intercourse. It is difficult to imagine a more anti-political tract.

The novelist Viktor Pelevin is equally contemptuous of politicians and their *métier*. Pelevin, a Buddhist who regularly retires for a period of contemplation, has produced savage satires of Soviet history and contemporary Russian society. *Omon Ra* describes a space mission being organised in the USSR. The cosmonauts are inducted into a chaotic training programme and it is found that the living quarters in the orbital craft have been designed too small. Pelevin tells how the men are put into hospital to have their legs amputated. Thus reduced, they can fit into the craft and bring glory to themselves and their country.[24]

Pelevin is just as hostile to today's Russia. His *Generation 'P'* declares on its first page:

> All commercial trademarks mentioned in the text are the personal
> property of their respected owners, and their rights are retained.
> The titles of products and the names of politicians do not refer to
> the corresponding market products and relate only to projections
> of elements of commercial–political informational space forcibly
> induced as objects of the individual mind.[25]

This mumbo-jumbo hits the disingenuous tone maintained throughout
the chapters. The materialism of contemporary culture is derided: 'Once
upon a time there really was a happy young generation which smiled
at the summer, the sea and the sun – and chose Pepsi.'[26] The main
character, a certain Tatarski, is a cynical operator in the advertising
industry. When his clients ask him to devise a slogan for a soft-drink
company, he has to compete in a business whose adverts blend the
techniques of Western commercialism and the contents of nineteenth-
century Russian intellectual culture. A slogan invented for the Gap chain
of retail shops runs:

> RUSSIA WAS ALWAYS NOTORIOUS FOR THE GAP
> BETWEEN CULTURE AND CIVILISATION.
> NO MORE CIVILISATION.
> THE ONLY THING THAT REMAINS IS THE GAP.
> THE WAY THEY SEE YOU.[27]

As Tatarski climbs to riches and power, he encounters Yeltsin, Berezovski and other leading Russian figures, and the rottenness of life after
communism is revealed.

But Pelevin leaves his readers doubting that there is any prospect of
salvation for Russia. The one thing that Tatarski, despite his literary skill,
finds he cannot compose is a plan for national redemption:

> At first the task seemed to him a simple one but sitting at the table
> he realised with horror that nothing, absolutely nothing was enter-
> ing his head. Even the sketching-board, to which he turned in
> despair, did not help, when the hands of the watch went past
> midnight.[28]

The 'Russian Question', for Pelevin, is a joking matter but also a matter
for despair.

Not all books, of course, are as sophisticated as *Generation 'P'*, and
most sales do not involve works of 'high culture'. Thrillers, romances
and soft pornography are highly popular. And yet even many of those
readers who prefer the less demanding kinds of prose are eager to

consider descriptions of Russia's contemporary plight. Detective and spy thrillers have continued to be printed in vast print-runs by Soviet publishing houses since 1991. Some examples of this literature are written with impressive verve and with realistic depictions of the Russian criminal milieu. Whereas publishers once rushed to translate Arthur Conan Doyle, Agatha Christie and Raymond Chandler, they now tend to support Russia's own writers. Domestic pulp fiction has acquired an enormous market and every city has makeshift street-stalls selling the latest publications, often in 'pirated' editions. Alexandra Marinina's publishers alternately advertise her as the 'Russian Agatha Christie' and as a writer whose books 'are not reminiscent of Anglo-Saxon analogies and all the more strongly whet the reader's appetite'.[29] The author's real name is Marina Alexeeva; she herself worked as a lieutenant-colonel in the Moscow police force. Her regular heroine, Anastasia Kamenskaya, is also a lieutenant-colonel, who tracks down gangs of murderers, drug peddlers and fraudsters from her office at 38 Petrovka.[30]

Along with several film directors, Marinina helped to pioneer discussion of the role of women in contemporary Russia.[31] She does not idealise her female characters. On the contrary, Lieutenant-Colonel Kamenskaya is in many ways an unprepossessing figure. She is gauche in conversation. She is unattractive to most men. She has a chronic back problem and a troublingly low sugar count. But her very ordinariness is part of her appeal to both male and female readers. She does not want to be glamorous: she is essentially just a 'normal' Russian person living and working in difficult conditions.

Yet the commercial success of Marinina's thrillers stems mostly from her extraordinary knowledge of Russian criminal behaviour and from her skill in putting together complex, unnerving plots. She is liked for her exposure of the 'mafioso' gangs. Implicitly she condemns the way the country has been changing; but no claim is made that things were better in the Soviet period. Nor does she propose solutions for the current Russian imbroglio. Characteristically Marinina is not so committed to feminist notions that she denies the need for Lieutenant-Colonel Kamenskaya to have burly male colleagues by her side. Physical violence in the thrillers is perpetrated by the men. Kamenskaya's most radical social habit is her refusal to wear make-up; and she hates going shopping. Thus the Kamenskaya series is escapist fiction enhanced by sharp observation of life on Moscow streets. And although few thriller writers can match Marinina's style and expertise, her shunning of the higher affairs of state is the norm in much pulp fiction. Russian counter-intelligence officers in spy thrillers continue to be depicted as national heroes in a hostile world, but the patriotic message is buried deep in the action: the blatant political messages in the thrillers written in Brezhnev's time are rare nowadays.

Rock music, perhaps surprisingly, is the popular genre which most directly tackled the 'Russian Question'. And it has done this much more enthusiastically than outstanding exponents of classical music such as the composer Alfred Schnittke, who emigrated in 1990 and whose various compositions avoided themes of political import. All this is a residue of the late Soviet years. As Gorbachëv sought to win active support from the youth of the USSR, he allowed greater freedom for TV editors to include music of all kinds – old and new, Soviet and foreign, sentimental and critical – in their programmes. Not all performers showed much interest in politics. One of the most popular singers, Alla Pugachëva, stuck to themes of love and day-to-day concerns. As magnificent a rock survivor as Tina Turner in the USA, Pugachëva is still mobbed in the streets by her fans and even her wedding is commemorated in newspapers.[32] Her plangent style turned her into a figure of glitzy earthiness. But there were others who wanted to extend the tradition of social critique which had been sustained in the Brezhnev period by poet-balladeers such as Bulat Okudzhava and Vladimir Vysotski. Under Gorbachëv there were many rock bands eager to highlight the malaises of Soviet society and the possibilities of betterment. This propensity was maintained after 1991, even though its prominence appears on the decline as it competes with rap, garage, hip hop, punk, heavy metal and 'boy bands'.

Among the outstanding singer-songwriters is Boris Grebenshchikov, leader of Akvarium, who combines the traditions of American blues and Russian balladry. In his album *Navigator* there is the verse:

> Just when you think you're building, the whole thing flies apart;
> Just when you feel like talking, you talk such utter rot.
> If you cannot take up drinking, truly nothing will work out.
> But the drink is no good either, it sends you howling like a wolf –
> For no reason at all.[33]

Grebenshchikov's work brilliantly expresses the pain of life in Russia since the late 1980s. Gorbachëv told Russians they were involved in 'restructuring', Yeltsin that they were constructing from scratch. The reality for most Russians has always been much harsher and Grebenshchikov sings for them.

In 1994 he brought out an album entitled *Kostroma, Mon Amour*. Kostroma, an old industrial town in north-central Russia, is a very unlikely place to be wistful about; but Grebenshchikov used its ordinariness in order to emphasise that the country has suffered unduly in its past. This theme is resumed in another song entitled '8200':

> Eight thousand two hundred versts of emptiness,
> And still there's nowhere for me to stay the night with you.
> I would be happy if it wasn't for you,
> If it wasn't for you, my motherland.
>
> I would be happy, but it makes no odds any more.
> When it's sky-blue everywhere else, here it's red.
> It's like silver in the wind, like a sickle to the heart –
> And my soul flies above you like a Sirin.[34]

These are wonderful stanzas. They start with the singer seemingly referring to a girlfriend, but it turns out that he wants to spend the night with Russia. And Russia is unhappy. Russia is red with despair and a sickle is pressed to her heart. Grebenshchikov uses the colour red and the sickle (reminiscent of the hammer-and-sickle emblem) in a negative fashion to indicate his rejection of the Soviet past. Instead of kilometres, he uses the tsarist measure of length, the *versta*. He also sings ancient pagan Russia. Sirin was a Slavonic mythical creature, half-woman and half-bird. Although the song is depressing in its message, it beautifully evokes the vast mysterious wastes of the Russian Federation.[35]

The contrast between Grebenshchikov's suggestiveness and the didacticism of the older generation of the intelligentsia is unmistakable. Solzhenitsyn's latest writings illustrate the point. On deciding to abandon *The Red Wheel*, he let some finished fragments appear in print. One of them is about Marshal Zhukov before and during the Second World War; and breaking with the conventional portraiture, Solzhenitsyn depicts Zhukov as a ruthless thug willing to sacrifice the lives of any number of the men under his command.[36] The story has little literary merit. Solzhenitsyn's purpose was more political than stylistic: he aimed to discredit all aspects of the USSR's past, including those which continue to enjoy the Russian government's approval. As he has got more elderly, he has concentrated upon his work as a pamphleteer. The recent booklet *Russia in the Shadows* discusses concerns that have been constant for several years. Russia, according to Solzhenitsyn, requires spiritual regeneration, the rule of law, truly local self-government and gradual, peaceful change. The West in his eyes is hostile to Russia both as a cultural presence and as an external economic and military force. He insists that Russia's humiliation can be reversed solely by the efforts of her people. These are the political statements of a prophet who has given up believing in the power of his artistry.[37]

And so the culture of the creative arts in the Russian Federation is diverse. It has nationalists and anti-nationalists, traditionalists and modernists, realists and satirists. It speaks with many tongues. This is to be welcomed in itself; but it also means that artistic culture cannot unify society in the way that optimistic Russian advocates of the arts once took for granted. A liberated culture is a culture that suggests and questions. Such a culture cannot indoctrinate. Sometimes it seems that artistic intellectuals had a more fulfilling role when they operated in fear of an oppressive state. Times have changed and few people any longer assume that literature, painting, music or cinema will decisively affect Russia's ability to reform itself.

PART FOUR

IN THE RUSSIAN DEPTHS

17. FEDERATION AND THE REGIONS

Kalmykia is a corporation now.

Kirsan Ilyumzhinov, President of Kalmykia, 1995[1]

Russia's reformers have always imposed central policies knowing that success would depend on co-operation and initiative being shown from below. Catherine the Great, who exchanged letters with Voltaire, knew her reforming policies would founder unless local support was forthcoming. The same insight was shared by Alexander II in the nineteenth century – and indeed by Alexander Kerenski and Mikhail Gorbachëv in the twentieth. Even Vladimir Lenin and Joseph Stalin, extreme centralisers, saw that change had to proceed from the depths as well as from on high.

The Russian Federation, according to the Constitution of 1993, is a combination of 'equal subjects' joined together by a federal structure. These subjects include eighty-nine units: republics, regions, provinces, cities of 'federal significance', autonomous districts and an autonomous region. The powers of the Federation are paramount but the various republics are allowed their own constitutions and legislation and the other subjects can pass their own laws.[2] The subjects have immense freedom on their territories so long as they stay within the limits of federal legislation. This is in line with Yeltsin's commitment before ousting Gorbachëv in 1991. However much Gorbachëv conceded to 'the localities', Yeltsin always claimed that it was inadequate. Travelling round the RSFSR, he urged the republican leaders in particular to 'gobble up as much autonomy as you can handle'. Throughout 1992 he insisted that he had meant what he said. The Russian government set up a State Committee for National Policy with the status of a ministry. Federal principles were expounded and the Minister of the State Committee, Valeri Tishkov, was someone who for years had argued that the interests of the non-Russians should be looked after better than previously. He had in mind the inception of a federation that was federal not just in words but in reality – and he said so.

Tishkov came to office ready for action. Since 1988 he had been Deputy Director of the Institute of Ethnography in the USSR Academy of Sciences. He was a prominent Soviet academic and had campaigned for Gorbachëv to protect the interests of the non-Russians. Based in the dingy three-storey building on Dmitri Ulyanov Street in southern Moscow, he and his colleagues had had to use great care when criticising Russian nationalist tendencies inside the Soviet communist leadership. But they had courageously highlighted the resentment in those many parts of the country where various ethnic groups lived side by side in large concentrations. Tishkov did not merely want to be in office; he wished to make a practical impact on the process of necessary reform.

Among his ideas was that each national group should be enabled to organise itself across the entire Russian Federation. He was alert to the danger that the Russian Federation might turn into a state that gave privileges to the ethnic Russians at the expense of the other peoples. But he also criticised the inherited Constitution of the RSFSR, which in practice had allowed the nation bearing the name of a given republic within the RSFSR to exercise disproportionate influence over the republic's affairs. Tishkov, who was influenced by the ideas of Austrian Marxism before the First World War, argued that Lenin's advocacy of small, territorially based administrative units was a recipe for local oppression. He failed to explain how his scheme for the organisation of national groups would fit into the Constitution of the Russian Federation. But his earnest wish was to solve the 'national question' – or rather the 'national questions' – by means of peaceful negotiation; and he insisted that the nations of the North Caucasus should be treated with particular care. His aim was that all national and ethnic groups across the Russian Federation should adopt some kind of general civic identity. Tishkov never quite explained how big the 'Russian' ingredient should be in this identity; but he unequivocally declared that each group should simultaneously be free to explore and affirm its specific history, traditions and consciousness.

The RSFSR's structure was a legacy of the early revolutionary years. The first attempt to set up an internal republic occurred in 1919 in the land inhabited by Tatars and Bashkirs. It was a failure. Tatar and Bashkir residents fought a war against each other. Both the Bashkirs and the Tatars also fought the local Russians. The Tatar-Bashkir Republic was quickly abandoned. But the idea of an array of national republics within the RSFSR was maintained; and although the central party and governmental bodies dominated policy and its implementation, the republics were not without power in schooling, the press, health and social amenities.

The RSFSR itself had been but one Soviet republic in the federal constitutional structure created in the early 1920s. But there was never any genuine federalism under Lenin: the Soviet republics did not jointly confer sovereignty upon the central state with the right to withhold it if that state transgressed its constitutional authority. In most ways, then, the RSFSR and other Soviet republics were kept under strict and unchallengeable control by the central bodies of the USSR; and the various internal units of the RSFSR – its republics, regions, provinces – were also under the direct control of the same bodies. This was made possible by the maintenance of a centralised communist party, based in Moscow, across the entire USSR. Under Stalin, furthermore, the leaderships of both the other Soviet republics of the USSR and the autonomous republics within the RSFSR were typically accused of 'bourgeois nationalism' and shot, and the interests of the local Russians were vigorously enhanced. Khrushchëv withdrew the weapon of terror, but his frequent sackings of personnel maintained an environment of political uncertainty. Only in the 1970s, when Brezhnev relaxed the pressure, did leaders in the Soviet republics (and to some extent in the RSFSR's internal republics) assert themselves again. No longer dreading they might lose their jobs, they tended to recruit amongst their own national group. The titular nationality was privileged in political promotion and economic benefaction.

Punishments were meted out for perceived excesses. Petro Shelest lost his job as First Secretary of the Communist Party of Ukraine for overdoing the indulgence to ethnic Ukrainians. Overt nationalism was curbed and any hint of hostility to Russia and the Russians was suppressed. But by and large the trend was for national self-assertiveness to grow. This happened under Brezhnev and, because of his political decentralisation, Gorbachëv.

Gorbachëv insisted that his purpose was to introduce a properly voluntary form of federalism in the USSR. But it was not to be, and the USSR broke up into fifteen independent states. Yeltsin had to start the negotiating process all over again within the RSFSR. Still at the height of his popularity, he urged the republics to sign a Federal Treaty in March 1992. Not only Chechnya under Djokar Dudaev but also the Tatarstan of

Mintimer Shaimiev refused the request. Tatarstan is an area of 68,000 square kilometres and has a large Moslem minority and Tatar cultural traditions stretching back for centuries. It is also an important site for industry and oil extraction. Shaimiev pushed his case to the limit, demanding recognition of the Republic of Tatarstan as an independent state. All the trappings were put into place. At Shaimiev's behest a 'state anthem' was composed on the basis of a melody attributed to People's Artist of the Republic of Tatarstan Rustem Yakhin and instrumentalised by Professor Rubin Abdulun. The law passed by the Cabinet of Ministers on 27 August 1993 stated that 'respect [for it] is the duty of each of its citizens' and that during its performance 'the public stands up while listening'.[3] Shaimiev's constitutional recalcitrance was a serious matter and he prohibited his administration from co-operating in arranging the referendum on the Constitution in December 1993.[4]

In deference to Shaimiev, Yeltsin withdrew his forces from Tatarstan in 1992.[5] The presence of ethnic Russian conscripts in Kazan was thought an unnecessary risk, and so Moscow accepted Shaimiev's commitment to keeping order with the republic's own troops. This was done despite the high proportion of Russians in Tatarstan's population. Other republics too were relieved of their Russian army garrisons. And for a time Tatarstan even banned Moscow-based banks from setting up branches in Kazan.[6]

Yet it was Shaimiev who became the first republican leader to sign a treaty with Moscow. This occurred in February 1994. Kabardino-Balkaria followed in June and Bashkortostan in August. Yeltsin presented this as a triumph for the territorial integrity and political sovereignty of the Russian Federation. Nothing could have been further from the truth. This was a period of governmental weakness in Moscow: the State Duma elections of the previous year had shocked Yeltsin when his favoured parties failed to get a majority. Shaimiev struck a deal with the central government allowing Tatarstan to keep the lion's share of profits from the taxation of the republic's enterprises. The treaty between the Russian Federation and Tatarstan did not even recognise the precedence of the Constitution and laws of the Federation over those of the republic.[7] Yeltsin and Chernomyrdin signed none the less. They wanted no further trouble with the republics – or at least they wanted to be able to deal with troublesome republics one by one. They signed dozens of individual treaties with them without worrying whether the contents broke the very Constitution which they had striven hard to get accepted in the December 1993 referendum.

Although Yeltsin, Chernomyrdin and Shaimiev put their names to the Russo-Tatarstani treaty, the parliaments of the Russian Federation and Tatarstan failed to ratify the act of signature. It is by no means clear that the treaty has any constitutional force.[8] But at least the Russo-Tatarstani treaty has been published and discussed. The same is not true for several other republics. Whereas Shaimiev has printed his treaty in a sumptuous booklet, other leaders have done little to explain their deals with Moscow. The consequence is that no one could examine the constitutionality of treaties before they came into effect. Yuri Skuratov, State Procurator until his dismissal in 1999, frequently challenged them, but to no avail. The Constitutional Court has been less active and even less effectual. Presidents have gone on signing whatever treaties they wished and the rule of constitution and law has been flouted time and time again.

The results were messy. Tatarstan stipulated in 1998 that its citizenship law was independent of any prescriptions by the Russian Federation. This was close to a declaration of state independence. Chechnya, of course, brought invasion on itself after asserting that it had seceded from Russia. The war of 1994–6, during which tens of thousands were killed, ended in an armed stalemate brokered by Alexander Lebed; and it was agreed to leave open the constitutional status of Chechnya within the Russian Federation until 2001.[9] Yet the Chechen government calmly affirmed that the republic would be subject to the Shariat Law. The rights of non-Moslems were suppressed; even those Moslems who objected were ignored. Chechnya became an Islamic administration in flagrant contradiction of the Federal Constitution. Other republics have behaved with scarcely less militancy. Bashkortostan and eight other republics have laid down that holders of public office should have competence in both Russian and the language of the titular people of the republic. This seems reasonable at first sight. But the menacing possibilities become obvious when we consider that, for instance, the Bashkirs – after whom Bashkortostan takes its name – constitute only 22 per cent of the republic's population. Understandably the other peoples of Bashkortostan feel that their constitutional rights have been disregarded.[10]

The republics and their leaders have no serious commitment to federalism.[11] At no time have they felt obligated; always they have made demands. Their interpretation of federalism is as a means of maximising political and economic concessions from Moscow. The idea that the republics should be pooling their sovereignty in the central government in return for guarantees of republican autonomy in lesser matters of rule has been absent. No one can pretend that the central authorities have not deserved the scorn of the republican leaders. Yeltsin and his ministers often behaved quite disgracefully. But two wrongs do not make a right.

With some justification, ministers have anyhow increasingly regarded the republics as lawless fiefdoms of the local presidents. It was only a matter of time before Moscow retaliated. Since nearly all ministers are ethnic Russians, there is an element of nationalism in this – and the intellectual crudity of many in Yeltsin's entourage added fuel to this centralising drive. Not everyone in Yeltsin's administration had given up hope that a properly federalist system might be created. Valeri Tishkov was the prime reformer. But he had few serious supporters in the government and soon felt isolated. In October 1992 he resigned his ministerial post in the State Committee for National Policy in October 1992 and his role as advocate of system and clarity was taken by Ramazan Abdulatipov, who was somewhat more amenable to compromise with his opponents. Like Tishkov, Abdulatipov wanted federalism in practice as well as in words. Hailing from Dagestan in the south of the Russian Federation, he had risen, under Gorbachëv, to the post of Chairman of the Council of Nationalities of the Supreme Soviet of the USSR. He argued that the interests of the non-Russian citizens were in urgent need of protection through new legislation; and for this purpose he prepared a document, *The Concept of the State National Policy of the Russian Federation*, in late 1992.[12]

Abdulatipov agreed with Tishkov that the interests of the non-Russians were not best served by the granting of unconditional power to the republics. Coming from Dagestan, a republic of extraordinary ethnic variety, he understood the danger of letting a republic fall into the hands of a particular nationality. The domination of Tatarstan by Tatar politicians even though Tatars constitute only 48 per cent of the population must surely have been in his mind. Another consideration for Abdulatipov was the sensitivity of Russians. He affirmed that demographic factors meant that Russians would remain 'the basic support' of the state. But somehow a civic version of statehood had to be built. Abdulatipov therefore called for 'the cultivation of a feeling of Russian [*rossiiskii*] patriotism';[13] and if the Russians could be reassured by such an orientation, he declared, it would be easier to make the reforms necessary for the improvement of the conditions and prospects of the other peoples. He worked indefatigably for this approach to be accepted by government and Duma. The warning he gave was blunt: without national and ethnic harmony, the Russian Federation is unworkable.

The non-Russians in Abdulatipov's opinion need their own national and ethnic facilities in Moscow. He suggested a Council of Nationalities as well as an All-Russia (*Vserossiiskii*) House of the Peoples of Russia. Each people of the Russian Federation arguably ought to receive 'national-cultural autonomy' and be enabled to organise themselves across the length and breadth of the Russian Federation.[14] He insisted that the peoples repressed by Stalin in 1943 should have their full rights restored. Many wounds from the old Soviet days have yet to be tended. But Abdulatipov had to struggle for years before he convinced Yeltsin and the Russian government. It was not until 15 June 1996 that the President consented to sign the draft *Concept* which Abdulatipov had pressed upon him since 1992.[15] The date was remarkable. It was just twenty-four hours before the first round of the Presidential elections of that year, and almost certainly Yeltsin was striving – at the last moment – to gather votes from those electors who were not Russian and who had not yet decided whom to support in the ballot. This gives a large hint that Yeltsin was not genuinely committed to the contents of the *Concept*. He wanted votes and would do anything to get them. Abdulatipov had nothing genuinely solid to celebrate.

Meanwhile the process of disintegration has continued. Kalmykia offers a striking example. This is a republic in Russia's south whose population according to the 1989 census was 45 per cent Kalmyk and whose religion, until the militant atheist campaigns of the 1930s, was Buddhist. In the Second World War the Kalmyks were judged by Stalin to be pro-German and – in a week of brutal repression – were rounded up and deported to Siberia and North Kazakhstan. The same fate befell the Chechens, Crimean Tatars, Meshketian Turks, Balkarians, Karachai and Volga Germans. Thousands died of hunger and disease on the rail journey. Thrown out of the trains at their destination, they were left to fend for themselves in the bleakest conditions imaginable. Shelter had to be constructed without saws and hammers. Food had to be foraged from the unknown forests. All the time they were kept under surveillance. Once a fortnight the Kalmyk families had to trudge to the nearest NKVD office, usually many miles away, to prove that no one had attempted to escape, and if someone had died, the corpse had to be dragged along to prove that death had occurred.[16] With Khrushchëv's denunciation of

Stalin in 1956, the uprooted Kalmyks were permitted to return to their ancestral lands.

As the USSR collapsed, no one expected this most cowed republic to assert itself against Moscow. Yet within a couple of years this is precisely what happened. Kalmykia acquired a President, Kirsan Ilyumzhinov, of great eccentricity. He had always been a troublemaker. The director of his kindergarten wanted to expel him and he smoked illicitly at secondary school. Despite his record, he got a place at Moscow's prestigious State Institute of International Relations; but then a fellow student denounced him to the KGB for his delinquent lifestyle and opinions. Nevertheless he somehow – and this is extraordinary and as yet unexplained – managed to get a job in a Soviet-Japanese company in 1989 and eventually became a millionaire. When presidential elections were called in Kalmykia in 1993, he decided to stand with a slogan not notable for modesty: 'Without me the people is incomplete.'[17] He won a handsome victory. His promise to donate money to every inhabitant of Kalmykia did him no harm. He fostered a resurgence of Kalmyk language and culture, and Tibetan monks came to revive Buddhism in the republic.[18] But Ilyumzhinov left nothing to chance; and although he claimed to be law-abiding and incorruptible, there was plentiful reason to doubt his word. Fraud became endemic in the republic and political assassinations of his adversaries have not been unknown since his rise to Presidential office.

Ilyumzhinov is not the only authoritarian republican leader, only the most authoritarian. Less flamboyant but also ruthless is Bashkortostan's President Murtaza Rakhimov, who has systematically eliminated opposition in disregard for the Constitution. Nor has he been shy about giving affront to Moscow. A case in point was his activity in the December 1999 election. When Moscow-based national TV stations started to expose his various wrongdoings, he simply cut off their local transmission facilities. The censorship lasted throughout the end of his clique's successful electoral campaign.

In any case, it is not just central politicians who resent the influence of the national republics in the new Russia. The various provincial units – the *oblasti* and *kraya* – have suffered under the recent economic pressures. Among them are several provinces which, in the communist period, had access to the portals of power and privilege. Great cities and their surrounding provinces were beneficiaries of state budgetary dispositions. It was claimed with justification that the First Secretary of the average party province committee (the *obkom* secretary) was like a local tsar. Or indeed like a local general secretary. Nor were the collective feelings of such leaders ignored with impunity after Stalin's death. Khrushchëv fell in 1964 in large measure because he had annoyed the province-level secretaries. He had sacked many and caused all of them to feel insecure in their posts. He had obsessively reorganised the institutions of local power. His successor Leonid Brezhnev learned from Khrushchëv's experience. Wisely he spent hours on the telephone consulting these same secretaries as he developed policy. It was from the ranks of the local party secretaries that Khrushchëv, Brezhnev, Gorbachëv and Yeltsin emerged in the middle of their careers.

Provincial leaders have understandably been disconcerted by the greater ability of the national republics to tweak the ear of the Russian president and the Kremlin ministers.[19] In some places there is territorial revanchism. For example, leading figures in Orenburg Province have suggested that its old boundaries – when it incorporated parts of what is now Bashkortostan and independent Kazakhstan – were more sensible than its present ones.[20] This is not merely a sense of envy. It also flows from the need of the leaders to prove themselves in the eyes of their business lobbies and their electorates. They need to be able to protect the interests of the province and to be seen to do so. In constitutional terms they have the same rights as the national republics. They are listed equally as 'subjects of the Russian Federation'.[21] But the sequence of the list is significant – or is felt to be significant. First come the national republics and then the provinces. Another point is worth noting. When Yeltsin sought to extend his authority in 1992, he appointed his own plenipotentiary representatives to the regions of the Russian Federation.[22] For the most part these representatives were attached to the provinces and Yeltsin left the national republics with their existing rulers. He also went on courting the favour of the rulers of the republics. The fact that a ministry – the Committee for Nationality Affairs – was established to look after the interests of non-Russian minorities while no parallel body protected the Russian provinces was further grist to the mill of resentment.

The result was a series of attempts by provinces to get together to assert themselves against the Kremlin. In extreme cases this has been accompanied by a secessionist campaign. The names of the potential breakaway states in the early 1990s included 'Siberian Agreement', the 'Urals Republic', the 'Far East and Trans-Baikal' and even the 'Big Volga'.[23] The same had occurred in Siberia and the Urals in the Civil War. It had looked distinctly possible then that the vast territory from the Urals eastwards might break away permanently from Lenin's Russia. Developments after 1991 followed this precedent. The declaration of the Urals Republic, based in Yekaterinburg, affronted Yeltsin, who had spent his early career in the city, and he came close to sacking Sverdlovsk Province Governor Eduard Rossel as punishment.[24]

But little has come of these challenges to the Kremlin and the Urals Republic has proved a flash in the pan. In the Civil War the regional republics were simply terminated by the Red Army. No such outcome has been necessary in the ethnic Russian provinces since the collapse of the USSR. Not only regions but even particular provinces lack the cohesive identity that several national republics have mustered. Their secessionism is rhetorical. The fact is that out of the eighty-nine republics, regions and provinces of the Russian Federation only about a dozen are net contributors to the federal fiscal revenues. The rest are dependent on largesse from Moscow to keep their administration, economy and social services in operation.[25] Regional leaders alternate between threatening to secede and claiming that only they can stop secession from taking place: both are tactics to obtain increased help. Once upon a time it was a matter of pride and self-interest for the *obkom* party boss to lobby Moscow for political and financial support for all his province's towns and villages and their economic enterprises. Now the relations of a market economy dominate the situation. It is a market economy distorted by the violence and corruption which accompanied its emergence in the 1990s. The tacit 'rules of the game' that characterised the Soviet political regime in the post-Stalin period have been torn up.

The brighter provincial leaders understand this and co-operate with the Kremlin in pursuit of a more efficient balance of central and local politics. This is what Eduard Rossel, Sverdlovsk Province governor, said in interview:

> Enormous might resides with us in the regions and then there are the federal organs of power (*vlast'*) which sit in Moscow. They do things, but they do them in isolation from the opinions of the regions. The introduction of one or two or even fifty representatives [from the regions] into the government, even the complete replacement of the government with a cabinet of ministers from the regions won't solve things. Because we need to keep contact with the government. Recommendations coming from us – from below – must be worked on at the level of government. The federal organs of power, some of them openly and others behind closed doors, are

administering Russia and the regions have been left to themselves;
in reality we have been abandoned by the government since 1990.[26]

Rossel is an economic reformer who could have entered Yeltsin's cabinet
if he had desired. He worked hard to reorganise the administrative
structures in Yekaterinburg so as to attract investment. He could have
done a lot more to stop criminal groups from installing themselves.
Nevertheless he justifiably lamented the inattention of central politicians
to his reasonable requests.

Whereas the President and government signed treaties with the
national republics from 1994, two more years passed before any such
agreement was made with any Russian province. The first to sign an
agreement, indeed, was Sverdlovsk Province (whose centre is Yekaterinburg) in January 1996. This precedent was followed by Nizhni Novgorod,
Kaliningrad, Irkutsk and Rostov-on-Don.[27] Deals were done with the
elected governors which guaranteed local autonomy as well as a degree
of central control. The scheme was extended to other provinces. In
July 1997 treaties were signed with Bryansk, Chelyabinsk and Magadan
Provinces.

Bryansk and Chelyabinsk were interesting cases since their earlier
leaders had been critics of Yeltsin and his government – and the Bryansk
governor Yuri Lodkin had been deposed by Yeltsin in the political crisis
in October 1993 by Presidential Decree No. 1453. Lodkin had had it
coming to him. He had given a promise to his friend Khasbulatov
that the Supreme Soviet could be relocated to Bryansk if Yeltsin closed
it down in Moscow. (Khasbulatov and Lodkin did not anticipate that
things would go as far as a siege of the White House.) Yeltsin's decree
appointed V. Karpov as Acting Governor. The problem was that Karpov
was on the road from Bryansk to Moscow and could not be telephoned.
At the very same time Lodkin, sensing that something was afoot, was on
the same road and travelling back to Bryansk. The police were instructed
to stop all Moscow-bound Volga cars and find Karpov. Soon he was
discovered and told to go back to Bryansk as the President's man.
Karpov needed much persuading that this was not a 'provocation'
organised by the opposite political side; and when he got back to Bryansk
he was confronted by Lodkin, who refused to leave his office and
arranged a public demonstration on his own behalf.[28] Only the definitive
victory of Yeltsin in Moscow enabled Karpov to eject Lodkin.

Yeltsin had removed unequivocal political enemies such as Lodkin
from provincial leadership. But he still had difficulties with governors

who simply insisted on running an administration in defiance of the Kremlin's policies. The most troublesome figure was Yevgeni Nazdratenko of Primorski Region on the Pacific coast. Appointed by Yeltsin in May 1993, he quickly demanded unusual levels of state subsidy. He also imposed his appointees at lower grades of the administrative hierarchy. Opposition was crushed, and it was only under intense pressure from Moscow that he submitted his leadership to the test of an election. Once in power, he had become a tyrant with extraordinary ambitions. He took it upon himself to comment on Russian foreign policy. First he denounced the 1992 Russo-Chinese treaty, then he ordered the security forces to clear his region of Chinese illegal immigrants. His vexations were ceaseless. The Primorski Region was a byword for corruption under his rule and foreign businessmen were threatened with losing their trading rights unless they complied with his demands. There have also been arrests of Russian businessmen, including some associated with the Moscow-based 'oligarch' Anatoli Chubais. Nazdratenko's behaviour toward Chubais, a politician of immense influence, reveals the degree of local assertiveness possible in the Russian Federation.

Nazdratenko could have been handled differently. Yeltsin and his ministers chose to limit their interference to the withdrawal of material support for the Primorski Region: breakdowns of electricity and gas supplies have been frequent. But Nazdratenko remained imperturbable. He probably benefited from the sense of Moscow politicians that a strong political leader, however corrupt and undemocratic, is needed in this region abutting a sensitive border. Not until Putin became President was Nazdratenko finally compelled to leave office, and even then he was not brought to trial for corruption but instead was offered alternative high-ranking employment as head of the State Committee for Fisheries.[29]

In any case not all the difficulties facing the government are of its own making. Russia is more like a continent than a country and there is a huge variety of conditions. Some provinces are primarily industrial, others are agricultural. In several provinces of the Russian Federation there is an abundance of rare natural resources and a few provinces have sustained their manufacturing enterprises. But elsewhere there is little in the way of raw materials or marketable goods. There are provinces where a variety of ethnic groups cohabit whereas in others it is the Russians who are the vast majority. Differences exist between one province and another in density of population and proximity to the main transport routes. And while some provinces enjoy a temperate climate, others are at the mercy of extremely long and cold winters. Provinces approach the government for assistance with a wide range of needs that make the formulation of a systematic 'provincial policy' a very tricky task.

It is an environment that has perplexed rulers of Russia across the centuries. The tsars before 1917 and the communist party leaders through to 1991 sometimes came to power with simplistic notions about policy; but nearly always they were pushed into recognising the complexity of the administrative needs of the vast territory under their rule.

None the less even when the difficulties are taken into account, a botched job has been made; and the local politicians have reason to think that a corrupt nexus of Kremlin politicians and high financiers has worsened their plight. The chairman of the 'Union for the Rebirth of the North', T. Karatsuba, has written:

> Of course, the districts of the Russian North cannot stand outside the general process of the transition to market relations. Yet it is impermissible for our North to be subjected to methods of a colonial approach or of 'the Wild West'. In the eyes of some businessmen and bankers from this country and abroad the Russian North is merely a new, convenient source of profits and the object of a game at stock exchanges and auctions ... Thus, for example, the famous Norilsk conglomerate with its mountain of wealth – whose annual production is valued at 3.5 milliard dollars – was sold by the privatisation officers for 170 million dollars. Or take the Yakutia diamonds. It was not long ago that diamond mining produced one milliard dollars annually for the state budget. But the new shareholding owners have turned the business upside down, debts have mounted and the federal government has been compelled to take emergency measures to save the sector from complete ruin. This is why the special conditions of the North require the optimal combination of market mechanisms and dependable state control.[30]

This sort of comment is very frequent nowadays and virtually commands a consensus among political leaders, campaigners and journalists of the provinces.

They stress that some parts of the country will undergo social and material degradation until the government recognises its responsibilities. Yuri Spiridonov, head of the Komi Republic, has argued:

> The North doesn't need privileges but equal starting conditions. These – and not the tax delivery quotas – need to be equalised. For this to happen the burden of the rising costs in the North, which

the northerners bear by themselves, must be taken up by the entire federation.[31]

Such a plea is a throwback to the Soviet era, when the state offered financial inducements to people to work in the less hospitable zones. (The inducements were not universally available: the Gulag prisoners were given no choice about serving out their sentences in the labour camps of the Russian North.) There is little sign that the present government intends to grant Spiridonov's requests.

The way out of this situation is hard to imagine, especially since most ministers have geared their policy to letting 'the market' decide what benefits should accrue to any region across the Russian Federation. Provinces have been left to their own devices. The government has stepped in to assist when emergencies have occurred, and has offered finance to stave off total bankruptcy. But economic regeneration is seen as a matter for the provinces themselves. The vicious circle appears unbreakable. The government declines to provide a system of geographically differentiated subsidy to economically depressed areas. At the same time it interferes by selling off huge economic assets. It also fails, spectacularly, to impose an environment of law and order that might induce foreign investors to offer partnership to native Russian enterprise. There is a degree of ideological zeal in this. Ministers have been committed to a form of capitalism that downgrades the role of the state. There is also much governmental indifference. Moscow is looked after; the rest of the country is treated as an unfortunate appendage that tiresomely refuses to look after itself.

There have been suggestions that the solution is for republics and provinces to designate themselves as special economic zones. The model proposed for this is present-day Hong Kong. Advocates have suggested that the extraordinary problems of Kaliningrad would be answered by such a reform. Kaliningrad, despite belonging to the Russian Federation, is 250 miles from the next province in Russia. The city's original name was Königsberg, which was part of the German Empire before the First World War and was separated from Germany by the Danzig Corridor after the Treaty of Versailles. After the Second World War, Königsberg was annexed to the USSR. In culture and architecture it retained its German aspect after the flight of most of its German inhabitants in 1944 and the expulsion of the remainder in 1947.[32]

After 1991 Kaliningrad was separated from Russia by newly independent Lithuania and Belarus. This left the province perilously isolated. Its energy supplies came in large measure from Lithuania. Its transport links crossed Lithuania and were at the mercy of Lithuanian passport controls. The Russian government made menacing noises to Lithuania, but did little to help the inhabitants of Kaliningrad province more concretely. Muscovite inaction was the norm and Kaliningrad became a by-word for the neglect of the provinces by the central state authorities. As industry and agriculture fell into decline, the city struggled to survive. Its port became a centre for criminal activity. Car smuggling was turned into the leading commercial enterprise. Drug trafficking has been rife. Prostitution and HIV-Aids infection have plagued the life of the city. The Kaliningrad governor, Leonid Gorbenko, did little to combat these trends and was widely suspected of colluding with the criminal gangs. His xenophobic utterances scared off foreign investment (even though German entrepreneurs had expressed a willingness to return to the area). He paid only rare visits to Germany. Although the BMW automotive company set up operations in Kaliningrad, the main source of revenue from Germany were the busloads of tourists – and Gorbenko's rhetoric did little to increase their annual influx. His departure from office, however, did not lead to much improvement in the situation.

Only in October 1999 did the Russian government apply serious thought to Kaliningrad. When its members belatedly drew up its strategy on the European Union, Putin declared the province as 'the pilot region within the framework of Euro-Russian co-operation'.[33] At least a beginning has been made in opening up Russia's more depressed provinces to injection of capital from the countries of the West. Perhaps the fact that Putin's wife is a native of Kaliningrad has alerted him to the acuteness of the local problem. More plausible is the hypothesis that Putin is concerned about the deep rift between the Kremlin and the 'localities'; he is, if nothing else, a committed centralist and aims at an economy that is not merely metropolitan but also national.

Yet the government has no comprehensive plan to regenerate the republics and provinces. Putin's initiatives in policy have been focused in the direction of asserting central governmental control. He began by suspending laws passed in Ingushetia, Bashkortostan and the Amur Region in contravention of the Constitution. Murtaza Rakhimov, the President of Bashkortostan, was left in no doubt that the days of care-free republican legislative activity were over – and in June 2000 the Prosecutor-General Vladimir Ustinov gave republics one month to bring their laws into conformity with those of the Russian Federation.[34] Putin also issued a decree to divide the Russian Federation into seven large regions. To each region he appointed his own 'plenipotentiary representative' to supervise the agencies of police, security and tax collection. The capitals of the regions are Moscow, St Petersburg, Yekaterinburg, Rostov-on-Don, Nizhni Novgorod, Novosibirsk and Khabarovsk. What is noticeable is that none of the regional capitals lies within a 'national' republic.[35] Putin has chosen Russian provincial capitals. In none too subtle a fashion he warned that the assertiveness of Tatarstan, Bashkortostan and other republics will no longer be tolerated. President Shaimiev of Tatarstan, who was accustomed to bragging that 97 per cent of his electorate voted for and supported him,[36] meekly commented that the decree would 'help the president to perform his constitutional duties more efficiently'.

Shaimiev's docility was not unconnected with the increased powers sought and obtained by Putin to dismiss regional leaders found to have acted unconstitutionally or corruptly. Putin's spokesmen opined that the security services have evidence against several such leaders. Until 2000 there was much complacency about the Kremlin in both the 'national' republics and the Russian provinces; it was reminiscent of the USSR under Leonid Brezhnev. As long as no overt insult was made to the Kremlin and its policies, then the localities were left alone. But Putin is a recentraliser.

The 'Russian' provinces too are placed under the scrutiny of his plenipotentiary representatives. The functions of supervision are vaguely defined, but clearly it is Putin's wish to have an agency capable of imposing compliance with the Kremlin's instructions. The reaction of the general public has been positive. Even Putin's adversaries have signalled a guarded approval. Communist party leader Gennadi Zyuganov expressed unease mainly because the decree did not spell out its principles exactly; but he had no doubt about the need for some such reform: 'It is extremely important to restore the vertical system of authority and normal control over the country as some of the regional leaders have in fact turned into khans and sheikhs.'[37] The 'national' republics have more to fear than the 'Russian' provinces. Some of the republics threw down a gauntlet to the Kremlin in the 1990s, and Putin has not forgotten this. Their ability to insist on their rights as constituent members of a voluntary federation has been curtailed. Presidential authority has been strengthened at their expense. This has happened, however, only at the level of policy. In practice it has yet to be seen whether the unruly regions can be brought to heel. Laws have been passed in the provinces and republics which contradict the Federal

Constitution and its laws. Outrageous thievery and corruption persist. Charlatans still hold posts as republican presidents or provincial governors.

Yet the main difficulty remains the same. The Kremlin has failed to conduct a feasible strategy for economic regeneration. Yeltsin allowed 'the localities' to operate autonomously while failing to insist on respect for constitutionality at the centre or in the localities. The result was the formation of criminal cliques without interest in the improvement of the situation – and the electorate's resentment of the political and economic elites has naturally increased. There is a long history here. Since the centralisation of tsarist power under Ivan the Terrible in the fifteenth century there has been a litany of complaints from the provinces that Moscow has failed to supply the means for social recovery. Russian history, for one reason or another, has conformed to a cyclical pattern. Periods of devolution have been frequent. The year 1917 was an extreme example under Alexander Kerenski, but Russian rulers such as Alexander II, Mikhail Gorbachëv and Boris Yeltsin have also insisted that any successful reform requires 'initiative from below'. Sooner or later there is a reaction to this. Centralism nearly always supersedes a slackening of the Kremlin's control. Peter the Great, Vladimir Lenin, Joseph Stalin and, since 1999, Vladimir Putin have nailed their colours to the mast of authoritarianism.

What is already clear is that the reform agenda of 1991–2 has been frustrated and, indeed, substantially abandoned. Optimists felt that the republics and provinces held the key to success and that the prospects were good if the Kremlin handled things with sensitivity. Evidently this sensitivity was not maintained. But equally important was the lack of resolve among the republican and provincial elites to pursue a positive course of change. The sins of commission and omission at the centre have proliferated outside Moscow. The second tier of power in Russia has just as crooked timber as the first.

18. RUSSIAN TOWN, RUSSIAN VILLAGE

It could have been the Russian paradise,
This land of Yaroslavl.
But the tractors have crucified
Each and every rut here.

Vladimir Kornilov, 'Russian Paradise'[1]

The situation is not much more encouraging in the towns and villages. Russians, like most Western observers, are preoccupied by metropolitan politics. The Romanov dynasty was overthrown by workers and soldiers on the streets of the capital Petrograd. The seat of power was transferred to Moscow in March 1918. The Kremlin was the ultimate citadel defended by the communists in the Civil War. The great internal disputes of the communist party took place in Moscow in the 1920s; and when Stalin issued his commands from the capital in the 1930s, the rest of the country trembled. At his death the popular disturbances most feared by his successors were those which occurred in the avenues near Red Square on the day of his funeral. If crowds could not be controlled in Moscow, the regime would totter. In August 1991 the Committee for the State of Emergency, acting to bring the reforms of Gorbachëv to a halt, focused their efforts on the capital. When Yeltsin mounted a tank outside the White House and denounced the Committee, he showed an audacity that thousands of onlookers started to emulate. The attempted coup collapsed into farce and Moscow's example was picked up by the rest of the country. Events in the capital were crucial in following years. The attack on the White House by Yeltsin's forces in October 1993 was a decisive moment in his Presidency.

Not for nothing have Russian rulers since time immemorial referred to places outside the capital – villages, towns, regions or even whole countries – as 'the localities' (*mesta*). In the tsarist and Soviet periods, even Ukraine was just one of these localities. What happened in the capital took massive precedence over every matter, tiny or large, that happened elsewhere.

The economic development of Russia since 1991 has reinforced this attitude. Moscow has an affluence unseen in any other city: whereas the average income in the capital is nine times higher than the level of mere subsistence, it is actually lower than that level in Ingushetia, Dagestan and Tyva.[2] The limousines cruise its boulevards. The shops of foreign parfumiers, clothes designers and sports-goods suppliers sparkle throughout the central precincts. Rich businessmen are everywhere, frequently accompanied by armed bodyguards and sumptuously dressed young women. Illustrious old buildings have been renovated. The Hotel Metropol has the appurtenances of luxury rivalling any such facility for the well-heeled traveller across the world. Even St Petersburg looks tawdry by comparison, not having had the lavish funds available to its predecessor and successor as Russia's capital. Moscow has the energy of privilege. Its mayor in the post-communist years has been Yuri Luzhkov. With his gleaming forehead, piercing eyes and aggressive comportment he let it be known that he regards his post as only one rung lower than the Presidency. The statuary of the new Moscow reflects his determination and confidence as well as his dubious artistic taste. Moscow still stands alone. It is like Holland in the European Union, a state on its own within a broader political and economic entity.

Yet the preoccupation with the metropolis is a bit of a paradox. The demographic statistics of the Russian Federation illustrate this: towns with fewer than 100,000 inhabitants constitute the majority of the population and yet their electoral weight plays little part in the calculation of central politicians. Almost no endeavour is made to prioritise the regeneration of such places – or perhaps we should say 'localities'. The reasoning is crude. The politicians of the Kremlin know from experience that a last-minute subsidy during a Presidential electoral campaign will suffice to win the support of local elites. In any case the ascendant leadership in Moscow has the capacity to fiddle the results of any election. The trick is not to overdo things, but rather to invent just enough political support to keep the ascendancy intact. All this is taken for granted nowadays. The towns and cities of Russia are thrown back on their own resources after the local elites have done whatever they can to extract handouts from the government. This in turn increases the tendency towards 'boss'-type politics. Once a town's mayor has emerged as a competent administrator, there is characteristically a widespread acceptance of his dominance. The mayor can then disburse favours in such a way as to increase his influence over the local economy and the local press and TV. The urban electorates conclude that little has changed in politics since the demise of the communist order and the rule of the first party secretary.[3]

Yet the scene in the towns has changed. In the Soviet years they were drab places, and walls were plastered with gloomy pictures of the Politburo and with excerpts from Lenin's writings. Usually the streets were free from litter and graffiti; but pavements and tarmac were often in shocking disrepair and office and residential accommodation was in a shabby state.

The introduction of the market economy has brightened up the urban landscape and long-neglected items of architecture have been restored. This has been a boon for the Russian Orthodox Church. In Voronezh, fewer than a score of ecclesiastical buildings were left standing by the end of Khrushchëv's rule. Only one of these was permitted to function as a church. Several were used as warehouses. The Orthodox Church's campaign to re-equip them for solemn use has been vigorous. Gold paint gleams again on the cupolas and internal redecoration has restored icons and frescoes. Voronezh, we might note, is a pauper in comparison with wealthy Moscow and the reconstruction of its secular buildings has been slow. But a start has been made; the cities are more colourful than they have been for decades. Not all of this is for the better. The absence of neon advertising signs in towns in the Soviet period made a positive contrast with Western garishness. But Marxist-Leninist slogans were ubiquitously visible in daytime. Their removal makes a pleasant change even if they have been substituted by the temptations of consumerism. Once it was impossible to escape Lenin, now Coca-Cola is omnipresent.

Yet the general condition of cities leaves a lot to be desired. Only a few of them have benefited from the results of economic reform. Notable among these is Nizhni Novgorod. In tsarist times it was the site of an annual Great Fair. Standing at the confluence of the rivers Volga and Oka, Nizhni Novgorod was Russia's greatest inland port and attracted half a million visitors from mid-July through to early September. There was no more picturesque scene in the country as merchants from the Volga region and indeed Russia thronged the thoroughfares. The make-shift booths and stalls offered an astonishing range of goods. Customers could find everything from the most advanced machinery to traditional hunting knives and baskets of felt shoes and leather belts. Many of the

11/2000

новая цена

0,99 Ls

ISSN 1407-0545

9 771407 054002

журнал для женщин

Мстислав Ростропович

Поцелуи non stop

Джулия Робертс

неукрощенная красотка

Обесчестить женщину

настоящее удовольствие для русского мужчины

Триумф серой мышки

красивая и умная обречена на поражение

Грузинская любовь

посла Ее величества

Быть при мужчине — сомнительная ценность

Сделай с женой что хочешь!

наш эксперимент

11. Western-style cover of upmarket women's magazine.
Lead article on the classical musician Mstislav Rostropovich is titled:
'Kisses non-stop'. (*Limit*, November 2000)

Пора ли начинать террор? стр. 5

ДУЭЛЬ

№43(90)
декабрь
1998

ЗА ОТВАГУ
СССР
1998

ГАЗЕТА БОРЬБЫ ОБЩЕСТВЕННЫХ ИДЕЙ - ДЛЯ ТЕХ, КТО ЛЮБИТ ДУМАТЬ

- **Хайль, СТАРОВОЙТОВА!** стр.2
- **Израиль в тисках АНТИСЕМИТИЗМА** стр. 3
- **Научные СТРАДАНИЯ** стр. 4
- **Универсальное ОРУЖИЕ** стр. 6
- **Новости из-за БУГРА** стр. 7
- **Ах, куклы, КУКОЛКИ** стр. 8

21 декабря состоится возложение венков и цветов к месту захоронения И.В. Сталина, посвященное 119 годовщине со дня рождения. Сбор в 12.00 у входа в Александровский сад.

Свод моральных понятий, по которым живет общество, обязан быть в энциклопедии и энцик-   ДОСТОИНСТВО   полностью исключены. Отнюдь это считалось крамолой.

12. Issue of nationalist newspaper celebrates Stalin's birthday. Top line reads: 'Is it time to start the terror?' (*Duel'*, December 1998)

13. 'Choose whomever you want . . .' Newspaper speculates on the race to succeed Yeltsin and shows leading politicians disguised as animals. Starting clockwise from the bottom lefthand corner, they are Boris Fëdorov, Anatoli Chubais, Yuri Luzhkov, Sergei Stepashin, Viktor Chernomyrdin and Grigori Yavlinski. Vladimir Putin was not included, just weeks before he became Acting President.

14. Nationalist newspaper denies that American President Bush, holding a fork of rockets and a knife of 'globalism' will dominate Russia. Among the heap of corpses below the map of Russia are a Teutonic Knight, Frederick of Prussia, Napoleon Bonaparte and Adolf Hitler. (*Sovetskaya Rossiya*, 7 February, 2002)

15. Putin, wearing a Texan hat and an American flag, carries a grinning Yeltsin along the path of reform. Neither notices they are on the edge of an abyss. (*Sovetskaya Rossiya*, 21 March 2002)

16. 'Are there reserves in Russia for acceleration?' While President Putin is on horseback, poor Prime Minister Kasyanov – in charge of the economy – has to ride a tortoise. (*Argumenty i fakty*, April 2002)

17. Political disagreement at chess game. First player says: 'You can't make that move! I'll take your king!' His opponent replies: 'So what! I'll declare a republic and go on playing.' (*Taim-aut/Sportklub*, May 2001)

18. Bank assistant to inexperienced robber: 'The chairman of the bank has told us only to hand over money to organised crime!' (*Literaturnaya gazeta*, 19 June 1996)

19. Financial transfers, Russian style. Criminal carries placard: 'Money doesn't smell if it's well laundered!' (*Literaturnaya gazeta*, 22 May 1996)

20. Convict is marched off to prison. One of his guards says: 'There's something familiar about your face! I think I voted for you!' (*Literaturnaya gazeta*, 15–21 December 1999)

entrepreneurs had trudged their way to the city through the blistering summer heat with their entire stock on their back. The more prosperous among them transported products by cow, horse or even by camel. Christians mingled with Moslems. Nizhni Novgorod was a bubbling broth of self-confidence. And competing with the stall-holders were religious zealots, pie-men, flower-sellers, fortune-tellers, thieves and prostitutes. All human life in Russia was represented at the Great Fair. The city flourished. Its local authorities sanctioned the construction of proud churches, municipal offices, banks and a railway station in a *fin de siècle* style incorporating traditional Russian motifs. Nizhni Novgorod combined Russia ancient and modern.

The city lost its Great Fair at the end of the 1920s and its very name in 1932. Vivacity gave way to sombreness. After the Second World War a huge factory complex sprang up connected to the defence sector. Once the most welcoming place in the Russian Empire, Nizhni, renamed Gorki, was declared a 'closed city' which no foreigner was allowed to visit. Mighty Nizhni became an obscure centre, important mainly for its armaments production and its supply of promotees to the supreme party leadership. At one time or another, Politburo members such as Vyacheslav Molotov, Lazar Kaganovich, Anastas Masikoyan and Andrei Zhdanov had run the communist party and government machines in Nizhni Novgorod (Gorki).

From 1991 Nizhni Novgorod resumed its old name and much of its old *élan*. The Fair had been revived a couple of years earlier and was a success. Under the leadership of Boris Nemtsov, Nizhni Novgorod became a byword for commitment to the market economy and to 'openness'. Nemtsov himself is a new Russian *Wunderkind*. Born in 1959, he took an excellent degree in mathematics and clearly could have had an illustrious academic career. He is of Jewish descent but, out of prudence or conviction, has joined the Orthodox Church. He easily won the contest for the Nizhni governorship in December 1995 by standing as a politician who is beholden to no one:

> No, I'm not a bureaucrat. I'm an elected governor. It's a wholly different status. I have none of those bureaucratic habits and I don't need to accommodate myself to anyone. Until the elections, the elections for the governorship, naturally I was a bureaucrat. Nevertheless my inclination towards independence and freedom was on display. Yes, of course I recognised that at any moment, at any second I could lose my place. This very chair. This armchair. But

there's something that's more important: the knowledge that you're responsible for many, many people.[4]

This populism is not unusual in Russia, but Nemtsov with his boyish good looks and photogenic family can handle himself better than most. His prose occasionally overloads the sugar-spoon: 'A decent person is someone who cannot commit betrayal.' With more than a touch of self-regard he adds: 'Great people are those who make history. Jesus Christ, Aristotle, Leonardo da Vinci, Peter [the Great], Sakharov, Einstein . . .'[5]

Nemtsov is not universally admired in the city. His was the first local campaign to hold public auctions to sell off municipally owned enterprises. This won plaudits from the government in Moscow, but in Nizhni there were crowds of protestors. Prime Minister Gaidar and the minister in change of privatisation, Anatoli Chubais, flew to the city to show their support for Nemtsov.[6] The auction went ahead. So too did Nemtsov's plan to allow private enterprises to be created without the need to undergo a lengthy process of registration by the city council administration – a process that was not only slow and unpredictable but also notorious for enabling bureaucrats to extract bribes from would-be businessmen. Some firms succeeded in Nizhni, others failed. The reformers emphasised that this was normal in the operation of a market economy. They also stressed that nearly all local firms had been failing before they had been privatised. Anyway, if a factory director refused to allow his enterprise to be sold off, he was usually condemning it to a slow death. In order to reconstruct Nizhni's pattern of industry and trade there was little alternative to privatisation, and Nemtsov and his adherents had the sense to appreciate this and the charm and determination to do something about it.

Such was his success with the international financial world that in March 1997 Nemtsov was asked by Yeltsin to leave Nizhni and become his Deputy Prime Minister in Moscow. Speculation was rife that he might succeed Yeltsin as President. This did not occur. In fact he was dropped from the government altogether in one of the reshuffles in August 1998. But even this brief elevation of a 'provincial', as he proudly called himself, was a sign that developments in the localities were taken seriously in Moscow.

What is clear is that some places have been much better able than others to cope with the economic and political transformation. Nizhni Novgorod had many advantages. It was well placed in the network of Russia's transport and communications. It had both industry and agriculture. It had a history, albeit a distant one, of economic pride and resilience. Its urban landscape is remarkably well preserved and is loved by its citizens. In Nemtsov there was a dynamic leader who knew what he wanted and had a chance to try to obtain it. Even so, Nizhni's economy did not benefit all its inhabitants, and in July 2001 the electorate chose not a reformer but the communist party candidate as its new governor. This was a popular verdict on the effects of the Nemtsov years. And if economic change has caused hardship and discontent in Nizhni, it has been still more painful and resented elsewhere. Cities in the Russian North and Far East have had an especially grim time. From the 1930s the Soviet regime offered material incentives to settlers – and when this did not work satisfactorily, it used the convict labourers of the Gulag to build the settlements that were to become the local townships. Under Khrushchëv, still higher wages and the promise of cheap food and housing were used as an attraction. Nowadays, however, state economic planning is no more. The result has been a decline in wages. There has also been a fall-off in maintenance of standards in industry and construction. Karelia, Archangel Province and the Primorski Region have notably suffered.[7]

Their troubles have taken a similar shape. Food shortages are no longer a serious problem in the shops, but the cost of living is considerably higher than in Moscow and St Petersburg. Unemployment too has increased. Its main immediate cure has not been the one wanted by the central and local authorities: an exodus of residents to more affluent parts of the Russian Federation. For example, Chukotka in the Far East had the Federation's highest proportion of unemployed workers in 1992. Within three years, as the result of migration, it had the second lowest. The average income of the residents in such areas collapsed from the late 1980s. In November 1997, it has been reckoned, people in Moscow earned about six times the amount needed locally for subsistence. In Tyva, by contrast, the financial income of households was estimated at about two-thirds of the minimum for physical survival. It is true that the official statistics are far from being wholly reliable. But probably the average Russian monetary income was a little more than double what was required for subsistence. This is hardly cause for congratulation; plainly there are many regions where the effects of Yeltsin's economic reforms have been baleful.[8]

Money, of course, is not the sole criterion of material well-being. Another is access to affordable housing. Here the picture is somewhat more encouraging. By 1994 about 46 per cent of Russian houses and apartments had been privatised. In most cases the tenants took full possession of the title deeds without the need for substantial expenditure.

There has to be a caveat about this. Residents of prime sites in great cities are frequently subject to intimidation once they have taken up private ownership. Criminal gangs have moved into the property market and harass people into selling up their homes at a knockdown price. There have been murders of residents who declined to co-operate. Another negative effect is that many apartment blocks, which were poorly maintained in the Soviet period, have fallen into dreadful disrepair. The housing stock is not what it was. But there are positive aspects that must not be overlooked. In particular, the restrictions on the construction of private houses in the countryside – dachas (*dachi*) or, in the case of the bigger ones, the so-called *kottedzhi* – have been relaxed. All over the rural area the fashion for building wooden and brick residences has spread. There is no longer a shortage of planks, tiles, plaster and cement; anyone can obtain them so long as the market price can be paid on the spot. The new owners are able to mark out vegetable gardens and keep chickens, pigs or cattle. Private housing has been a boon to the general public. To that extent the move towards the market has been beneficial.

Yet the material standard of living cannot be gauged solely by recorded monetary income and housing provision. Much that goes on in the economy is handled through barter. A lot also proceeds through the exchange of currency notes but without passing into the vaults of banks that are accessible to tax inspectors. Savings are often stashed away at home. The collapse of the Russian financial system in August 1998 served to increase the distrust of both government and banks. So things are not quite as bad as they appear in the publications of the state statistics agency, Goskomstat.

It is this economic frailty that explains the reluctance of regions and municipalities, despite their frequent accusations against the Russian Federal Government, to ignore the Kremlin's wishes. There have been recurrent threats of secession. Siberia's politicians toyed with the idea. In the Volga Region, too, the cry went up that the connection with the rest of Russia ought to be broken. But this has been the merest rhetoric. Secessionist ideas were last touted in 1917–18 when Russia was engulfed in Civil War – and they came to nothing. So much less likely, then, that Russian cities will band together and secede. Sporadic attempts have been made to form unions of towns for limited mutual assistance. Thus there is an Association of Closed Towns. Such towns were those in the

USSR which foreigners were forbidden to visit. Usually they had industrial enterprises of a sensitive military kind and Stalin, sharing the
long-standing Russian official suspiciousness, wanted no prying eyes in
the vicinity. Similarly there is an Association of Historic Towns. There is
even an Association of Scientific Towns.[9] But unions of this sort have
had no serious impact on the general situation. Towns flourish or decline
by their own efforts.

Without governmental assistance, in any case, urban administration
would enter bankruptcy. The municipalities cannot raise loans abroad
because of their abysmal creditworthiness.[10] The only option for them is
to lobby the Moscow ministries. Not only loans are needed but also
agreement to postpone payment of tax arrears or even to write them off.
If such a situation fails to tame the 'localities', then the government
may quietly indicate it will find ways to disrupt supplies of basic utilities
such as electricity, oil or gas. Another point of pressure is the avail-
ability of food in the local shops. Not all areas, even in conditions of
a market economy, have succeeded in keeping bread, milk, meat and
vegetables on the shelves without assistance from ministries in Moscow.
A recording of a telephone message was given to the press in early
2000, purporting to show that Anatoli Chubais had ordered that direct
threats should be made to the governors of regions and cities during the
December 1999 Duma elections. Failure to secure seats for candidates
supporting Yeltsin would allegedly have had dire practical consequences.
The authenticity of the message has not been proved beyond peradven-
ture. But there can be little doubt that political bosses in towns and
villages are made aware of the adverse consequences likely to flow from
non-compliance with the President's demands.

What is also clear is that the corruption and cynicism are not
confined to the Kremlin. When in 1994 the Presidential Administration
was trying to prepare the legislation for local self-government, it met
considerable resistance from the already established authorities in several
of those localities. The prospect of elections was feared by those who
stood even the slightest chance of losing them. They had influential
support in the Council of the Federation, where both the 'national'
republics and the Russian provinces are represented. The Council
rejected Yeltsin's project three times. It was passed into law only in
September 1995.[11] Not every obstacle to democratic development lies
in the government.

And hard though it is to regenerate the towns, it is even more
difficult to do anything about the villages. The great changes in Russia

in the twentieth century started in the towns and the villages have followed the urban example. Soviet propaganda from 1930s – and indeed official propaganda since the fall of communism in 1991 – emphasised that Russia was a predominantly urban and industrial country. Yet this is a distortion of reality. The urban part of the population became a majority only in the 1959 census. Even today 38 per cent of Russian citizens live in the countryside. In terms of occupational structure it is still the case that 15 per cent of adults in employment have jobs in agriculture. This is an enormous figure. Even India has a lower proportion employed in agriculture: 5 per cent. When sociologists and political scientists examine society outside the Kremlin, they often take a random town and leave the impression that 'typical' Russia is being explored. But the Russian countryside is so large a part of the inhabited country that it is wrong to ignore it and its problems – and it is time to look at them now.

The heart was knocked out of the villages in the 1930s with the forcible mass collectivisation of agriculture. The more prosperous peasants – pejoratively designated as *kulaki* ('fists') who held the rest of the peasantry in their exploitative grasp – were thrown off their land and the most unfortunate among them were deported to Siberia or Kazakhstan. The churches were closed or, in thousands of cases, demolished. Priests were killed. Millions of villagers starved to death, especially in Ukraine, southern Russia and Kazakhstan. Others fled the rural catastrophe and took up employment in the towns.

A structure of collective farm administration was established in the early 1930s. The state announced yearly quotas of grain and other produce for delivery to the towns and the quotas had to be met even when the result would be malnutrition in the villages. The rural standard of living collapsed. It fell to the lowest depths in the Second World War in the zone of German occupation. But even after the end of military hostilities the recovery of agriculture and social life in the countryside was slower than in the urban settlements. There remained an incentive for ambitious young people to get an education and leave the countryside. There was always corruption on the collective farms. Their chairmen managed them to suit their personal interests. There was always a deficit of decent amenities. It was not rare for a *kolkhoz* grocery shop to have bare shelves. And it was unknown for villages to have premises for hairdressing, cobbling, carpentry or electrical goods. Library facilities were extremely thin on the ground. Some villages were fortunate in having a 'house of culture' where there were opportunities for recreational meetings. But such villages were also decidedly few.

I saw this for myself as a postgraduate student in Leningrad in 1974. Taking the local electric train westward out to the villages beyond twenty-five kilometres, then the legal limit for visitors from abroad, I wandered into a hamlet deep in snow and mud where foreigners seemed never to have been since the German invasion in 1941.

It is difficult to convey the full sense of barrenness. Even in poverty-ridden India I have not seen such a desert of amenities. In the early 1960s it had been Khrushchëv's ambition to aggregate villages into local 'agrotowns' with the full urban provision of fuel, goods, accommodation, cafeterias and shops. (Not that Soviet cities at that time were well provided with amenities by the standards of the rest of the world.) Khrushchëv bulldozed ancient settlements in pursuit of this aim and conducted a campaign of what might aptly be called rural cleansing. Like a lot of communist leaders, essentially he hated the old countryside and, as an agricultural moderniser, wanted to transform it into something like the towns and cities where he felt most comfortable. The consequence was the ultimate stage in the depeasantisation of Russia. Among Russian nationalists Stalin is hated for the mass collectivisation of agriculture, but often is given high marks by the same people for his elevation of the USSR to the position of military superpower. Khrushchëv is awarded no such compensatory judgement. Many continue to regarded him as an ignorant and crude wrecker of the best traditions of Mother Russia.

One thing catching the eye in the little hamlet I visited was the shoddy condition of the buildings. Alongside the traditional wooden structures there was a grocery shop. On its shelves, when eventually it opened hours after the prescribed daily schedule, there was little that anyone might want to purchase. There was hardly anything at all to buy. Bread was available. Tea was on sale and there was a Jurassic slab of chocolate. The only surprise was that the bread had not all gone. In the last years of the USSR the subsidy of food products amazingly made it economical for rural householders to use wheat and rye loaves as fodder for their livestock. Near the shop, across a road as muddy as the tracks described by Nikolai Gogol or Mikhail Sholokhov, was a water pump. Lenin coined the phrase that 'communism equals Soviet power plus electrification'. There was little sign of any advance having been made since the 1920s. The water was drawn up from a well. The electrical current supplied to the village was inoperative on that dark winter's day. The shop was a contradiction in terms; it offered goods to consumers which it had never – not once, so far as it could be gathered from conversations with the villagers – obtained for sale.

The official policies adopted to improve the rural situation left things worse than before. Younger villagers became even keener to leave for the towns. The age structure on the farms became tilted ever more towards the older generation, and women provided a larger proportion of the workforce. The demoralisation of rural inhabitants deepened. Under Brezhnev there was a degree of relief as the restrictions on small private plots of land were somewhat relaxed. Prices paid to farmers for their products were raised. But the general situation, as many a Soviet social investigator – including Raisa Gorbachëva in her published dissertation entitled *The Way of Life of the Collective Farm Peasantry: A Sociological Study* – confirmed, was grim.[12]

The traditional culture of the Russian village, though, has not entirely disappeared. The dependence of collective-farm workers upon their little private plot meant that horticultural skills remain with nearly all inhabitants of the countryside. Everyone knows how to plant and harvest potatoes, onions, garlic, carrots, cabbages and parsley. Everyone can recognise edible mushrooms and look after chickens (although the husbandry of horses and cattle is a more specialised skill). During the Great Patriotic War of 1941–5 most people would otherwise have perished – and life was not a great deal easier in the late 1930s and in the years of post-war economic and social recovery. The permission granted in 1932 to sell surplus products at the official *kolkhoz* markets in the towns provided a very welcome boost to the incomes of rural families. The villagers have also preserved their lore about the weather and the land. The fact that the communist regime's promises of a modern material infrastructure were empty has compelled rural inhabitants to fend for themselves in constructing and repairing their homes. The old expertise in handicrafts has stayed in place. Some villagers are more competent than others and the result is that commercial exchange of goods and services never vanished from the countryside. Barter was and is a part of everyone's life.

The music and dancing of old Russia has also lasted better in the countryside than in the towns. Folksongs retain a strong appeal, strong enough to outmatch the 'light entertainment' offered by television and radio.[13] Some of the pre-revolutionary crafts, too, have survived. The delicate woollen shawls of Orenburg Province, mentioned in the nineteenth century by Ivan Turgenev and Anton Chekhov, are still produced.

But more has been lost than saved. Although religious faith has endured, its presence is of an attenuated kind. The clergy disappeared from the villages in the 1930s as executions and deportations took their toll. The Orthodox Church has been working hard to reinstate itself in the countryside; but it still has only one priest for every three rural parishes.[14] The peasantry never had a close knowledge of the Bible and the city-based ecclesiastical hierarchy regularly complained about the ignorance of its own priesthood in the countryside. Although Christianity survived, its popularity declined. Without priests or even a church building, many collective farmers gave up Orthodoxy. Meanwhile old pagan superstitions flourished. Today there are even witches in the countryside. Folk magical customs endure. The reasons for this are a matter of guesswork, but probably the ancient beliefs have offered a crucial solace to citizens of the Russian Federation during decades when Christian belief and practice was the object of official persecution. It may well be, furthermore, that by imposing Marxism-Leninism through the schools and the media, the authorities turned the population against communism and made a fading set of popular superstitions more attractive than they would otherwise have become.

Yet the communist period has left its mark. Soviet official festivals gradually worked their way into popular consciousness and the Victory Day celebration has proved especially attractive. Stalin meanly refused to allow a day off work for the occasion. But the memory of its celebration in 1945 had never been forgotten. Stalin's successors restored Victory Day as a full festival to general acclaim.

The ethnographers investigated the phenomenon in the 1970s. G. S. Maslova's research took her to the depths of Ryazan Province: 'The old women mark each 9 May, Victory Day ... They bake pancakes, pies, buns ... They finish a requiem and say a prayer for those killed in the war.' Elsewhere, in the town of Nizhni Tagil, there were similar acts of commemoration:

> The buses going in the direction of the cemetery were packed and there was an endless stream of people moving along the road to the cemetery. More than an hour before the designated time the cemetery was filled with people of various ages ... During the solemn meeting there was a tense silence, many of those present were sobbing. The participants placed wreaths and bouquets of

flowers on the graves of the fighters. Not one grave was left forgotten. In accordance with the old folk tradition ... barley was sprinkled on all the graves and cakes and sweets were placed on them.[15]

Nowadays open celebrations of the Christian calendar have returned to town and countryside. Easter, Whitsun and Christmas are the most popular. This is happening with the encouragement, obviously, of the Orthodox Church. But often the initiative comes from the rural populace.[16]

These signs of vivacity are outweighed by the negative side of life in the countryside. Few commercial appeals are aimed at the farmers. Monthly magazines such as *Sam* cater for the owners of dachas more than for full-time agriculturists.[17] They have bright photographs of patio paving, parasols, rabbit-hutches and lawn-mowers. They give advice for making garden sheds which are sometimes more decorative than functional. They provide designs of 'dacha divans'. For the most part, however, government and media have abandoned the Russian countryside to its own impoverished devices.

Conditions have worsened for most rural inhabitants. The wages of agricultural workers are about a third of what is earned by industrial workers (who themselves are hardly well off) – and the gap is widening.[18] The state ceased being involved in the trade of farm products within three years after the USSR's collapse; it also sought to transfer its own property in land to the farms themselves. Subsidies from the government for equipment and fertilisers were cut back. For the first time since the late 1920s, the authorities no longer issued instructions about the management of large farms. The *kolkhozes* and *sovkhozes* were denationalised. Yeltsin wanted them to be broken up and their working households to set up independent holdings. Small private farms were the objective. He was trying to do what the last great conservative politician before the First World War, Pëtr Stolypin, wanted. The Ministry of Agriculture provided basic advice about the legal procedures and Nizhni Novgorod was used as an experimental province and as a model. Yet the results were dispiriting. By the mid-1990s the number of private owners of farms had stabilised at around a quarter of a million.[19]

Most collective farms, in fact, have simply been re-designated as agricultural co-operatives and have retained all their land intact. Although such co-ops trade their harvest on the open market, the structure of management is not very different from what it was under communism. Changes in working practices have been kept to a minimum. Farm managers have retained their jobs.[20]

And so although the state no longer owns and regulates agriculture, the transformation of the Russian countryside has yet to take place. The reluctance of entrepreneurial individuals and their households to set up separate private farms is understandable. 'Separators' have to cope on their own resources and fuel, fertilisers and finance are difficult to obtain. Many new farms have failed to make a profit. There is also much hostility from fellow villagers. Sometimes this has spilled over into vendettas ending in physical violence, and usually the victims are those who have left the former collective farm.[21] Often it does not need to come to a fight. All manner of peaceful obstruction has been put in the way of the creation of small farms. The officials of local government are past masters at thwarting the demands of central ministries by insisting on excessive adherence to bureaucratic requirements. Most of the countryside's working people prefer familiarity to innovation – and they have plenty of cause to worry about the uncertainties of private agriculture.[22] Faced with the mixture of indifference and recalcitrance, Yeltsin eased the pressure. Apart from anything else, he could not afford a struggle that might lead to a disruption of food supplies to the towns.[23]

Nevertheless the rural scene has not been entirely static. Gone is the state's close control over agricultural technique, production and distribution. The Kremlin had set quotas for collective farms to deliver to governmental procurement agencies and appointed the functionaries in command of the rural economy. It had also financed and organised the construction of schools, shops, bakeries, kindergartens and housing. Since 1991 the state has left agriculture to its own devices. Farms now make their own decisions about crops, equipment and marketing. By the mid-1990s, moreover, the government felt able to order a drastic reduction in the level of subsidies. State financial resources for the programme for residential accommodation in 1994 were only 37 per cent of those resources available in 1990.[24]

The change in relations between town and countryside also leaves something to be desired. This is a perennial difficulty. When peasants in the First World War felt they were being poorly paid for their harvest, they withdrew from the usual markets. Shortages in food supplies to the towns were among the reasons for the urban strikes and demonstrations that brought about the collapse of the Romanov dynasty in the February 1917 Revolution. The Provisional Government's failure to provide for the cities helped the communists to advance on power in October 1917. But then the communist regime encountered difficulty. Peasants revolted when the communists grabbed grain and conscripts in the Civil War. Stalin sought to bury the problem by the forcible mass collectivisation of agriculture in the late 1920s. But the subsequent inefficiency of the Soviet farming system left urban and rural inhabitants in a dreadful plight. The energies of Khrushchëv and Brezhnev were devoted to the securing of improvement; but the annual grain harvest remained a factor of acute political importance through to the end of the USSR – and precious little was modified in the general pattern of relations between the towns and the villages.

What happens now is that urban inhabitants seek to build more dachas in the countryside. Many are young people who have left the other states of the former Soviet Union and, in the absence of urban jobs and homes, have opted for rural residence and work.[25] There is not exactly a flood of newcomers. Yet a greater number of townspeople than at any time since before 1917 are trying to set themselves up in the countryside.

Another common sight is the farm lorry parked in an urban suburb or near a railway station. The driver has to be quick and surreptitious; even in Putin's Russia permission is needed before trading can legally commence. The lorry may be loaded to the roof with potatoes, cabbage or beetroot. (Usually it is potatoes.) Bags will be pulled to the back of the vehicle and the driver will shout out the price. There has been nothing like it since the last free marketplace in Moscow – the Sukhar-ëvka – was closed down in the Civil War. Bulk purchases of agricultural produce now take place without the interference of the Ministry of the Interior or indeed the KGB. Elderly peasant women come in from the countryside with sacks of parsley or garlic or even – yet again – potatoes. They used do this on the sly. Now they sit by the roadside and, if the police prove difficult, they bribe them. But times are changing. Official policy from 1917 was greatly hostile to private commerce. When it took place, more often than not it was on the black market. Nowadays trading is permitted and encouraged by government, and a dynamic relationship between town and countryside is emerging.

Certainly this has a long way to go before Russia acquires the complexion of a contemporary capitalist economy. The food-processing sector remains primitive. The transport system to the countryside is abysmal. The population in the villages has a disproportionate number of old and demoralised citizens. But the comparison with the towns flatters to deceive. Russian towns and cities, apart from Moscow the Great and perhaps St Petersburg and Nizhni Novgorod, have yet to be regenerated. The cold hand of communism also lies across them. It is likely to remain there for many years to come.

19. CLASS AND THE 'NEW RUSSIANS'

The workers' barracks were a wooden leaky building. Ours had been constructed in 1949. It had already tipped on its side and gone mouldy ... But people live there to this day. There's an outside toilet. The dump for the toilet props up the ceiling in the winter.

V. V. Strokanev, 1998[1]

The ramifications of such developments are plain to see. The society of the Russian Federation since 1991 is extremely stratified in power and material well-being. While the economy has been shrinking, the distribution of income has become ever more unequal. Yeltsin's early vision of a 'humane' and 'civilised' environment for a growing market economy has been disappointed. Capitalism of the most primitive kind has been battened on to Russia; the rich have got richer, the poor ever poorer and more numerous. Nearly two-fifths of the population were reckoned to live in poverty by the last year of the twentieth century. The data may overestimate the problem.[2] But a problem certainly exists: government, police and organised crime contrive to make the chasm between wealth and poverty unbridgeable.[3]

The USSR, too, had a social hierarchy. At the apex stood the Party General Secretary and his comrades in the Politburo. These were the supreme beneficiaries of the Soviet political order. They could command any institution or individual and their orders would be obeyed. There were no constitutional restraints. Their formal material reward was not very high. Leonid Brezhnev's monthly salary was 800 rubles, not even three times the income of a tram-driver. But the unofficial perks were huge. Party Politburo members had personal chauffeurs and domestic servants. They had dachas, situated in special cantonments near Moscow out of the gaze of ordinary people. They had access to secret Kremlin shops in which the prices were set artificially low and where foreign goods – unobtainable on the streets of Moscow – could be bought. They could travel abroad. Whenever they fell ill, they were treated in one of the Kremlin clinics where the facilities were better than in any other Soviet medical facility. They could hunt for bears and deer in Siberia and take holidays in North Caucasus spa towns or on the beaches of Crimea. Brezhnev himself was a car enthusiast and welcomed the gift of limousines from visiting foreign dignitaries. Life was sweet for the Kremlin's inner elite.[4]

At the opposite end of the range (if we exclude the miserable inmates of the Gulag camp) was the manual worker. Male or female, they were lucky if their town had sufficient meat and vegetables for general consumption. In principle it was possible for everyone to buy a car; but in practice there was a years-long waiting list. Clothes were highly standardised. Housing was grim. There was no escape from the endless demands of ill-rewarded, grinding work unless people had exceptional talent and conspicuous loyalty to the official political authorities. For women it was even worse – worse by far – than it was for men, who have always done very little around the house in Russia. It would be wrong to overlook the achievements of Soviet communism. Only a tiny minority of society lacked food, shelter, clothing, health-care and employment. A basic minimum of welfare was available almost universally. But the discrepancy in conditions between the complacent, upholstered life of the Politburo and the gruelling circumstances in factories or on collective farm was extreme.

None the less, the social polarities of the USSR were not as distant from each other as is the case today. Mikhail Gorbachëv had a Presidential dacha built in Foros in Crimea; it was luxurious by Soviet standards, but bore little comparison to the villas constructed by millionaires in the West (and anyway, as Raisa often pointed out to him, he did not own it personally). Although he could commission the most superb local craftsmanship, Gorbachëv never had international levels of perfection available to him. This became clear after 1991 when the Russian *nouveaux riches* began to construct homes for themselves in the countryside outside the big cities. These residences are usually called *kottedzhi*. The English-derived word has implications of modesty which have been lost in Russia. The Russian rich are super-wealthy. They have a level of income unparalleled in the country's history since the tsarist era. When they travel around the Russian Federation – or even when they take a ride in their limousines to the *kottedzhi* or to a select restaurant – they take armed bodyguards. Their children are not safe from kidnappers. The rivalries between financial bosses led to contract killings in the 1990s.

The last time this sort of thing happened was in the 1920s, when private traders used Lenin's New Economic Policy to get rich quick and to enjoy their wealth while they could. But the hole-in-the corner businessmen of that period did not trade on world markets. They did not hire dozens of armed protectors. They did not act as if they, rather than the government, had the right to prescribe state policy. They could not buy ministers. They did not holiday in Rimini or buy French châteaux and Hampstead villas. They had no access to confidential Cypriot, Swiss or British bank accounts for the purposes of money laundering.

The businessmen of the 1920s defied the statisticians through their determination to avoid paying their taxes – and we can only guess at how thoroughly they succeeded in defrauding the People's Commissariat of Finances. The same is true today but on a truly enormous scale. In October 1996 it was announced that Anatoli Chubais had been appointed to an All-Russian Extraordinary Commission for Strengthening Tax and Budget Discipline. The Commission's acronym was 'VChK', which was the same as that of the feared secret police in Lenin's time; this was deliberate: Yeltsin wanted to imply that the pursuit of wrongdoing would be remorseless. But there were two difficulties here. One was the sheer complexity of current fiscal problems, which had been allowed to accumulate for several years: the backlog of arrears defied analysis by whole regiments of tax gatherers. The other was that Chubais had already made a personal fortune while working for the President and was not obviously the ideal person to cleanse the channels of corruption in the Russian Federation. The new rich in Russia do not have a record of moral uprightness. They have no conscience about the plight of the poor; and although they talk patriotically, they treat Russia like a colony to be exploited. While hating communism, they desire a regime that will secure their privileges just as the communist regime guaranteed the lifestyle of the *nomenklatura*. They are ruthless, but also a little desperate.

I met one of the bankers of the new Russia in 1998. He had no training in financial services but was a journalist by profession and had worked his way up the hierarchy of the Komsomol – the communist party's youth organisation – in the 1980s, marrying a beautiful woman who came from a family of the Soviet political *nomenklatura*. The USSR's collapse induced him to switch careers. His is a bright, forceful personality and he has a sharp analytical mind. From being a rather sensitive individual he quickly turned into a commercial predator. His tales about how he enforced his contracts took the breath away. Absolutely no leeway was given to creditors who failed to comply exactly with the terms of their loans. Shakespeare's Shylock could have taken lessons from him.

He and his family travelled around in a heavily built Landcruiser with a couple of burly armed bodyguards. As we entered a plush rural restaurant, he was greeted like a lord. The walls were decorated with wooden folkloric items. The waiters wore smart costumes that owed much to an idealised image of the ancient Russian peasantry. The food was as lavish as in the feast scene from Goncharov's novel *Oblomov*. But the talk was depressing. The banker's son had had to be sent abroad, to the United Kingdom, for his physical security during the years of his education – and like many such lads, he had to obey his parents about what kind of profession he should aspire to. It was not going to be enough to be a financier. The question inside the family was which field of financial operations the boy should occupy. The banker was rich beyond his childhood dreams. He and his wife were hospitable and kindly towards old friends. But they did not feel secure in today's Russia. They genuinely dreaded that 'the Reds' might make a comeback and that the tables of the market economy might be overturned. More than that: they were afraid that the struggle for profit in the new Russia might prove fatal for the banker or one of his close relatives.

The crooked path taken to prosperity by most 'new Russians' means that they are even less open to scholarly investigation than were the members of the communist *nomenklatura*. No serious data exists about the Russian rich. Such persons do not fill in forms and do not respond to questionnaires. What we know is based mainly on indirect evidence. Throughout the 1990s the International Monetary Fund was alarmed that huge tranches of its loans to Russia disappeared into the pockets of the 'new Russians' and from their pockets into secret bank accounts abroad. Perhaps half of the foreign financial assistance has disappeared in this way.

Wealthy Russians flaunt their riches in the grossest fashion; and they are unembarrassed about using shops advertising 'elite goods' or buying apartments described as 'elite homes'.[5] Their wish to be seen as cultured members of the world of international business is a standing joke. Once upon a time the pretentiousness of Brezhnev was the butt of popular humour. Now it is the beneficiaries of the country's emergent capitalism who are mocked. The satire is merciless. For example:

A new Russian spots a poster on a lamp-post advertising the Mozart horn concerto and asks his girlfriend whether she'd like to go with him. His girlfriend, priding herself on her education, demurs: 'Are you sure we can? Didn't Mozart say clearly that the concerto's not for us but for the horn?'

This is humour of a type familiar in other countries. But elsewhere it is typically aimed at national or regional minorities or at groups in society deemed unusually incompetent at looking after themselves. No one has any doubt that the 'new Russians' can look after themselves. They are notorious for helping themselves to the assets of the entire country. This makes the jokes all the more remarkable. Popular contempt for the unalterable ignorance of the Russian elite is extraordinary. Only black humour of this sort, perhaps, makes the existence of the very wealthiest fellow citizens a little more bearable to the general population.

What is especially galling is the fact that few 'new Russians' have risen from the depths of society. Most of them come from fairly comfortable Soviet backgrounds. In advance of the collapse of the USSR, hurried arrangements were made amidst the central and local *nomen-klaturas* to exploit the commercial opportunities about to become available. A few super-rich financiers such as Boris Berezovski had been academics. Gusinski had been a theatre director. The others had typically held political and economic posts of some importance. The Komsomol supplied a number of rising businessmen. It would seem that, being younger and more flexible in their outlook than their parents, they had less inhibition about declaring themselves in favour of capitalism.

The chutzpah of a figure such as Berezovski caught the eye. His early career was spent as an obscure but talented mathematician in the USSR Academy of Sciences' Institute of Management in Moscow, but he was quick to understand the economics of the market. He started by taking a stake in the car manufacturing industry. His firm, LogoVAZ, imported a large number of automobiles for sale to Russians. From this vantage point he bought shares in the privatised television station, Ostankino. When the newspaper *Nezavisimaya gazeta* ran into financial trouble in 1995, he stepped in and bought it. Berezovski's trading empire grew exponentially. His financial group diversified still further by setting up a bank and buying up properties in Switzerland and the United Kingdom. It also took a large stake in the fuel sector of the economy, especially gas and oil. The breadth of his interests across manufacturing, the media, export trade and finance was staggering. Nor was Berezovski slow to consolidate himself politically. The Yeltsin family entrusted its growing wealth to his care and he in turn took posts in public life. In 1998 he was appointed Secretary of the Commonwealth of Independent States; and behind the scenes he played a part in decisions on policy towards Chechnya. He even negotiated the release of foreigners held hostage by Chechen criminals. And it was Berezovski who helped to put together the coalition of rich financiers who provided the funds necessary for Yeltsin's electoral campaign in the first half of 1996.[6]

Berezovski and his associates became known as 'the oligarchs'. It was widely believed that it was they rather than the government who really ruled the country. Other members of the oligarchy became equally notorious: Roman Abramovich, Pëtr Aven, Vladimir Gusinski, Mikhail Khodorkovski and Vladimir Potanin – and they were joined by Anatoli Chubais. Until Putin's accession to the Presidency, they were politically imperturbable. They worried more about the relations they had with each other than about any threat from the authorities. Apparently Berezovski and Gusinski are alleged to have arranged assassination attempts on each other.[7] But they dominated the economy and they let everyone know it.

They exacted a price for the financial support they gave to Yeltsin. The electoral campaign was an example. Although the legal spending limit for Presidential candidates was $3 million, it is plausibly assumed that vastly more than that was collected for Yeltsin. Perhaps $500 million was secretly funnelled towards him.[8] In return the contributors secured the existing capitalist framework against the possibility of a return to power by the communists under Gennadi Zyuganov. They also bailed out the government's budget. But as usual there was a price to pay. As part of the deal, the 'oligarchs' were given temporary ownership of the controlling shares in the chief companies working in the lucrative mining areas. The nickel industrial sector was a particular attraction.[9] These acquisitions became permanent when the government could not pay off the loans on time. Thus the 'oligarchs', while rescuing Yeltsin, piled up the mountains of their wealth higher and reinforced the dependence of the political establishment upon their favour. It is true that individuals among them encountered difficulties under Putin from 2000. Berezovski felt compelled to resign his seat in the State Duma and flee abroad. Gusinski spent several weeks in prison before he too took refuge outside Russia. Chubais found his business interests no longer easy to protect.[10] But the essential characteristics of Russian capitalism endured.

The 'oligarchs' are the vanguard of an army of 'new Russians'. This is the popular term for those thousands of people who have flourished in the market economy after capitalism. Like the 'oligarchs', they are rarely people who previously were crane-drivers or *kolkhozniki*. Many were second-grade *apparatchiki*.[11] Others were criminal elements in the old Soviet days. What distinguishes all of them is their quick-wittedness and ruthlessness. They saw chances in the late 1980s. They had no ideological inhibitions. They had few restraining ties of a practical kind. If they were acquainted with the people of supreme power, they were not so close to them that they needed to kow-tow to them.

Indisputably the Russian Federation's economic leadership is far from being simply a reborn version of the highest strata of the Soviet *nomenklatura*. Nor is it a solidified social stratum. Why this should be so is a matter of opinion. One reason, surely, is that not all members of the old central and local *nomenklaturas* were either interested in promoting their individual interests in personal profit-making or sufficiently skilled if indeed they were so interested. The Soviet administrative system, as nobody should forget, had always let the Devil take the hindmost; the ruthless pursuit of self-interest was the norm. Furthermore, some members of the *nomenklaturas* were in a better position than others to make the most of the collapse of communism. Persons working in the Department of Administration of Affairs in the Central Committee had the opportunity to expatriate finance by setting up foreign firms and acquiring party funds for their operation. Another institution that could commercially aggrandise itself was the Komsomol. But there were also individuals who had no special organisational base yet did well in the milieu of the market economy. If communism had not collapsed, their skills would have remained undeveloped. But communism did collapse. And their skills had a chance to develop.

Often they matured in a vicious fashion. The complex but tight relationship between private business, the state and criminal gangs is demonstrated in the difficulties experienced by a pharmaceutical company in St Petersburg. When the owner tried to seek redress against a rival company, he discovered that he could not rely upon a fair decision from the local political authority; and in the end he had to approach his own 'roof' – the contemporary term for a criminal gang offering 'protection' for a company's interests in return for a regular portion of the profits:

> Our boss did some investigation, and he discovered that the head of the state committee was closely linked to our main local rivals.

So going to the authorities would have been pointless. What was to be done? Naturally he went to our 'roof'. They negotiated with the 'roof' of our rivals, and sorted out the whole thing between them. We didn't even have to pay anything extra – they said it was covered by our regular payment, that's what it was for. Generous of them, you could say ... Without question the state committee head is also under a 'roof'. Who are our roof? I couldn't tell you. I try not to get too close to such things.[12]

The Russian elite at all levels is an amalgam of economic, political and criminal elements. This is a sorry and intractable state of affairs. Criminal gangs are loosely described as 'mafias'. It is not a satisfactory term. The Mafia in Sicily, like Cosa Nostra and 'Ndragheta in the Italian south, are largely regional organisations which brook no competition in their respective territories. The Russian 'mafias' are much more disparate. Or at least they are as yet. They also have a strong admixture of leaders and members who are not ethnic Russians. In the early 1990s the viciousness of the Chechen bands was a cause of much hostile commentary. Such an admixture would be unthinkable in Palermo or Naples. Nor is there any 'code of honour' among the Russian criminal gangs. But similarities, too, exist. The Russian and Italian mobsters resemble each other in buying up politicians in pursuit of profit. They are also sentimental about their dead members. In Russia, indeed, it is the criminal elites which have sustained an art which for a while looked as if it was going to be lost: the embalming of corpses. Experts who used to be employed in keeping Lenin's remains in a more or less respectable condition now find work making slain gangsters look presentable before interment.

But what about the workers? This is the group of people at the opposite end of the social system. Under communism they were meant to benefit from the official policies; indeed they appeared in Marxist-Leninist propaganda as the very vanguard of a society marching towards the perfection of that society. The reality was very different. Pay was poor and the chances of promotion grew smaller as the existing political, economic and administrative elites sought to secure jobs for their own offspring. The welfare facilities were universally available but extremely rudimentary. The sole consolation was that discipline at work was lax: drunkenness, unpunctuality and a general lack of conscientiousness were common. But life was otherwise tough for the working class in town and countryside.[13]

One thing that has yet to undergo universal change is the working routine. Laxity of work discipline has persisted. An example from Sakhalin Island, off the eastern coast of Siberia, illustrates the point. At a fish-packing factory, the workers start drinking vodka at eleven o'clock in the morning before any labour at all is performed.

> The ladies in the cleaning section were having their own problems staying vertical, hence the first conveyor belt did not roll in until approximately two [in the afternoon], after what was two and a half hours of concerted resting. With the first fish, there was a lethargic twenty-minute display of worker honour, followed by a forty-five-minute rest and the sampling of the atrocious Azerbaijani wine *Agdam*. We returned to work for thirty-five, then rested for another thirty. This continued more or less until five, when we parted for an hour for dinner. By six o'clock the fish was on its eighth hour and indeed a great deal of it had accumulated over the course of the day. This began a somewhat stricter regime with more sporadic breaks, marked by the consumption of quantities of beer obtained over the dinner hour. By eleven the stalwart had graduated to the graver heavy-duty gut rot, *samogon*.[14]

Samogon is illicitly distilled spirit, usually vodka. Like the Irish poteen, it is sometimes made incompetently and can cause blindness.

The hard-drinking of Russian workers was notorious from travellers' accounts over several centuries and from the classic novels of Tolstoi and Dostoevski. It drew little comment after 1917, when the 'proletariat' was officially hailed as a vanguard of revolutionary consciousness and sobriety. The reality is that Russians continued to drink as hard after as before the October 1917 Revolution. Intermittent official campaigns against excessive consumption of alcohol, from the 1920s through to the 1980s, only made things worse. Usually the authorities restricted the opening hours of vodka sellers and raised the price. The response of drinkers was to distil their own tipples – and often the result was fatal in as much as a poisonous sort of alcohol was produced.

The situation of the Sakhalin fish-packers is not typical of workers everywhere in the Russian Federation. The fish-run there is an annual affair; the excitement is extraordinary and a festival atmosphere prevails. And at least the fish-packers have work. Many citizens of the Russian Federation no longer have jobs. In mid-2000 nearly 12 per cent of persons of working age were reckoned to be completely without gainful employment. This amounts to nearly nine million people.[15] The situation is much worse than as recorded by the official labour exchanges, who have only 1.3 million persons on their books. Most of the unemployed men and women see no point in registering themselves since payment of their social benefits is seldom honoured – and in any case it has been fixed below half the amount thought necessary for mere subsistence. Unemployment benefit was niggardly in the Soviet period. It remains so today, but the difference is that the USSR provided jobs for everyone of working age. Hardly anyone lacked a job and wages and salaries were paid regularly and on time. The contrast with conditions in the Russian Federation is stark.

The average monthly pay at the end of the twentieth century was a pittance: $60.[16] But nowadays even people who have reasonable salary tariffs can find themselves in difficulties. Many employers, when faced with declining revenues, ask employees to go over to shorter working weeks and accept a cut in pay. Another tactic is to request workforces to take extended holidays. In 1999 this was the fate of nearly one-tenth of those persons with jobs. Worse still is the situation of people who turn up for work every day and yet fail to be paid at the end of the month. In 1997–8, arrears affected between half and two-thirds of the working population. There was some improvement in 1999, when the government needed to show the electorate it could do something about social problems in advance of the Duma and Presidential elections. Neverthe-less pay arrears remain a widespread difficulty. One-fifth of employed people in 2000 were owed substantial sums by their offices or enterprises. The effect on morale in society has been catastrophic. Everywhere there is an air of uncertainty, resentment, complaint and barely contained fury. An old Soviet joke used to run as follows: 'We pretend to work and they pretend to pay us.' Now even if the workers work, there is sometimes hardly a pretence at paying.

At least twelve million Russian citizens have therefore turned to 'second jobs'. Some manage to make a profit trading on the streets, but this is no long-term solution unless individuals earn enough to leave the first job behind. Often, however, the jobs are of a menial nature. Almost always they are offered without the minimal rights of employment, safety and health. For most people the second job simply adds to the pressures of life. It exhausts them. It is certainly a safety valve for tensions that would otherwise be uncontainable. But the valve has become the object of general complaint. Surely, Russians say, 'normal' conditions have to be restored to them; the easy working conditions of the 1970s are remembered with nostalgia. Surely, Russians say, the government ought to be doing things to make this happen. But the humane market economy which Boris Yeltsin promised to construct has not emerged from the drawing-board. The scams of the rich and powerful have triumphed. Russians have little or no stake in the capitalist structures. The voucher-based privatisation of the early 1990s pleased few. Most citizens still feel betrayed. 'We've got nothing left to lose,' a popular saying goes, 'and they're threatening to take even that away.'

There are several reasons why many workers have been kept on the books of business enterprises. But among them was a financial incentive at the level of local government to maximise the number of employees.[17] This legislative quirk has meant that people are on the books of firms without doing any work for them – and of course this makes it easy for them to moonlight. A tacit concordat among government, employers and employees persists. It cannot last for ever. But at the moment there are stimuli in Russian laws inhibiting rapid transformation. The legacy of the USSR has not vanished a decade after the collapse of the Soviet multinational state.

Meanwhile the standard of living for a large number of Russians has fallen to depths unplumbed since the 1940s. By early 1999, months after the August 1998 financial collapse, 38 per cent of citizens languished below the officially recognised poverty line. The subsequent partial recovery of the economy eased the situation, and the poor now constitute only 30 per cent of the population. This is the same proportion as in the earlier years of the decade.[18] The result is that over forty million people receive incomes below the requirements of subsistence. Certain categories of society have continued to receive support from state welfare agencies. These include military invalids as well as veterans of the 'Great Patriotic War' and subsequent wars. Benefits are also available for single mothers, for the disabled and for persons who risked their lives in the Chernobyl nuclear disaster. In none of these categories is the money adequate for a comfortable life; it was insufficient in the communist years and remains so in the present day. But the situation of the recipients is at least better than it is for most of the Russian poor. The state lacks the revenues it had under communism to guarantee a minimum level of welfare for all citizens. Social benefits nowadays constitute merely 2 per cent of the country's gross domestic product. This is woefully short of what is required to alleviate misery.

The state has made clear that it envisages no increase in its provision in the foreseeable future. If a citizen wishes to obtain money from the state, the easiest option is therefore to seek registration in one of the special categories. The result has been a sharp rise in the number of officially recognised disabled men and women. No doubt the deterioration in living conditions in the past twenty years has affected the general state of health in society; but this cannot be the sole reason: another is that Russians have been fiddling the system.

Nevertheless the authorities have been careful to avoid most people being left to fend entirely for themselves in the new market economy. Fifty-two per cent of average household expenditure in 1999 went on purchases of food for the home. Only 1.6 per cent was spent on rents or mortgages for accommodation.[19] This to a large extent reflects the decision of Yeltsin's cabinets to transfer ownership from the state into the hands of existing tenants. By 1999, according to official records, 56 per cent of the country's housing stock had become the private 'property of citizens'.[20] But other items of household expenditure are equally odd for a capitalist system. Russian families lay out only 0.7 per cent of their income on electricity, 0.6 per cent on gas and 0.6 per cent on central heating.[21] Local telephone calls are virtually free of charge – thus Russian callers can still have their customary interminable conversations. A town bus trip in many large cities in 2001 cost only four rubles (which was equivalent to about thirteen US cents). The cosy relationship between the state and the various massive utilities companies has not only made a few directors rich beyond their dreams; it has also enabled ministers to insist that residents should not – at least during the early years of the establishment of a market economy – have to pay a genuine commercial price for their domestic fuel.

This gives the lie to claims by opposition politicians (and many Western commentators) that the economic policy of governments under Yeltsin and Putin have been committed to unrestrained 'shock therapy'. Fear of the potential for general social disorder has been constant. Shocks have been administered, but they have been carefully calculated so as to fall short of pushing most people below the level of subsistence. Even Gaidar in 1992 was wary of adverse popular reaction. Things are quite bad enough, but they are not as bad as they could be.

And if we are searching for the extreme antithesis of the Berezovskis and the other 'oligarchs', we should not be looking at the employed workers and farmhands. There is a class of people still lower in the social hierarchy: the beggars. They stand on the main streets, their hands outstretched. Sunshine or snowstorm, they stand there. Some have their own pitch. For practical reasons the subterranean walkways in city centres are a favourite spot as are the gateways of churches. No one knows the number of the indigent and homeless. But about their piteous condition there can be no doubt. These people are destitute and are living completely on the charity of strangers. Their mode of begging has nothing in common with the sort often found in the West. If a young man asks for alms, he will not be healthy and certainly he will not curse passers-by if they fail to hand over some money. More likely he will be an amputee survivor of the Afghan War or of one of the military campaigns in Chechnya. If a young woman begs, more often than not she will be surrounded by several of her children. If she is lucky, she and her family will be living in a railway carriage or a hut on the city outskirts.

Most beggars, however, are pensioners, amputees, alcoholics or homeless mothers with young children. Their clothes are tattered, their footwear bedraggled. Sometimes they cross themselves in the fashion of the Orthodox Church; always they are grateful for whatever is given to them. Their posture is indescribably humble. They behave like characters out of Soviet dramas about the horrors of tsarism – and perhaps this is why their demeanour is as it is: until the late Soviet years under Gorbachëv it was entirely forbidden to beg on the streets. When beggars returned to the scene, they behaved like mendicant characters in historical films and plays. Russians today are charitable to those who accost them for alms. This is a society where life is tough for almost everyone, and the assumption is made that anyone who needs to beg must perforce have had misfortunes in life still greater than the average.

Yet the life of most beggars is exceptionally tough. Sleeping rough in the Russian winter breaks the health of all of them in the end. The police have regular campaigns to clear them out of the railway carriages, tramcars and Metro walkways. Shops in the cities do not welcome their presence in their doorways. The churches distribute alms to the destitute, but not on a scale that has much influence on the situation. The state, inheriting the facilities available in the communist years, built no hostels for the urban homeless – and many public buildings have been privatised. City councils are in financially straitened circumstances and have not prioritised this sector of welfare provision; in the larger conurbations, indeed, the effort is concentrated upon discouraging non-residents from trying to stay in the locality. The authorities confine their care to the bare minimum: they send their lorries round the streets each morning and, as the litter is removed from the pavements, so too the beggars who have died in the night are loaded up and carted off to the crematoria. There is almost no commentary on this in the press or on TV. It is too normal a phenomenon to invite discussion.

There can be no doubt whatever about the bitter resentment in society. Russians detest what they regard as the robbery of state assets that took place from the early 1990s. And they hate their own humiliation. Russia under the USSR was always a country of deeply entrenched inequalities. These have increased since the fall of the Soviet Union. For the present, robber capitalism rules.

20. A SOCIETY DISCLOSED

Wife: Darling, I must tell you the latest news: there are soon
   going to be three of us.
Husband: Oh, how wonderful, sweetheart! I'm so happy!
Wife: Yes, Mum has just written to say she's coming to live
   with us.

Yevgeni Petrosyan, comedian, 1995

The social changes of recent years were the result of developments through the 1990s. But they also had roots in the late Soviet period. Many changes took place over many decades and were simply less visible than they now are. Society in the USSR, far from being static, was increasingly diverse. This was not understood abroad largely because the statements of successive communist leaders and their propagandists were taken too seriously. Reality was also occluded from us by an understandable preoccupation during the Cold War with matters of politics, diplomacy and security. Thus when spokesmen claimed that aspirations and conditions were uniform across the USSR, the tendency abroad was to assume that the communist party and the KGB had truly homogenised society by eliminating the phenomena at variance with Marxism-Leninism.

   Nothing could be further from the truth. Loose threads dangled from all sides of the social fabric of the USSR. Although relations between men and women in Soviet society were meant to be egalitarian, in reality the men lived at the expense of their womenfolk. They did almost no housework. They left childcare to the mothers. They got drunk. Many of them beat their wives. They took it for granted that if a sudden and unwelcome pregnancy occurred, their women should take themselves off and get an abortion. Men had preferential treatment at work when promotion became a possibility. Certain employment niches were available to females. They moved into medical and teaching posts in substantial numbers – the salary level in both professions was low. At a lowlier level they worked as snow clearers, house painters, street sweepers, shop assistants and farm labourers. In the Soviet Union women had equality, but it was equality of compulsion to enter paid employment. They suffered from inequalities of recruitment, reward and promotion, and there was the expectation that they would continue to carry out the main domestic tasks without their husbands lifting a finger to help.

The lot of women has not significantly improved. Feminists have tirelessly protested about this, and some of them have tried to bring about practical change. Their organisations are not confined to Moscow. In Murmansk, for example, there is the Congress of Women of the Kola Peninsula. Its programme of activities include supplementary basic education for women, refuge-hostels and telephone help-lines. The Congress aims to modify attitudes among men. In its own words, it is dedicated to 'the gender enlightenment of the population'.[1]

This adoption of Western trends is not the only sign of change – and feminists have been powerless to arrest less salubrious developments. Little public restraint prevents women offering themselves for sexual gratification. In the Soviet Union there was pressure on them to appear decorous and to avoid any salacious behaviour. Prostitution existed, but for the most part it was kept off the streets. There was even a prohibition on a Miss USSR competition. Nowadays things are very different. Whores are readily available in hotel foyers; restaurants regularly put on strip-tease cabarets, and in 1999 a strip-tease weather forecasting programme was introduced to a national TV channel. Serious newspapers often carry images of naked young women. The female condition and sexual allure are considered co-extensive. Even the more severe feminists are likely to agree that 'a woman shouldn't lose her femininity'.[2] So lipstick, perfume and flirtatiousness are accepted by more or less everyone as essential for womankind. Elegant coats and colourful, figure-enhancing dresses are virtually obligatory for those who can afford them. In the Soviet period there was a pent-up longing among women to express themselves in a fashion unapproved by Marxism-Leninism. And the media in post-communist Russia have been happy to indulge and encourage such an aspiration.

Women continue to face difficulties in the home. The deterioration in material conditions since the late 1980s has been widespread and this has added to the load of pressure on family life.[3] Husbands are not behaving noticeably better towards their wives. Over-indulgence with alcohol has been a problem in Russia for centuries as it has in many countries where drinking to get drunk rather than drinking as an accompaniment to a family meal has been traditional.

The fact that Yeltsin's governments kept a low tax on vodka has led to an increase in alcoholism, especially among men. Excise duty was raised somewhat in February 2000, but a bottle of distilled liquor is still cheaper than the most basic *vin de table*. To some extent this is the result of the disintegration of the USSR, since the vine-growing areas were mainly in Ukraine, Moldova and Georgia. None the less this should not have inhibited commerce since 1991. The main reason is the yearning of so many Russians for the traditional relief from melancholy: strong alcoholic spirit. Commercial inducements have been cunning. Nowhere in the world is there a greater love of the bottle; only Finland and a few other countries of northern Europe rival Russia. As a popular saying puts it: 'Vodka is the enemy of the people, but our people has no fear of its enemies.' The playfulness is taken to extremes in the marketing of a special Zhirinovski Vodka with a logo depicting the leader of the Liberal-Democratic Party. Politics and cirrhosis of the liver go together in Russia. It is mainly men who are the hard drinkers. The consequence, as ever in Russian history, is that wives have to deal with the problems at home. Without women, the entire social order would collapse. Thus it always has been.

Some things, however, have got easier. Contraceptives, including both the pill and condoms, are more readily available than in the Soviet period; and condoms are no longer made to a thickness as if intended for re-use as football bladders. Unfortunately the price is too high for most couples and abortion remains the practical alternative. Meanwhile there is encouragement on TV and in the press for women to assert their rights. A party called Women of Russia has contested elections. Several women, most notably the late Galina Starovoitova, have become prominent in public life in her own right and not just as a token of the regime's formal pretension to being fair to women; and women have also proved more adaptable than men to the demands of the economy's new service sector.

One thing that has not changed is the obligation of men to show admiration for their loved ones on International Women's Day, 8 March each year. The giving of a bouquet is the barest acceptable minimum. Some men, breaking the habits of the rest of the year, do the washing up for their spouses. Woe betides the husband who forgets to mark the day in some such fashion. Since the fall of communism there has been discussion of the range of women to whom it is advisable to give a present. Even *Auto Mechanic* magazine takes part in the debate:

> Whom to give a present to? First define the degree of closeness. Is she your wife, lover, comrade in the Liberal-Democratic Party of Russia [led by Zhirinovski] or someone you met only yesterday? And remember: you can give to a person close to you almost anything, including money. (Relationships in which money is given before acquaintance is made are not classifiable as close. *Ed.*) But there's practically nothing you can give a new acquaintance.[4]

International Women's Day has long been criticised by feminists as the exceptional phenomenon which proves the rule of 'male chauvinism' in Russian culture, but perhaps the jocular comments of a male-oriented car magazine indicate that masculine complacency may be beginning to wane a little – or perhaps the comments are merely 'laddish' cynicism.

The single aspect of life in which women have the advantage over men is in delayed death. By 1994, on average they lived fourteen years longer – a staggering discrepancy. The average age of male mortality in that year was fifty-seven.[5] Very many men do not reach the age of retirement. The environmental pollution, the decline in health-care provision and increased consumption of nicotine and alcohol have worsened living conditions.[6] There are rising problems with HIV infection as well as with the spread of addiction to heroin and cocaine. It would seem that men are more liable to be affected, especially by diseases associated with alcoholism and smoking, than women – and perhaps men are also more likely to work in more dangerous industrial conditions. Even so, it is striking that the discrepancy has as yet caused no great public outcry in Russia or elsewhere.

Simultaneously there has been a steady fall in the population. The year 1999 alone, according to the State Statistical Committee, witnessed a decrease by 0.5 per cent. Between 1992 and the beginning of 2000 the Russian Federation underwent a net loss of 2.8 million inhabitants; this is almost 2 per cent of the population and is a serious concern for the authorities. Nor can the fall be explained by emigration. Although the exodus of Jews to Israel continues, there were only 215,000 emigrants of all ethnic groups in 1999. Meanwhile there were 380,000 immigrants into the Russian Federation; almost all of them came from other countries of the former Soviet Union where conditions for Russians have become irksome. Thus the demographic question is unlikely to be resolved in the near future. At the moment there are nearly one and a half times more deaths than births, and the trend seems set to continue since most young married couples can ill afford to have more than one or two children.[7] Both partners in any marriage are under pressure to stay in employment for as long as possible. Unfortunately the facilities for childcare in kindergarten have become more restricted as economic privatisation has proceeded; and the construction of larger apartments has yet to have an impact on the lives of most families.

There has been a slight subsequent recovery in mortality rates, but in 1999 the average age of death of adult males was still only sixty.[8] By the late 1980s the USSR had been approaching Western levels, and men were dying at the age of sixty-four and women at seventy-five.[9] Old age was easy in the last years of the Soviet period. The pension was pitiful. Men retired at sixty, women at fifty-five; but most people, unless they could live off the income of their families, sought to go on working. In some professions, such as teaching and medicine, this was not unduly difficult. For industrial workers, however, it was frequently necessary to take menial jobs. Men acted as hotel doormen. Women could get employed as cloakroom attendants; in hotels they might serve as concierges: veteran visitors to Russia will recall the ferocious female enforcers of order and morality who kept a *samovar* on the boil in their office.

Such work was boring and ill-paid, but facilitated a degree of integration in society. The old in the USSR were not regarded as parasitical; they had the respect of the younger generations – and the importance of the grandmother in the raising of children was generally acknowledged. This did not stop people making jokes about this. A popular street refrain (*chastushka*) ran as follows:

> Granny loved her granddaughter so much,
> She put a landmine in her bed
> One night there were two powerful explosions –
> The little granddaughter also loved her granny.[10]

But 'gallows humour' of this sort was a way of relieving the tensions of domestic life lived in a cramped apartment. It did not indicate basic disrespect for the older generation. Without help from grandparents, most married couples with children could not have coped with the demands of their professional jobs. Single parents were under still greater pressure. The result was that cultural values were transmitted by people of pensionable age with an effectiveness that frustrated the efforts of official communist propagandists. Marxism-Leninism was thwarted much more by the traditional ideas of Soviet grannies than by the diffusion of overt political dissent.

Grandparents continue to have influence, but it is threatened by the calamitous trend in demography. Increasingly the expectancy of Russian citizens is to die in middle age and so not even reach the point of retirement. The diseases that kill them are familiar. Heart attacks, cirrhosis of the liver and emphysema as well as cancer are widespread. The physical threat is bad enough. But there is also a precipitous fall in the morale of citizens. Russia is not a hopeful country.

There is a psychological and social texture to this that Russians feel even if they do not often comment on it. From the late 1930s through to the mid-1980s the rulers of the USSR suggested that older people knew what was best for society in general and the young in particular.[11] How strange this was for us Westerners, brought up with assumptions about the 'generation gap'. One only had to walk out on a Soviet street without a hat on a snowy day for some elderly person to shout: '*Molodoi chelovek!*' ('Young person!') The words were delivered with a confidence that pensioners should be listened to; and there would follow an impromptu lecture on the need to conserve energy by wrapping the entire body in padding. The fact that older people had fought in the war added to their authority. Military invalids were allowed to go straight to the front of shop queues and parades of veterans, proudly wearing their medals, were frequent. Whereas in the West there was a cult of youth, in the USSR there was respect for experience tempered in the heat of patriotic defence and economic progress. It was considered improper to ignore the elderly in the fashion typical in Western industrial countries.

But already in the 1960s this was changing, albeit slowly, as the younger generation began to assert its right to behave and enjoy itself as it wanted without permission from its elders – and already much impetus for this came from the West. Rock music could be heard on foreign radio stations no longer jammed by the Soviet authorities. Foreign visitors became more frequent on the streets of Moscow and Leningrad, and privileged groups of Soviet citizens were allowed to go on holiday tours to Europe and North America. The youth of the USSR increasingly resented the contrast between the constraints laid upon them and the freedoms of their Western counterparts.

This feeling also had a Russian source. Even in Stalin's time there was cult of the young. Stalin was adulated as the wise patriarch in *Pravda* and *Izvestiya*; but the same newspapers fêted dashing young aviators, footballers, writers and scientists. Record-breaking milkmaids, coal-miners and railway-engine drivers, most of them being fresh out of school or training institute, had their photographs on the front page of *Pravda* and *Izvestiya*. This continued in subsequent years, even when the geriatric Brezhnev, Andropov and Chernenko held supreme political office. Furthermore, the young people themselves had never been as effectively suppressed in their behaviour as the official media liked to pretend. Non-conformist behaviour had been a problem for the authorities throughout the twentieth century. Young peasants coming to the towns for industrial employment under both Nicholas II and Stalin were notorious for their outbreaks of delinquency;[12] and the alienated youngsters sometimes took to the politics of rebellion. Lenin's communists in 1917 were known as a party disproportionately composed of the younger workers. And when clandestine political groups were formed immediately after the Second World War with the purpose of getting rid of Stalin, their members were almost always students. Even in the USSR there were signs of a 'generation gap'.

Indeed by the 1960s there were gangs of male adolescents who imitated the Western Teddy boys and their drainpipe trousers, winkle-picker shoes and slicked-down hairstyles. These were the *stilyagi*, whose aggressiveness towards 'decent' Soviet people became notorious. Of course, not everyone needed to join the *stilyagi* in order to behave 'anti-socially'. Western-style rock music became widespread and, by the 1980s, soft and hard drugs were part of 'the scene'.

Even when Khrushchëv and Brezhnev were in power, the authorities felt compelled to come to terms with the alienation from the regime felt by so many young people. Predictably this was done in a highly manipulative fashion. For example, Khrushchëv allowed Soviet publishing houses to translate the American novelists Ernest Hemingway and John Steinbeck and to print their works in large editions. Permission had been given because such authors criticised the workings of liberal democracy and the market economy. Hemingway and Steinbeck became great favourites with the reading public. But their popularity rested less on their critique of American capitalism than on their endorsement of the principle of personal pleasure. Nobody in Russia since the poet-balladeer Sergei Yesenin in the 1920s had written so lovingly about the pleasures of the bottle, women and carousing. Soviet literature with its insistence upon civic duty and self-denial had no equivalent. In the USSR even the novels of British authors Arthur Conan Doyle and Agatha Christie – which in their native land had the reputation for being rather quaint and stilted – were read for their cameos of gaiety as much as for their crime-based thrills. The 'West' became a metaphor for freedom and fun.

Another channel of Western influence was popular entertainment. Not all of this was limited to the USA and other Great Powers. For example, there were the footballing heroes of Brazil in successive World Cups. What an unregimented type of soccer Pelé, Garrincha and their team-mates played! Later, under Brezhnev, there were visits from British rock stars such as Elton John. Beatles LPs were smuggled through Soviet customs and copied on to cassette-tapes; the popular appeal of a lifestyle not subject to subordination, inquisition and indoctrination was obvious.

Gorbachëv personally kept himself apart from this trend; his preference in culture was for literary classics, Lenin and symphonies. But as the trend grew in the 1990s, it proved hard for politicians to ignore the political influence of young people as electors. Yeltsin was the first to sense this. Unlike previous leaders, he avoided giving moral sermons to young people. In the 1996 Presidential electoral campaign, moreover, he attended on stage a rock concert in Rostov-on-Don. Despite his chronic cardiac condition he joined some teenagers and wiggled about in a creditably modern fashion. His aides doubted the political efficaciousness of his impromptu dance. Alexander Korzhakov, his bodyguard and aide at the time, sourly noted – admittedly after being sacked by Yeltsin – that the vote for Yeltsin in the Rostov territorial constituency was lower than in the rest of the country. Perhaps it was for this reason that when Bill Clinton asked Yeltsin to join other leaders of the G8 countries at a Chuck Berry concert, Yeltsin refused.

Likewise Putin has declined to ingratiate himself with the young except in so far as he emphasises his physical fitness and love of sport. Wild horses, however, would not drag him on to a stage to dance under the gaze of TV viewers. For him, the pomp and ceremony of office are essential to the dignity of state. It is also a matter of character: his wife has revealed that outward displays of enjoyment and affection are not in his nature.

But even the puritanical Putin would be powerless to counteract social trends that long existed in the deep tissues of Soviet life. The removal of the old constraints on behaviour has spread to social relations. Not all Russians lived or live in 'normal' families. Sexual preferences have publicly become ever more diverse. Gays and lesbians have until recently had to act with extreme discretion. Stalin, trying to re-orientate state policy towards the need for more children to be born and reared, placed a legal ban on homosexual activity in 1934 on pain of judicial sentences to forced labour in the Gulag. This was the position through the remaining years of the Soviet period and indeed until the law was repealed in April 1993. But of course 'gays' always existed. In certain professions they were – as in the West – always heavily represented. Ballet-dancers and actors were well known for this. But 'campness' in public discourse was virtually unknown. The predominant assumption was that heterosexuality was the universal norm and no Soviet communist leader, TV commentator or press journalist ever dared to contradict this. Nor probably did any of them want to: popular traditions and the official political line coincided on this matter. Homosexuality was despised and feared and gays and lesbians continued to be extremely secretive.

The hostility to gays amongst the general public has not faded. In 2000 it was found that three-fifths of Russian citizens still found homosexuality intolerable. Only 2 per cent saw it as acceptable behaviour.[13] Gays are known as 'light blues' (*golubye*). This is the Russian word, but increasingly they are referred to as *gei* in imitation of the English word.

Gays and lesbians have their clubs mainly in the big cities. In St Petersburg, for instance, there is *Tsifry*, which advertises its attractions on the Internet:

> The leader among gay-clubs. Open daily except for Mondays. *Tsifry* is just too good to be available only to men: mirrors everywhere, ventilation; it has a condom-dispensing machine and a good kitchen. The musical format is Eurodance (40%), Russian pop (40%), Techno (20%). Inside everything is of Eurostandard. At the doors outside there's a crowd like outside the Hotel Metropol in the Soviet period. The bouncers are ferociously strict. But any attempts to exclude 'straights' (heterosexuals) with their girl friends (entrance charge for ladies is up to 360 rubles) are ineffectual . . . Now the only place inaccessible for ladies is 'the dark room': bare walls, a platform covered with linoleum, obscure silhouettes and confused wailing . . . In November there should be the opening of an intimate bar on the upper floor with sixty places exclusively for men.[14]

Such an advertisement was unimaginable a very few years ago. Gays do not usually invite attention; quite the reverse: they are discreet about their activities. As abroad, Russian gays have certain parks, lavatories and particular streets where they meet. Theirs is no longer the love that cannot speak its name. Individual choice of lifestyle, including sexual orientation, is now a principle of Russian social behaviour even if it is not respected universally.

Inevitably, though, freedom of choice in a market economy is conditioned by financial capacity. Most people cannot afford to go to restaurants, night-clubs or even the cinema, and the purchase of books or CDs remains difficult for many. Consequently book-reading habits, for example, have changed only slowly.[15] Public libraries continue to be important in society, but their budget for new accessions has fallen drastically. A recent survey of borrowings revealed the following ranking of favourite authors:

1	James Hadley Chase	12	G. Benzoni
2=	Valentin Pikul	13=	N. Leonov
	Agatha Christie		Edgar Rice Burroughs
4	Alexandre Dumas	15=	Nikolai Nekrasov
5	Fëdor Dostoevski		A. Adamov
6	Lev Tolstoi	17	Mikhail Sholokhov
7	Erle Stanley Gardner	18	Viktor Astafev
8	Mikhail Bulgakov	19=	Micky Spillane
9	Harold Robbins		Arthur Conan Doyle
10=	Yulian Semënov		Maxim Gorki
	Georges Simenon		

This is not very different from rankings made in the late Soviet years. Harold Robbins's works show less concern for moral propriety than was customary; but the presence of Dostoevski, Tolstoi, Bulgakov, Sholokhov and Gorki shows that popular respect for 'high' culture persists: buses are still filled with passengers avidly reading the great literature of the past. But if the works of the brilliant young novelists and poets – and indeed writers of the latest thrillers and romantic fiction – were on the library-shelves, they too would probably figure on the list of favourites.[16]

At any rate it is not only at the level of individuals that Russian society has changed. It has also evolved in its organisational units. By mid-1996 there were more than 58,000 'voluntary' associations – and of them about 3,000 covered the Russian Federation as a whole.[17]

Many such organisations were Moscow-based in the *perestroika* years and this continues to be true. But in the 1990s there was also a proliferation of them in the provinces. Some organisations are idiosyncratic to the point of being bizarre. The Russian Federation even has its own adjunct of the Burnley Football Club Supporters' Society.[18]

But many organisations have at the same time been dedicated to the extension of civil rights and to ecological protection.[19] There is also a steady shift towards social charity: activists campaign for assistance for the disabled, for one-parent families, for families with many children, for the destitute. Gradually there is a growing public awareness of the problems.[20] This began with encouragement from Gorbachëv, who licensed the weekly *Moscow News* and the illustrated magazine *Ogonëk* to shine their spotlight onto the insalubrious corners of social life in the USSR. The revelations continued in the Yeltsin Presidency. Little groups of campaigners dedicated to the correction of abuses sprang up. Some were ecological, others were architectural. Some dealt with political scandals such as the treatment of conscripts in the armed forces. There were also intellectual and religious associations. Such bodies were regarded as potential seeds of a civil society in the USSR.[21]

Yet they sprouted in an inclement environment. The Soviet political leadership from Lenin onwards eliminated any autonomous associations that might challenge the regime. Total central control from the Kremlin was the objective – and Stalin in the 1930s extirpated every single social body outside the state's direct authority. His method was sometimes to liquidate organisations and sometimes to replace them with those of his own creation. There was a moderate regrowth of autonomy in the somewhat freer atmosphere under Khrushchëv and Brezhnev. Most of the new associations survived because the Politburo decided to tolerate them. Clubs for sport and culture were formed. The central political authorities had not always anticipated which games, pastimes and hobbies would attract people; and so it was left to individual enthusiasts to set them up for themselves with whatever finances and buildings they managed to acquire.

Oriental forms of unarmed physical combat became popular with many men of an athletic disposition. Examples were judo (favoured by the young Vladimir Putin) and tae kwon do. Also of growing popularity were those sports which the regime had refused to subsidise. One such was rugby football. The authorities stinted for nothing in subsidising soccer, which even had clubs run by the KGB; but they overlooked other games popular in Europe and North America. There were also cultural groups, some of which came close to challenging the political status quo. Russian nationalists began to set up unofficial bodies for the conservation of the country's architecture. They were outraged that communist leaders had demolished cathedrals and churches; quietly they issued pamphlets extolling their beauty. These informal associations could at last flourish under Gorbachëv. Announcements of meetings and invitations to membership began to appear on walls for the first time since the 1920s. Independent trade unions were founded. Political organisations also appeared. Among the first was the Democratic Union, which aimed to enhance civic freedoms in the USSR. In 1990 the Liberal-Democratic Party of Vladimir Zhirinovski was accorded recognition as a political party. The Soviet Union seemed to be acquiring the intermediate organisations that had long been missing in leisure, sport, culture and even politics.

Not all of them have survived intact. A Federation of Independent Trade Unions of Russia continues to exist. Formed with the purpose of replacing the official Soviet trade union organisations, the Federation unites forty-three unions. It boasts a membership of forty-five million men and women. This means that already 100 million people have deserted the union movement since the mid-1980s; for the communist order made it virtually compulsory for individuals to join. The Federation, furthermore, exaggerates its present strength – and it would be interesting to know exactly how many members really pay their dues.[22] Production in most industries has collapsed in the past few years. It would be staggering if people had not drawn the conclusion that unions are no more able than in the Soviet period to bring about an improvement of their working and living conditions. This idea is confirmed by what is known about the tripartite negotiations undertaken by the Federation, the government and employers' associations.[23] These negotiations were heralded as a means whereby the unions might secure guarantees for their members' rights. But the positive results for workers have been minuscule, and the Federation has acquired a reputation for having a cosy relationship with the political and economic elites.

By 1998 this situation became embarrassing even for the Federation and its leaders called a general strike for 7 October. Even before the economic collapse in August, the unions were annoyed by the government's failure to enforce the payment of wages. Nevertheless the local branches trod carefully in approaching their members for participation in the strike. In Petrozavodsk, for example, the Karelian Republic Committee for Collective Actions supported the plan to withdraw labour but recognised that it could not simply issue instructions: it had to make a tactful appeal:

> The question of participation or non-participation in this strike must be decided individually by each worker. If you're minded to

defend your rights to work and payment, please help in the defence
of the economic interests of those workers like yourself – and join
the ranks of the strikers.[24]

The general strike duly took place. It was supported best in Moscow, but
elsewhere hardly at all. It had no impact on the policies of government.
This was hardly unexpected. The financial crash of August 1998 was fresh
in the memory of workers. It was far from clear that most businesses
would survive. Fear of unemployment was consequently greater than the
determination to obtain higher wages.

Strikes have had a greater impact when a particular industrial sector
has been the target. But even the miners, who have taken action more
effectively than any other group of workers, have failed to secure durable
improvements. Collective action is no longer as popular as in the late
1980s. Few societies can remain for years at a high pitch of excitement,
and the Russian Federation is no exception. In any case, workers have
an exhausting daily life. Most of them are too worried about feeding and
clothing themselves to wish to take part in affairs outside the family or
the workplace.

Another factor is the history of communist repression. In the 1930s
those Soviet citizens who had a record of outspokenness, even at the
lowliest local level, had a disproportionately high chance of being
arrested. Anyone who dared to criticise Stalin was doomed if an informer
happened to be present. When Stalin died, the malnourished inmates
of the Karaganda forced-labour camp rose against their guards; and it
took tanks and military aircraft to suppress them. In July 1962, under
Khrushchëv, there were urban disturbances when the Politburo raised
the prices of foodstuffs. In Novocherkassk a popular rebellion needed
the Soviet army to put it down. It is true that Gorbachëv encountered
difficulty with strikes. From the late 1980s the miners of the Kuzbas
withdrew their labour more than once. Strikes have not been unknown
since the fall of the USSR. But they have been rare and ill supported
despite the efforts of the Russian Communist Party to agitate for workers
to protest against their shabby treatment by government and employers
under both Yeltsin and Putin. When in 1998 the Kuzbas miners went on
strike and even stopped the local railway network from working,[25] it was
the exception to the general pattern. The labour movement in contemporary Russia is a toothless old dog; but many of its teeth were pulled
before the Second World War.

And in general the financial and organisational framework for organised civil associations is very shaky. Potential members of trade unions and other bodies are often too poor to pay their dues. The same conditions that cause people to complain are the conditions that prevent them from doing much about them.

But there is more to it than this. Russia and the other countries of the Commonwealth of Independent States were pressed into the mould of the communist state for decades longer than was true for East European states. Lenin founded the Soviet Union but it was Stalin in the Second World War who introduced communism to Eastern Europe. This discrepancy has had a profound consequence. In Poland, Czechoslovakia, Hungary and the German Democratic Republic there remained a popular memory of earlier times. There was also a profound resentment at the presence of the Soviet army on the national soil and at the compulsory political and cultural prostration before the USSR. In Poland and Hungary the Catholic Church continued to offer a haven for people who refused to adopt communism as their credo; in the German Democratic Republic the same resistance was shown by the Lutheran Church. In Poland there was a political expression of the national rejection of communism. This arose in the 1970s with the emergence of the Solidarity independent trade-union movement under the Gdansk electrician Lech Wałęsa. On a more modest scale Vaclav Havel led the Civic Forum movement in the 1980s in Czechoslovakia. Without a massive, brutal programme of repression there was no means of eliminating these growths of civil society in at least some of the countries of the Eastern Bloc.

In Russia things were never going to happen as propitiously.[26] The political, social, intellectual elites had been deeply affected by seven decades of communist rule. The memory of the tsarist period had faded. Although the communist dictatorship was introduced and consolidated by much violence, this was not the work of a handful of communists but of a vast number of Russian communist volunteers. Russians did far more to consolidate Russian communism than Poles or Czechs did in Eastern Europe. The potential for a national movement of anti-communism was all the smaller in Russia.

And so we are left with a picture of a society disclosing itself. Like photographic paper in the developing-bath, the long-hidden trends of Soviet social life have began to produce their images in the light of Russian post-communism. The demographic process is inexorable. In terms of family, generations and gender there has been a steady revelation of the largely unacknowledged trends of the Soviet period. This process is going to take many years to reach its end. The complexities of life are deep-rooted and social relationships will almost certainly follow an idiosyncratic course in Russia regardless of the policies and will of its rulers. For Russians this process contains fewer surprises than for foreign observers, especially those observers who lack acquaintance with the country's history. The sociology of new Russia has to be searched for in the old USSR. Russian citizens are living out what previously they lived within. But they are doing this inside a framework that neither they nor their rulers – past or present – anticipated. The foundations of the old order have been undermined. The carapace of politics has been shattered and the building beneath it has been altered beyond recognition.

21. RUSSIA IN PRIVATE

Ultimately the contemporary person experiences a deep mistrust of practically everything not connected with the devouring or spewing out of money. This takes the outward appearance of life becoming more and more boring while people get more calculating and drier ... In fact there's no diminution of the emotions in human life.

Viktor Pelevin, *Generation 'P'* (2000)

And yet all was not yet lost. At the base of Russian society there have been changes since 1991 that only the most cynical observer would not welcome. Despite all the disappointments, much in life has improved. Thankfully the improvement is unlikely to prove reversible.

The thing that most sharply differentiates communist Russia from Russia after communism is not economics or politics. It is the scope for privacy. I went to Russia in the month after the August 1991 coup. Everyone was still mentally digesting the momentous events: the arrest of the Committee for the State of Emergency, Gorbachëv's return from detention in Crimea and Yeltsin's rise to political dominance. Some of my friends felt pleased, others were rather disoriented. The most ecstatic acquaintance was someone who had not seemed unduly bothered about the KGB in the late 1980s. What she said over the phone in September 1991, therefore, took me by surprise. She said it no longer mattered what we talked about and that she was sure that 'the organs' were no longer listening to us. As she put it later, she felt she could at last have a genuinely private life. Russians could decide for themselves what they wished to think, say or do. The authorities had made attempts at 'mass mobilisation' even under Gorbachëv, who lectured and cajoled people in the traditional communist fashion. Individual choice had not been respected. The violin string snapped when the coup was thwarted on August; privacy in personal life at last became a reality.

This achievement remains insecure and partial. 'The organs' still operate, especially since the accession to power of former KGB operative Vladimir Putin. The Russian Federation has never realised the fullness of civil rights vouched by the Constitution. The security agencies are not the only problem. Rights of citizens are routinely trampled upon by criminal gangs, big business and local administrative personnel.

Manifold difficulties confront ordinary citizens. Although the legal requirement to have written permission to live in a particular town has been rescinded, local authorities in Moscow and other cities continue to limit individual choice by the way they apply the rules on the 'registration' of urban inhabitants.[1] Russians also lack the right to deny entrance into their homes by the police. The authorities merely have to possess – or to say they possess – 'grounds to suppose' that an illegal act has been committed and they can go into any premises without a warrant. The inviolability of the individual – a general liberal principle – is only weakly established. Anyone failing to stop on the street at a militiaman's whistle faces either a legal penalty of up to fifteen days in prison or the informal need to pay a bribe. Nor is private property secure from threat. The authorities are permitted by law to deprive someone of their apartment simply by declaring it a hazard to public safety. Thus citizens have to beware whenever their interests conflict with the objectives of members of the elites; and even when no such clash exists, there remains little opportunity for a private life for those millions of families still residing in *kommunalki*.

Administrative arbitrariness and dishonesty endure. This is evident in the unlikeliest places, including the agony uncle's column in the car magazine *Avtomir* ('Car World'). The columnist is Dmitri Kirillov. What makes him unusual is the fact that he is also Head of the Propaganda Department in the Main Administration of the Interior Ministry. In a recent issue, a thirty-four-year-old woman from Vladimir wrote to him: 'What concretely should the ordinary driver do if an employee of the Interior Ministry openly asks for a bribe, and how should subsequent proof be offered about the fact of the extortion?' Kirillov advised her to ring a confidential help-line. Another reader – a man in his twenties – enquired whether the police were right to insist that his car should be re-registered after he moved his place of abode from the north to the west of the city's limits. Kirillov confirmed that the police were correct. A third question came from a fifty-four-year-old native of Yekaterinburg who needed to renew his lost driving licence after moving to Moscow. Did he have to return to Yekaterinburg to get proof that he had passed his test? Kirillov explained that it could be done in Moscow so long as the driver had kept 'a whole range of documents'. Petty restrictions and requirements remain a basic feature of existence in Russia.[2]

Meanwhile the principle of the equality of all citizens has undergone attrition. The government of the Russian Federation scrapped the old Soviet insistence that people should identify themselves by nationality in the passports. But in April 2001 a State Duma committee proposed that individuals should have the right to specify their national origin if they so desired. This idea stemmed originally from demands made in the national republics; but Russian politicians too supported it since it would give Russians a chance to assert themselves.[3] The maltreatment of persons from the North Caucasus has intensified since 1991. They have regularly been cast out of Moscow and other cities – and this trend began before the first Chechen War was started. The persecution became intense after Chechen terrorists were blamed for blowing up three apartment blocks in Moscow in September 1999.

Yet the popular fear of politicians and policemen is nothing like what it was in the Soviet period. The reason why we hear so little about such an improvement is that it is something already taken for granted.[4] Understandably, Russians think more about the undeniable inadequacies of political and economic changes since 1991. But this has involved neglect of an immense achievement. When Russians close their doors, they are left to their own devices, and it is at home that they are at their most relaxed. The questionnaires on popular attitudes back this up. Eighty per cent of citizens of the Russian Federation, it is reported, 'frequently feel' they have something in common with their families. Seventy-four per cent say the same about their friends. Such a finding is pretty self-evident. Yet it is noteworthy that only 53 per cent attest to a feeling of commonality with persons of similar opinions and beliefs. The figure is 52 per cent with reference to persons of the same generation and 51 per cent in relation to 'comrades at work'. Nationality has a still smaller influence. Forty-five per cent often feel commonality with persons of the same national group. Significantly, only 28 per cent have this feeling with fellow citizens of the Russian Federation (*rossiyane*).[5] It is clear that there is no wide sense of belonging to the new Russian state: the main positive relationships for citizens are those with their family and with their friends.

Yet the size of the groups giving succour in times of difficulty is now much more restricted than before. A woman from the Kuzbas put this starkly in the late 1990s:

Eight or nine years ago the collective was different; we were more organised. We socialised together, celebrated holidays and birthdays together. We even went to the circus together. Not now. People have become closed and aggressive. Previously, if one of us had a baby we would all go along and see it. We'd help out if need be. We went along when someone died.[6]

What this appears to mean is that people can no longer rely on the larger low-level grouping – the workforce, the local communist party organisation or the trade union – which used to be supported by the state. The mines are on the verge of closure. The communists are ghosts of their former selves. The trade union movement is frail. Cliental systems are still important when individuals need help to survive an emergency.[7] But not all the old patrons can assist in the old way; and new patrons are not always available. Relatives and friends do not universally have the influence to fill the gap.

The media give a picture of the gathering gloom. Abortion, divorce, suicide, mental breakdown, hooliganism, mugging, alcoholism and drug addiction are troublesome phenomena. They existed before 1991. They have continued to increase since the collapse of the USSR. And in the press and on television there is endless reportage of the crisis in society – and in the organs of the foreign press and TV the emphasis falls heavily upon such phenomena.

No one would deny that these phenomena are of great importance. They are in the forefront of the minds of Russian citizens when they are asked about life in the Russian Federation today. But this does not signify that all is ill with the country. Russians can now enjoy themselves, however modestly, more freely than in times gone by. Television is their main form of leisure. In contrast with the old days, they have a degree of choice about what they watch. The national channels compete with each other for viewers. ORT is engaged in rivalry with NTV. In the republics, too, there are local channels; and many Russians are sufficiently well off to subscribe to foreign satellite services such as CNN and BBC World. At the same time, however, the demands of viewers themselves have had an impact on the contents of programmes. The popular interest in politics which surged over Russia in the late 1980s is a spent tide. Discussions about public affairs have been relegated to late slots in the evening programme schedule. What people chiefly want is escapist entertainment. Television executives need the advertising revenues and supply what the viewers require.

Easily the favourite type of TV entertainment is the soap opera. The Mexican series *The Rich Also Cry* was the first to grip the imagination of Russians. In the early 1990s there were days when two-fifths of the population of the Russian capital tuned into the saga of love, divorce, suicide and business in the air-conditioned apartment blocks of exotic Mexico. Apparently across the former USSR as a whole there were times when 100 million viewers were sitting in front of their television sets watching *The Rich Also Cry*. When Veronica Castro, one of the stars, visited the Bolshoi Theatre in Moscow, a crowd of exuberant fans mobbed her.[8] The leading character Marianna acquired such popularity that her very foreign name became one of the most popular for new-born girls in Russia.[9] Russian viewers love the lavish lifestyle, the emotional entanglements and the abrupt reversals of fortune. When the Australian soap opera *Neighbours* was tried out in Russia, it failed to gather the same following. Although *Neighbours* is not known for its gritty social realism, it is down-to-earth enough for viewers in Russia to prefer the soap operas of Central America.[10] Russians want fantasy; and when Australian middle-class café owners or their teenage offspring – however beautiful or handsome they may be in beachwear – experience problems with repairing their cars or finding the money to buy fashionable clothes, the reminders of life in Russia are too hurtful. Better a Mexican millionaire than an antipodean grease monkey.

Yet although foreign first names have become popular, so too have ancient Russian ones. Yaroslav, Rodion and Vyacheslav[11] are old names that fell into desuetude at least until the last years of the USSR (despite the fact that Vyacheslav Molotov was a prominent Soviet politician). Indeed a vogue exists for the recovery of old Russia and songs, tales, crafts and antique books are sought after with zeal.

Also widespread is a keen interest in astrology. All newspapers employ 'star-gazers'. Even specialist magazines have their pages of predictions. An example is the Scorpio entry in *Auto Mechanic* in May 2000:

> The Scorpio in all his conscious and unconscious life wages an uncompromising struggle for social justice and technical perfection. Scorpio-Drivers, when they occupy an active position in life, never walk or drive past ignoring inadequacies. They are always people of principle and are constantly demanding of those around them. For example, they expect to find no short measures or wrong fuel grades at petrol stations; they expect competence from car-service

workmen and honesty from car dealers; they expect car inspectors to show impartiality and also a knowledge of the highway code. In traffic queues you'll easily spot the gleaming eyes on the faces of Scorpio drivers, which are marked with bruises and scratches, and their vehicles often have torn or punctured tyres, shattered windows and bodywork with cuneiform images of Russian Esperanto [sic!]. Scorpios have a difficult life and need understanding and care. Love them with all your heart and you will bring closer our radiant future.[12]

This entry is dotty by any standards: the astrologer even forgot to give a prediction for readers.

The point is that Russians can indulge themselves in ways that were officially denied them in the Soviet period. The *Auto Mechanic* magazine has a zany and contemporary aspect while other kinds of superstition are of a more traditional kind. Fortune-telling with playing cards or by palmistry has been legalised and is increasingly popular.[13] Many of the old folk practices never left the overt behaviour of Russians. People sat down and lifted their feet off the floor before setting out on a long journey. They stroked taps of running water when they wished something to happen. They took care not to walk underneath ladders. Now these practices are seen ever more frequently in Russia.

Some people even resort to witchcraft, especially in the villages. The witches are of both the black and the white variety. Old Russia's legacy, with its curious mixture of pagan and Christian beliefs, is resurfacing in a contemporary form. People in the towns and cities are also attracted to the ancient lore as well as to new and foreign cults such as Voodoo. The national weekly TV guide *Seven Days* carries adverts for occult services:

- Anna – hereditary sorceress. Highly effective elimination of female rival. Free amulet '2001'. I'll get back your loved one within a single day. Sexual attachment for ever. 100 per cent guarantee. 249–43–24.
- Healer. Fortune-telling. Love charms, evil eye, healing, business. Exit from any desperate situation. 116–24–46.
- Shaman – all services. 315–08–77.
- 'Adonai' Parapsychology Centre. Superpowerful, high-professional curses. Guarantee. 729–03–03.
- Pëtr Smelov – High Archbishop of Black Magic. Your loved one will come crawling on his knees to you. Dry up your tears –

magic is all-powerful. Immediate result. 500 per cent guarantee. With no adverse health effects! Consultation on all questions – free! 928–14–96, 924–85–05.

- Voodoo. One-day spell. 396–63–37.[14]

This is clearly a commercial sector that has benefited from the removal of the controls maintained in the Soviet period. Witchcraft is one of the few areas of economic growth in Russia since the fall of communism.

No longer are people embarrassed about this. Filipp Kirkorov, husband of singer Alla Pugachëva, tells that he was taken to see the 'wise woman' (*baba*) Vanga when as a baby he was ill with mumps. Vanga reassured his parents that all would be well. But then:

> Naturally Mama asked her: 'What's going to happen to happen to my son in the future? Who's going to be his wife?' 'I see your son on a high mountain with a metal stick in his hands,' said Vanga, 'and he's waving it.' Mama was in shock: either a skier or ... It would never have occurred to a sane person to imagine then that the high mountain might be a musical Olympus and the stick a microphone. In relation to the second question 'Who's the wife?', Vanga answered: 'The first woman he sees when you go home.' Mama was terrified: 'Does this mean he's going to marry me?' And so we go back home and I'm still unconscious and everyone's cautiously waiting for me to open my eyes. I open my eyes and see Mama, and she is utterly distressed because Vanga had unimpeachable authority ... But at that moment they were showing a 'Golden Orpheus' programme from Bulgaria on TV. When I woke up they were just announcing: 'Alla Pugachëva is performing.'

Such stories are nowadays not rare in the newspapers.

In any case, witchcraft is not something the Russian Orthodox Church regards with equanimity. It had faced a similar problem before 1917; but priests in that distant period thought superstitions were a vestige of the rural past eradicable through efficient religious instruction. (Actually, many parish priests also shared the superstitious beliefs.) It is difficult for today's Church to be quite so optimistic. Popular interest has turned witchcraft into a growing commercial business and perhaps as many as a hundred training schools exist for witches: the nature of the profession makes precision impossible. Antiquarianism alone did not foster this resurgence. Witchcraft's prevalence gives an index of the pressures on Russians to fend for themselves in a harsh, volatile environment. No institution, organisation or social group supplies the assistance needed in the emergencies afflicting individuals and their families. The official welfare agencies are in disarray. Certainly the Church conducts charitable activity, but it concentrates its efforts on the restoration of its properties and the preaching of the gospel. The armed forces are notoriously negligent of their duties of care towards conscripts and their families. Nor is there a network of strong intermediate organisations between the government and the individual citizen to make life more tolerable. Understandably, many Russians turn to customary beliefs and practices. Despair speaks the language of tradition.

Thus if an eighteen-year-old conscript goes missing in action in Chechnya and the authorities are not energetic in looking for him, his mother might well resort to a seer. If the hospital fees for a wife's illness are beyond the means of the family, a husband might turn to the services of a faith-healer. And what about the husband who engages in adultery or in domestic physical violence? Some wives have gone to the local witch and paid her to put a spell on the miscreants.[15] Prophets, quacks, seers and fortune-tellers fulfil a useful social function. By deploying 'magical' knowledge or 'supernatural' power, they are relieving the mental aches of clients. They give solace to lonely, disoriented or helpless people.

This does not mean that Russians are attracted solely by escapism and superstition. Russia is not awash with floods of irrationality. On the contrary, news programmes are still very popular, especially when events of crucial national importance are occurring. Viewers are fairly discriminating. When the first of Yeltsin's Chechen Wars was started up in 1994, many viewers watched NTV rather than the state television stations. It was obvious to such people that the government was purveying a very biased version of the situation in Grozny.[16] In the second war, which began in October 1999, the government barred the access of journalists to the military front (and the newspapers and television, including NTV, were in any case favourable to the campaign). The more affluent of Russian citizens could and did turn to foreign broadcasting stations: CNN, the BBC World Service, Voice of America and Deutsche Welle.

The resentment of the Russian people at attempts to indoctrinate them is not confined to politics. While welcoming the influx of foreign goods, Russians do not approve of the imported marketing techniques. They have retained their dislike for what they regard as profiteering – and, sometimes, even for profits in general. Before 1917 there was popular distrust of 'speculation'. Capitalism was a dirty word even before the socialists used it pejoratively. And so Yeltsin, as he introduced capitalism to Russia, carefully avoided calling it by its name. The MMM pyramid-selling scandal of 1994, when tens of thousands of investors lost their life savings, confirmed the popular assumption that all businessmen are crooks to a greater or lesser extent. There remains a feeling that capitalist economics are alien to Russian culture. Neologisms such as *biznes*, *menedzhment*, *partnërstvo* and *diling* have been taken from the lexicon of Western commerce, and those Russians who do not benefit from the collapse of the communist economy resent them. The 'market' is viewed as a kind of barbarian invasion destroying traditional values. The language tells Russians all they think they need to know: capitalism cometh from abroad and capitalism has done them harm.

Yet there is double-thinking here. Patriotism only counts for so much; Russians, even the most xenophobic among them, want to enjoy what they see as the higher standards of existence in the rest of the world. Material conditions have been too hard over many decades for Russian people to aspire to an ascetic style of life. (Solzhenitsyn is the exception.) Products made in Russia come with labels asserting that they are made 'to the European standard' or 'to the American standard'. Or else they are put on sale with fake foreign labels.

Soviet citizens, being accustomed to attempts to deceive them, have turned to satire. History remains a sensitive matter. As if needing to exorcise the grim doctrines of Soviet communism, people still delight in laughing at Lenin:

> The telephone rings at the Smolny Institute [where the communists started the October 1917 Revolution]:
> 'Hello, is that the Smolny Institute?'
> 'Yes, indeed. How can we help you?'
> 'Do you have any vodka in your cellars?'
> 'No, I'm afraid we don't keep any.'
> 'In that case I wonder whether you know a place that has the stuff?'
> 'Well, you could try the Winter Palace, you know.'
> 'Hurrah! Let's storm the Winter Palace!'

Thus a snub was delivered to communist mythology, which held that the storming of the Winter Palace was an action of heroic purity by the party and the working class that completed the October 1917 Revolution in Petrograd. Snubs are directed with equal frequency at recent and current rulers. Jokes about Yeltsin and Putin abound, and it is said that Russians have more sites devoted to humour on the Internet than any other nation. The custom of enlivening a conversation with the latest political quip did not die with the demise of communism.

Another way to lighten life's burdens is gardening; indeed it is vital for the survival of many millions of families. The scale of horticultural activity is enormous. In the early Soviet years, after the famine of 1921–2, urban inhabitants too were officially encouraged to sow vegetables on communal patches of land. Often a factory would make allotments available to its employees. This tradition was resumed during and after the Second World War, when many areas of the USSR would have suffered still greater malnutrition if they had had to rely entirely upon supplies from the state. Yeltsin himself recalled how his family planted potatoes in the late 1940s to survive. Yet the allotments were small, and it was almost impossible to gain permission, after Stalin's mass collectivisation of agriculture, for private house construction. Dachas were owned only by the very few. It took until 1991 for this to change and, as usual, the first moves were not especially legal. Russia's vast spaces beyond the edges of the towns were colonised by people wanting to ensure they would not starve even if they could not get their wages. Allotments became common and were proudly maintained. Wherever there was unused land, residents put up rough sheds and started to plant and sow their vegetables, herbs and flowers.

If they could leave an elderly family member nearby to act as guard, they also brought their livestock with them. Hens, pigs and even cattle were quartered on the allotments. Not all families had the time for such excursions. The weekly *Arguments and Facts* reported an extraordinary case. A couple with four children filled their flat with five dogs, several cats, a goat, a parrot, some geese, guinea pigs and, improbably, a female bear. The family was determined that if the economy were to slump, it would have a plentiful supply of fresh meat.[17] In any other country its collection of live animals would be called a zoo.

Not all animals are kept to be eaten. Pets have become a craze across the Russian Federation. At every newspaper kiosk there are magazines dedicated to advice on the breeding and rearing of dogs and cats. Among them is *Drug* ('Friend'). Whereas many magazines are recycled foreign productions, *Drug* is very much a Russian item. It contains plenty of ideas based on German and British experience, but always with a view towards the specific requirements of Russians and their dogs. An editorial was entitled: 'A sausage always helps in times of trouble.'[18] Another piece bemoaned the near extinction of native breeds, notably the Nenets reindeer dog (which, apparently, is the only herding dog indigenous to the Russian Federation).[19] Space was also given to the supporters of a new political party, A Million Friends, which has promoted the interests of dog owners and campaigns for the repeal of the law against tail-cropping. National pride has been asserted in an article on 'the Russian view on the Western "lessons" of dog rearing'. The complaint was made: 'And so it has turned out that we Russians are forever being instructed by someone – whether it's in politics, economics, building or dog-rearing.'[20]

The editor remains frank about the problems. What Russians lack, he says, is not expertise but money. Pets are costly. If we take account of the cramped living conditions in the apartment blocks, it is clear that the craze must have sprung from a deeply felt need among Russians. The reason can only be conjectured. Possibly it is that most Russians are only second-generation urban dwellers and have retained desire to have animals around them. Another is that pets are a status symbol cheaper than a house, car or Gucci clothing. Nevertheless the pets, too, are expensive. They have to be fed and most Russian citizens are hard pressed to buy enough decent food even for themselves.[21]

Hobbies in general have become a passion. The forms of leisure legally pursued in the USSR were rather few; chess, Russian skittles (*gorodki*), skiing, hunting and crosswords were well to the fore and the authorities catered for them adequately. The chess masters of the USSR were fêted as world-class performers; the game had its dedicated magazines and chess clubs existed in every city district. Furthermore, the state provided facilities for most Olympic sports without charge. But not all recreations had this support. In Stalin's time any activity with an overt international connection might result in arrest and dispatch to the Gulag. Practitioners of Esperanto were treated as spies. Even philatelists were imprisoned if they went beyond collecting only Soviet stamps. After 1953, when Stalin died, things were eased and hobbies were not punished. Nevertheless there were massive gaps in official provision. Knitting, sewing, clothes-making, carpentry, fishing, gardening and card tricks had to be learned from expert friends. Printed instruction manuals were few and far between. Not even all sports were adequately nurtured. Again the official choice was biased: communism stuck with football, ice hockey, basketball, gymnastics and athletics. The avoidance of rugby and cricket is comprehensible: Russia was no more a colony of the United Kingdom than was the USA. But less understandable was the frigidity towards field hockey, judo and other types of sport popular elsewhere.

Since 1991 there has been an explosion of hobby activities. The word *khobbi* has entered the lexicon without the usual dreary complaints from the likes of Solzhenitsyn that Vladimir Dal's pre-revolutionary dictionary did not include it. Magazines have been founded for each leisure activity and, as in the West, there is intense commercial competition among them. Television has joined in. Early on weekday mornings and at weekends there are programmes offering practical counsel on gardening, carpentry, pets and antiques.

The TV stations and the press advise, too, on lifestyles. This had also been done in the later Soviet years, when books on etiquette and comportment, on culinary expertise and hairdressing, were common.[22] Bizarrely, Glavlit – the censorship authority – even sanctioned the publication of *Parkinson's Law*. The motive was that Professor Parkinson demonstrated the oppressive conditions of life and work under capitalism, but Russian readers understood that the bureaucratic techniques described by him were still more obvious in the hypertrophied institutions of the USSR. People in the 1970s were encouraged to be clean-faced, high-permed, neatly dressed and rather prim. The approved lifestyle was never hip, cool, or exploratory. It was regimentative, and it was subject to a discipline prescribed uniformly by the communist party. All this has changed. The advice from television, radio and the press stresses the possibilities for Russians to be as affluent as peoples elsewhere already are. Hair-style, clothes, rock music, consumer industrial products and even vodka are presented as being automatically better if they are of foreign provenance. Russians are alerted to whatever is modish abroad by print and broadcast media which quickly report on Western fashions; and the more prosperous citizens avidly buy the advertised products.

But an ambivalence has grown up about this. Several products from the Soviet years such as 'Belomorkanal' *papirosy* continue to be produced. *Papirosy* are cigarettes with an open cardboard-tube end instead of a filter, designed for soldiers or workers to smoke while wearing gloves in icy temperatures. The 'Belomorkanal' is the White Sea Canal built by Gulag convict labour in the 1930s. Thousands of prisoners died of malnutrition and exhaustion; and the work was so botched that the water was too shallow for use by ships. But the eponymous *papirosy* were (literally) handy in cold weather. Despite years of anti-Stalin exposures in the late 1980s, the 'Belomorkanal' smoking brand remains a popular choice in the town kiosks.[23]

There are also many new brands of products making their appeal through Russian patriotism. Vodka bottles bear the images of Peter the Great, the two-headed Romanov eagle or even Ivan the Terrible. Boxes of chocolates are named after the poet Alexander Pushkin and the cosmonaut Yuri Gagarin. But the market is also flooded by foreign brands. Wines from Italy and France are paraded. More than occasionally there is reasonable suspicion that the labels are fictitious: the wholesalers have judged that a Russian label would diminish sales. Other products, too, attract Russian consumers. Snickers bars, Kelloggs cornflakes and Bic ballpoint pens are on sale even in deepest Siberia. Rock music CDs from the USA and the UK are also found in all cities. Once upon a time the pride of the Melodiya shop was the compilation LP of Lenin's speeches or the record of some classical symphony or other played by a Soviet orchestra. Now Russian consumers can obtain virtually any CD that enters the Western pop charts – and since most of the examples are pirated copies made in Russia or Bulgaria, the usual price is considerably lower than in the West.

Of equal importance is the fact that Russians with money have ready access to the latest IT equipment. Under communism this met official obstruction. Photocopiers and – as this sector of the scientific revolution expanded in the West – automatic inter-city telephones, personal computers and satellite TV receivers were treated as potentially subversive equipment. This situation started to be reversed only under Gorbachëv.

Now Russians are taking to the Internet enthusiastically. In mid-2000 about seven million people across the Russian Federation made regular use of it. They use the Internet not only for electronic mail but also for the world's Web sites, and it is hard to envisage how any government would succeed in withdrawing this freedom. The average age of users is thirty. They are keen to stay in touch with global trends. At the same time they want Russian data in the Russian language. Russia's entrepreneurs have responded to the demand and companies such as Rambler and Yandex are catering efficiently for the local particularities of Internet usage. Russians have a penchant for reading anecdotes and jokes: no other nation has recorded so many 'hits' on such Web sites. In other ways the usage is typical for an economy involved in the expansion of private commerce. Small businesses are heavy users. The Internet enables them to surmount many of the defects in communication, transport and administration in Russia; it also makes them less reliant upon the assistance and co-operation of official authorities. The fact that some electronic mail servers offer their facilities free of charge and that local telephone calls are free has been a huge stimulus to the trend.[24]

Also among the changes begun under Gorbachëv and continued ever since was a flurry of low-brow publishing. The moral restraints in place since the 1920s were swept away. Pornography flooded on to the bookstalls. By the 1990s there were Russian versions of *Playboy* and *Penthouse* magazines. Russians can now buy sexually titillating material just as openly as in the West. All this, for better or worse, has become normal.

Yet there are also tendencies in the opposite direction. Many Russians cling to values of respectability. Efforts to improve the manners of society were made in the USSR from the 1920s onwards.[25] Books advised on how to arrange the home and office. The tone was instructional. Such an approach is out of keeping with the contemporary Russian attitudes. No one any longer takes kindly to being lectured to. But magazines offering counsel on the 'cultured' (*kul'turnyi*) life are published in large print-runs. One such is *My Comfortable Home*, which regularly sells 100,000 copies each month. It is largely a puff for various retail companies specialising in domestic products. But the competition page in the May 2000 issue signals the aspirations of the readership. A twenty-four-piece cutlery set was the prize for answering these questions:

1. On which side of the plate should a soup spoon be placed?
   ☐ On the left
   ☐ On the right
   ☐ To the top

2. Which side of the plate should the knife blade face?
   ☐ The right
   ☐ The left
   ☐ The bottom

3. How many prongs are on a dessert fork?
   ☐ Two
   ☐ Three
   ☐ Four[26]

The prices of domestic items in *My Comfortable Home* are quite beyond most people's incomes. For example, a rudimentary little pine table is advertised at over $40 – more than the average worker's weekly wage.[27] But as in the West, magazines are bought as frequently for fantasy as for the realistic possibility of achievement.

And something has happened to Russian culture that seemed inconceivable only a short time ago: Russians now buy slimming magazines. Throughout Russian history the preoccupation of most people was to get enough food for survival. Malnutrition affected millions of Russia's inhabitants in the Civil War. Food shortages returned in the early 1930s as a result of Stalin's campaign for agricultural mass collectivisation. Between five and six million people perished. Hitler's invasion of the USSR in 1941 led to the occupation of the richest arable land by the Wehrmacht. The sieges of Leningrad and Stalingrad became bywords for starvation, and the rest of Russia eked out a miserable existence. Conditions in the villages remained grim after 1945 and the Soviet state's economic priorities did not include the rapid improvement in supplies of food to the towns; and although Khrushchëv and Brezhnev had policies which increased the food intake, the variety of products remained narrow: rationing was reintroduced in many towns in the 1970s. Consequently Soviet citizens did not quickly adopt the faddishness that has spread in the West. For too long they had been involuntary vegetarians, and the chance to eat meat was seized enthusiastically.

But this attitude has faded among those who can afford an improved diet. Once it was only ballerinas, gymnasts and athlete runners who were slim, and Russians counted themselves healthy only if they were well covered with flesh. Now female beauty is perceived to require a quasi-skeletal form; it has become the dream of most women, including the middle-aged, to reduce their weight. The knitting magazine *Sandra* carries patterns for pullovers which will fit only individuals with the figures of catwalk models; and *Sport-klub*, despite being a monthly publication dedicated to physical fitness, has endorsed the hostility to bodily exercise expressed by the British fashion model Naomi Campbell: 'I hate gymnastics.'[28] The magazine *Shape* caters for enthusiasts (or should we call them victims?) who aspire to such a condition. Most of its advice, as in North America and Western Europe, is couched in terms of sensual excitement and personal development. Significantly, the very name of this particular magazine is printed in the Latin rather than the Cyrillic alphabet.

Another avenue of escape from politics is provided by organised religion. In the Soviet period it was risky to profess religious faith, especially when Stalin was instructing the NKVD to kill or send to the Gulag those clerics – Christian, Moslem or Jewish – who were still ministering to their congregations. Yet when a census was organised in 1937, 57 per cent owned to belief in a deity of some kind. The real statistic, surely, was much higher. The communist state continued to harass Christianity, Islam, Buddhism and Judaism after the Second World War. But the persecution, which intensified under Khrushchëv, faded under his successors; and from 1988, when Gorbachëv promoted the Russian Orthodox Church's millennial celebration of the conversion of the eastern Slavs to Christianity, the resurgence of religious belief was beyond doubt. In the 1990s the revival of religion attracted many Russians. In the ethnic Russian provinces, according to a recent survey, 59 per cent described themselves as 'believers' or said they 'believed in God'.[29]

The question arises of how much difference is made by the religious resurgence to the thought and behaviour of most people in the Russian Federation. The answer appears to be that it makes only a little difference. Attendance at church has ceased its recent growth. Only 2 per cent of citizens go to Sunday services on a weekly basis.[30] People agree that the Orthodox Church in particular deserves a larger degree of trust than any other institution.[31] But the enthusiasms of most citizens lie with family, friends, domesticity and leisure and not with God.

And so I come to the climax of this book. Democratisation and marketisation have spectacularly failed the Russians. The grand project promoted by the Yeltsin team in 1991–2 has fallen by the wayside, and many of the things that his government originally opposed have been restored to favour. The new elites, emerging partly from the old communist *nomenklatura*, have exploited their opportunities with ruthlessness. Nevertheless, popular life has an internal vivacity and variety that should not be overlooked. Below the level of the political and economic elites, society in the Russian Federation is molten. Herein, perhaps, lies the main hope for the future. Russians want a society different from the one they live in. They are attracted to some ideas from abroad; this is true even about those who deny that foreign models have anything attractive about them. The influence of 'the West' has been deep and did not start with the collapse of the Soviet Union.[32] On the other side of the debate, it is clear that even the 'Westernisers' (*zapadniki*) have much about them that is as much 'Russian' as Western. This is true of individuals and is equally true of social groups and society as a whole. Nearly all Russians now aspire to a society that somehow follows the contours of the country's traditions.

What is undeniable is that hope and initiative exist in this country that is widely reported as being inert and hopeless. There is vibrancy in the Russia of the people. It is not the well-heeled, well-fed and well-housed Russia of expensive magazines. It is not a Russia that speaks with a sophisticated voice and acts with a groomed set of manners. Popular Russia exists beyond the gaze of most foreign journalists. It even eludes appreciation by native Russian commentators. But the vibrancy of New Russia is strong – and one day, perhaps, it will be allowed freedom to transform the country from the bottom to the top. Russia is long overdue its quiet revolution.

22. FUTURE UNCERTAIN

Well, are you telling me we're living badly at the moment? What's worse than what it was once before?

Former *kolkhoz* female worker, 1997

Most of the bolder promises of 1991–2 have been dashed. They were always going to be difficult to realise. The small group of reformers had to rely too much upon Yeltsin, who was not as committed to reform as he at first appeared. His health and attitude degenerated after attaining supreme office, and from the apparent protagonist of the people's cause he turned into an embarrassment to every Russian. His political apparatus resembled a medieval court – or a den of racketeers – more than the engine of a contemporary state. Corruption in the Kremlin, moreover, was paralleled in every official institution and at all territorial levels of the hierarchy of government. Politicians wallowed in their opportunities to get rich and exploit others. Russia became a milch cow for its rulers.

Yet at the fall of the USSR the ruling group under Yeltsin had a loose but broadly coherent set of objectives: they aimed at universal civil rights, political democracy, a market society, ideological pluralism, cultural freedom, inter-ethnic tolerance and civic nationhood. The route towards these objectives had not been planned, and this was part of the difficulty. But the reformers also ran into obstructions that were not of their own making. They could not govern without a degree of consent from the administrative cadres of the collapsed Soviet state. They also inherited a ruined economy. Moreover, Russian society did not feel the need to come out on to the streets in support of the changes espoused by the reformers. Unfortunately there were no alternative institutions with enough authority to counteract the situation. Communism had undermined civil society. The consequence was that Church, army, Academy, schools and media were poor at buttressing the case for reform; and the new political parties were more interested in polemics and parliamentary time-serving than in constructive opposition to Yeltsin's establishment. A common national purpose in such circumstances was likely to elude attainment.

The country's history made a bad situation worse. The Soviet decades – and the previous centuries of Imperial rule – weighed against the prospects of basic betterment. Administrative structures impeded the reformers. So, too, did the persistence of popular scepticism about rulers; this made difficulties not only for Yeltsin but also, despite his initial popularity, for Putin. Political and economic circumstances remained depressing. Problems of daily life reinforced the inclination of most people to cleave to methods of survival that had served them in earlier times. Clientelism remained a favoured mode of social organisation. Informal and illegal methods of coping with adversity grew in strength.

Yeltsin's speech of resignation was an epitaph for his early hopes of reform. Much had been achieved, but much more had fallen short of the official objectives – and much had been done that ran in the opposite direction. Beside him was a decorated Christmas tree: the scene was arranged for jollity. But seated at his desk, the aged President had to press out the words:

> Dear friends, my dear ones, today I am wishing you New Year greetings for the last time. But that is not all. Today I am addressing you for the last time as Russian President. I have made a decision. I have contemplated this long and hard. Today, on the last day of the outgoing century, I am retiring.

He tried to explain his unexpected decision:

> I am standing down earlier than scheduled. I have realised that I have to do this. Russia must enter the new millennium with new politicians, new faces, new intelligent, strong and energetic people. As for those of us who have been in power for many years, we must go. Seeing with what hope and belief people voted during the Duma elections for a new generation of politicians, I understood that I had done the main job of my life. Russia will never return to the past. Russia will now always be moving forward. I must not stand in its way, in the way of the natural progress of history.

The sight of the supreme leader calmly relinquishing power was unprecedented in Russian history. In the twentieth century there had been some leaders – Lenin, Stalin, Brezhnev, Andropov and Chernenko – who died in office. But several had not been so lucky. Nicholas II had been overthrown in the February 1917 Revolution, and year later he and his family were murdered by the communists. Khrushchëv had been thrown out of power by a conspiracy of his close comrades in October 1964. Gorbachëv had been ejected from the Kremlin at the end of 1991 by Yeltsin. Neither Khrushchëv nor Gorbachëv suffered any violence, but they did not leave of their own volition. Yeltsin's departure was – as has to be assumed until evidence is produced to the contrary – by personal choice.

There was an untoward side to this: Yeltsin was handing power to Putin as if it was his patrimony, and he made it virtually certain that Putin would win the Presidency in the forthcoming election. Yeltsin was stretching the Constitution to its limit. None the less there was humility in his words to his fellow citizens as he acknowledged his responsibility for many of Russia's current ills:

> Today, on this incredibly important day for me, I want to say more personal words than I usually do. I want to ask you for forgiveness, because many of our hopes have not come true, because what we thought would be easy turned out to be painfully difficult. I ask you to forgive me for not fulfilling some hopes of those people who believed that we would be able to jump from the grey, stagnating, totalitarian past into a bright, rich and civilised future in one go. I myself believed in this. But it could not be done in one fell swoop. In some respects I was too naive. Some of the problems were too complex. We struggled on through mistakes and failures. At this complex time many people experienced upheavals in their lives. But I want you to know that I never said this would be easy. Today it is important for me to tell you the following. I also experienced the pain which each of you experienced. I experienced it in my heart, with sleepless nights, agonising over what needed to be done to ensure that people lived more easily and better, if only a little. I did not have any objective more important than that. I am leaving. I have done everything I could.

Yeltsin ended tenderly:

> In saying farewell, I wish to say to each of you the following. Be happy. You deserve happiness. You deserve happiness and peace. Happy New Year, Happy New Century, my dear people.

In the same breath he announced that he was handing over power to Prime Minister Putin until the forthcoming Presidential elections. He declared that Putin and his contemporaries were capable, in a way he himself was no longer, of carrying the country forward. His patriarchal strength was fading. It was time for the next generation to throw up a new and younger leader.

In fact he and his regime had not failed in every aspect. Elections had been held regularly even though Yeltsin had been tempted to suspend them in 1996. The market economy, once introduced, was made ineradicable. In most regions of Russia there was no use of the armed forces, and Russia did not invade any neighbouring country. Citizens were largely left alone by the state authorities and interference in the affairs of individuals and families was reduced. Freedom of expression, organisation and assembly was respected in the main, despite the violent struggle of October 1993. Reform had not been mere rhetoric. It had become a reality, and it would be only a very foolhardy President who might seek to roll back several of these changes. Popular enjoyment of them is altogether too influential, albeit invisible if we judge the matter only on the basis of what is said by Russians to opinion pollsters. What Gorbachëv started and Yeltsin consolidated is something that is reversible solely at some risk by their successors. The achievements of reform ought not to be ridiculed.

Yet disappointment has grown among Russians that the transformation of society promised in 1991–2 has not been achieved. The basic requirements of most people are simple. They want decent wages and jobs. They want secure access to food, clothing, shelter, health-care, education and physical safety. They want a clean environment. They want to be festive on the great days of the Russian calendar, but generally their wish is for a quiet, untroubled and even unexciting life. They would like their football and ice hockey teams to win more matches than they lose. They desire amusing and instructive television programmes. They long for a country to be proud about. They want to bring up their children with a reasonable hope of a better future than they themselves face. They want rulers and employers who treat them with respect. They would love to see Russia re-establish herself as a power in the world, but not if this might involve external war. They want peace. Neither Yeltsin nor his successor Putin has pulled off this transformation – and no one expects it to happen in the years immediately ahead.

Russians remain discontented. The deterioration in so many aspects of their life has been appalling and the harshness of life is evident in town and countryside. The real income of citizens has plummeted since 1984, the last year before the process of economic change was initiated by Gorbachëv. It may even be that things will get worse before they get better. Unemployment is a growing problem. Although most people have homes, are adequately clothed and are educated free of charge, it is not impossible that such a situation will deteriorate. The process is still at an early stage. An empire – the USSR – has fallen apart. Support for imperial restoration has been unpopular even though surveys indicate a residual and growing nostalgia for the Brezhnev period. The disappearance of the Soviet welfare state, however inadequate it was, is regretted. Shame is felt about the country's political and economic decline and about the humiliation of Russia in the 'near and far abroad'. Some Russians want to acquire a 'strong leader' even if this means a diminution of individual political and economic rights. But as yet thought has not turned into action, and the electorate has voted more for moderation than for extreme political and military solutions.

Things have moved on since 1999. Putin has pushed policies further in the direction of reconciling New Russia with the old Soviet order. Where Yeltsin had set out to resume the links with the tsarist past, Putin wants the communist period to be accorded respect. More than Yeltsin, too, he has asserted Russian interests and honour against the demands of the USA. His unapologetic defence of the invasion of Chechnya contrasted with the mumblings of Yeltsin; and the attempt to muzzle criticism of the government, displayed in the persecution of the 'oligarchs' Gusinski and Berezovski, broke with the line of the Gaidar and Chernomyrdin cabinets. But the scope of resultant change has as yet been small. The moves to tame the republics and provinces have come to little. The adjustments of economic policy show no sign of bringing about benefit to most citizens. In the light of all this it would be foolish to discount the possibility of popular unrest. Russians have been an enduring people. They have been remarkably passive in recent years: change had to come from on high – or else it would not have occurred at all in the late 1980s and early 1990s. But this may not always be so. Enough damage has been done to material conditions and to feelings to give grounds for long-term concern about the stability of Russian state and society.

The tragedy is that things need not have turned out like this. Russia is in dynamic flux. Below the surface of conservatism it throbs with excitement and innovation. Unfortunately the ministers and businessmen have an incentive to keep everything as it is. They benefit from it materially; they sense no pressing stimulus to introduce a legal order and social justice. But most ordinary Russians are frustrated. Their private lives are busy and productive and they could and should have been led by a government which appreciated their potential. With Yeltsin they had someone who talked this way but proceeded to preside over a regime of extreme corruption. With Putin they have someone whose preoccupation with order is greater than his concern for fairness and legality. It is a wasted historic opportunity. All the enthusiasm that goes into domestic and cultural activity could have been diverted into public affairs. The building of a 'civil society' of intermediate organisations of collective self-representation could have been cultivated. The longer this opportunity is neglected, the harder it will be to make a success of it. Time is not on Russia's side.

It may be that such an endeavour always had little chance of success. There was always too much improvisation and too little commitment. But the project for reform did exist. Yeltsin's team were loath, for their own cynical reasons, to acknowledge how much had already been accomplished under Gorbachëv. Admittedly Gorbachëv had not been very clear about his changing purposes; he appeared to have turned into a social-democrat, yet he refused to lead off his section of the Soviet communist party into a separate party in the open cause of putting an end to communism. Yeltsin was much clearer. There was no verbal fumbling in his rejection of the communist past. He and his ministers condemned the October 1917 Revolution and the regime established by Lenin. Decommunisation was the avowed aim. Unlike Gorbachëv, Yeltsin did not want a gradual evolution of state and society away from Leninism (and indeed Gorbachëv did not wish to reject Lenin, at least his own sanitised image of him). Yeltsin aimed at an abrupt rupture with communism. There was meant to be an immediate and comprehensive 'transition'.

But why did the country lose its way so quickly, veering from the chosen path at many crucial points? One reason is obvious. As Gorbachëv had warned, Yeltsin was not a steady and reliable driver. His intellectual and physical decline, moreover, was more drastic than anyone had expected; and his associates did not make up for his deficiencies. Instead they too often played upon his weaknesses: his ministers became notorious for their material self-seeking. Chernomyrdin's promotion of the interests of the gas sector of industry, where he had recently been the chairman of Gazprom, was the nadir in the failure to separate private profit from public service. Few ministers left office with their reputation for probity intact. Gaidar was a notable exception, but he was hardly a popular favourite: he had incurred hatred for the harshness of the economic transformation. More typical was the meta-morphosis of a figure such as Anatoli Chubais, who started out as an honourable privatising reformer and steadily turned into a complacent profiteer. Gradually the objectives of 1991–2 were lost by the wayside. The temptations of corruption overcame the bright hopes of the minis-ters who had broken up the USSR and engaged in the transition from communism.

But the country's condition in 1991 always made an arduous transi-tion likely. Advice poured in from abroad. Some of it was well-meaning. Some of it only appeared to be so: not every foreign government or economic-interest group wished to see Russian power restored in Europe, Asia and the rest of the world. There was talk about the 'end of history'. It was said that a 'new world order' had supplanted the dangers of the Cold War and that Russia simply had to do the things that had become normal elsewhere. This was always fanciful. The number of countries that have both sound economies and solid democracies remains small. In any case Russia faced special problems. Democratisa-tion in countries such as Spain and Chile took place on the basis of an existing capitalist economy; and transitions from communism in Poland, the Czech Republic and Hungary were to the accompaniment of a national consensus. Everything about the Russian reform project was always going to be difficult.

The advice from abroad was given in a period of liberal-capitalist triumphalism; it took little account of the country's unique past and exceptional current features. The first problem was one of territorial definition. It was not easy to answer the question 'What is Russia?' Under the tsars there was confusion of 'Russia' with the Russian Empire; under the communists there was an entity called the RSFSR, but its boundaries were recurrently redrawn. Russians had reason to query whether they should regard the Russian Federation as 'Russia'. Linked to this was the problem of Russian national identity. Neither the tsars nor the communists had given Russians a clear sense of who they were. Instead they encouraged the Russian people to identify themselves with, successively, 'the people' of the Russian Empire and the USSR. Russian-ness was not allowed free development – and the consequence is that Russians today have a lingering sense that their identity is bigger than anything they can ever aspire to be by themselves. The imperial syn-drome has yet to be outlived and its survival is facilitated by Russia's ethnic complexity even after the USSR's demise. The wars in Chechnya have shown the dangers of the situation.

Problems of territorial truncation and of national and cultural confusion were compounded by the troublesome bequest of history. The Soviet experience gave a steel-edged hardness to the less congenial aspects of tsarism. Distrust of official authority, already deep, became extreme. The organisational units of civil society were frail before 1917 and were smashed to smithereens under Lenin and Stalin. Political discourse in the late years of the Romanov monarchy had a tendency towards crude polemics. This was turned into an absolute norm after 1917 as Marxism-Leninism arrogated a monopolistic position of correctitude. Meanwhile popular fatalism remained strong. The rebelliousness of 1905–6 and 1917–22 was eliminated and although active resistance occurred on a sporadic basis, the authorities were able to contain the rebels without undue difficulties. Russian nationalism was held in check under tsars and commissars. Attempts to excite it have attracted little general support since 1991. Nationalist revanchism has also had little support, at least as yet, at successive national elections. The citizens of Russia have accepted rather than welcomed the disintegration of the USSR. They have resigned themselves to the demands of their two Presidents, first Yeltsin and then Putin.

Meanwhile Russia's armies remain a shambles and her government understands that in order to go on receiving IMF assistance it needs to be cautious in diplomacy. Even the 'near abroad' has been penetrated by the operations of foreign powers. Turkey and Iran have become an economic presence in the former Soviet republics of the Transcaucasus and Central Asia, and Islamic armed groups from Afghanistan and the Near East have made a nuisance of themselves in Chechnya. American oil companies have set themselves up in Kazakhstan and elsewhere. Intermittently the Russian Federation has asserted itself as an independent power. Relations with Iraq and Serbia were maintained in a fashion that annoyed the USA; but the downfall of Slobodan Milošević in Belgrade has restricted Moscow's influence. Although Putin has declared himself unwilling to continue the process of nuclear disarmament if the USA develops a new anti-missile programme, he has yet to put his words into practice. The New York terrorist massacre in September 2001 did something to restore Russian influence and status in the world; but this happened in a fashion that was less than helpful to the improvement of political, social and economic conditions in Russia.

So where does the country go from here? There is an image in

Nikolai Gogol's novel *Dead Souls* of a carriage being dragged along by a wild team of horses. Gogol, nineteenth-century master of phantasmagoria, was suggesting that the Russia of tsars and peasants, policemen, society dames and priests was a vehicle hurtling through history without a known destination. This is an image that Russians have often picked up since the disturbance to the Soviet order began in the mid-1980s. *Glasnost* and *perestroika* flung the carriage out of control despite Gorbachëv's best efforts, and the post-communist stage of the journey has been even more disrupted with Yeltsin and Putin at the reins. The havoc has not ended. The hope must be that the drivers start to consult the passengers about the route to be taken.

NOTES

Introduction

1. W. Laqueur, *The Fate of the Revolution: Interpretation of Soviet History*.
2. See in particular the editorials in *The Times*, the *Guardian*, *Le Monde*, *Die Zeit*, the *Washington Post* and *La Stampa* in the first week of January 1992.
3. R. Suny, *Revenge of the Past. Nationalism, Revolution and the Collapse of the Soviet Union*. See also V. Zaslavsky, *The Neo-Stalinist State: Class, Ethnicity and Consensus in Soviet Society*.
4. R. Service, 'Muddle no longer enough as Gorbachëv stumbles', *The Times*, 27 June 1990. It took some effort to persuade the page editor that the RSFSR had its own ethnic tensions and that this would continue to be a problem.
5. R. Service, 'Is Yeltsin really another Czar?', *Daily Mail*, 28 December 1991.
6. J. Linz and A. Stepan, *Problems of Democratic Transition and Consolidation. Southern Europe, South America, and Post-Communist Europe*. See also G. O'Donnell, P. Schmitter and L. Whitehead (eds), *Transitions from Authoritarian Rule*; G. O'Donnell, 'Illusions about Consolidation'; K. Thelen, 'Historical Institutionalism in Comparative Politics'; F. Zakaria, 'The Rise of Illiberal Democracy'.
7. S. Whitefield and G. Evans, 'Class Markets and Partisanship in Post-Soviet Russia: 1993–1999'; S. Whitefield, 'Social Responses to Reform in Russia' in D. Lane (ed.), *Russia in Transition*.
8. A. Brown, 'Transnational Influences in the Transition from Communism'; A. Brown, 'Vladimir Putin and the Reaffirmation of Central State Power'; S. M. Fish, 'Democratization's Requisites: The Postcommunist Experience'; S. Fish, *Democracy from Scratch: Opposition and Regime in the New Russian Revolution* – see also his *Democracy from Scratch*.
9. J. Higley, J. Pakulski and W. Wesolowski, 'Introduction: Elite Change and Democratic Regimes in Eastern Europe' in *idem* (eds), *Postcommunist Elites and Democracy in Eastern Europe*; P. G. Roeder, 'Varieties of Post-Soviet Authoritarian Regimes'. See also H. Eckstein and F. J. Fleron et al., *Can Democracy Take Root in Post-Soviet Russia?*; J. Hough, *Democratization and Revolution in the USSR*; J. Lloyd, *Rebirth of a Nation*; G. Lapidus, *The New Russia*. More generally see G. A. Almond and S. Verba, *The Civic Culture*.

10. D. Rustow, 'Transitions to Democracy', pp. 341–63. This is a topic that has attracted only glancing attention. Exceptions are V. Tolz, *Inventing the Nation*; T. McDaniel, *The Agony of the Russian Idea*. On general questions of nationhood see B. Anderson, *Imagined Communities*; J. Armstrong, *Nations before Nationalism*; J. Breuilly, *Nationalism and the State*; E. Gellner, *Nations and Nationalism*; E. Hobsbawm, *Nations and Nationalism Since 1870*; E. Hobsbawm and T. Ranger (eds), *The Invention of Tradition*; M. Hroch, *Social Preconditions of National Revival in Europe*; A. D. Smith, *The Ethnic Origins of Nations*; A. D. Smith, *National Identity*; E. Weber, *Peasants Into Frenchmen*. Useful case studies are L. Colley, *Britons*; P. D. Curtin, *The Image of Africa*; I. N. R. Davies, *The Isles*; E. Weber, *Peasants Into Frenchmen*.

11. This tightly contested topic is treated in A. Gerschenkron, *Economic Backwardness in Historical Perspective*; J. Barrington Moore, *Social Origins of Dictatorship and Democracy*; S. P. Huntington, *The Clash of Civilizations*.

12. See the contributions to G. A. Hosking and R. Service (eds), *Reinterpreting Russia*.

13. V. Bunce has put this case militantly in 'Should Transitologists be Grounded?'. See also her *Subversive Institutions*.

14. See contending accounts by S. F. Cohen, *Failed Crusade:. America and the Tragedy of Post-Communist Russia*; M. Goldman, *Lost Opportunity: What Has Made Economic Reform in Russia So Difficult?*; T. Gustafson, *Capitalism Russian-Style*; P. Hanson, 'What Sort of Capitalism is Developing in Russia?'; J. Hellman, 'Winners Take All. The Politics of Partial Reform in Postcommunist Transitions'; P. Reddaway and D. Glinski, *The Tragedy of Russia's Reforms: Market Bolshevism Against Democracy*; J. Sachs and K. Pistor (eds), *The Rule of Law and Economic Reform in Russia*.

15. A. Przeworski, *Democracy and the Market*; A. Przeworski, et al., 'What Makes Democracies Endure?'. See also L. C. B. Pereira, J. M. Maravall and A. Przeworski, *Economic Reform in New Democracies*.

16. A recent exception is L. Aron, *Boris Yeltsin: a Revolutionary Life*, which eulogises Yeltsin as the Russian Abraham Lincoln.

17. For general studies of changing social mores see N. Elias, *The Civilising Process*; C. Geertz, *The Interpretation of Cultures*; E. Gellner, *Conditions of Liberty: Civil Liberty and its Rivals*; E. Gellner, *Plough, Sword and Book*; J. S. Migdal, *Strong Societies and Weak States. State-Society Relations and State Capabilities in the Third World*.

18. A. Kappeler, *Russland als Vielvölkerreich: Entstehung, Geschichte, Zerfall*; G. Hosking, *Russia: People and Empire, 1552–1917*; R. Service, *A History of Twentieth-Century Russia*.

1. For A New Russia

1. M. S. Gorbachëv, *Zhizn' i reformy*, vol. 2, p. 621; A. Grachëv, *Gorbachëv*, p. 419.
2. B. Yeltsin, *Against the Grain*, pp. 152–5.
3. B. Yeltsin, *The View from the Kremlin*. pp. 111–12.
4. Gorbachëv, *Zhizn' i reformy*, vol. 1, pp. 5–8.
5. A. Brown, *The Gorbachev Factor*, pp. 10–11.
6. *Nezavisimaya gazeta*, 27 November 1991.
7. Ibid., 14 December 1991.
8. *Izvestiya*, 23 and 28 April 1992, 12 May 1992, 11 June 1992, 23 July 1992, 20 August 1992, 1 October 1992, 24 December 1992.
9. M. Wyman, *Public Opinion in Post-Communist Russia*, pp. 93–5.
10. Yeltsin, *Against the Grain*, p. 16.
11. Ibid., pp. 21–2.
12. Yeltsin, *The View from the Kremlin*. p. 95.
13. Yeltsin, *Against the Grain*, p. 20.
14. Ibid., p. 26.
15. Ibid., p. 56.
16. Ibid., p. 192.
17. L. Sukhanov, *Shest' let s Yel'tsinym*, p. 33.
18. Yeltsin, *Against the Grain*.
19. 'Nadoeli lyudyam skazki./Khvatit zhit' nam po ukazke./Yel'tsin znaet, chto nam nuzhno./Golosui za Borya druzhno.': Yu. M. Baturin, et al., *Epokha Yel'tsina: ocherki politicheskoi istorii*, p. 118.
20. J. Lloyd, *Financial Times*, 19 December 1991.
21. For example, neither *Nezavisimaya gazeta* nor *Izvestiya* – two of the best sources of news in the months in question – regularly reported Yeltsin's big speeches.
22. See Yeltsin's aide-memoire written before the Fifth Congress of People's Deputies of the RSFSR: Baturin et al., *Epokha Yel'tsina*, pp. 175–7.
23. V. Kostikov, *Roman s prezidentom*, p. 52; A. Korzhakov, *Boris Yel'tsin*, p. 120; Baturin et al., *Epokha Yel'tsina*, p. 807 (which also mentions that V. F. Kadatski and K. V. Nikiforov were added to the speech-writing group: see p. 203).
24. Baturin et al., *Epokha Yel'tsina*, p. 803.
25. Kostikov, *Roman s prezidentom*, pp. 169 and 229–30.
26. Korzhakov, *Boris Yel'tsin*, p. 326.
27. R. Service, 'Boris Yeltsin: Politics and Rhetoric, 1991–1992'.
28. Radio Rossii, 11 September 1991: *SWB*, 13 August 1991.
29. Radio Mayak, 28 August 1991: *SWB*, 30 August 1991.
30. USSR TV Channel One, 29 December 1991: *SWB*, 31 December 1991.
31. *RTR*, 28 October 1991: *SWB*, 30 October 1991.
32. USSR TV Channel One, 29 December 1991: *SWB*, 31 December 1991.

33. Radio Mayak, 28 August 1991: *SWB*, 30 August 1991.
34. Radio Mayak, 28 August 1991: *SWB*, 30 August 1991.
35. USSR TV Channel One, 29 December 1991: *SWB*, 31 December 1991.
36. Radio Rossii, 11 September 1991: *SWB*, 13 August 1991; *RTR*, 28 October 1991: *SWB*, 30 October 1991.
37. Radio Mayak, 28 August 1991: *SWB*, 30 August 1991.
38. Radio Rossii, 29 August 1991: *SWB*, 31 August 1991.
39. Radio Rossii, 11 September 1991: *SWB*, 13 August 1991.
40. Radio Rossii, 11 September 1991: *SWB*, 13 August 1991.
41. Kanal Rossii, 11 January 1992: *SWB*, 13 January 1992.
42. Radio Rossii, 17 October 1991: *SWB*, 19 October 1991.
43. USSR TV Channel One, 24 August 1991: *SWB*, 26 August 1991.
44. Radio Rossii, 17 October 1991: *SWB*, 19 October 1991. The word he used for farmers was *fermery*.
45. Service, 'Boris Yeltsin: Politics and Rhetoric, 1991–1992'.
46. Radio Rossii, 11 September 1991: *SWB*, 13 August 1991.
47. In the twelve speeches made in the six months after the August 1991 coup Yeltsin referred to 'the West' only three times (and in only two speeches): see Service, 'Boris Yeltsin: Politics and Rhetoric, 1991–1992'.
48. USSR TV Channel One, 29 December 1991: *SWB*, 31 December 1991.
49. Service, 'Boris Yeltsin: Politics and Rhetoric, 1991–1992'.
50. *Izvestiya*, 30 November 1992.
51. See B. Anderson, *Imagined Communities*; E. Gellner, *Nations and Nationalism*; E. Hobsbawm, *Nations and Nationalism Since 1870*.

2. What is Russia?

1. 'Svoboda' in G. S. Smith (ed. and tr.), *Contemporary Russian Poetry*, p. 48.
2. From 1936 the title was changed to the Russian Soviet Federative Socialist Republic. The reason for this modification was ideological pedantry, consisting in the changed relative emphasis attached to the words 'Socialist' and 'Soviet'. Such were the joys of Marxism-Leninism. Thus it had been since 1936. The name in both versions was anyhow usually abbreviated to an acronym: the RSFSR. See R. Service, *History of Twentieth-Century Russia*, pp. 84 and 561.
3. Brokgauz and Efron (pubs), *Entsiklopedicheskii slovar'*, vol. 54, map following p. 360.
4. But see M. Bassin on the distinction between 'Russia' and 'Siberia': 'Inventing Siberia: Visions of the Russian East in the Early Nineteenth Century'. See also M. Bassin, 'Russia Between Europe and Asia: The Ideological Construction of Geographical Space'; S. Becker, 'Russia Between East and West: the Intelligentsia, Russian National Identity and Asian Borderlands'.

5. H. Seton-Watson, *The Russian Empire, 1801–1917*, pp. 51–62, 172–3 and 438–45.
6. It ought to be noted, however, that some maps – such as in the Brokgauz and Efron encyclopedia (see n. 3 above) – treated 'European Russia' as a territory including Ukraine, Belorussia, Lithuania and eastern Poland: see vol. 54, especially the map following p. 360.
7. N. F. Bugai, *L. P. Beriya – I. Stalinu: 'Soglasno Vashemu ukazaniyu'*, pp. 56 ff.
8. I. V. Stalin, *Sochineniya* (ed. R. H. MacNeal), vol. 15, pp. 203–4.
9. *Istoricheskii arkhiv*, no. 1 (1992), pp. 48–9.
10. A. B. Veber et al. (eds.), *Soyuz mozhno bylo sokhranit'*, p. 14.
11. R. Service, *Lenin: A Political Life*, vol. 3, *The Iron Ring*, pp. 92–5.
12. Ibid., pp. 274–82.
13. From 1918 to 1924 it was designated as the *Rossiiskaya Kommunisticheskaya Partiya*.
14. F. Chuev (ed.), *Molotov. Poluderzhavnyi vlastelin*, pp. 508–9.
15. Service, *History of Twentieth-Century Russia*, p. 367.
16. A. Brown, *The Gorbachev Factor*, p. 208. See also J. Dunlop, *The Rise of Russia and the Fall of the Soviet Empire*.
17. See his funeral speech for the four victims of the abortive coup: USSR Central TV, 24 August 1991: *SWB*, 26 August 1991; and his speech to the Congress of Compatriots: Radio Mayak, 28 August 1991: *SWB*, 30 August 1991.

3. Who are the Russians?

1. A. Zinoviev, 'Moi dom', p. 46.
2. *Rossiisskii statisticheskii ezhegodnik. Ofitsial'noe izdanie 2000*, p. 65.
3. I am aware that the Orthodox Church, which most peasants belonged to, had privileges; my point is that the Russian peasants did not have a sense that they were privileged – and indeed in secular respects they were right.
4. G. Hosking, *Russia: People and Empire*, chapter 3.
5. A. V. Buganov, *Russkaya istoriya v pamyati krest'yan XIX veka i natsional'noe samosoznanie*. See also M. Cherniavsky, *Tsar and People: Studies in Russian Myths*.
6. E. W. Clowes et al. (eds), *Between Tsar and People: Educated Society and the Quest for Public Identity in Late Imperial Russia*.
7. J. Brooks, *When Russia Learned to Read*.
8. H. F. Jahn, 'For Tsar and Fatherland? Russian Popular Culture and the First World War' in S. P. Frank and M. D. Steinberg (eds), *Cultures in Flux*, pp. 140–6.
9. O. Figes and B. Kolonitskii, *Interpreting the Russian Revolution. The Language and Symbols of 1917*; R. Service, *Lenin: A Political Life*, vol. 2, *Worlds in Collision*, pp. 223–38.

10. P. Gatrell, *A Whole Empire Walking*, pp. 199–201.
11. O. H. Radkey, *Russia Goes to the Polls: the Election to the Russian Constituent Assembly, 1917*, pp. 16 and 18–19.
12. K. Simonov, *Glazami cheloveka moego pokoleniya*, p. 37.
13. M. Lewin, *The Making of the Soviet System*, pp. 275–6 and 305.
14. S. White, *Political Culture and Soviet Politics*, p. 35.
15. N. F. Bugai, *L. P. Beriya – I. V. Stalinu: 'Soglasno Vashemu ukazaniyu'*, pp. 56 ff.
16. *Gde u russkikh gosudarstvo?*, p. 20.
17. J. Anderson, *Religion, State and Politics in the Soviet Union and the Successor States*, p. 55.
18. See J. Dunlop, *The Faces of Contemporary Russian Nationalism*.
19. V. Kozlov, *The Peoples of the Soviet Union*, p. 203. It must be added that the figures for ethnic Russians in the RSFSR (or indeed the USSR) were not made available. But given the fact that 83 per cent of the RSFSR population in 1979 were ethnic Russians, it is highly unlikely that they did not make a substantial contribution to the level of inter-marriage: see ibid., p. 66.
20. Calculated from the table in *SSSR. Entsiklopedicheskii spravochnik*, p. 21.
21. The figures are given for the 1979 census in V. Kozlov, *The Peoples of the Soviet Union*, pp. 86–8.
22. This figure is calculated from the date provided ibid.
23. Ibid.
24. R. Service, *A History of Twentieth-Century Russia*, p. 192.
25. O. Karpenko, 'Byt' "nastional'nym": strakh poteryat' i strakh poteryat'sya. Na primere tatar Sank-Peterburga' in V. Voronkov and I. Os'val'd (eds.), *Konstruirovanie etnichnosti. Etnicheskie obshchiny Sankt-Peterburga*, pp. 556–7.

4. Public Images, 1800–1991

1. M. M. Gromyko, *Mir russkoi derevni*, p. 5.
2. H. Rogger, *National Consciousness in Eighteenth-Century Russia*; A. Kappeler, *Russland als Vielvölkerreich*; G. Hosking, *Russia: People and Empire, 1552–1917*.
3. N. Riasanovsky, *Nicholas I and Official Nationality*, p. 74.
4. Hosking, *Russia: People and Empire*, pp. 431–7.
5. Ibid., pp. 5–6 and 68–9.
6. N. Riasanovsky, *Russia and the West in the Teachings of the Slavophiles*.
7. Struve himself was a former Marxist: see R. Pipes, *Struve: Liberal on the Left, 1870–1905*. See also his *Struve:. Liberal on the Right, 1905–1944*.
8. See below, pp. 152–3.
9. N. M. Karamzin, *Istoriya rossiiskogo gosudarstva*.
10. For a survey of the 'Western' theme see M. Malia, *Russia under Western Eyes. From the Bronze Horseman to the Lenin Mausoleum*.

11. *The Russian Experiment in Art, 1863–1922*; R. C. Ridenour, *Nationalism, Modernism and Personal Rivalry in Nineteenth-Century Russian Music*; M. Slonim, *Russian Theater from Empire to Soviets*; E. Valkenier, *Russian Realist Art: the Peredvizhniki and Their Tradition*.

12. A. Blok, 'Skify', in *Sochineniya*, pp. 263–4. For his articles on such subjects see pp. 407–95.

13. G. Uspenskii, Polnoe sobranie sochinenii.

14. A. Walicki, *Russian Social Thought: An Introduction to the Intellectual History of Nineteenth-Century Russia*, chs 12 and 18; E. Acton, 'The Russian Revolutionary Intelligentsia and Industrialisation'.

15. R. Service, *Lenin: A Political Life*, vol. 3, *The Iron Ring*, p. 180.

16. Ibid., pp. 180 and 274–82.

17. A. Luukkanen, *The Party of Unbelief: The Religious Policy of the Bolshevik Party, 1917–1929*, chs 3–4.

18. Prokofiev returned only in the 1930s.

19. Service, *A History of Twentieth-Century Russia*, p. 137.

20. A. Blyum, *Za kulisami 'Ministerstva Pravdy'*, p. 79.

21. J. Barber, *Soviet Historians in Crisis, 1928–1932*, pp. 57–66 and 73–5. This historical bias included an attempt to erase episodes from popular consciousness. Thus the Soviet authorities erected no monument to those who were killed or maimed in the First World War: C. Merridale, *Night of Stone. Death and Memory in Russia*, p. 123.

22. N. Ustryalov, *Pod znakom revolyutsii*.

23. N. S. Trubetskoi, *K probleme russkogo samosoznaniya: sobranie statei*.

24. N. Berdyaev, *The Russian Idea*.

25. I. Il'in, *O soprotivlenii zlu siloyu: The Trial of the Socialist Revolutionaries*. Moscow, 1922.

26. M. Jansen, *A Show Trial under Lenin*; A. Liebich, *From the Other Shore: Russian Social-Democracy after 1921*.

27. Barber, *Soviet Historians in Crisis*, pp. 57–66 and 73–5.

28. G. Hewitt, 'Aspects of Language in Georgia (Georgian and Abkhaz)', p. 132.

29. T. Shanin, *The Awkward Class: Political Sociology of Peasantry in a Developing Society, 1910–1925*.

30. Service, *A History of Twentieth-Century Russia*, p. 205.

31. Barber, *Soviet Historians in Crisis*, pp. 139–40. See also M. Agurskii, *Ideologiya natsional-bol'shevizma*.

32. *Pravda*, 16 January 1937.

33. I. V. Stalin, *Sochineniya*, vol. 15, p. 204.

34. M. Friedberg, *Russian Classics in Soviet Jackets*, pp. 32–56.

35. Service, *A History of Twentieth-Century Russia*, pp. 317–18.

36. Y. M. Brudny, *Reinventing Russia: Russian Nationalism and the Soviet State, 1953–1991*, ch. 2.

37. Ibid., p. 127.

38. L. N. Gumilëv, *V poiskakh vymyshlennogo tsarstva*.

39. V. Bukovskii, *Moskovskii protsess*, pp. 82 ff.

40. R. Service, 'Mikhail Gorbachev as Political Reformer' in R. Hill and J. Dellenbrant (eds), *Gorbachev and Perestroika* (London, 1989), p. 30.
41. R. Service, 'Gorbachëv's Reforms: The Future in the Past'.
42. Service, *A History of Twentieth-Century Russia*, pp. 478–9.

5. Soviet Legacies

1. Ye. Gaidar, *Gosudarstvo i evolyutsiya*, p. 164; A. B. Chubais, *Privatizatsiya po-rossiiski*, p. 54.
2. See the decrees of 23 August, 25 August and 6 November 1991: Yu. M. Baturin et al., *Epokha Yel'tsina: ocherki politicheskoi istorii*, p. 231.
3. Ibid., p. 232.
4. K. Williams, 'The Rhetoric of Lustration'; see also his 'A Scorecard for Czech Lustration'.
5. R. Sakwa, *Russian Politics and Society*, p. 84.
6. *Moskovskaya pravda*, 11 August 1998.
7. M. Voslensky, *Nomenklatura: The Anatomy of the Soviet Ruling Class*, pp. 1–5.
8. T. H. Rigby, 'The Origins of the Nomenklatura System', pp. 84–5.
9. T. H. Rigby, *Political Elites in the USSR: Central Leaders and Local Cadres from Lenin to Gorbachev*.
10. G. Gill (ed.), *Elites and Leadership in Russian Politics*; G. Gill, *The Dynamics of Democratisation: Elites, Civil Society and the Transition Process*; O. Kryshtanovskaya and S. White, 'From Soviet *Nomenklatura* to Russian Élite'; D. Lane and C. Ross, *The Transition from Communism to Capitalism: Ruling Elites from Gorbachev to Yeltsin*; S. Solnick, *Stealing the State. Control and Collapse in Soviet Institutions*.
11. Gaidar, *Gosudarstvo i evolyutsiya*, p. 164.
12. See Chapter 8.
13. R. Service, *The Bolshevik Party in Revolution: A Study in Organisational Change*, pp. 119–20.
14. N. Timasheff, *The Great Retreat*.
15. *Istoricheskii arkhiv*, no. 3 (1993), pp. 117 and 130–4.
16. B. Grushin, *Chetyre zhizni Rossii v zerkale oprosov obshchestvennogo mneniya*, vol. 1, pp. 73–88.
17. A. Inkeles and R. M. Bauer, *The Soviet Citizen: Daily Life in a Totalitarian Society*.
18. Grushin, *Chetyre zhizni*, vol. 1, pp. 533–40.
19. M. McAuley, *Bread and Justice: State and Society in Petrograd, 1917–1922*, pp. 170–1.
20. Agence Française Presse, 24 November 2000: report on St Petersburg.
21. Rigby, *Political Elites in the USSR*. See also V. Dunham, *In Stalin's Time: Middle-Class Values in Soviet Fiction*.

22. G. Hosking, *Russia: People and Empire, 1552–1917*.
23. R. Service, *A History of Twentieth-Century Russia*, pp. 219, 225–6 and 242.
24. On Gorbachëv's early appointments see A. Brown, *The Gorbachev Factor*, pp. 104–10.
25. T. Vorozheikina, 'Clientelism and the Process of Political Democratization in Russia'; V. E. Bonnell and G. W. Breslauer, 'Informal Networks, Collective Action and Sources of (In)stability in Russia: a Brief Overview'; R. Service, 'Boris El'cin: Continuità e Mutamento di un Rivoluzionario Democratico'.
26. The prime instance was the removal of Gennadi Burbulis in 1993.
27. M. Afanas'ev, *Klientelizm i rossiiskaya gosudarstvennost'*.
28. N. Gevorkyan et al., *Ot pervogo litsa. Peregovory s Vladimirom Putinym*, p. 76.
29. See below, p. 135. See also M. Afanas'ev, *Klientelizm i rossiiskaya gosudarstvennost'*.
30. Service, *The Bolshevik Party in Revolution*, pp. 171–4.
31. Brown, *The Gorbachev Factor*, ch. 2.
32. K. Simis, *USSR: Secrets of Corrupt Society*; A. Ledeneva, *Russia's Economy of Favours: Blat, Networking and Informal Change*. See also V. Shlapentokh, *Public and Private Life of the Russian People: Changing Values in Post-Stalin Russia*; and V. Shlapentokh, 'Russia: Privatisation and Illegalisation of Social and Political Life'.
33. R. Service, *Lenin: A Biography*, pp. 321–2.
34. See below, pp. 221–2.
35. D. Moon, 'The Problem of Social Stability in Russia, 1598–1998'.
36. I. Chubais, *Ot Russkoi idei – k idee Novoi Rossii*, p. 29.
37. M. I. Dubrovin, *Angliiskie i russkie poslovitsy i pogovorki v illyustratsiyakh*, pp. 64, 78, 83, 101, 108, 130, 135.
38. R. Conquest, *The Great Terror: A Reassessment*, chs 7–8.
39. N. Lampert, *Whistleblowing in the Soviet Union: Complaints and Abuses under State Socialism*.
40. Yu. A. Polyakov, V. B. Zhiromskaya and I. N. Kiselëv, 'Polveka molchaniya', p. 69.
41. B. Kerblay, *Modern Soviet Society*, pp. 282–3.
42. S. White, *Political Culture and Soviet Politics*, p. 133.
43. On the survival of old patterns of thought and behaviour see G. Hosking and R. Service (eds), *Reinterpreting Russia*, especially the chapter by D. Moon, 'The Problem of Social Stability in Russia, 1598–1998'.
44. Probably the vividness of his family's memory was enhanced by the fact that the authorities in the USSR did so much to erase certain historical episodes, such as the famine and terror of the early 1920s, from public discussion. See C. Merridale, *Night of Stone. Death and Memory in Russia*, pp. 199–200, on the attempt to avoid the commemoration of the victims of the later famine of 1932–3. There is an interesting account of the highly

personal memory of the past kept by Buryat villlages regardless of official Soviet historiography in C. Humphrey, *Marx Went Away – But Karl Stayed Behind*, pp. xiii–xiv and xvi.

45. When we met again many years later, he had no idea about the effect he had had on me, and equally I had no idea what an experience it had been for him to meet a 'Westerner' for the first time.

6. The New Russian State

1. A. M. Yakovlev, *Striving for Law in a Lawless Land. Memoirs of a Russian Reformer*, p. 225.
2. R. Sakwa, *Gorbachev and His Reforms: 1985–1990*, p. 263.
3. *Soyuz mozhno bylo sokhranit'*, p. 146.
4. He won in the teeth of the refusal of several Soviet Republics – Armenia, Estonia, Georgia, Latvia, Lithuania and Moldova – to open polling booths on their territory.
5. *Soyuz mozhno bylo sokhranit'*, pp. 146–7.
6. *Johnson's List*, 28 January 2001.
7. A. Grachëv, *Gorbachëv*, p. 409.
8. M. S. Gorbachëv, *Zhizn' i reformy*, vol. 1, p. 5.
9. Ibid., pp. 6–7.
10. Ibid., p. 5.
11. Ibid.
12. *Komsomol'skaya pravda*, 27 May 1992.
13. Yakovlev, *Striving for Law in a Lawless Land*, p. 132.
14. Ibid., pp. 141–2.
15. *Rossiiskaya gazeta*, 6 May 1993.
16. Ibid.
17. S. White et al., *How Russia Votes*, pp. 90–2.
18. *Rossiiskie vesti*, 22 September 1993.
19. Ibid., 25 December 1993.
20. V. Kostikov, *Roman s prezidentom*, p. 267; *Izvestiya*, 4 May 1994.

7. Popular Opinion

1. *Nezavisimaya gazeta*, 12 June 1992.
2. Ibid., 30 May 1992.
3. Ibid., 25 September 1991.
4. VTsIOM: January–February 1995.
5. *Monitoring obshchestvennogo mneniya. Ekonomicheskie i sotsial'nye peremeny*, no. 2 (52), 2000, p. 82.
6. Ibid.

7. See S. White, *Political Culture and Soviet Politics*.
8. *NG-Szenarii*, January 2000.
9. Ibid.
10. Ibid.
11. Ibid.
12. *Sovetskaya Rossiya*, 6 May 1993.
13. B. Grushin, *Chetyre zhizni Rossii v zerkale oprosov obshchestvennogo mneniya*, vol. 1, pp. 84–111.
14. D. Marples, *Belarus: A Denationalised Nation*.
15. P. Baev, *Russia's Policies in the Caucasus*; I. Bremmer and R. Taras (eds), *New States. New Politics. Building the Post-Soviet Nations*; L. Jonson, *Keeping the Peace in the CIS: The Evolution of Russian Policy*; David D. Laitin, *Identity in Formation. The Russian Speaking Populations in the Near-Abroad*; A. Lieven, *Chechnya. Tombstone of Russian Power*; D. C. M. Lieven, *Empire. The Russian Empire and Its Rivals*; D. Lynch, *Russian Peacekeeping Strategies in the CIS Region*.
16. N. Melvin, *Russians Beyond Russia: The Politics of National Identity*, pp. 130–3.
17. S. White et al., *How Russia Votes*, pp. 52–3.
18. Ibid., p. 46. See also A. G. Zdravomyslov, *Sotsiologiya rossiiskogo krizisa*, p. 73.
19. A. Brown, *The Gorbachev Factor*, pp. 104–9.
20. M. P. Perrie, *The Image of Ivan the Terrible in Russian Folklore*.
21. See above, p. 110.
22. It is true that not all the respondents to the questionnaire were Russian. Consequently some of the respondents must be non-Russians. None the less it is significant that many Russians are not worried whether or not their president belongs to the same national group as themselves. See V. N. Ivanov and M. S. Gutseriev, *Rossiya i regiony*, pp. 128.
23. Ibid., pp. 128–9.
24. *Monitoring obshchestvennogo mneniya. Ekonomicheskie i sotsial'nye peremeny*.
25. M. Wyman, *Public Opinion in Post-Communist Russia*, p. 90.
26. *Kommersant*, 6 April 2000.
27. Wyman, *Public Opinion in Post-Communist Russia*, pp. 190–1.
28. Zdravomyslov, *Sotsiologiya rossiiskogo krizisa*, p. 75.
29. R. Rose, 'Floating Parties and Accountability: A Supply-Side View of Russia's Elections' in A. Brown, *Contemporary Russian Politics: A Reader*, p. 216.
30. M. K. Gorshkov et al., *Osennii krizis 1998 goda: rossiiskoe obshchestvo do i posle*, pp. 16–19 and 40.
31. Ibid., pp. 16–19.
32. In the case of Yeltsin it was substantially lower: whereas 25 per cent of the over-sixties judged him negatively, only 16 per cent of those under the age of thirty did the same: Ivanov and Gutseriev, *Rossiya i regiony*, pp. 40 and 44.

33. A. Zdravomyslov, 'O natsional'nom samosoznanii rossiyan', *Monitoring obshchestvennogo mneniya*, January–February 2001, p. 51. At the same time the percentage of people declaring themselves 'citizens of the USSR' fell from 15 to 11: ibid., p. 50.

34. Lieven, *Chechnya*, pp. 46–52.

35. See below, pp. 152–3.

36. People of the same generation come at 52 per cent and people at place of work at 51 per cent.

37. Zdravomyslov, *Sotsiologiya rossiiskogo krizisa*, p. 114.

38. Ibid., p. 121.

39. Ibid., p. 120.

40. A. R. Aklaev in L. M. Drobizheva et al., *Demokratizatsiya i obrazy natsionalizma v Rossiiskoi Federatsii 90-kh godov*, pp. 138–9. The results are similar for Sakha-Yakutia: ibid.

41. Ibid., pp. 138–9.

42. *Ekonomicheskie i sotsial'nye peremeny: monitoring obshchestvennogo mneniya*, no. 1 (1994) pp. 56–7.

43. See below, pp. 235–41.

44. *Ekonomicheskie i sotsial'nye peremeny: monitoring obshchestvennogo mneniya*, no. 1 (1994) pp. 56–7.

8. Masters of Red Square

1. N. Gevorkyan et al., *Ot pervogo litsa: razgovory s Vladimirom Putinym*, p. 51.

2. Yu. M. Baturin et al., *Epokha Yel'tsina: ocherki politicheskoi istorii*, p. 798.

3. B. Yeltsin, *The View from the Kremlin*, pp. 180–1 and 236.

4. O. Poptsov, *Khronika vremën 'Tsarya Borisa'*, p. 391.

5. V. Kostikov, *Roman s prezidentom*, p. 19.

6. Ibid., p. 38.

7. P. Klebnikov, *Godfather of the Kremlin: Boris Berezovsky and the Looting of the Kremlin*, pp. 201–2.

8. Ibid., p. 119.

9. B. Yeltsin, *Midnight Diaries*, pp. 18–34.

10. V. Kostikov, 'Stanet li skazka byl'yu?', p. 4; Baturin et al., *Epokha Yel'tsina*, p. 798.

11. Kostikov, *Roman s prezidentom*, pp. 193–4.

12. Kostikov, 'Stanet li skazka byl'yu?', p. 4.

13. A. Korzhakov, *Boris Yel'tsin: ot rassveta do zakata*, pp. 210–12.

14. M. S. Gorbachëv, *Vlast' i reformy*; A. Karaulov, *Plokhoi nachal'nik: grustnaya kniga*, p. 105.

15. Kostikov, *Roman s prezidentom*, p. 240.

16. Ibid., p. 8. See also G. Breslauer, 'Boris Yeltsin as Patriarch'.

17. Korzhakov, *Boris Yel'tsin: ot rassveta do zakata*, p. 75.

18. L. Aron, *Boris Yeltsin. A Revolutionary Life*, ch. 3, provides a hagiographical but indispensable account of the emergent local party leader.

19. Poptsov, *Khronika vremën 'Tsarya Borisa'*, p. 397.

20. Kostikov, *Roman s prezidentom*, p. 304.

21. L. Shevtsova, *Yeltsin's Russia: Myths and Reality*.

22. S. White et al., *How Russia Votes*, p. 123.

23. P. Chaisty, 'Legislative Politics in Russia', p. 112.

24. See K. Dawisha and B. Parrott, *Democratic Changes and Authoritarian Reactions in Russia, Ukraine, Belarus and Moldova*; M. Urban, V. Igrunov and S. Mitrokhin, *The Rebirth of Politics in Russia*; M. A. Weigle, *Russia's Liberal Project: State–Society Relations in the Transition from Communism*; S. White, *Russia's New Politics. The Management of a Post-Communist Society*.

25. O. Kryshtanovskaya and S. White, 'From Soviet *Nomenklatura* to Russian Élite', p. 728.

26. J. Kampfner, *Inside Yeltsin's Russia*, pp. 2–13.

27. Baturin et al., *Epokha Yel'tsina*, p. 764.

28. See O. Davydov on the Yeltsin–Gaidar relationship in V. Tret'yakov (ed.), *Rossiiskaya elita*, p. 42.

29. Korzhakov, *Boris Yel'tsin*, p. 404; N. P. Medvedev, *'Novye' na Staroi ploshchadi*, p. 167.

30. Chaisty, 'Legislative Politics in Russia', p. 113. See also P. Chaisty, 'Democratic Consolidation and Parliamentary Reform in Russia, 1990–93'.

31. Korzhakov, *Boris Yel'tsin*, p. 317.

32. Yeltsin, *Midnight Diaries*, p. 23.

33. Ibid.

34. Ibid., p. 23.

35. V. Nekrasov, *MVD v litsakh*, pp. 351–2.

36. Yeltsin, *Midnight Diaries*, p. 25: my modified translation.

37. Klebnikov, *Godfather of the Kremlin*, p. 277.

38. Baturin et al., *Epokha Yel'tsina*, p. 759.

39. Ye. Primakov, *Gody v bol'shoi politike*, p. 106.

40. Y. M. Brudny, 'Continuity or Change in Russian Electoral Patterns?', p. 173.

41. Chaisty, 'Legislative Politics in Russia', pp. 114–15; Brudny, 'Continuity or Change in Russian Electoral Patterns?', p. 173.

42. B. Yeltsin, Resignation Speech of 31 December 1999: *Midnight Diaries*, pp. 386–7.

43. V. Putin, Inauguration Speech of 7 May 2000: Russian television, 7 May 2000 (reproduced in *SWB*, 8 May 2001).

44. See also his address to the Federal Assembly, 8 July 2000: RTR.

45. Gevorkyan et al., *Ot pervogo litsa*, p. 174.

46. See the more detailed account below, pp. 223–5.

47. See Medvedev, *'Novye' na Staroi ploshchadi*, p. 167 for Yeltsin's hatred of 'the Reds'.

9. Economising on Reform

1. A. Korzhakov, *Boris Yeltsin: Ot rassveta do zakata*, p. 310.
2. A. Lukin, *The Political Culture of the Russian 'Democrats'*, p. 296.
3. See above, pp. 129–30.
4. Yu. M. Baturin et al., *Epokha Yel'tsina: ocherki politicheskoi istorii*, p. 204.
5. See below, pp. 171 and 264.
6. See below, pp. 223–5.
7. See above, pp. 24–6.
8. A. Åslund, *How Russia Became a Market Economy*, p. 43.
9. A. B. Chubais, *Privatizatsiya po-rossiiski*, p. 54; Ye. Gaidar, *Gosudarstvo i evolyutsiya*, p. 164.
10. *Ekonomicheskaya zhizn'*, no. 4, 1993, p. 13.
11. B. Yeltsin, *The View From The Kremlin*, uses the term as a chapter heading, p. 145.
12. J. Eatwell et al., *Transformation and Integration: Shaping the Future of Central and Eastern Europe*, pp. 73 and 76.
13. See below, pp. 288–9.
14. See below, pp. 302–3.
15. P. Klebnikov, *Godfather of the Kremlin: Boris Berezovsky and the Looting of the Kremlin*, p. 96.
16. Ibid.
17. *Programma uglubleniya ekonomicheskikh reform v Rossii*.
18. *Izvestiya*, 20 August 1992, p. 2.
19. Klebnikov, *Godfather of the Kremlin*, p. 135.
20. N. Moser and P. Oppenheimer, 'The Oil Industry: Structural Transformation and Corporate Governance', p. 301.
21. Chubais, *Privatizatsiya po-rossiiski*, pp. 47, 98 and 100.
22. The literature on the alternative possible routes of economic reform is extensive. See Åslund, *How Russia Became a Market Economy*; C. Davis, 'The Russian Economic Crisis and Western Aid'; M. Feshback and A. Friendly, *Ecocide in the USSR*; C. Freeland, *Sale of the Century: The Inside Story of the Second Russian Revolution*; C. Gaddy, *The Price of the Past: Russia's Struggle with the Legacy of a Militarized Economy*; M. Goldman, *Lost Opportunity: What Has Made Economic Reform in Russia So Difficult*; B. Granville and P. Oppenheimer (eds), *Russia's Post-Communist Economy*; P. Reddaway and D. Glinski, *The Tragedy of Russia's Reforms: Market Bolshevism Against Democracy*; P. Rutland, 'Privatisation in Russia'; J. Sachs and K. Pistor (eds), *The Rule of Law and Economic Reform in Russia*; S. Solnick, *Stealing the State. Control and Collapse in Soviet Institutions*; P. Sutela, 'Insider Privatisation in Russia'.
23. Klebnikov, *Godfather of the Kremlin*, p. 129. See below, p. 232.
24. See below, p. 288.
25. Baturin et al., *Epokha Yel'tsina*, p. 239.

26. *Den'*, no. 50, 1992, p. 1.
27. A. G. Zdravomyslov, *Sotsiologiya rossiiskogo krizisa*, p. 163.
28. See above, p. 128.
29. *Konstitutsiya Rossiiskoi Federatsii*, p. 3.
30. See below, Chapter 10.
31. A. Lieven, *Chechnya. Tombstone of Russian Power*, p. 14.
32. Ibid., p. 176.
33. Freeland, *Sale of the Century*, pp. 166–8.
34. See below, p. 160.
35. See V. Tolz, *Russia: Inventing the Nation*, p. 256.
36. See below, p. 183.
37. Freeland, *Sale of the Century*, pp. 292–9.
38. B. Granville, 'The Problem of Monetary Stabilisation', p. 127. See V. Tik-homirov, 'The Second Collapse of the Soviet Economy: Myths and Realities of the Russian Reform'; M. K. Gorshkov et al., *Osennii krizis 1998 goda: rossiiskoe obshchestvo do i posle.*
39. *Nezavisimaya gazeta*, 14 January 2000: interview with Sergei Stepashin.
40. E. Huskey, 'Overcoming the Yeltsin Legacy', p. 88. See also his 'Political Leadership and the Center–Periphery Struggle'. See also below, pp. 273–4.
41. *Monitoring obshchestvennogo mneniya. Sotsial'nye i Ekonomicheskie Pere-meny*, no. 6 (50), November–December 2000, pp. 84–5.
42. A. Brown, 'Vladimir Putin and the Reaffirmation of Central State Power', p. 48.
43. P. Akopov, 'Obshchestvenniki v Kremle', *Izvestiya*, 13 June 2001. The Russian term for Civic Forum is *Grazhdanskii Forum.*

10. Bloodbath in Chechnya

1. See above, pp. 62–3.
2. For further discussion see S. Layton, *Russian Literature and Empire: The Conquest of the Caucasus from Pushkin to Tolstoy.*
3. J. Klier, *Imperial Russia's Jewish Question, 1855–1881.*
4. G. Hosking, *Russia: People and Empire, 1552–1917*, pp. 376–96.
5. I. Fleischhauer, 'The Ethnic Germans under German Rule', p. 96.
6. This attitude was at the heart of Khrushchëv's Party Programme of 1961: *Dvadtsat' vtoroi s''ezd Kommunisticheskoi Partii Sovetskogo Soyuza*, vol. 3, p. 303.
7. L. Gatanova et al., *Rossiya i Severnyi Kavkaz: 400 let voin*, pp. 10–11.
8. R. Service, *A History of Twentieth-Century Russia*, p. 114.
9. A. Avtorkhanov, 'The Chechens and the Ingush during the Soviet Period', p. 47.
10. A. Lieven, *Chechnya. Tombstone of Russian Power*, pp. 58–60.
11. *Konstitutsiya Rossiiskoi Federatsii*. The previous Constitution of the RSFSR was no less antagonistic to the local establishment of Shariat law.

12. Lieven, *Chechnya*, pp. 85–6.
13. It cannot be discounted that Grachëv wanted an invasion so as to cover up the illegal sales of Russian military equipment he had allegedly sanctioned.
14. Lieven, *Chechnya*, pp. 124–5.
15. Ibid., p. 144.
16. L. Belin, 'Political Bias and Self-Censorship in the Russian Media', p. 324. See also O. Dobrodeev's open letter in *Argumenty i fakty*, no. 15, April 2001.
17. European Union Capacity Development in Election Monitoring, *Briefing Document*, no. 1: Stavropol region, 3 March 2000.
18. *Nezavisimaya gazeta*, 14 January 2000: interview with Sergei Stepashin.
19. It was frequent to witness the police doing this on Moscow streets, and it is not uncommon in certain parts of the city today.
20. N. Gevorkyan et al., *Ot pervogo litsa*, p. 137.
21. A. Lieven, 'Through a Distorted Lens: Chechnya and the Western Media', *Current History*, October 2000.
22. Gevorkyan et al., *Ot pervogo litsa*, pp. 133–7.
23. Ibid.
24. O. Dobrodeev: open letter in *Argumenty i fakty*, no. 15, April 2001.
25. He did, however, allow for the possibility that in the long run Chechnya might be granted independence: Gevorkyan et al., *Ot pervogo litsa*, p. 135.
26. See above, p. 133.
27. RTR: 11 April 2001; *Kommersant*, no. 122, 13 July 2001.

11. Russia in the World

1. A. Pravda (ed.), *The End of the Outer Empire: Soviet–East European Relations in Transition, 1985–1990*.
2. S. White, *Russia's New Politics*, p. 222.
3. Yu. M. Baturin et al., *Epokha Yel'tsina: ocherki politicheskoi istorii*, p. 470.
4. A. Kozyrev, *Preobrazhenie*, p. 125.
5. N. Melvin, *Russians Beyond Russia. The Politics of National Identity*, ch. 3.
6. D. Marples, *Belarus: A Denationalised Nation*.
7. V. Baranovsky, 'Russia: A Part of Europe or Apart from Europe?', p. 441.
8. Y. Borko, 'EU/Russia Co-operation: The Moscow Perspective' in J. Baxendale et al., *The EU and Kaliningrad*, p. 59.
9. See below, pp. 272–3.
10. *Izvestiya*, 12 September 2001.
11. B. Nemtsov, *Washington Post*, 1 October 2001. Nemtsov, as leader of the Union of Right Forces, opposed Putin's war in Chechnya.

12. Official Transmission

1. S. Webber, *School, Reform and Society in the New Russia*, p. 135. See also J. Sutherland, *Schooling in the New Russia. Innovation and Change, 1984–1995*.
2. 'Konkurs "Ideya dlya Rossii"', *Rossiiskaya gazeta*, 30 July 1996, p. 1.
3. 'Est' proroki v svoëm Otechestve', ibid.
4. Ibid., 31 December 1996, p. 1.
5. Ibid., 17 September 1996, p. 5.
6. E. Mickiewicz, *Changing Channels and the Struggle for Power in Russia*, p. 218.
7. Ibid., p. 229.
8. 'Spravka', *Izvestiya*, 31 August 2001.
9. A. Tolstoi, *Russkii kharakter*.
10. M. Yu. Lermontov, *Stikhotvoreniya*, vol.1, p. 213.
11. It would anyhow be wrong to think that Soviet education involved only texts of Russian provenance and patriotic content. The curriculum stipulated that all ten-year-olds should read Hans Christian Andersen. In the next year they had to read extracts of Homer as well as Robert Louis Stevenson. Then in class seven, for twelve-year-olds, extracts of Cervantes's *Don Quixote* were compulsory. Through to the age of sixteen, Soviet schoolchildren were expected to sample Molière, Byron, Goethe, Balzac and Shakespeare. Generally, therefore, Russian pupils already had an education involving both patriotism and world literature even in the Soviet period. See J. Muckle, *A Guide to the Soviet Curriculum*, pp. 116–23.
12. *Perechen' uchebnikov i uchebnykh posobii, rekomendovannykh Ministerstvom obshchego i professional'nogo obrazovaniya Rossiiskoi Federatsii na 1999/2000 god*.
13. D. Mendeloff, 'Demystifying Textbooks in Post-Soviet Russia', pp. 16–20.
14. R. Davies, *Soviet History in the Yeltsin Era*, part 3.
15. Among the most popular Western historical textbooks are G. Hosking, *Istoriya Sovetskogo Soyuza*, and N. Werth, *Istoriya Sovetskogo gosudarstva*. Neither, however, has been accorded the imprimatur of the Ministry of Education's approval.
16. *Izvestiya*, 29 May 1989.
17. A. N. Bokhanov, et al., *Istoriya Rossii. XX vek*, pp. 5–6.
18. Ibid., p. 3.
19. *Rossiiskaya gazeta*, 1 April 1998: editorial.
20. *Komsomol'skaya pravda*, 12 February 1992.
21. O. Poptsov, *Khronika vremën 'Tsarya Borisa'. Rossiya, Kreml'. 1991–1995*.
22. V. Shenderovich, *Kukly-2*, p. 3.
23. Yu. Vasil'ev, *Rossiiskaya gazeta*, 6 November 1999.
24. N. Gevorkyan et al., *Ot pervogo litsa. Peregovory s Vladimirom Putinym*, p. 39.
25. Ibid.

26. Speech of 14 December 2001.
27. See below, pp. 211–12.
28. *Izvestiya*, 31 August 2001.
29. Ye. Korop, 'Uchebniki pereputali s agitkami', *Izvestiya*, 30 August 2001; A. Angelevich, 'Grifomany', *Izvestiya*, 31 August 2001. Not only the work edited by Dmitrenko but also O. V. Volobuev, V. V. Zhuravlëv and A. N. Nenarokov, *Istoriya Rossii. XX vek* were criticised.
30. *Izvestiya*, 31 August 2001.
31. Ibid.
32. Information conveyed to the author in 1989 by one of the involved historians.
33. See above, pp. 108–10.

13. Symbols for Russia

1. Yu. Shkuratov, *Variant drakona*, p. 60.
2. *Moskovskie novosti*, November 2000.
3. N. A. Sobelev and V. A. Artamonov, *Simvoly Rossii*, p. 201.
4. Ibid., p. 141.
5. I witnessed some of these unsavoury scenes.
6. It ought to be added that although the city has been renamed, the province remains *Leningradskaya oblast'*.
7. M. Gray, *Blood Relative*, pp. 48–65 and 78–9.
8. B. Yeltsin, *The View from the Kremlin*, pp. 145–8: this passage gives an account of Russian political predecessors.
9. B. Slutsky, *Things That Happened*, pp. 58–9.
10. *Segodnya*, 8 November 1999.
11. B. Zemtsov, 'Prazdnik, kotoryi uzhe ne s nami', *Nezavisimaya gazeta*, no. 79 (2141), 29 April 2000.
12. *Rossiiskaya gazeta*, 10 May 1995.
13. Ibid., 14 March 1995.
14. D. Volkogonov, *Etyudy o vremeni. Iz zabytogo, nezamechennogo, nepechatannogo*, p. 357: letter to Yeltsin, dated 4 February 1994.
15. See above, pp. 108–9.
16. *Superal'manakh narodnykh AiForizmov*, p. 54.
17. *Komsomol'skaya pravda*, 8 December 2000.
18. *Rossiiskaya gazeta*, no. 248, 30 December 2000.
19. *Komsomol'skaya pravda*, 8 December 2000
20. The few who had read the basic literature, which was almost entirely Western, were of the second rank in the government – Valeri Tishkov is an example, and it is significant that he resigned from the government in October 1992. All this contrasts with the process of economic reform. Gaidar and others had read a little Hayek and Samuelson when they

introduced a market economy. Whether this improved the formulation and execution of policy is a moot point.

14. Understating the Case

1. O. Poptsov, *Khronika vremën 'Tsarya Borisa'*, p. 397.
2. R. Sakwa, *Gorbachev and his Reforms, 1985–1990*, pp. 219–20. See also J. Ellis, *The Russian Orthodox Church. Triumphalism and Defensiveness*.
3. V. Kostikov, *Roman s prezidentom*, pp. 240–1.
4. This compromise still holds: *Izvestiya*, no. 61, 6 April 2001. Alexi II, however, has indicated a wish for agricultural land adjacent to monasteries to be given back to the Church so that monks might be able to sustain themselves materially: ibid.
5. B. Yeltsin, *Against the Grain. An Autobiography*, p. 15.
6. See above, pp. 202–3.
7. G. Fagan, 'Kremlin Doesn't Trust Orthodox Leaders', *Keston News Service*, 7 September 2001.
8. A. Gentleman, 'Russian Crusaders Take to the Railways', *Guardian*, 20 October 2000.
9. VTsIOM, *Monitoring obshchestvennogo mneniya*, no. 6, 2000.
10. Ibid.
11. J. Lloyd, *Rebirth of a Nation*, pp. 117–21.
12. *Soldat udachi. Zhurnal dlya sil'nykh i zhestkikh muzhchin*, no. 4 (67), 2000.
13. G. Hosking, *The Awakening of the Soviet Union*.
14. T. Zaslavskaya, 'The Novosibirsk Report', *Survey*, no. 28/1 (1984).
15. I owe this quotation to the evocation of contemporary Siberia by Colin Thubron, *In Siberia*, p. 67.
16. See below, pp. 223–4.
17. P. Goldschmidt, 'Jewish Identity in Russia Today'.
18. Z. Gitelman, 'Promised Land': St Antony's College Russian and East European Centre seminar, 2 November 1998. The number refers to the period 1989–98.
19. See above, p. 135.
20. Open letter of Oleg Dobrodeev: *Argumenty i fakty*, no. 15, April 2001, p. 8. On the travails of the media see L. Belin, 'Political Bias and Self-Censorship in the Russian Media'.
21. *Segodnya*, 29 May 2000.
22. *Moskovskie novosti*, 2 June 2000.
23. NTV, 6–7 April 2001.
24. *Profil'*, no. 13, 9 April 2001.
25. V. Tret'yakov, *Nezavismaya gazeta*, 7 April 2001.
26. *Den'*, 26 July/1 August 1992.

27. A. Brown, *The Gorbachev Factor*, p. 321. See L. McReynolds, *The News Under Russia's Old Regime*; J. Murray, *The Russian Press from Brezhnev to Yeltsin*.
28. *Dochki-Materi*, no. 5, April 2000.

15. The Politics of Ideas

1. G. Zyuganov, *Rossiya i sovremennyi mir*, p. 16.
2. For a survey see J. Lester, *Modern Tsars and Princes. The Struggle for Hegemony in Russia*.
3. G. Zyuganov, *Rossiya – moya rodina. Ideologiya gosudarstvennogo patriotizma*; V. Zhirinovskii, *Poslednii brosok na yug*; Ye. Gaidar, *Gosudarstvo i evolyutsiya*; A. Lebed', *Za derzhavu obidno*; G. Yavlinksii, *Krizis v Rossii: konets sistemy? Nachalo puti*. See also B. Yeltsin, *Against the Grain*; B. Yeltsin, *The View from the Kremlin*; B. Yeltsin, *Midnight Diaries*; N. Gevorkyan et al., *Ot pervogo litsa. Peregovory s Vladimirom Putinym*. Chernomyrdin's 'Idea of Russia' competition, held in *Rossiiskaya gazeta*, is discussed above on pp. 183–5.
4. Ye. Gaidar, *Gosudarstvo i evolyutsiya*.
5. G. Yavlinksii, *Krizis v Rossii: konets sistemy? Nachalo puti*; G. Yavlinksii, *O rossiiskoi politike. Vystupleniya i stat'i* (see especially pp. 42, 67 and 88–9).
6. Zyuganov, *Rossiya i sovremennyi mir*, pp. 17–18.
7. G. Zyuganov, *Veryu v Rossiyu*.
8. *Poslednii brosok na yug*, p. 90.
9. Ibid.
10. E. Klepikova and V. Solovyov, *Zhirinovsky. The Paradoxes of Russian Fascism*, p. 71.
11. *Poslednii brosok na yug*, p. 125.
12. *Materialy V S''ezda LDPR, 2 aprelya 1994*, p. 19.
13. S. Kuleshov and V. Strada, *Il fascismo russo*, pp. 229–38.

16. Culture for the Nation

1. D. A. Prigov, *Napisannoe c 1990 po 1994*, p. 22.
2. J. Andrew, *Writers and Society During the Rise of Russian Realism*.
3. Among the works by them published since 1991 are: N. Berdyaev, *Dukhovnye osnovy russkoi revolyutsii: opyt 1917–1918 gg.*; N. Berdyaev, *Dukhovnyi krizis intelligentsii; Mirosotserzanie Dostoevskogo*; L. N. Gumilëv, *Ot Rusi do Rossii*; L. N. Gumilëv, *Chërnaya legenda: druz'ya i nedruz'ya Velikoi Stepi*; L. N. Gumilëv, *Ritmy Evrazii*; I. Il'in, *Put' k ochevidnosti*; N. M. Karamzin, *Istoriya rossiiskogo gosudarstva*. Some of these works were published in the Gorbachëv period in the USSR – and Karamzin even earlier.
4. See above, pp. 75–6.
5. A. Solzhenitsyn, *Rossiya v obvale*, p. 5.

6. See in particular *Krasnoe koleso*, section 4, part 1.

7. See his *August 1914* and *November 1916*.

8. V. Soloukhin, *Pri svete dnya*.

9. D. Volkogonov, *Lenin: politicheskii portret*. See especially vol. 1, pp. 9–34. Volkogonov's own earlier biography of Stalin, *Stalin: Triumf i tragediya*, was kinder to its subject than the author came to like; a comprehensive denunciation of Stalin, written in equally accessible language, was given by the playwright Edvard Radzinski in his biography *Stalin*.

10. I. Glazunov, *Vechnaya Rossiya*.

11. V. Astaf'ev, *Proklyaty i ubity*.

12. D. Likhachëv, *Kniga bespokoistv. Vospominaniya, stat'i i besedy*, p. 240.

13. Ibid., p. 226.

14. D. Likhachëv, *Razdum'ya*, p. 208.

15. S. Lipkin, *Zapiski zhil'tsa*.

16. V. Makanin, *Kavkazskii plennyi*.

17. S. Bodrov (dir.), *Plennik Kavkaza*.

18. N. Mikhalkov (dir.), *Otomlennye solntsem*.

19. See above, pp. 211–12.

20. V. Khotinenko (dir.), *Musul'manin*.

21. 'Svoboda' in G. S. Smith (ed. and tr.), *Contemporary Russian Poetry*, p. 48.

22. Ibid., p. 218.

23. M. Shatunovskii, *The Discrete Continuity of Love* in N. Perova and A. Tait (eds), *New Russian Writing*, no. 7 (1994), p. 161.

24. V. Pelevin, *Omon Ra*.

25. V. Pelevin, *Generation 'P'* , whose title appears in Latin script, is translated into English as *Babylon*. See p. 7.

26. Ibid., p. 11.

27. Ibid., p. 92.

28. Ibid., pp. 198–9.

29. See the dustjacket of A. Marinina, *Za vsë nado platit'*.

30. C. T. Nepomnyashchy, 'Markets, Mirrors and Mayhem: Alexandra Marinina and the Rise of the New Russian *Detektiv*', pp. 166–82.

31. For a survey of such themes see B. Heldt, *Terrible Perfection*; C. Kelly, *A History of Russian Women's Writing, 1820–1992*; R. Marsh (ed.), *Gender and Russian Literature*; R. Marsh (ed.), *Women and Russian Culture: Projections and Self-Perceptions*.

32. *Argumenty i fakty*, no. 15, April 2001.

33. Boris Greben'shchikov, 'Maëtsya', song from *Navigator* (1995).

34. Boris Greben'shchikov, '8200', song from *Kostroma, Mon Amour*.

35. J. P. Friedman and A. Weiner, 'Between a Rock and a Hard Place' in A. M. Barker (ed.), *Consuming Russia*, pp. 130–1.

36. A. Solzhenitsyn, 'Dva rasskaza'.

37. Solzhenitsyn, *Rossiya v obvale*, pp. 1–5 and 32.

17. Federation and the Regions

1. P. Severtsov, *Kirsan: The Universal President.*
2. *Konstitutsiya Rossiiskoi Federatsii,* article 5.
3. Cabinet of Ministers, The Republic of Tatarstan: resolution 512, 27 August 1993.
4. L. M. Drobizheva, *Asimmetrichnaya federatsiya,* p. 17.
5. Conversation with Professor L. M. Drobizheva: St Antony's College, Oxford, 8 June 2000.
6. V. V. Koroteeva, ch. 5 in L. M. Drobizheva et al., *Demokratizatsiya i obryady natsionalizma v Rossiiskoi Federatsii 90-kh godov,* p. 211.
7. Drobizheva, *Asimmetrichnaya federatsiya,* pp. 17–18; *Suverennyi Tatarstan,* pp. 33–9.
8. J. Kahn, 'What Is the New Russian Federalism?' in A. Brown (ed.), *Contemporary Russian Politics,* p. 380.
9. A. Lieven, *Chechnya,* pp. 142–3.
10. J. Kahn, 'Russia's "Federal" Façade': St Antony's College, Oxford Russian and East European Centre Seminar (10 May 1999).
11. G. Smith (ed.), *Federalism: the Multiethnic Challenge.*
12. R. Abdulatipov et al., *Natsional'naya politika Rossiiskoi Federatsii: ot kontsepsii do realizatsii,* p. 33.
13. Ibid., p. 19.
14. Ibid., pp. 23 and 50.
15. Ibid., pp. 3 and 23.
16. K. Ilyumzhinov, *Ternovyi venets prezidenta,* p. 118. I am grateful to Jeff Kahn for drawing the works of and about Ilyumzhinov to my attention.
17. Ibid., pp. 12, 90, 133 and 150. See also Severtsov, *Kirsan.*
18. I am grateful to Jonathan Aves for his account of a visit to Kalmykia.
19. On the provinces since 1991 see J. Andrew and K. Stoner-Weiss, 'Regionalism and Reform in Provincial Russia'; P. Hanson, 'Understanding Regional Patterns of Economic Change in Post-Communist Russia'; P. Kirkow, 'Regional Warlordism in Russia: the Case of Primorskoi Krai'; P. Kirkow, *Russia's Provinces: Authoritarian Transformation versus Local Autonomy?*; M. McAuley, *Russia's Politics of Uncertainty*; N. Melvin, 'The Consolidation of a New Regional Elite: the Case of Omsk, 1987–1995'; K. Stoner-Weiss, *Local Heroes: The Political Economy of Russian Regional Government*; D. Zimine and M. J. Bradshaw, 'Regional Adaptation to Economic Crisis in Russia: the Case of Novgorod Oblast'.
20. G. Kosach, 'Orenburg: regional'naya mifologiya vo vzaimodeistvii s sosedyami' in A. Malashenko (ed.), *Chto khotyat regiony?*, p. 84.
21. *Konstitutsiya Rossiiskoi Federatsii,* p. 24.
22. A. M. Yakovlev, *Striving for Law in a Lawless Land,* p. 155: 15 July 1992.
23. N. Gorodetskaya and V. Todres, *Segodnya,* 11 November 1993.

24. N. P. Medvedev, *'Novye' na Staroi ploshchadi. Kremlëvsko-provintsial'nye istorii*, pp. 144–6.
25. V. N. Ivanov, *Rossiya: tsentr i regiony*, issue 3, p. 16
26. *Nezavisimaya gazeta*, 3 June 1997, p. 4.
27. S. P. Peregudov et al., *Gruppy interesov i rossiiskoe gosudarstvo*, p. 184.
28. Medvedev, *'Novye' na Staroi ploshchadi*, pp. 154–60.
29. E. Huskey, 'Political Leadership and the Center–Periphery Struggle', p. 129.
30. *Izvestiya*, 21 June 1997, p. 2.
31. *Dom i otechestvo*, 17–23 May 1997, p. 3.
32. Conversation with Neil Taylor.
33. R. Nyberg, 'The EU and Kaliningrad' in J. Baxendale et al. (eds), *The EU and Kaliningrad: Kaliningrad and the Impact of EU Enlargement*, p. 54. D. Gowan, 'Russia and the European Union': St Antony's College, Oxford, Russian and East European Centre Seminar (10 May 2000).
34. *Izvestiya*, 1 June 2000.
35. *Rossiiskaya gazeta*, 16 May 2000.
36. *Nezavisimaya gazeta*, 26 March 1996.
37. *Interfax* report: 14 May 2000.

18. Russian Town, Russian Village

1. G. S. Smith (ed. and tr.), *Contemporary Russian Poetry*, p. 44.
2. P. Hanson, 'Regional Income Differences', p. 418.
3. On local government see T. H. Friedgut and J. F. Kahn (eds), *Local Power and Post-Soviet Politics*; L. Gil'chenko, 'Reforma mestnoi vlasti v Rossii' in Ye. V. Alferova (ed.), *Gosudarstvennaya vlast' i mestnoe samoupravlenie v Rossii*.
4. B. Nemtsov, *Provintsial*, pp. 21–2.
5. Ibid., p. 29.
6. A. B. Chubais, *Privatizatsiya po-rossiiski*, pp. 98–100.
7. P. Hanson, 'Understanding Regional Patterns of Economic Change in Post-Communist Russia'.
8. Ibid.
9. L. Gil'chenko, 'Reforma mestnoi vlasti v Rossii', p. 19.
10. P. Hanson, 'Understanding Regional Patterns of Economic Change in Post-Communist Russia'.
11. Gil'chenko, 'Reforma mestnoi vlasti v Rossii', pp. 11–12.
12. A. Brown, *The Gorbachëv Factor*, pp. 33–4.
13. Yu. V. Arutyunyan et al., *Russkie: etno-sotsiologicheskie ocherki*, pp. 263–4 and 266.
14. Conversation with the Rev. Michael Bourdeaux, 13 November 2000.
15. Arutyunyan et al., *Russkie: etno-sotsiologicheskie ocherki*, p. 316.
16. Ibid., p. 330.

17. See *Sam. Zhurnal domashnikh masterov*, no. 5, 2000; implausibly this magazine claims to have the farmer as well as the *dachnik* in its sights.
18. S. K. Wegren, *Agriculture and the State in Soviet and Post-Soviet Russia*, p. 125.
19. J. Channon, *Agrarian Reforms in Russia, 1992–1995*, pp. 1–5.
20. Wegren, *Agriculture and the State*, pp. 13 and 73.
21. C. Humphrey, *Marx Went Away – But Karl Stayed Behind*, p. 464.
22. C. Leonard, 'Rational Resistance to Land Privatization: The Response of Rural Producers to Agrarian Reforms in Pre- and Post-Soviet Russia', pp. 607–18.
23. Wegren, *Agriculture and the State*, p. 229.
24. Ibid., pp. 113 and 123.
25. Ibid., p. 237.

19. Class and the 'New Russians'

1. Interview in L. Lopatin (ed.), *Rabochee dvizhenie Kuzbassa v vospominani-yakh ego uchastnikov i ochevidtsev*, p. 64.
2. See the discussion by B. Granville and P. Oppenheimer in their *Russia's Post-Communist Economy*, p. 19.
3. J. Kampfner, *Inside Yeltsin's Russia, Corruption. Conflict. Capitalism*; O. Kryshtanovskaya, 'Rich and Poor in Post Communist Russia'.
4. M. Voslensky, *Nomenklatura*, pp. 1–5.
5. *Kommersant-Dom*, 12 April 2001.
6. P. Klebnikov, *Godfather of the Kremlin: Boris Berezovsky and the Looting of the Kremlin*, chs 2–6.
7. Ibid., p. 154.
8. A. Lieven, *Chechnya. Tombstone of Russian Power*, p. 14.
9. Ibid., p. 176.
10. See above, pp. 135–6.
11. O. Kryshtanovskaya and S. White, 'From Soviet *Nomenklatura* to Russian Élite'.
12. Lieven, *Chechnya*, p. 159.
13. D. Filtzer, *Soviet Workers and the Collapse of Perestroika: the Soviet Labour Process and Gorbachev's Reforms, 1985–1991*.
14. This and the following details come from the anthropological account by Bruce Grant, *In The Soviet House of Culture: A Century of Perestroikas*, p. 25.
15. Carnegie Moscow Center, Briefing No. 4, April 2000: T. Maleva, 'What Sort of Russia Has the New Russian President Inherited?'.
16. A. Lushin and P. Oppenheimer, 'External Trade and Payments', p. 279.
17. J. Eatwell et al., *Transformation and Integration: Shaping the Future of Central and Eastern Europe*, pp. 73 and 76; S. Commander and Andrei Tolstopyatenko, 'The Labour Market', p. 335.
18. Maleva, 'What Sort of Russia Has the New Russian President Inherited?'.

19. *Sotsial'noe polozhenie i uroven' zhizni naseleniya Rossii. Ofitsial'noe izdanie*, pp. 138–9.
20. Ibid., p. 305.
21. Ibid., pp. 138–9.

20. A Society Disclosed

1. Kongress Zhenshchin Kol'skogo Poluostrova: http://www.owl.ru/win/women/org002/.
2. H. Goscilo, '*Domostroika* or *Perestroika*', in T. Lahusen and G. Kuperman, *Late Soviet Culture. From Perestroika to Novostroika*, p. 237. See also L. Attwood, *The New Soviet Man and Woman: Sex Role Differentiation in the USSR*.
3. H. Pilkington, *Generation, Gender and Identity*; V. Sperling, *Organising Women in Contemporary Russia: Engendering Transition*.
4. *Avtomekhanik*, March 2000, p. 37.
5. V. Shkol'nikov et al., *Neravenstvo i smertnost' v Rossii*, p. 10.
6. Ibid., p. 82.
7. Agence France Presse, 21 February 2000.
8. Carnegie Moscow Center, Briefing No. 4, April 2000: T. Maleva, 'What Sort of Russia Has the New Russian President Inherited?'.
9. *Rossiiskii statisticheskii ezhegodnik. Ofitsial'noe izdanie 2000*, p. 53.
10. S. McMillin and A. McMillin, 'Any Colour, So Long As it Is Black', p. 7.
11. N. Timasheff, *The Great Retreat: The Growth and Decline of Communism in Russia*.
12. Ibid.
13. APN report: 6 June 2000: report by Yelena Bashkirova, director of ROMIR Research Centre.
14. http://www.club69.gay.ru:8084/press/pulse_sept99.html.
15. Of course, books are not the only reading matter; and newspapers are full of new ideas and material. But then again even the level of newspaper purchase is much lower than in the late 1980s.
16. See pp. 244–53. See also S. Lovell, *The Russian Reading Revolution: Print Culture in the Soviet and Post-Soviet Eras*.
17. *Rossiya*, June 1997, p. 25. These were bodies which registered themselves with the official authorities, and not every organisation bothered itself with the legal nicety. By mid-1999 the number had risen to 3,500: S. P. Peregudov et al., *Gruppy interesov i rossiiskoe gosudarstvo*, p. 152.
18. Information supplied by Mr Rick Byrch, sports teacher and fellow camper by Lake Garda, summer 2000.
19. Peregudov et al., *Gruppy interesov i rossiiskoe gosudarstvo*, pp. 152–3.
20. Ibid., p. 156.
21. A. White, *Democratisation in Russia under Gorbachev, 1985–1991: the Birth of a Voluntary Sector*.

22. Peregudov et al., *Gruppy interesov i rossiiskoe gosudarstvo*, p. 167.
23. Ibid., pp. 171 ff.
24. *Severnyi kur'er* (Petrozavodsk), 13 August 1998, no. 152 (23199).
25. S. Ashwin, *Russian Workers*, p. 1.
26. On the general problems of civil society see E. Gellner, *Conditions of Liberty: Civil Liberty and its Rivals*.

21. Russia in Private

1. Editorial comment in *Argumenty i fakty*, no. 15, April 2001.
2. *Avtomir*, no. 17, 25 April 2001, p. 30.
3. *Moskovskaya pravda*, no. 64, 6 April 2001.
4. On the importance of unstated assumptions in daily existence see M. de Certeau, *The Practice of Everyday Life*.
5. M. K. Gorshkov et al., *Osennii krizis 1998 goda: rossiiskoe obshchestvo do i posle*, p. 40.
6. S. Ashwin, *Russian Workers*, p. 52.
7. See M. Afanas'ev, *Klientelizm i rossiiskaya gosudarstvennost'* . More generally see L. Roniger and A. Günes-Ayata (eds), *Democracy, Clientelism, and Civil Society*.
8. F. Ellis, 'The Media as Social Engineer' in C. Kelly and D. Shepherd (eds), *Russian Cultural Studies*, p. 220.
9. Ye. A. Zemskaya, *Russkii yazyk kontsa XX stoletiya (1985–1995)*, p. 11.
10. Ellis, 'The Media as Social Engineer', p. 220.
11. A. V. Suslova and A. V. Superanskaya, *O russkikh imenakh*, p. 91.
12. *Avtomekhanik*, March 2000, p. 47.
13. See F. Wigzell, *Reading Russian Fortunes: Print Culture, Gender and Divination in Russia Since 1765*.
14. *Sem' dnei. TV-programma*, no. 8, 19–25 2001.
15. I. Traynor, *Guardian*, 3 June 2000.
16. E. Mickiewicz, *Changing Channels and the Struggle for Power in Russia*.
17. 'Chetyre lapy na kvadratny metr', *Argumenty i fakty*, no. 23, 1997, p. 2.
18. *Drug*, no. 4 (78), 2000, p. 4.
19. Ibid., p. 6.
20. Ibid., p. 34.
21. A. M. Barker, 'Going to the Dogs' in A. M. Barker (ed.), *Consuming Russia*, pp. 270–1.
22. C. Kelly, *Refining Russia*, ch. 5. Those who are interested in hairdressing literature and similar subjects should go to the University of Keele Library, which in the late 1970s had an enlightened policy of purchasing such books.
23. I have to add, however, that on a trip in April 2001 I found that the 'Belomorkanal' *papirosy* were kept out of the main windows of the kiosks. Would-be purchasers had to ask specially for them.

24. J. Cooper, 'ru.net: Russia and her Real "Virtual" Economy': St Antony's College, Oxford, Russian and European Centre Seminar (12 June 2000).

25. Kelly, *Refining Russia*, p. 286.

26. *Moi uyutnyi dom*, no. 5, 2000, p. 29.

27. Ibid., p. 22.

28. *Sandra. Vyazanie*, no. 4, 2000; *Sport-klub*, no. 5, 2000.

29. K. Kääriäinen and D. Furman, *Religiosity in Russia in the 1990s*, pp. 28–75.

30. Ibid.

31. See above, p. 216.

32. See above, p. 65.

BIBLIOGRAPHY

This bibliography is divided between primary and secondary sources and it has sometimes been a matter of fine judgement about which section should hold particular works. Please note that only those sources are included which have been used in the book.

PRIMARY SOURCES

Current Periodicals

Argumenty i fakty (Moscow)
Avtomekhanik (Moscow)
Avtomir (Moscow)
Den' (Moscow)
Dochki-Materi. Ezhenedel'noe prilozhenie k 'AiF' (Moscow)
Dom i otechestvo (Moscow)
Drug (Moscow)
Duel' (Moscow)
Guardian (London)
Istoricheskii arkhiv (Moscow)
Izvestiya (Moscow)
Keston News Service (Oxford)
Kommersant (Moscow)
Kommersant-Dom (Moscow)
Komsomol'skaya pravda (Moscow)
Lilit. Zhurnal dlya zhenshchin (Moscow)
Moi prekrasnyi sad (Moscow)
Moi uyutnyi dom (Moscow)
Monitoring obshchestvennogo mneniya (VTsIOM: Moscow)
Moskovskaya pravda (Moscow)
Moskovskie novosti (Moscow)

Nezavisimaya gazeta (Moscow)
Novyi mir (Moscow)
Profil'. Populyarnyi delovoi zhurnal (Moscow)
Rossiiskaya gazeta (Moscow)
Rusistika (Rugby)
Rybach'te s nami (Moscow)
Rybolov-klub (Moscow)
Sad svoimi rukami (Moscow)
Sam. Zhurnal domashnikh masterov (Moscow)
Sandra. Vyazanie (Moscow)
Segodnya (Moscow)
Sem' dnei. TV-programma (Moscow)
Sever'nyi kur'er (Petrozavodsk)
Soldat udachi. Zhurnal dlya sil'nykh i zhestkikh muzhchin (Moscow)
Sport-klub (Moscow)
Zavtra (Moscow)

Web sites

Kongress Zhenshchin Kol'skogo Poluostrova: www.owl.ru/win/women/org002/
www.club69.gay.ru:8084/press/pulse_sept99.html
www.gazeta.ru
www.informika.ru/text/
www.keston.org
www.polit.ru
www.pravitelstvo.gov.ru
www.prezident.ru
www.pw1.netcom.com/~merezhko/ordersandmedals.html
www.rambler.ru
www.yandex.ru
www.zyuganov.ru/1/1.asp

Films and Music

Andrei Rublëv (dir. A. Tarkovskii: 1964)
Brat (dir. A. Balabanov: 1996)
Boris Greben'shchikov, *Navigator* (1995)
Boris Greben'shchikov, *Kostroma, Mon Amour* (1994)
BG [Boris Gebenshchikov], *Russkii al'bom* (1995)
Kalina krasnaya (V. Shuksin: 1974)
Musul'manin (dir. V. Khotinenko: 1995)
Osobennosti natsional'noi okhoty (dir.A. Rogozhkin: 1995)
Otomlennye solntsem (dir. N. Mikhalkov: 1994)

Plennik Kavkaza (dir. S. Bodrov: 1996)
Pokayanie (dir. T. Abuladze: 1986)
Yurii Shevchuk, *Aktrisa vesna* (1993)
A. Schnittke, *Tak zhit' nel'zya* (dir. S. Govorukhin: 1990)
Urga (dir. N. Mikhalkov: 1990)

Printed Works

R. Abdulatipov, *Rossiiskii federalizm: opyt stanovleniya i strategiya perspektiv* (Moscow, 1998)
R. Abdulatipov et al., *Natsional'naya politika Rossiiskoi Federatsii: ot kontsepsii do realizatsii* (Moscow, 1997)
Yu. Afanas'ev, *Sovetskoe obshchestvo: vozniknovnenie, razvitie, istoricheskii final* (Moscow, 1997), vols. 1–2
N. Anisov (ed.), *Russkii kharakter. Rasskazy sovetskikh pisatelei* (Moscow, 1988)
V. Astaf'ev, *Proklyaty i ubity* (Moscow, 1994)

Yu. M. Baturin, A. L. Il'in, V.F. Kadatskii, V. V. Kostikov, M. A. Krasnov, A. Ya. Lifshits, K. V. Nikiforov, L. G. Pikhoya and G. A. Satarov, *Epokha Yel'tsina: ocherki politicheskoi istorii* (Moscow, 2001)
N. Berdyaev, *Dukhovnye osnovy russkoi revolyutsii: opyt 1917–1918 gg.* (Moscow, 1998)
N. Berdyaev, *Dukhovnyi krizis intelligentsii* (Moscow, 1998)
N. Berdyaev, *Mirosotserzanie Dostoevskogo* (Moscow, 2001)
N. A. Berdyaev, *The Russian Idea* (London, 1947)
B. Berezovskii, 'Polnyi tekst otkrytogo pis'ma deputata Gosudarstvennoi Dumy Borisa Berezovskogo prezidentu Vladimiru Putinu', *Gazeta.ru*, 18 May 2000.
A. Blok, *Sochineniya* (Moscow, 1946)
A. N. Bokhanov, M. M. Gorinov, V. P. Dmitrenko, *Istoriya Rossii. XX vek* (Moscow, 2000)
Buker v Rossii. Finalisty Russkoi Bukerskoi premii, 1992–1995 (eds. L. Zakovorotnaya et al.: Moscow, 1997)
V. Bukovskii, *Moskovskii protsess* (Moscow, 1996)
G. Burbulis, *Stanovlenie novoi russkoi gosudarstvennosti: real'nosti i perspektivy* (Moscow, 1996)

A. B. Chubais, *Privatizatsiya po-rossiiski* (Moscow, 1999)
F. Chuev (ed.), *Molotov. Poluderzhavnyi vlastelin* (Moscow, 1999)

V. P. Dmitrenko (ed.), *Istoriya Rossii. XX vek* (Moscow, 2000)
V. P. Dmitrenko, V. D. Yesakov and V. A. Shestakov, *Istoriya Otechestva. XX vek* (Moscow, 1998)

F. M. Dostoevskii, *Polnoe sobranie sochinenii* (Moscow, 1972–88), vols 1–30

Dvadtsat' vtoroi s''ezd Kommunisticheskoi Partii Sovetskogo Soyuza. 17–31 oktyabrya 1961 goda. Stenograficheskii otchët (Moscow, 1962), vols. 1–3

Brokgauz and Efron (pubs), *Entsiklopedicheskii slovar'* (ed. I. Ye. Andreevskii: St Petersburg, 1890–1904), vols 1–82

Ye. Gaidar, *Gosudarstvo i evolyutsiya* (Moscow, 1995)

Ye. Gaidar, *Dni porazhenii i pobed* (Moscow, 1997)

N. Gevorkyan, N. Timakova and A. Kolesnikov, *Ot pervogo litsa. Peregovory s Vladimirom Putinym* (Moscow, 2000)

I. Glazunov, *Vechnaya Rossiya* (n.d.)

I. Goncharov, *Oblomov* (Moscow, 1934)

M. S. Gorbachëv, *Perestroika. New Thinking for My Country and the World* (London, 1987)

M. S. Gorbachëv, *Zhizn' i reformy* (Moscow, 1995), vols 1–2

A. Grachëv, *Gorbachëv* (Moscow, 2001)

M. M. Gromyko, *Traditsionnye normy povedeniya: formy obshcheniya russkikh krest'yan XIX v.* (Moscow, 1986)

M. M. Gromyko, *Russkie: semeinyi i obshchestvennyi byt* (Moscow, 1989)

M. M. Gromyko, *Mir russkoi derevni* (Moscow, 1991)

L. N. Gumilëv, *V poiskakh vymyshlennogo tsarstva* (London, 1970)

L. N. Gumilëv, *Ot Rusi do Rossii* (St Petersburg, 1992)

L. N. Gumilëv, *Ritmy Evrazii* (Moscow, 1993)

L. N. Gumilëv, *Chernaya legenda: druz'ya i nedrugi Velikoi stepi* (Moscow, 1994)

I. Il'in, *O soprotivlenii zlu siloyu* (Berlin, 1925)

I. Il'in, *Put' k ochevidnosti* (Moscow, 1993)

K. Ilyumzhinov, *Ternovyi venets prezidenta* (Moscow, 1995)

N. M. Karamzin, *Istoriya rossiiskogo gosudarstva* (Moscow, 1989)

N. M. Karamzin, *Istoriya rossiiskogo gosudarstva* (Moscow, 1993–4), vols 1–6

J. Kates (ed.), *In the Grip of Strange Thoughts. Russian Poetry in a New Era* (Newcastle-upon-Tyne, 1999)

A. Kokh, *The Selling of the Soviet Empire: Politics and Economics of Russia's Privatisation. Revelations of the Principal Insider* (New York, 1998)

Konstitutsiya Rossiiskoi Federatsii (Moscow, 1993)

A. Korzhakov, *Boris Yel'tsin: ot rassveta do zakata* (Moscow, 1997)

V. Kostikov, *Roman s prezidentom* (Moscow, 1997)

V. Kostikov, 'Stanet li skazka byl'yu?', *Argumenty i fakty*, no. 14, April 2001

S. Kovalëv, 'Putin's War', *New York Review of Books*, 10 February 2000.

A. Kozyrev, *Preobrazhenie* (Moscow, 1995)

V. Kustyllo, *Zapiski iz Belogo Doma, 21 sentyabrya – 4 oktyabrya 1993* (Moscow, 1993)

A. Lebed', *Za derzhavu obidno* (Kirov, 1995)

M. Yu. Lermontov, *Izbrannye proizvedieiya v dvukh tomakh* (Moscow, 1963), vols 1–2

D. Likhachëv, *Kniga bespokoistv. Vospominaniya, stat'i, besedy* (Moscow, 1991)

D. Likhachëv, *Razdum'ya* (Moscow, 1991)

D. Likhachëv, *Zametki o russkom* (Moscow, 1981)

S. Lipkin, *Zapiski zhil'tsa* in *Novyi mir*, nos. 9–10 (1992)

L. Lopatin (ed.), *Rabochee dvizhenie Kuzbassa v vospominaniyakh ego uchastnikov i ochevidtsev* (Moscow, 1998)

M. MacFaul and A. Ryabov, *Rossiiskoe obshchestvo: stanovlenie demokraticheskikh tsennostei* (Moscow, 1999)

V. Makanin, 'Kavkazskii plennyi', *Novyi mir*, no. 4 (1995)

V. Makanin, 'Bukva "A"', *Novyi mir*, no. 4 (2000)

A. Marinina, *Za vsë nado platit'* (Moscow, 2000)

Materialy V S''ezda LDPR, 2 aprelya 1994 (Moscow, 1994)

V. Mau, *Ekonomika i vlast'. Politicheskaya istoriya ekonomicheskoi reformy v 1985–1994* (Moscow, 1995)

N. P. Medvedev, *'Novye' na Staroi ploshchadi. Kremlëvsko-provintsial'nye istorii* (Moscow, 1997)

F. M. Mukhametshin and R. T. Izmailov (eds), *Suverennyi Tatarstan* (Moscow, 1997)

Nekotorye voprosy protokol'noi praktiki (no named editor: Moscow, 1997)

B. Nemtsov, *Provintsial* (Moscow, 1997)

V. Pelevin, *Omon Ra: povest'* (Moscow, 1992)

V. Pelevin, *Generation 'P'* (Moscow, 2000)

Perechen' uchebnikov i uchebnykh posobii, rekomendovannykh Ministerstvom obshchego i professional'nogo obrazovaniya Rossiiskoi Federatsii na 1999/ 2000 god (Moscow, 1999)

N. Perova and A. Tait (eds), *New Russian Writing*, no. 7 (Moscow, 1994)

R. G. Pikhoya, *Sovetskii Soyuz: istoriya vlasti. 1945–1991* (Moscow, 2000)

O. Poptsov, *Khronika vremën 'Tsarya Borisa'. Rossiya, Kreml'. 1991–1995* (Moscow, 1996)

D. A. Prigov, *Napisannoe c 1990 po 1994* (Moscow, 1994)

Ye. Primakov, *Gody v bol'shoi politike* (Moscow, 1999)

E. Radzinskii, *Stalin* (Moscow, 1997)

Rossiisskii statisticheskii ezhegodnik. Ofitsial'noe izdanie 2000 (Moscow, 2000)

Rossiya v tsifrakh. Ofitsial'noe izdanie Goskomstata Rossii (Moscow, 2000)

G. Shakhnazarov, *S vozhdyami i bez nikh* (Moscow, 2001)

M. Shatunovskii, *The Discrete Continuity of Love*: excerpt in N. Perova and A. Tait (eds), *New Russian Writing*, no. 7 (1994)

V. Shenderovich, *Kukly-2* (Moscow, 1998)

V. A. Shestakov, *Rossiya v 1992–1998 gg. Dopol'nitel'nye materialy k uchebniku 'Istoriya Otechestva. XX vek* (Moscow, 2000)

K. Simonov, *Glazami cheloveka moego pokoleniya* (Moscow, 1990)

Yu. Skuratov, *Variant drakona* (Moscow, 2000)

B. Slutsky, *Things That Happened* (edited, translated, and with an introduction and commentaries by G. S. Smith: Birmingham, 1998)

G. S. Smith (ed. and tr.), *Contemporary Russian Poetry. A Bilingual Anthology* (Indiana, 1993)

A. K. Sokolov, *Lektsii po sovetskoi istorii, 1917–1940* (Moscow, 1995)

V. Soloukhin, *Pri svete dnya* (Moscow, 1992)

A. Solzhenitsyn, *August 1914* (London, 1971)

A. Solzhenitsyn, *Letter to Soviet Leaders* (Glasgow, 1975)

A. Solzhenitsyn, *Krasnoe koleso. Povestvovanie v otmerennykh srokakh* (Paris, 1983 ff.)

A. Solzhenitsyn, *Kak nam obustroit' Rossiyu* (Leningrad, 1990)

A. Solzhenitsyn, 'Dva rasskaza', *Novyi mir*, no. 5 (1995)

A. Solzhenitsyn, *Rossiya v obvale* (Moscow, 1998)

A. Solzhenitsyn, *November 1916* (London, 1999)

Sotsial'noe polozhenie i uroven' zhizni naseleniya Rossii. Ofitsial'noe izdanie (Moscow, 2000)

I. V. Stalin, *Sochineniya* (Moscow, 1946–53), vols 1–13

I. V. Stalin, *Sochineniya* (ed. R. H. MacNeal: Stanford, 1967), vols 14–16.

L. Sukhanov, *Tri goda s prezidentom. Zapiski pervogo pomoshchnika* (Riga, 1992)

Superal'manakh narodnykh AiForizmov. Zolotaya seriya (no named editor: Moscow, 1999)

V. A. Tishkov, *Ocherki teorii i praktiki etnichnosti v Rossii* (Moscow, 1997)

A. Tolstoi, *Russkii kharakter* in N. Anisov (ed.), *Russkii kharakter: Rasskazy sovetskikh pisatelei* (Moscow, 1998)

L. N. Tolstoi, *Sobranie sochinenii* (Moscow, 1960–65), vols 1–20

N. S. Trubetskoi, *K probleme russkogo samosoznaniya: sobranie statei* (Paris, 1927)

G. Uspenskii, *Polnoe sobranie sochinenii* (Moscow, 1908), vols 1–6

N. Ustryalov, *Pod znakom revolyutsii* (2nd revd edn: Harbin, 1920)

A. B. Veber, et al. (eds.), *Soyuz mozhno bylo sokhranit'. Belaya kniga. Dokumenty i fakty o politike M.S. Gorbachëva po reformirovaniyu i sokhraneniyu mnogonatsional'nogo gosudarstva* (Moscow, 1995)

D. Volkogonov, *Stalin: triumf i tragediya* (Moscow, 1989), vols 1–2

D. Volkogonov, *Lenin: politicheskii portret* (Moscow, 1994), vols 1–2

O. V. Volobuev, V. V. Zhuravlëv and A. N. Nenarokov, *Istoriya Rossii. XX vek* (Moscow, 2001)

A. M. Yakovlev, *Striving for Law in a Lawless Land. Memoirs of a Russian Reformer* (Armonk, 1996)

G. Yavlinksii, *Krizis v Rossii: konets sistemy? Nachalo puti* (Moscow, 1999)

G. Yavlinksii, *O rossiiskoi politike. Vystupleniya i stat'i* (Moscow, 1999)

B. Yeltsin, *Against the Grain. An Autobiography* (London, 1990)

B. Yeltsin, *The View from the Kremlin* (London, 1994)

B. Yeltsin, *Midnight Diaries* (London, 2000)

V. Zhirinovskii, *Poslednii brosok na yug* (Moscow, 1993)

A. Zinov'ev, 'Moi dom', in *Gomo sovetikus/Moi dom-moya chuzhbina* (1991)

G. Zyuganov, *Rossiya i sovremennyi mir* (Moscow, 1995)

G. Zyuganov, *Veryu v Rossiyu* (Moscow, 1995)

G. Zyuganov, *Rossiya – moya rodina. Ideologiya gosudarstvennogo patriotizma* (Moscow, 1996)

SECONDARY SOURCES

E. Acton, 'The Russian Revolutionary Intelligentsia and Industrialisation', in R. Bartlett (ed.), *Russian Thought and Society, 1800–1917* (Keele, 1984)

M. Afanas'ev, *Klientelizm i rossiiskaya gosudarstvennost'* (Moscow, 1997)

Yu. Afanas'ev, *Sovetskoe obshchestvo: vozniknovnenie, razvitie, istoricheskii final* (Moscow, 1997), vols. 1–2

M. Agurskii, *Ideologiya natsional-bol'shevizma* (Paris, 1980)

Ye. V. Alferova (ed.), *Gosudarstvennaya vlast' i mestnoe samoupravlenie v Rossii* (Moscow, 1998)

G. A. Almond and S. Verba, *The Civic Culture: Political Attitudes and Democracy in Five Nations* (Princeton, 1963)

B. Anderson, *Imagined Communities. Reflections on the Origins and Spread of Nationalism* (London, 1991)

J. Andrew, *Writers and Society During the Rise of Russian Realism* (London, 1980)

J. Andrew and K. Stoner-Weiss, 'Regionalism and Reform in Provincial Russia', *Post-Soviet Affairs*, no. 4 (1995)

C. Andreyev, *Vlasov and the Russian Liberation Movement: Soviet Reality and Émigré Theories* (Cambridge, 1987)

J. Armstrong, *Nations before Nationalism* (Chapel Hill, 1982)

L. Aron, *Boris Yeltsin: a Revolutionary Life* (London, 2000)

V. A. Artamonov, *Gerb i flag Rossii, X–XX veka* (Moscow, 1997)

Yu. V. Arutyunyan et al., *Russkie: etno-sotsiologicheskie ocherki* (Moscow, 1992)

S. Ashwin, *Russian Workers. The Anatomy of Patience* (Manchester, 1999)

A. Åslund, *How Russia Became a Market Economy* (Washington, DC, 1995)

L. Attwood, *The New Soviet Man and Woman: Sex Role Differentiation in the USSR* (London, 1990)

A. Avtorkhanov, 'The Chechens and the Ingush during the Soviet Period', in M. Broxup (ed.), *The North Caucasus Barrier: The Russian Advance towards the Muslim World* (London, 1992)

P. Baev, *Russia's Policies in the Caucasus* (London, 1997)

V. Baranovsky, 'Russia: A Part of Europe or Apart from Europe?', in A. Brown (ed.), *Contemporary Russian Politics: A Reader* (Oxford, 2001)

J. Barber, *Soviet Historians in Crisis, 1928–1932* (London, 1981)

F. C. Barghoorn, *Soviet Russian Nationalism* (New York, 1956)

A. M. Barker, 'Going to the Dogs', in A. M. Barker (ed.), *Consuming Russia: Popular Culture, Sex and Society since Gorbachev* (Durham, NC, 1999)

A. M. Barker (ed.), *Consuming Russia: Popular Culture, Sex and Society since Gorbachev* (Durham, NC, 1999)

V. S. Barulin, *Rossiiskii chelovek v XX veka. Poteri i obreteniya sebya* (Moscow, 2000)

M. Bassin, 'Inventing Siberia: Visions of the Russian East in the Early Nineteenth Century', *American Historical Review*, no. 96 (1991)

M. Bassin, 'Russia Between Europe and Asia: The Ideological Construction of Geographical Space', *Slavic Review*, no. 50 (1991)

M. Bassin, *Imperial Vision. Nationalism and Geographical Imagination in the Russian Far East, 1840–1865* (Cambridge, 1999)

J. Baxendale et al. (eds), *The EU and Kaliningrad. Kaliningrad and the Impact of EU Enlargement* (London, 2000)

S. Becker, 'Russia Between East and West: The Intelligentsia, Russian National Identity and Asian Borderlands', *Central Asian Survey*, no. 4 (1991)

L. Belin, 'Political Bias and Self-Censorship in the Russian Media', in A. Brown (ed.), *Contemporary Russian Politics: A Reader* (Oxford, 2001)

J. Billington, *The Icon and the Axe* (London, 1966)

A. Blyum, *Za kulisami 'Ministerstva Pravdy'. Tainaya istoriya sovetskoi tsentury, 1917–1929* (St Petersburg, 1994)

V. E. Bonnell and G. W. Breslauer, 'Informal Networks, Collective Action and Sources of (In)stability in Russia: a Brief Overview', in V. E. Bonnell and G. W. Breslauer (eds), *Russia in the New Century. Stability or Disorder?* (Boulder, 2001)

V. E. Bonnell and G. W. Breslauer (eds), *Russia in the New Century. Stability or Disorder?* (Boulder, 2001)

Y. Borko, 'EU/Russia Co-operation: The Moscow Perspective', in J. Baxendale et al. (eds), *The EU and Kaliningrad: Kaliningrad and the Impact of EU Enlargement* (London, 2000)

S. Boym, *Common Places: Mythologies of Everyday Life in Russia* (Cambridge, MA, 1994)

I. Bremmer and R. Taras (eds), *New States. New Politics. Building the Post-Soviet Nations* (Cambridge, 1997)

G. Breslauer, 'Boris Yeltsin as Patriarch', *Post-Soviet Affairs*, no. 2 (1999)

J. Breuilly, *Nationalism and the State* (Manchester, 1985)

J. Brooks, *When Russians Learned to Read. Literacy and Popular Literature, 1861–1917* (Princeton, 1985)

A. Brown, *The Gorbachev Factor* (Oxford, 1996)

A. Brown, 'Transnational Influences in the Transition from Communism', *Post-Soviet Affairs*, no. 2 (2000)

A. Brown, 'Vladimir Putin and the Reaffirmation of Central State Power', *Post-Soviet Affairs*, no. 1 (2001)

A. Brown (ed.), *Contemporary Russian Politics: A Reader* (Oxford, 2001)

A. Brown and L. Shevtsova (eds), *Gorbachev, Yeltsin and Putin. Political Leadership in Russia's Transition* (Washington, DC, 2001)

M. Broxup (ed.), *The North Caucasus Barrier. The Russian Advance towards the Muslim World* (London, 1992)

Y. M. Brudny, *Reinventing Russia. Russian Nationalism and the Soviet State, 1953–1991* (Cambridge, MA, 1999)

Y. M. Brudny, 'Continuity or Change in Russian Electoral Patterns? The December 1999 – March 2000 Election Cycle', in A. Brown (ed.), *Contemporary Russian Politics: A Reader* (Oxford, 2001)

M. Buckley (ed.), *Perestroika and Soviet Women* (Cambridge, 1992)

N. F. Bugai, *L. P. Beriya – I. Stalinu: 'Soglasno Vashemu ukazaniyu'* (Moscow, 1995)

A. V. Buganov, *Russkaya istoriya v pamyati krest'yan XIX veka i natsional'noe samosoznanie* (Moscow, 1992)

V. Bunce, 'Should Transitologists be Grounded?', *Slavic Review*, no. 1 (1995)

V. Bunce, *Subversive Institutions. The Design and Destruction of Socialism and the State* (Cambridge, 1999)

I. A. Butenko, *Chitateli i chtenie na iskhode XX veka: sotsiologicheskie aspekty* (Moscow, 1997)

M. de Certeau, *The Practice of Everyday Life* (Berkeley, 1988)

P. Chaisty, 'Democratic Consolidation and Parliamentary Reform in Russia, 1990–93', *The Journal of Legislative Studies*, no. 4 (1997)

P. Chaisty, 'Legislative Politics in Russia', in A. Brown (ed.), *Contemporary Russian Politics: A Reader* (Oxford, 2001)

J. Channon, *Agrarian Reforms in Russia, 1992–1995* (London, 1995)

M. Cherniavsky, *Tsar and People: Studies in Russian Myths* (New York, 1969)

I. Chubais, *Ot Russkoi idei – k idee Novoi Rossii. Kak nam preodolet' ideinyi krizis?* (Moscow, 1997)

V. Clark, *Why Angels Fall: A Portrait of Orthodox Christianity from Byzantium to Kosovo* (London, 2000)

S. Clarke, *Conflict and Change in the Russian Industrial Enterprise* (London, 1996)

S. Clarke, *The Formation of a Labour Market in Russia* (London, 1999)

E. W. Clowes, S. D. Kassow and J. L. West (eds), *Between Tsar and People: Educated Society and the Quest for Public Identity in Late Imperial Russia* (Princeton, 1991)

S. F. Cohen, *Failed Crusade: America and the Tragedy of Post-Communist Russia* (New York, 2000)

L. Colley, *Britons. Forging the Nation, 1707–1837* (New Haven, 1992)

S. Commander and Andrei Tolstopyatenko, 'The Labour Market', in B. Granville and P. Oppenheimer (eds), *Russia's Post-Communist Economy* (Oxford, 2001)

W. Connor, *The National Question in Marxist-Leninist Theory and Strategy* (Princeton, 1984)

R. Conquest, *The Great Terror: A Reassessment* (London, 1992)

J. Cooper, 'ru.net: Russian and her Real "Virtual" Economy': St Antony's College, Oxford, Russian and European Centre Seminar (12 June 2000)

P. D. Curtin, *The Image of Africa* (Madison, 1964)

I. N. R. Davies, *The Isles* (London, 1999)

R. Davies, *Soviet History in the Yeltsin Era* (London, 1997)

C. Davis, 'The Russian Economic Crisis and Western Aid', *The World Today*, no. 12 (1998)

C. Davis, 'The Health Sector: Illness, Medical Care and Mortality', in B. Granville and P. Oppenheimer (eds), *Russia's Post-Communist Economy* (Oxford, 2001)

K. Dawisha and B. Parrott, *Democratic Changes and Authoritarian Reactions in Russia, Ukraine, Belarus and Moldova* (Cambridge, 1997)

L. M. Drobizheva, *Asimmetrichnaya federatsiya: vzglyad iz tsentra, respublik i oblastei* (Moscow, 1998)

L. M. Drobizheva, et al., *Demokratizatsiya i obrazy natsionalizma v Rossiiskoi Federatsii 90-kh godov* (Moscow, 1996)

L. M. Drobizheva and M. S. Kashuba (eds), *Traditsii v sovremennom obshchestve: issledovaniya etnokul'turnykh protsessov* (Moscow, 1990)

M. I. Dubrovin, *Angliiskie i russkie poslovitsy i pogovorki v illyustratsiyakh* (Moscow, 1993)

P. Dukes, *World Order in History. Russia and the West* (London, 1996)

P. J. S. Duncan, *Russian Messianism. Third Rome, Holy War, Communism and After* (London, 2000)

V. Dunham, *In Stalin's Time: Middle-Class Values in Soviet Fiction* (Cambridge, 1976)

P. Dunleavy and B. O'Leary, *Theories of the State: the Politics of Liberal Democracy* (London, 1987)

J. Dunlop, *The Faces of Contemporary Russian Nationalism* (Princeton, 1983)

J. Dunlop, *The Rise of Russia and the Fall of the Soviet Empire* (Princeton, 1993)

J. Eatwell et al., *Transformation and Integration. Shaping the Future of Central and Eastern Europe* (London, 1995)

H. Eckstein and F. J. Fleron et al., *Can Democracy Take Root in Post-Soviet Russia?* (Oxford, 1998)

N. Elias, *The Civilising Process* (Oxford, 1978)

F. Ellis, 'The Media as Social Engineer', in C. Kelly and D. Shepherd (eds), *Russian Cultural Studies: An Introduction* (Oxford, 1998)

J. Ellis, *The Orthodox Church: A Contemporary History* (Bloomington, 1986)

J. Ellis, *The Russian Orthodox Church. Triumphalism and Defensiveness* (London, 1996)

R. D. English, *Russia and the Idea of the West. Gorbachëv, Intellectuals and the End of the Cold War* (New York, 2000)

G. Evans and S. Whitefield, 'Identifying the Bases of Party Competition in Eastern Europe', *British Journal of Political Science*, no. 4 (1993)

M. Feshback and A. Friendly, *Ecocide in the USSR* (London, 1992)

O. Figes and B. Kolonitskii, *Interpreting the Russian Revolution. The Language and Symbols of 1917* (New Haven, 1999)

D. Filtzer, *Soviet Workers and the Collapse of Perestroika: the Soviet Labour Process and Gorbachev's Reforms, 1985–1991* (Cambridge, 1994)

S. Fish, *Democracy from Scratch: Opposition and Regime in the New Russian Revolution* (Princeton, 1994)

S. M. Fish, 'Democratization's Requisites: The Postcommunist Experience', *Post-Communist Affairs*, no. 3 (1998)

I. Fleischhauer, 'The Ethnic Germans under German Rule', in I. Fleischhauer and B. Pinkus, *The Soviet Germans Past and Present* (London, 1986)

S. P. Frank and M. D. Steinberg (eds), *Cultures in Flux. Lower-Class Values, Practices and Resistance in Late Imperial Russia* (Princeton, 1994)

C. Freeland, *Sale of the Century. The Inside Story of the Second Russian Revolution* (London, 2000)

M. Friedberg, *Russian Classics in Soviet Jackets* (New York, 1962)

T. H. Friedgut and J. F. Kahn (eds), *Local Power and Post-Soviet Politics* (New York, 1994)

J. P. Friedman and A. Weiner, 'Between a Rock and a Hard Place', in A. M. Barker (ed.), *Consuming Russia: Popular Culture. Sex and Society since Gorbachev* (Durham, NC, 1999)

C. Gaddy, *The Price of the Past: Russia's Struggle with the Legacy of a Militarized Economy* (Washington, DC, 1996)

M. Galleotti, *Afghanistan. The Soviet Union's Last War* (London, 1995)

L. Gatanova et al., *Rossiya i Severnyi Kavkaz: 400 let voiny* (Moscow, 1999)

P. Gatrell, *A Whole Nation Walking: Refugees in Russia During World War I* (Indiana, 1999)

Gde u russkikh gosudarstvo? Sovremennye problemy i veroyatnye napravleniya razvitiya natsional'nogo ustroistva Rossiiskoi Federatsii (no named author: Irkutsk, 1993)

C. Geertz, *The Interpretation of Cultures* (New York, 1973)

E. Gellner, *Nations and Nationalism* (Oxford, 1983)

E. Gellner, *Plough, Sword and Book* (London, 1988)

E. Gellner, *Conditions of Liberty: Civil Liberty and its Rivals* (London, 1994)

E. Yu. Genieva et al., *Chitayushchaya Rossiya. Mify i real'nost'. Po materialam rossiiskoi nauchno-prakticheskoi konferenstii. Moskva, 1996* (Moscow, 1997)

A. Gerschenkron, *Economic Backwardness in Historical Perspective: A Book of Essays* (New York, 1965)

L. Gil'chenko, 'Reforma mestnoi vlasti v Rossii', in Ye. V. Alferova (ed.), *Gosudarstvennaya vlast' i mestnoe samoupravlenie v Rossii* (Moscow, 1998)

G. Gill, *The Dynamics of Democratisation: Elites, Civil Society and the Transition Process* (London, 2000)

G. Gill (ed.), *Elites and Leadership in Russian Politics* (London, 1998)

P. Ginsborg, *L'Italia del tempo presente. Famiglia, società civile, Stato: 1980–1996* (Turin, 1998)

Z. Gitelman, 'Promised Land': St Antony's College, Oxford, Russian and East European Studies Centre Seminar (2 November 1998)

M. Goldman, *Lost Opportunity: What Has Made Economic Reform in Russia So Difficult* (New York, 1994)

P. Goldschmidt, 'Jewish Identity in Russia Today': St Antony's College, Oxford, Oxford University Russian Society lecture (17 February 1999)

M. K. Gorshkov, A. Yu. Chepurenko and F. E. Sheregi, *Osennii krizis 1998 goda: rossiiskoe obshchestvo do i posle* (Moscow, 1998)

H. Goscilo, '*Domostroika* or *Perestroika*', in T. Lahusen and G. Kuperman, *Late Soviet Culture. From Perestroika to Novostroika* (Durham, NC, 1993)

H. Goscilo and B. Holmgren, *Russia. Women. Culture* (Bloomington, 1995)

B. Grant, *In The Soviet House of Culture: A Century of Perestroikas* (Princeton, 1995)

B. Granville, 'The Problem of Monetary Stabilisation', in B. Granville and P. Oppenheimer (eds), *Russia's Post-Communist Economy* (Oxford, 2001)

B. Granville and P. Oppenheimer (eds), *Russia's Post-Communist Economy* (Oxford, 2001)

C. Gray, *The Russian Experiment in Art, 1863–1922* (2nd edn.: London, 1986)

M. Gray, *Blood Relative* (London, 1998)

B. Grushin, *Chetyre zhizni Rossii v zerkale oprosov obshchestvennogo mneniya*, vol. 1, *Zhizn' 1-ya. Epokha Khrushchëva* (Moscow, 2001)

T. Gustafson, *Capitalism Russian-Style* (New York, 1999)

W. Hahn, *Postwar Soviet Politics. The Fall of Zhdanov and the Defeat of Moderation, 1946–1953* (Ithaca, 1982)

P. Hanson, 'What Sort of Capitalism is Developing in Russia?', *Communist Economies and Economic Transformation*, no. 1 (1997)

P. Hanson, 'Understanding Regional Patterns of Economic Change in Post-Communist Russia': St Antony's College, Oxford, Post-Communist Regions in Transition seminar (25 January 2000)

P. Hanson, 'Regional Income Differences', in B. Granville and P. Oppenheimer (eds), *Russia's Post-Communist Economy* (Oxford, 2001)

B. Heldt, *Terrible Perfection: Women and Russian Literature* (Indiana, 1987)

E. Hellberg-Hirn, *Soil and Soul. The Symbolic World of Russianness* (Aldershot, 1998)

J. Hellman, 'Winners Take All. The Politics of Partial Reform in Postcommunist Transitions', *World Politics*, no. 2 (1998)

G. Hewitt, 'Aspects of Language in Georgia (Georgian and Abkhaz)', in M. Kirkwood (ed.), *Language Planning in the Soviet Union*

J. Higley, J. Pakulski and W. Wesolowski, 'Introduction: Elite Change and Democratic Regimes in Eastern Europe', in *idem* (eds), *Postcommunist Elites and Democracy in Eastern Europe* (London, 1998)

R. Hill and J. Dellenbrant (eds), *Gorbachev and Perestroika* (London, 1989)

A. Hilton, *Russian Folk Art* (Bloomington, 1995)

E. Hobsbawm, *Nations and Nationalism Since 1870* (Cambridge, 1990)

E. Hobsbawm and T. Ranger (eds), *The Invention of Tradition* (Cambridge, 1983)

L. Holmes, *Post-Communism. An Introduction* (Durham, NC, 1997)

G. Hosking, *The Awakening of the Soviet Union* (London, 1990)

G. Hosking, *Russia: People and Empire, 1552–1917* (London, 1997)

G. Hosking and R. Service (eds), *Russian Nationalism Past and Present* (London, 1998)

G. Hosking and R. Service (eds), *Reinterpreting Russia* (London, 1999)

J. Hough, *Democratization and Revolution in the USSR, 1985–1991* (Washington, DC, 1997)

M. Hroch, *Social Preconditions of National Revival in Europe: A Comparative Analysis of the Social Composition of Patriotic Groups among the Smaller Nations* (Cambridge, 1985)

C. Humphrey, *Marx Went Away – But Karl Stayed Behind* (Ann Arbor, 1998)

S. P. Huntington, *The Third Wave: Democratisation in the Late Twentieth Century* (Norman, OK, 1991)

S. P. Huntington, *The Clash of Civilizations* (New York, 1996)

E. Huskey, *Presidential Power in Russia* (New York, 1999)

E. Huskey, 'Overcoming the Yeltsin Legacy: Vladimir Putin and Russian Political Reform', in A. Brown (ed.), *Contemporary Russian Politics: A Reader* (Oxford, 2001)

E. Huskey, 'Political Leadership and the Center–Periphery Struggle: Putin's Administrative Reforms', in A. Brown and L. Shevtsova (eds.), *Gorbachev, Yeltsin and Putin. Political Leadership in Russia's Transition* (Washington, DC, 2001)

A. Inkeles and R. M. Bauer, *The Soviet Citizen. Daily Life in a Totalitarian Society* (Cambridge, MA, 1959)

V. N. Ivanov (ed.), *Rossiya: tsentr i regiony*, issue 3 (Moscow, 1999)

V. N. Ivanov and M. S. Gutseriev, *Rossiya: tsentr i regiony* (Moscow, 1998)

H. F. Jahn, 'For Tsar and Fatherland? Russian Popular Culture and the First World War', in S. P. Frank and M. D. Steinberg (eds.), *Cultures in Flux: Lower-Class Values, Practices and Resistance in Late Imperial Russia* (Princeton, 1994)

H. F. Jahn, *Patriotic Culture in Russia during World War I* (Ithaca, 1995)

M. Jansen, *A Show Trial Under Lenin. The Trial of the Socialist-Revolutionaries. Moscow, 1922* (The Hague, 1982)

L. Jonson, *Keeping the Peace in the CIS; the Evolution of Russian Policy* (London, 1999)

J. Kahn, 'Russia's "Federal" Façade': St Antony's College, Oxford, Russian and East European Centre Seminar (10 May 1999)

J. Kahn, 'The Parade of Sovereignties: Establishing the Vocabulary of the New Russian Federalism', *Post-Soviet Affairs*, no. 1 (2000)

R. Kaiser, *The Geography of Russian Nationalism in Russia and the USSR* (Princeton, 1994)

J. Kampfner, *Inside Yeltsin's Russia, Corruption. Conflict. Capitalism* (London, 1994)

A. Kappeler, *Russland als Vielvölkerreich: Entstehung, Geschichte, Zerfall* (Munich, 1992)

A. Karaulov, *Plokhoi nachal'nik: grustnaya kniga* (Moscow, 1996)

K. Kääriäinen and D. Furman, *Religiosity in Russia in the 1990s* (Helsinki, 2000)

O. Karpenko, 'Byt' "natsional'nym": strakh poteryat' i strakh poteryat'tsya. Na primere tatar Sankt-Peterburga', in V. Voronkov and I. Os'val'd (eds), *Konstruirovanie etnichnosti. Etnicheskie obshchiny* (St Petersburg, 1998)

C. Kelly, *A History of Russian Women's Writing, 1820–1992* (Oxford, 1994)

C. Kelly, *Refining Russia. Advice Literature, Polite Culture and Gender from Catherine to Yeltsin* (Oxford, 2001)

C. Kelly and D. Shepherd (eds), *Constructing Russian Culture in the Age of Revolution, 1881–1940* (Oxford, 1998)

C. Kelly and D. Shepherd (eds), *Russian Cultural Studies: An Introduction* (Oxford, 1998)

B. Kerblay, *Modern Soviet Society* (London, 1983)

O. Khakhordin, *The Collective and the Individual in Soviet Russia: A Study of Practices* (Berkeley, 1999)

P. Kirkow, 'Regional Warlordism in Russia: The Case of Primorski Krai', *Europe–Asia Studies*, no. 6 (1995)

P. Kirkow, *Russia's Provinces: Authoritarian Transformation versus Local Autonomy?* (London, 1998)

M. Kirkwood (ed.), *Language Planning in the Soviet Union* (London, 1989)

H. Kitschelt, Z. Mansfeldova, R. Markowski and G. Toka, *Post-Communist Party Systems. Competition, Representation, and Interparty Cooperation* (Cambridge, 1999)

P. Klebnikov, *Godfather of the Kremlin. Boris Berezovsky and the Looting of the Kremlin* (London, 2000)

E. Klepikova and V. Solovyov, *Zhirinovsky. The Paradoxes of Russian Fascism* (London, 1995)

J. Klier, *Imperial Russia's Jewish Question, 1855–1881* (Cambridge, 1985)

P. Kolstoe, *Russians in the Former Soviet Republics* (Bloomington, 1995)

G. Kosach, 'Orenburg: regional'naya mifologiya vo vzaimodeistvii s sosedyami', in A. Malashenko (ed.), *Chto khotyat regiony?* (Moscow, 1999)

V. Kozlov, *The Peoples of the Soviet Union* (London, 1988)

O. Kryshtanovskaya, 'Rich and Poor in Post Communist Russia', *Journal of Communist and Transition Politics*, no. 1 (1994)

O. Kryshtanovskaya and S. White, 'From Soviet *Nomenklatura* to Russian Élite', *Europe–Asia Studies*, no. 5 (1996)

S. Kuleshov and V. Strada, *Il fascismo russo* (Venice, 1998)

T. Lahusen and G. Kuperman, *Late Soviet Culture. From Perestroika to Novostroika* (Durham, NC, 1993)

Laitin, David D., *Identity in Formation. The Russian Speaking Populations in the Near-Abroad* (Ithaca, 1998)

N. Lampert, *Whistleblowing in the Soviet Union. Complaints and Abuses under State Socialism* (London 1985)

C. Lane (ed.), *Russia in Transition* (London, 1995)

D. Lane, 'The Gorbachev Revolution: The Role of the Political Elite in Regime Disintegration', *Political Studies*, no. 1 (1996)

D. Lane, 'The Transformation of Russia: The Role of the Political Elite', *Europe–Asia Studies*, no. 4 (1996)

D. Lane and C. Ross, *The Transition from Communism to Capitalism: Ruling Elites from Gorbachev to Yeltsin* (London, 1999)

G. Lapidus, *The New Russia* (Boulder, 1995)

G. Lapidus and V. Zaslavsky (eds), *From Union to Commonwealth: Nationalism and Separatism in the Soviet Republics* (Cambridge, 1992)

W. Laqueur, *The Fate of the Revolution. Interpretations of Soviet History* (London, 1967)

S. Layton, *Russian Literature and Empire. The Conquest of the Caucasus from Pushkin to Tolstoy* (Cambridge, 1994)

A. Ledeneva, *Russia's Economy of Favours: Blat, Networking and Informal Exchange* (Cambridge, 1998)

C. Leonard, 'Rational Resistance to Land Privatization: The Response of Rural Producers to Agrarian Reforms in Pre- and Post-Soviet Russia', *Post-Soviet Geography and Economics*, no. 8 (2000)

J. Lester, *Modern Tsars and Princes. The Struggle for Hegemony in Russia* (London, 1995)

M. Lewin, *The Making of the Soviet System. Essays in the Social History of Interwar Russia* (London, 1985)

M. Lewin, *The Gorbachev Phenomenon* (Berkeley, 1991)

O. S. Libova and L.V. Glukhova in E. Yu. Genieva et al., *Chitayushchaya Rossiya. Mify i real'nost'. Po materialam rossiiskoi nauchno-prakticheskoi konferentsii. Moskva, 1996* (Moscow, 1997)

A. Liebich, *From The Other Shore: Russian Social-Democracy After 1921* (Cambridge, MA, 1997)

A. Lieven, *Chechnya. Tombstone of Russian Power* (New Haven, 1998)

D. C. M. Lieven, *Empire. The Russian Empire and Its Rivals* (London, 2000)

J. Linz and A. Stepan, *Problems of Democratic Transition and Consolidation. Southern Europe, South America, and Post-Communist Europe* (Baltimore, 1996)

J. Lloyd, *Rebirth of a Nation. An Anatomy of Russia* (London, 1998)

S. Lovell, *The Russian Reading Revolution: Print Culture in the Soviet and Post-Soviet Eras* (London and New York, 2000)

V. Loupan, *Le Défi Russe* (Paris, 2000)

A. Lukin, *The Political Culture of the Russian 'Democrats'* (Oxford, 2000)

A. Lushin and P. Oppenheimer, 'External Trade and Payments', in B. Granville and P. Oppenheimer (eds), *Russia's Post-Communist Economy* (Oxford, 2001)

A. Luukkanen, *The Party of Unbelief. The Religious Policy of the Bolshevik Party, 1917–1929* (Helsinki, 1994)

D. Lynch, *Russian Peacekeeping Strategies in the CIS Region* (London, 1999)

A. Malashenko (ed.), *Chto khotyat regiony?* (Moscow, 1999)

T. Maleva, 'What Sort of Russia Has the New Russian President Inherited?', *Carnegie Moscow Center, Briefing*, no. 4, April 2000

M. Malia, *Russia under Western Eyes. From the Bronze Horseman to the Lenin Mausoleum* (Cambridge, MA, 1999)

D. Marples, *Belarus: A Denationalised Nation* (Amsterdam, 1999)

R. Marsh (ed.), *Gender and Russian Literature* (Cambridge, 1996)

R. Marsh (ed.), *Women and Russian Culture: Projections and Self-Perceptions* (New York, 1998)

T. Martin, 'The Russification of the RSFSR', *Cahiers du Monde Russe*, no. 1/2 (1998)

E. Mawdsley, *The Russian Civil War* (London, 1987)

M. McAuley, *Bread and Justice. State and Society in Petrograd, 1917–1922* (Oxford, 1991)

M. McAuley, *Russia's Politics of Uncertainty* (Oxford, 1997)

T. McDaniel, *The Agony of the Russian Idea* (Princeton, 1996)

M. McFaul, *Russia's 1996 Presidential Election: The End of Polarised Politics* (Stanford, 1997)

S. McMillin and A. McMillin, 'Any Colour, So Long As it Is Black: Cruel and Gallows Humour in Contemporary Russian Jokes, Anecdotes and Folklore', *Rusistika*, no. 23 (2001)

L. McReynolds, *The News Under Russia's Old Regime: the Development of a Mass-Circulation Press* (Princeton, 1991)

N. Melvin, *Russians Beyond Russia. The Politics of National Identity* (London, 1995)

N. Melvin, 'The Consolidation of a New Regional Elite: the Case of Omsk, 1987–1995', *Europe–Asia Studies*, no. 4 (1998)

D. Mendeloff, 'Demystifying Textbooks in Post-Soviet Russia', *Institute for the Study of Russian Education Newsletter*, no. 2 (1996)

C. Merridale, *Night of Stone. Death and Memory in Russia* (London, 2000)

E. Mickiewicz, *Split Signals. Television and Politics in the Soviet Union* (Oxford, 1988)

E. Mickiewicz, *Changing Channels and the Struggle for Power in Russia* (Oxford, 1997)

J. S. Migdal, *Strong Societies and Weak States. State–Society Relations and State Capabilities in the Third World* (Princeton, 1998)

J. R. Millar and S. L. Wolchik, *The Social Legacy of Communism* (Cambridge, 1994)

J. Miller, *Mikhail Gorbachev and the End of Soviet Power* (London, 1993)

D. Moon, 'The Problem of Social Stability in Russia, 1598–1998', in G. Hosking and R. Service (eds), *Reinterpreting Russia* (London, 1999).

J. Barrington Moore, *Social Origins of Dictatorship and Democracy* (London, 1967)

J. Morrison, *Boris Yeltsin. From Bolshevik to Democrat* (London, 1991)

N. Moser and P. Oppenheimer, 'The Oil Industry: Structural Transformation and Corporate Governance', in B. Granville and P. Oppenheimer (eds), *Russia's Post-Communist Economy* (Oxford, 2001)

R. G. Moser, The Impact of Parliamentary Electoral Systems in Russia', *Post-Soviet Affairs*, no. 3 (1997)

J. Muckle, *A Guide to the Soviet Curriculum: What the Soviet Child is Taught in School* (London, 1988)

J. Murray, *The Russian Press from Brezhnev to Yeltsin* (London, 1992)

G. Murrell, *Russia's Transition to Democracy: An Internal Political History, 1992–1995* (Brighton, 1997)

R. C. Nation, 'L'Iniziativa *National Missile Defense*', *Europea/Europe*, no. 2/3 (2001)

V. Nekrasov, *MVD v litsakh: ministry ot V. V. Fedorchuka do A. S. Kulikova. 1982–1998* (Moscow, 2000)

C. T. Nepomnyashchy, 'Markets, Mirrors and Mayhem: Alexandra Marinina and the Rise of the New Russian *Detektiv*', in A. M. Barker (ed.), *Consuming Russia: Popular Culture, Sex and Society since Gorbachev* (Durham, NC, 1999)

I. B. Neumann, *Russia and the Idea of Europe* (London, 1996)

R. Nyberg, 'The EU and Kaliningrad', in J. Baxendale, S. Dewar and D. Gowan (eds), *The EU and Kaliningrad. The Consequences of EU Enlargement on Kaliningrad* (London, 2001)

G. O'Donnell, 'Illusions about Consolidation', *Journal of Democracy*, vol. 7, no. 2 (1996)

G. O'Donnell, P. Schmitter and L. Whitehead (eds), *Transitions from Authoritarian Rule* (Baltimore, 1986)

G. di Palma, *To Craft Democracies: an Essay on Democratic Transitions* (Berkeley, 1990)

S. P. Peregudov, N. Yu. Lapina and I. S. Semenenko, *Gruppy interesov i rossiiskoe gosudarstvo* (Moscow, 1999)

L. C. B. Pereira, J. M. Maravell and A. Przeworski, *Economic Reform in New Democracies* (Cambridge, 1993)

M. P. Perrie, *The Image of Ivan the Terrible in Russian Folklore* (Cambridge, 1987)

L. Péter, '"East of the Elbe": The Communist Take-over and the Past', in R. Pynsent (ed.), *The Phoney Peace: Power and Culture in Eastern Europe, 1945–49* (London, 2000)

R. Pipes, *Struve. Liberal on the Left, 1870–1905* (Cambridge, MA, 1970)

R. Pipes, *Struve. Liberal on the Right, 1905–1944* (Cambridge, MA, 1980)

R. Pipes, 'Misinterpreting the Cold War: The Hardliners Had it Right', *Foreign Affairs*, no. 1 (1995)

H. Pilkington, *Generation, Gender and Identity* (London, 1996)

H. Pilkington, *Migration, Displacement and Identity in Post-Soviet Russia* (London, 1998)

A. Polonsky, *The Great Powers and the Polish Question, 1941–1945: A Documentary Study in Cold War Origins* (London, 1976)

Yu. A. Polyakov, V. B. Zhiromskaya and I. N. Kiselëv, 'Polveka molchaniya (Vsesoyuznaya perepis' naseleniya)', *Sotsiologicheskie issledovaniya*, no. 7 (1990)

D. Pospielovsky, *The Russian Church under the Soviet Regime, 1917–1982* (New York, 1984)

A. Pravda (ed.), *The End of the Outer Empire: Soviet–East European Relations in Transition, 1985–1990* (London, 1992)

A. Przeworski, *Democracy and the Market: Political and Economic Reforms in Eastern Europe and Latin America* (Cambridge, 1991)

A. Przeworski, M. Alvarez, J. A. Cheibub and F. Limongi, 'What Makes Democracies Endure?', *Journal of Democracy*, no. 1 (1996)

R. Putnam with R. Leonardi and R. Y. Nanetti, *Making Democracy Work. Civic Traditions in Modern Italy* (Princeton, 1993)

O. H. Radkey, *Russia Goes to the Polls: the Election to the Russian Constituent Assembly* (2nd edn: Ithaca, 1989)

P. Reddaway and D. Glinski, *The Tragedy of Russia's Reforms: Market Bolshevism Against Democracy* (Washington, DC, 2001)

N. V. Riasanovsky, *Russia and the West in the Teachings of the Slavophiles: a Study of Romantic Ideology* (Cambridge, MA, 1952)

N. V. Riasanovsky, *Nicholas I and Official Nationality in Russia, 1825–1855* (Berkeley, 1959)

R. C. Ridenour, *Nationalism, Modernism and Personal Rivalry in Nineteenth-Century Russian Music* (Ann Arbor, 1993)

T. H. Rigby, 'The Origins of the Nomenklatura System', in his *Political Elites in the USSR: Central Leaders and Local Cadres from Lenin to Gorbachev* (London, 1990)

T. H. Rigby, *Political Elites in the USSR: Central Leaders and Local Cadres from Lenin to Gorbachev* (London, 1990)

P. G. Roeder, 'Varieties of Post-Soviet Authoritarian Regimes', *Post-Soviet Affairs*, no. 1 (1994)

H. Rogger, *National Consciousness in Eighteenth-Century Russia* (Cambridge, MA, 1960)

L. Roniger, 'The Comparative Study of Clientelism and the Changing Nature of Civil Society in the Contemporary World', in L. Roniger and A. Günes-Ayata (eds), *Democracy, Clientelism, and Civil Society* (Boulder, 1994)

R. Rose, 'Floating Parties and Accountability: A Supply-Side View of Russia's Elections', in A. Brown (ed.), *Contemporary Russian Politics: A Reader* (Oxford, 2001)

D. Rustow, 'Transitions to Democracy', *Comparative Politics*, no. 2 (1970)

P. Rutland, 'Privatisation in Russia', *Europe–Asia Studies*, no. 7 (1994)

J. Sachs and K. Pistor (eds), *The Rule of Law and Economic Reform in Russia* (Boulder, 1997)

E. W. Said, *Orientalism* (London, 1995)

R. Sakwa, *Gorbachev and his Reforms, 1985–1990* (London, 1990)

R. Sakwa, *Russian Politics and Society* (2nd edn: London, 1993)

G. Schöpflin, *Politics in Eastern Europe* (Oxford, 1993)

A. Sella, 'An Army in Crisis', *The Soviet and Post-Soviet Review*, no. 1 (2000)

R. Service, *The Bolshevik Party in Revolution: A Study in Organisational Change* (London, 1979)

R. Service, 'Gorbachëv's Reforms: The Future in the Past', *Journal of Communist Studies*, no. 3 (1987)

R. Service, 'Mikhail Gorbachev as Political Reformer', in R. Hill and J. Dellenbrant (eds), *Gorbachev and Perestroika* (London, 1989)

R. Service, *Lenin: A Political Life*, vol. 2, *Worlds in Collision* (London, 1991)

R. Service, 'Boris El'cin: Continuità e Mutamento di un Rivoluzionario Democratico', *Europe/Europa*, no. 2 (1992)

R. Service, 'Boris Yeltsin: Politics and Rhetoric, 1991–1992': research paper delivered in St Antony's College, Oxford, 9 March 1992

R. Service, *Lenin: A Political Life*, vol. 3, *The Iron Ring* (London, 1995)

R. Service, *A History of Twentieth-Century Russia* (London, 1997)

R. Service, *Lenin: A Biography* (London, 2000)

H. Seton-Watson, *The Russian Empire, 1800–1917* (Oxford, 1967)

P. Severtsov, *Kirsan: The Universal President* (Moscow, 1996)

S. Shane, *Dismantling Utopia: How Information Ended the Soviet Union* (1994)

T. Shanin, *The Awkward Class. Political Sociology of Peasantry in a Developing Society, 1910–1925* (London, 1972)

L. Shevtsova, *Yeltsin's Russia: Myths and Reality* (Washington, DC, 1999)

V. Shkol'nikov, Ye. Andreev and T. Maleva, *Neravenstvo i smertnost' v Rossii* (Moscow, 2000)

V. Shlapentokh, *Public and Private Life of the Russian People: Changing Values in Post-Stalin Russia* (New York, 1989)

V. Shlapentokh, 'Russia: Privatisation and Illegalisation of Social and Political Life', *Washington Quarterly*, no. 1 (1996)

A. Shleifer and D. Treisman, *Without a Map. Political Tactics and Economic Reforms in Russia* (Cambridge, MA, 2000)

K. Simis, *USSR: Secrets of a Corrupt Society* (London, 1982)

M. Slonim, *Russian Theater from Empire to Soviets* (Cleveland, 1961)

A. D. Smith, *The Ethnic Origins of Nations* (Oxford, 1986)

A. D. Smith, *National Identity* (London, 1991)

G. Smith (ed.), *Federalism: the Multiethnic Challenge* (London, 1995)

N. A. Sobolev and V. A. Artamonov, *Simvoly Rossii* (Moscow, 1993)

S. Solnick, *Stealing the State. Control and Collapse in Soviet Institutions* (Cambridge, MA, 1998)

V. Sperling, *Organising Women in Contemporary Russia: Engendering Transition* (Cambridge, 1999)

SSSR. Entsiklopedicheskii spravochnik (ed. A. M. Prokhorov: Moscow, 1982)

R. Stites, *Russian Popular Culture. Entertainment and Society Since 1900* (Cambridge, 1992)

K. Stoner-Weiss, *Local Heroes: The Political Economy of Russian Regional Government* (Princeton, 1997)

R. Suny, *Revenge of the Past. Nationalism, Revolution and the Collapse of the Soviet Union* (Stanford, 1993)

A. V. Suslova and A. V. Superanskaya, *O russkikh imenakh* (Moscow, 1999)

P. Sutela, 'Insider Privatisation in Russia', *Europe–Asia Studies*, no. 3 (1994)

J. Sutherland, *Schooling in the New Russia. Innovation and Change, 1984–1995* (London, 1999)

A. J. Swan, *Russian Music and its Sources in Chant and Folk-Song* (London, 1973)

R. Taras (ed.), *Post-Communist Presidents* (Cambridge, 1997)

K. Thelen, 'Historical Institutionalism in Comparative Politics', *The Annual Review of Political Science 1999* (Palo Alto, 1999)

C. Thubron, *In Siberia* (London, 1999)

V. Tikhomirov, 'The Second Collapse of the Soviet Economy: Myths and Realities of the Russian Reform', *Europe–Asia Studies*, no. 2 (2000)

N. Timasheff, *The Great Retreat. The Growth and Decline of Communism in Russia* (New York, 1946)

V. Tolz, *Russia: Inventing the Nation* (London, 2001)

V. Tret'yakov (ed.), *Rossiiskuya elita. Psikhologicheskie portrety* (Moscow, 2000)

P. Truscott, *Russia First. Breaking With The West* (London, 1997)

M. Urban, V. Igrunov and S. Mitrokhin, *The Rebirth of Politics in Russia* (Cambridge, 1997)

E. Valkenier, *Russian Realist Art: the Peredvizhniki and Their Tradition* (Ann Arbor, 1977)

G. Vitkovskaya and A. Malashenko (eds.), *Neterpimost' v Rossii: starye i novye fobii* (Moscow, 1999)

N. K. Voevodenko (ed.), *Mestnoe samoupravlenie v Rossiiskoi Federatsii. (Regional'nyi aspekt)*, (Moscow, 1998)

V. Voronkov and I. Os'val'd (eds), *Konstruirovanie etnichnosti. Etnicheskie obshchiny* (St Petersburg, 1998)

T. Vorozheikina, 'Clientelism and the Process of Political Democratization in Russia', in L. Roniger and A. Günes-Ayata (eds.), *Democracy, Clientelism and Civil Society* (Boulder, 1994)

M. Voslensky, *Nomenklatura. The Anatomy of the Soviet Ruling Class* (London, 1984)

A. Walicki, *Russian Social Thought. An Introduction to the Intellectual History of Nineteenth-Century Russia* (Stanford, 1977)

S. L. Webber, *School, Reform and Society in the New Russia* (London, 2000)

E. Weber, *Peasants into Frenchmen: The Modernization of Rural France, 1870–1914* (Stanford, 1976)

S. K. Wegren, *Agriculture and the State in Soviet and Post-Soviet Russia* (University of Pittsburg, 1998)

M. A. Weigle, *Russia's Liberal Project: State–Society Relations in the Transition from Communism* (Pennsylvania, 2000)

Nicolas Werth, *Istoriya sovetskogo gosudarstva* (Moscow, 1992)

A. White, *Democratisation in Russia under Gorbachev, 1985–1991: the Birth of a Voluntary Sector* (London, 1999)

S. White, *Political Culture and Soviet Politics* (London, 1979)

S. White, *After Gorbachev* (Cambridge, 1993)

S. White, *Russia's New Politics. The Management of a Post-Communist Society* (London, 2000)

S. White, R. Rose and I. McAllister, *How Russia Votes* (London, 1997)

S. Whitefield, 'Social Responses to Reform in Russia', in D. Lane (ed.), *Russia in Transition* (London, 1995)

S. Whitefield, 'Partisan and Party Divisions in Post-Communist Russia', in A. Brown (ed.), *Contemporary Russian Politics: A Reader* (Oxford, 2001)

S. Whitefield and G. Evans, 'The Emerging Structure of Partisan Development in Post-Soviet Russia', in M. Wyman, S. White and S. Oates (eds), *Elections and Voters in Post-Communist Russia* (Cheltenham, 1998)

S. Whitefield and G. Evans, 'Class Markets and Partisanship in Post-Soviet Russia: 1993–1999', *Electoral Studies*, no. 2 (1999)

F. Wigzell, *Reading Russian Fortunes: Print Culture, Gender and Divination in Russia Since 1765* (Cambridge, 1998)

J. P. Willerton, *Patronage and Politics in the USSR* (Cambridge, 1992)

K. Williams, 'A Scorecard for Czech Lustration', *Central Europe Review*, no. 19 (1999)

K. Williams, 'The Rhetoric of Lustration', *The Masaryk Journal*, no. 1 (2000)

M. Wyman, *Public Opinion in Post-Communist Russia* (London, 1997)

M. Wyman, S. White and S. Oates (eds), *Elections and Voters in Post-Communist Russia* (Cheltenham, 1998)

F. Zakaria, 'The Rise of Illiberal Democracy', *Foreign Affairs*, no. 76 (1997)

T. Zaslavskaya, 'The Novosibirsk Report', *Survey*, no. 28/1 (1984)

V. Zaslavsky, *The Neo-Stalinist State: Class, Ethnicity and Consensus in Soviet Society* (Armonk, 1982)

A. Zdravomyslov, 'O natsional'nom samosoznanii rossiyan', *Monitoring obshchestvennogo mneniya. Sotsialn'ye i ekonomicheskie peremeny*, January–February 2001

A. G. Zdravomyslov, *Sotsiologiya rossiiskogo krizisa* (Moscow, 1999)

Ye. A. Zemskaya (ed.), *Russkii yazyk kontsa XX stoletiya (1985–1995)* (Moscow, 1996)

D. Zimine and M. J. Bradshaw, 'Regional Adaptation to Economic Crisis in Russia: the Case of Novgorod Oblast', *Post-Soviet Geography and Economics*, no. 5 (1999)

INDEX